D0990014

THE
RUSSIAN JEW
UNDER TSARS
AND SOVIETS

ALSO BY *Salo W. Baron*

A SOCIAL AND RELIGIOUS HISTORY OF THE JEWS
THE JEWISH COMMUNITY: ITS HISTORY AND STRUCTURE TO
THE AMERICAN REVOLUTION
MODERN NATIONALISM AND RELIGION

Edited by Salo Baron
BIBLIOGRAPHY OF JEWISH SOCIAL STUDIES, 1938-39
ESSAYS ON MAIMONIDES
FREEDOM AND REASON
JUDAISM, POSTBIBLICAL AND TALMUDIC PERIOD
(Joseph L. Blau, joint editor)
JERUSALEM: CITY HOLY AND ETERNAL
THE JEWS OF THE UNITED STATES, 1790-1840:
A DOCUMENTARY HISTORY
(Joseph L. Blau, joint editor)

THE

RUSSIAN JEW

UNDER TSARS
AND SOVIETS

by Salo W. Baron

RUSSIAN CIVILIZATION SERIES
GENERAL EDITOR *Michael T. Florinsky*

THE MACMILLAN COMPANY, NEW YORK
COLLIER-MACMILLAN LIMITED, LONDON

Copyright © Salo W. Baron 1964

All rights reserved—no part of this book may be reproduced in any form without permission in writing from the publisher, except by a reviewer who wishes to quote brief passages in connection with a review written for inclusion in magazine or newspaper.

First Printing

The Macmillan Company, New York
Collier-Macmillan Canada, Ltd., Toronto, Ontario

Library of Congress catalog card number: 64-20459

DESIGNED BY MARY A. BROWN

Printed in the United States of America

Acknowledgments

Every effort has been made to secure permission for quotation from the copyright owners, but in some cases it has been impossible to locate the owners. Grateful acknowledgment is due to the following for permission to quote selections from the works cited:

The American Jewish Committee, New York: Solomon M. Schwarz, *The Jews in the Soviet Union*, 1951. *The American Jewish Yearbook for 5667*, 1906-1907. *The Jews in the Eastern War Zone*, 1916.

Behrman House, New York: Edmond Fleg, *The Jewish Anthology*, 1925.

Block Publishing Company, New York: David Philipson, *Max Lilienthal, American Rabbi*, 1915.

Chapman and Hall, Limited, London: Julius F. Hecker, *Religion and Communism: A Study of Religion and Atheism in Russia*, 1933.

Chatto and Windus, Limited, London: Alexander Herzen, *My Past and Thoughts*, Vol. I, tr. Constance Garnett, 1924-1928.

Columbia University Press, New York: Isaac Levitats, *The Jewish Community in Russia, 1772-1844*, 1943.

Conference on Jewish Social Studies, New York: Moshe Perlmann, "*Razsvet* 1860-1861: The Origins of the Russian Jewish

DS
135
.R9
B28

Press." *Jewish Social Studies*, XXIV (1962). Koppel S. Pinson, "Arkady Kremer, Vladimir Medem and the Ideology of the Jewish Bund." *Jewish Social Studies*, VII (1945). Zosa Sjajkowski, "How the Mass Migration to America Began." *Jewish Social Studies*, IV (1942).

Crown Publishers, New York: B. Z. Goldberg, *The Jewish Problem in the Soviet Union: An Analysis and a Solution.* Copyright 1961 by B. Z. Goldberg. Used by permission of Crown Publishers, Inc.

Dawar, Tel Aviv, Israel: Elisha Rudin, *Bi-fe'at Nekhar*, 1938. Author's translation.

Fordham University Press, New York: N. S. Timasheff's translation from *Izvestia* of April 17, 1939. *Thought*, XX.

Harcourt, Brace & World, New York: Corliss Lamont, *The Peoples of the Soviet Union*, 1946.

Harvard University Press, Cambridge: *Continuity and Change in Russian and Soviet Thought*, edited by Ernest J. Simmons, 1955.

Hebrew Union College, Cincinnati, Ohio: David Philipson, "Max Lilienthal in Russia." *Hebrew Union College Annual*, XII-XIII, 1937-1938.

Horovitz Publishing Company, Limited (East and West Library), London: *Ahad Ha-Am: Essays, Letters, Memoirs*, tr. Leon Simon, 1946.

International Publishers, New York: Maxim Gorki, *Culture and the People* (English translation). *Lenin on the Jewish Question*, 1936. By permission of International Publishers Co., Inc.

The Jewish Publication Society, Philadelphia: Joseph L. Baron, *Stars and Sand*, 1943.

The Medieval Academy of America, Cambridge: *The Russian Primary Chronicle*, tr. Samuel H. Cross and Olgerd P. Sherbovitz-Wetzor, 1953.

The New York Times Company, New York: Harry Schwartz, "Moscow Papers Assail Writer" (English translation of an excerpt from Yevtushenko's *Babii Yar*), *New York Times*, September 28, 1961. Copyright © by The New York Times Company. Reprinted by permission.

Harold Ober Associates, New York: Catherine Drinker Bowen, *"Free Artist": A Story of Anton and Nicholas Rubinstein*, New York, Random House, 1939.

Frederick A. Praeger, Inc., New York: Betram Wolfe, *Khrushchev and Stalin's Ghost: Text, Background and Meaning of Khrushchev's Secret Report to the Twentieth Congress on the Night of February 24-25, 1956*, 1957.

Alma College Library
Alma, Michigan

Stanford University Press, Stanford, California: *Out of My Past: Memoirs of Count Kokovtsov*, edited by H. H. Fisher, 1935. Reprinted with permission of the publishers.

Yale University Press, New Haven, Connecticut: Louis Greenberg, *The Jews in Russia*, Vol. II, 1951.

Contents

Contents ix

Foreword

The Russian Jew: Under Tsars and Soviets is the fourth volume of the Russian Civilization Series to appear.

The remarkable change in Russia's international position since the Second World War has brought forth an unprecedented demand for information about the land of the Soviets, which the press, radio, and television—in their very nature—can satisfy but imperfectly. Russia, moreover, is a fascinating ancient country and there is much about her that an informed person might like to know, irrespective of the Soviets' recently acquired prominence.

Countless elements shape the life and policies of a nation and the more we know about Russia's past and present, the better are the chances of comprehending her correctly. It is a notable and regrettable fact that until quite recently Russian studies were neglected in the West. A generation ago interest in Russia was limited to a relatively small group of specialists and intellectuals; today there is a widespread and mounting demand for authoritative, dependable, and clearly presented information on tsarist Russia and the USSR. There are numerous books in English, some of them excellent, on the various aspects of the Russian scene, but other aspects have been unexplored or call for fresh consideration.

The Russian Civilization Series, which deals with both the prerevolutionary and the Soviet periods, is designed to meet, in part, this need. Each volume is written by a specialist in the field. The studies endeavor to maintain a high level of scholarship without being too technical and to present the information in an attractive style. Each volume is complete in itself and can be used independently of the other volumes in the Series.

The Russian Jew: Under Tsars and Soviets surveys a particularly dramatic and moving aspect of imperial and Soviet history. Dr. Salo W. Baron, emeritus professor of Jewish History, Literature and Institution history at Columbia Uni-

versity is a leading authority on Judaism and needs no introduction to those interested in historical studies. He has
written an absorbing book, well-organized, fully-documented,
and eminently readable, and he succeeds in conveying admir-
ably, and with great restraint, the feeling of the tragedy of
Israel under both the imperial and the Soviet regimes. His
distinguished volume throws much new light on a vital issue.

                    Michael T. Florinsky
                    General Editor, Russian Civilization Series
July 1964
Vevey, Switzerland

Preface

The story told in the following pages is both sad and heroic. Rarely was a people subjected to such sustained, unrelenting pressures as were the Jews under the tsarist regime. A powerful autocracy, employing its unlimited powers, combined strict segregation and sharp discrimination with fiscal exploitation and contemptuous treatment to force the Jews to abandon their ancestral mores and faith, and completely to submerge their identity within the religion and culture of the majority. Yet Russian Jewry successfully resisted both pressures and blandishments. Its great vitality came to the fore not only in its constant growth in numbers and intellectual vigor, but also in its ability to nurture from its manpower and spiritual resources the growing Jewish communities of the New World, Western Europe, and Palestine. One need but remember that in the 1920s many a Jewish *Landsmannschaft* in New York City exceeded in size the total population of the town from which its members had stemmed.

Paradoxically, Russian Jewry is at once one of the oldest and one of the youngest communities in Western Judaism. Many peripheral areas of the Soviet Union have been inhabited by Jews from the earliest days of the Christian era; in some cases long before their occupation by their present ethnic majorities. Yet the tsars peremptorily excluded Jews from their rapidly expanding Russian heartland and even after they had willy-nilly taken over hundreds of thousands of Jewish subjects residing in the territories of partitioned Poland in 1772-1795, the tsars succeeded, through the artifice of a Pale of Settlement, in admitting there only a select few to the very end of their regime. The history of Russian Jewry as such thus covers less than two centuries and is actually shorter than, for instance, that of the United States.

By repudiating tsarism and all it stood for, the Revolutions of 1917 seemed to usher in a new glorious era for all the oppressed minorities of the vast empire extending over one-sixth of the earth. Many Jews, in particular, were easily persuaded that the new society would not only establish a reign of social justice approximating their own old spiritual yearnings, but that it would also grant to its numerous ethnic minorities an unprecedented combination of full equality of rights and national autonomy. The new communist Jewish leadership, especially, was prepared to overlook the immediate hardships caused by the Communist Revolution—the undermining of the entire socioeconomic structure of their community, the disfranchisement of about one-third of their people, and the overthrow of their traditional institutions, viewing them all as but a transitional phase toward the fulfillment of their socialist dreams. But few realized that, by giving up their traditional moorings of the Jewish religion, Hebrew culture, and the Zionist ideal, they would sap the very energies which had theretofore maintained the strength of their people in the midst of adversity. Nor did many of them foresee that, even under the totally changed social structure, the anti-Semitic feelings of the Russian masses could reassert themselves under various guises. They also failed to anticipate the sharp reaction of a regime which, growingly nationalistic and imperialist, would look with suspicion upon the "cosmopolitan" connections of the Jewish people dispersed through many lands.

Moreover, before it had a chance to adjust itself to this novel situation, Russian Jewry went through the traumatic experience of the Nazi invasion and extermination. Deeply grateful to the Red Army in which it saw its actual savior, it meekly submitted to the Stalinist terror of 1948-52 which shattered whatever expectations it may have cherished for its postwar reconstruction.

It is small wonder, then, that, facing such world-shaking changes, the Russian Jews have not yet found their bearings. Theoretically still living under the illusion of equality plus autonomy, they face the stark reality of administrative discrimination, governmental and popular animosity, and novel assimilatory pressures. At the same time, taught by their own leaders that they must abandon some of the most essential elements of their millennial heritage, they have not yet found the way of resuming their old cultural progress, interrupted by half a century of alternating exalted expectations and abysmal despair. Yet, despite their numerous shattered illusions, it appears that this is not the "end of the road" for them, and that, in some as yet unpredictable fashion, they will, before very long, recover their ancient vitality to find some unprecedented solutions to the novel, intrinsically contradictory challenges of discrimination by, and assimilation to, one of the great nations of history.

In conclusion it is a pleasant duty for the author to express his thanks to those who have helped him to tell his story in its present form. He is indebted to Professor Michael T. Florinsky who, as General Editor of the Series, read the manuscript and offered a number of valuable suggestions. His secretary, Mrs. Rebecca Fischer, prepared the manuscript with painstaking care and assisted in seeing it through the press. Most of all, the author is indebted to his wife, Mrs. Jeannette Meisel Baron, for her tireless cooperation, encouragement, and constructive criticisms during the entire process of research, writing, and publication. Needless to say, these expressions of gratitude involve no delegation of responsibility.

S. W. B.

Yifat Shalom
Canaan, Connecticut
May 28, 1964.

THE
RUSSIAN JEW
UNDER TSARS
AND SOVIETS

❦ 1 ❦

Early Vicissitudes

LIKE MOST ANCIENT and medieval origins, those of the Jewish settlement in the present boundaries of the Soviet Union are shrouded in darkness. True, owing to persistent efforts of East-European archeologists, we now know a little more about the general ethnology and history of the early inhabitants of that area, particularly of its European segment. Because of the well-known limitations of archeological finds unaccompanied by inscriptions and literary documents, however, these early human settlements in European Russia are subject to conflicting hypotheses and for the most part are completely undatable. Nor can the racial and ethnic composition of that early population be clearly identified. Certainly, if any Jews appeared in those regions before the Christian era without leaving behind any literary or epigraphic traces, they could not easily be isolated as such from the rest of the population.

Nevertheless some early contacts may go back to the seventh century B.C. The vast conglomeration of peoples inhabiting eastern Europe in antiquity and going under the name of Scythians was not unknown to the ancient Israelites. Scythian invaders at one time actually reached the confines of neighboring Syria and, rightly or wrongly, many scholars have seen in them the embodiment of that "peril from the north" of which Jeremiah spoke, when he prophesied, "For I [the Lord] will bring evil from the north, and a great destruction"(4:6). Reciprocally, later Jewish traditions ascribed the first settlements of the Jews in southern Russia to the period of the First Exile. St. Jerome doubtless merely repeated an assertion heard from Jewish contemporaries that "the Assyrians and Chaldaeans had conducted the Jewish people into exile not only in Media and Persia but also in the Bosporus and the extreme north."[1]

Some medieval Jewish legends even spoke of displaced Canaanites at the time of Joshua's conquest of Palestine having gone all the way into Russia, just as others had settled in North Africa. From these legends may have stemmed the medieval Hebrew designation of Slavonic eastern Europe as Canaan, although Canaan's Hamitic descent was clearly contrasted in the Bible with the Japhetite ancestry of the Indo-European peoples. According to another explanation offered by medieval writers, including the famous twelfth-century traveler Benjamin of Tudela, that designation was derived from the slave trade which was so widely prevalent among the "Slav" nations.

ANCIENT SETTLEMENTS

We are on safer ground when we find Greek inscriptions pertaining to Jewish communities settled on the northern shore of the Black Sea in the early centuries of the Christian era. They reveal, as in many other areas within the *limes* of the ancient Roman Empire, the presence of organized Jewish communities which, while professing the Jewish religion, adopted the speech, the names, and even certain rituals from their Hellenized neighbors. A considerable number of Hebrew inscriptions from the Crimea have likewise come to light, but their reading and dating have long been suspect, because their original discoverer, Abraham Firkovitch, is known to have tampered with some texts for the glory of his own, the Karaite sect which, founded in the eighth century, had increasingly separated itself from the so-called "Rabbanite" majority of Jews. However, quite a few texts found by this learned and indefatigable traveler probably have greater historical merit than was attributed to them by an oversuspicious and overcritical generation of the late nineteenth century. From these borderlines of the declining Roman Empire venturesome Jewish individuals doubtless explored much of the interior of Russia, just as the Jews of

Armenia and northern Persia, including Khiva, had penetrated Asiatic territories adjacent to the Caspian Sea. Jewish
emigrés from the more advanced countries of western Asia
also early infiltrated the Caucasus, laying the foundations for
the so-called "Mountain Jews" whose peculiar mores and
rituals have long greatly impressed travelers and anthropol-
ogists.

The Jewish population in all these regions increased considerably after each of the recurrent Byzantine persecutions
and particularly after the total outlawry of Judaism, promulgated in each of the four centuries between the seventh and
the tenth. The warlike disturbances accompanying the
numerous campaigns between Rome or Byzantium on the
one hand, and Persia or the Great Caliphate on the other
hand, likewise forced many Jewish refugees to seek shelter
in these outlying, more pacific areas. In view of the slowness
and perils of personal communication, the settlers around the
Black and Caspian Seas often lost contact with the great
centers of Jewish learning in Palestine and Babylonia. They
harbored among them heterodox elements, including outright
sectarians such as Samaritans or Karaites. It was from a
Samaritan in Kherson, we are told, that St. Cyril, the apostle
of the Christian faith among the eastern Slavs, had learned
Hebrew. With the aid of Hebrew, Cyril was able to fashion
his new alphabet, the Cyrilitsa, for use in Russian and the
other eastern Slavonic languages. Perhaps even more pronounced was the impact of Hebrew on the related Glagolithic
alphabet used by other Slavs, including the Croats, as late as
the seventeenth century.

Most decisive was the Jewish influence on the rapidly
expanding Khazar Empire, which covered a large segment of
southern Russia from the lower Volga to the Crimea and
which for a time controlled many Slavonic tribes as well. This
influence attracted the attention of distant Arab geographers
and literary historians. Muqaddasi did not wish to sound
humorous when he described Khazaria as a large arid country, where "sheep, honey and Jews exist in large quantities,"
while the encyclopedic historian of Arabic literature, Ibn
an-Nadim, declared bluntly, "The Khazars use the Hebrew
script."[2] Not surprisingly, both Byzantium and the Caliphate

tried to draw the Khazar Empire into their respective orbits, the best method of securing such an alliance being the conversion of the desirable neighbor to one's own faith. But precisely because the Khazars wished to retain their neutrality, they repudiated both Christianity and Islam. To secure further noninterference, one of the Khazar rulers, Bulan, formally adopted the third monotheistic religon, Judaism (about 740). His example was followed by numerous Khazars, especially among the upper classes, although no effort was made to impose the Jewish religion upon the pagan masses or the Christian and Muslim minorities. In fact, religious toleration went so far that the supreme court of the empire allegedly consisted of two Jews, two Christians, two Muslims, and one pagan.

Nor was the Khazar Jewish faith a monolithic entity. Apart from continuing to embrace numerous sectarians, the Khazarian Jews displayed a peculiar kind of orthodoxy which was often at variance with the teachings and rituals accepted elsewhere. For a long time the very classics of Jewish literature were extremely scarce; they were familiar only to a small minority of the educated Jewish Khazars. In time, at least according to one of their kings, Obadiah, they succeeded in importing some eastern rabbis and teachers who helped to reestablish a measure of religious conformity and to raise the level of Jewish education. In any case, Jews whether of Jewish, Khazar, or other origin, became quite numerous in the Khazar districts and did not totally disappear even after the Khazars lost their imperial power and came under Russian and Tartar domination.

KIEVAN RUSSIA

Upon the destruction of Khazaria, the center of gravity of that entire area shifted to Kievan Russia. Kiev, admiringly called by a Western contemporary, Adam of Bremen, "the rival of Constantinople and the most shining gem of the Greek Church,"[3] entered the scene of world history upon the conversion to Christianity of its ruler Vladimir (980-1015). *The Russian Primary Chronicle* reports the story of this conversion in picturesque detail, relating in particular the debate which allegedly had taken place before the prince between representatives of the three world religions, Christianity, Islam, and Judaism. This is a replica of a similar discussion supposedly conducted two and a half centuries earlier in Khazaria before Bulan decided to adopt Judaism. This time, we are told, Vladimir rejected the Jewish arguments, primarily because the Jewish spokesman had purportedly replied to his question of where the Jews lived by saying:

> We do not [live in Jerusalem] for the Lord was wroth with our forefathers, and scattered us all over the earth for our sins, while our land was given away to the Christians. Thereupon Vladimir exclaimed: How then dare you teach others when you yourselves are rejected by God and scattered? If God loved you, you would not be dispersed in strange lands. Do you intend to inflict the same misfortune on me?[4]

Precisely because Christianity in its Greek-Orthodox form was but a recent growth and paganism was still deeply rooted in the Kievan people, the early Russian Church was quite intolerant toward Jews and the adherents of any faith other than their own. Most of its leaders were recruited from Byzantium, where religious intolerance had led to the reiterated outlawry of Judaism, although in other periods the Jewish communities were allowed to persist and at times even to flourish there. The first native Russian Metropolitan, Hilarion, outdid his local predecessors by writing a treatise contrasting "The Mosaic law and the Grace and Truth of Jesus Christ" (after 1051). He probably borrowed most of his arguments from St. Cyril's anti-Jewish polemical tract, since lost. When, under Byzantine pressure, he was deposed from his metropolitanate, he founded the famous Petcherskii (Cave) Monastery in Kiev in 1053, which soon became the main center of Russian Orthodox thinking. In his biography of the Byzantine Theodosius who served as its abbot from 1062 to 1074, the Russian chronicler Nestor tells us that the monk was searching out Jews in order to engage them in theological controversies, hoping to provoke them into inflicting upon him the coveted death of a martyr. That Judaism still represented a serious threat even to that monastery, however, is illustrated by another member, Nikita, who had allegedly tried to spread Jewish doctrines among his fellow monks, though he ultimately repented.

In the meantime Kiev's Jewish community grew in both size and affluence. In the twelfth century, and probably earlier, Jews lived in at least two quarters, in the so-called Podole and in the northeastern section, where in 1124 and 1146 a "Jewish gate" is mentioned in connection with some local disturbances. They were active in both business and politics. We are told that, after the death of Grand Duke Sviatopolk II (1093-1113), some Jews, as well as Kievan grandees, involved in that ruler's machinations, especially his salt monopoly, were attacked by the partisans of the newly elected Grand Duke, Vladimir II Monomakh (1113-25). Upon his tardy arrival Vladimir quickly restored order. Soon thereafter two influential Jews, Ephrem Moisevich and Anbal Yassin, figured prominently in a court conspiracy. But the majority seems to have remained neutral in these court conflicts and we hear of no retribution having been inflicted upon the community at large.

Culturally, too, the Kievan Jews made considerable progress. Although, like most other Jewish peripheral settlements of that period, that of the later Ukrainian capital remained inarticulate, we learn from incidental references in Western letters that it embraced some devotees of Jewish learning who were undoubtedly helped by visitors reaching Kiev from Central Europe. Occasionally, Kievan students addressed pertinent inquiries to distinguished rabbis abroad, while one, Moses of Kiev, is recorded in France as a pupil of the leading Western Jewish scholar of the twelfth century, Jacob ben Meir Tam. Moses was apparently also in communication with Samuel ben Ali, head of the important Jewish Academy of Baghdad.

Their relatively advanced educational level enabled the Jews also to exert continued religious influence upon the Russian people. In this period foundations were laid for the spread of those Judaizing Russian sects which were to play so prominent a role in the subsequent history of the Russian Church. Much of the checkered evolution of Russian sectarianism, which understandably shunned the light of day and was largely recorded by its bitter enemies, still is shrouded in darkness. But the presence of a flourishing minority, cultivating its rituals and insisting upon its religious diversity, necessarily helped to nurture deviationist trends among the deeply religious Russian masses. Obviously, this very impact evoked the hostility of the official Church which increased the vehemence of its anti-Jewish attacks and, before long, sought the complete elimination of this source of "contagion."

MUSCOVITE XENOPHOBIA

After the Mongol conquest we hear very little about Jews in any territories of European Russia, except in the Crimea. Here the Genoese received a concession to develop the harbor of Kaffa (Feodosia) from where they traded with, and even politically controlled, the neighboring areas for about two centuries (1260-1475). Jewish traders soon established there independent Rabbanite and Karaite communities, probably recruited in part from descendants of the old settlers under Khazaria. The Karaite community developed a special Tartar dialect in which a number of its literary documents were written even in recent generations. However, the figure of 4,000 houses, allegedly inhabited by the two Jewish groups in Kaffa, according to the traveler Johannes Schiltberger who had visited the Crimea between 1396 and 1427, is undoubtedly exaggerated.[5] Conditions became increasingly difficult in the fifteenth century as the expansion of the Ottoman Turks interposed a serious obstacle to the communications between Genoa and its Black Sea colonies. Although in 1449 the Republic specifically ordered the local authorities to extend full protection to Jews, as well as to Greeks and Armenians, and the Jewish community soon thereafter expressed special satisfaction with the Genoese chief of police Nicoloso Bonaventura, its economic status constantly deteriorated, causing many Jews to depart.

In the main centers of Russian life, however, particularly Novgorod and Moscow, there seem to have been but few Jews. The prevailing xenophobia of both the Russian masses and their rulers kept out the Jews and other foreigners. True, the Russian liberator from the Golden Horde, Ivan III (1462-

1505), made use of some Crimean Jews for his diplomatic negotiations with their khan. Curiously, one such Kaffa Jew, Khoza Kokos, tried to correspond with the Tsar in Hebrew, but he had to change, at Ivan's instance, to another language and script ("Russian or Mohammedan," that is Arabic) which was more readily understood in Moscow. Another Kaffan, Zechariah de Guizolfi, an Italian immigrant of Jewish descent who married a local princess and was styled the Prince of Taman, even thought of settling in Moscow.[6]

Amicable developments of this type were cut short, however, when another Zechariah (Skharia), a Kievan Jew, settled in Novgorod and started engaging in religious propaganda. This great commercial center, which had attracted many foreigners, became the scene of turbulent socioreligious controversies which led to the formation of new sects. The impact of Balkan Bogomilism, to be sure, like that of the ancient Christian gnosticism, from which it had stemmed, had many anti-Jewish implications. Yet Skharia quite willingly participated in the raging religious disputations. This mystery man, of obscure antecedents and with unknown objectives, apparently was so successful that, under his influence, a number of Novgorod nobles and clerics repudiated the divinity of Christ and the Trinitarian dogma, and insisted that the Messiah was yet to come. They also rejected the veneration of icons and adopted a number of other Jewish doctrines. Skharia was supported in these endeavors by two Jewish visitors from Lithuania. From Novgorod the heresy of *Judaizanti* spread also to Moscow. Ivan III himself brought back with him from a visit to Novgorod in 1479 two Judaizing priests whom he placed in two Moscow churches. Among the sympathizers with the new sect appeared such influential personalities as Ivan's daughter-in-law, Helena, and the chancellor, Fedor Kurizin. Alarmed, the Metropolitan of Novgorod, Gennadius, initiated a repressive action which, supported by the revered Joseph Sanin, founder of the Volokolamsk monastery, resulted in the decisions of several synods of the Russian Church between 1490 and 1504 condemning the Judaizing sect. Some apostates were publicly burned at the stake and the sect was again forced underground.[7]

Another characteristic incident occurred when Ivan III

invited an eminent Jewish physician, Messer Leon, who, because of internal squabbles in his community, had been banished from Mantua, to extend medical care to the royal family. To the misfortune of the boastful Jewish physician, he was unable to cure the Tsar's son, whereupon he was executed.[8]

Repressive measures of this kind continued under Ivan's successors, Vassilii Ivanovich (1505-33) and Ivan IV the Terrible (1533-84). Not only did the tsars try to keep out the Jews from their own possessions, but when Ivan IV conquered Polotsk he forced the Jews to adopt Greek Orthodoxy, while three hundred resisters were thrown into the Dvina. For generations thereafter a folk tale connected with this incident was being retold by the Jews of that region. Fortunately for the community the forced converts and other survivors could again publicly profess Judaism after the reconquest of Polotsk by Poland in 1579. Ivan also rejected all advances on the part of the Polish kings that he allow Polish-Jewish merchants to visit the Muscovite territories on business. He explained his refusal by claiming that the Jews were in the habit of importing "poisonous herbs" (tobacco?) into Russia and also of influencing the Russians to question their faith. In fact, in 1550 Ivan begged the Polish king, Sigismund August, never to raise that question again.

Nor was this merely a personal animus of the Tsar. His aversion to Jews and Judaism was shared by the Empire's grandees who wished to maintain the homogeneous Orthodoxy of their population against any foreign influences. International considerations reinforced that intolerant mood. At least Dimitrii Gerasimov, sent by Vassilii to Rome to try to coordinate the activities of the Greek-Orthodox and the Roman Catholic worlds against the Turkish menace, explained to the famous Renaissance publicist, Paolo Giovio, that Jews were not only thieves and generally harmful persons but that they also were responsible for teaching the Turks the art of manufacturing gun powder and cannons. During the great interregnum, after Ivan IV's death, the rumor that the false so-called second Dimitrii (1607-1608), a pretender to the Russian throne, was really a Jew was widely spread by his opponents and helped undermine his claims. When in 1610

the Polish Prince, Vladislav, was elected to the tsarist throne,
his adherents stipulated with him in advance that no churches
or chapels of the Catholic or any other non-Orthodox denomination should be allowed in Russia and no one should be induced to observe the Roman or any other ritual. "Jews must
not be admitted to the Muscovite Empire whether on business
or for any other purpose."[9] This anti-Jewish and antiforeign
agitation, including the rumors about Dimitrii's Jewish descent, emanated, in part, from the native Romanov family
distantly related to the previous Rurik dynasty, who, partially
through these methods, succeeded, in 1613, in securing the
throne for themselves. It is small wonder, then, that the new
tsars staunchly adhered to their predecessors' policy of keep-
ing the Jews away from their domains.

More serious were the anti-Jewish moves initiated by
Alexei Mikhailovich (1645-76). Drawn into the Cossack
uprisings against Poland, Alexei invaded the neighboring
provinces of Poland and Lithuania where his troops found
long-established and populous Jewish communities. No sooner
did the Russian army enter Moghilev than the commander
banished all Jews. Expecting the return of the Polish regime,
the latter tarried in leaving the city, but upon the approach
of the Polish troops many were massacred by the Russians.
Their Vitebsk coreligionists, perhaps forewarned, helped put
up a staunch defense. However, the city was captured and
most Jews were taken prisoner and sent back to the interior
of Russia. Ironically, these deportees formed the nucleus of
a new Jewish settlement, for even after the peace treaty of
1667 provided for an exchange of war prisoners, some of
them decided to remain in Russia. True, the government
renewed in 1676 the prohibition of Jewish settlement in
Moscow, but it could not quite prevent Jewish survivors of
the Cossack massacres and the Russian invasion in the border-
line areas, now permanently annexed by Muscovy, from
remaining in these localities.

SUPERFICIAL WESTERNIZATION

No significant change occurred even during the Western-
izing regime of Peter the Great (1682-1725). On principle,

Peter might have welcomed Jews, as he did many other foreigners in order to introduce Western methods of production
and Western science. However, he felt that his people were
not yet ripe for their admission. A story, perhaps apocryphal,
is told about Peter's interview with the pro-Jewish mayor of
Amsterdam, Nicolaes Witsen, during his visit to the Dutch
city in 1698. When Witsen transmitted to him a petition from
leading Amsterdam Jews for the admission of their coreligionists to his country, the Tsar readily conceded the advantages
of such a move but he claimed that "the time has not yet
come to bring these two nationalities together." He also felt
that, if admitted, Jews would greatly suffer from the hostility
of the Russian people.

Behind these rationalizations were concealed Peter's own
anti-Jewish prejudices. On another occasion, he is supposed
to have exclaimed, "They are all rogues and cheats; I am
trying to eradicate evil, not to increase it." The Tsar may have
been influenced also by the rumors concerning a ritual murder, allegedly committed by Jews of Gorodnia near Chernigov, in 1702. On the other hand, when during the Great
Northern War with Sweden, the Russian troops approached
in 1708 the city of Mstislavl, Peter, if we are to believe a
contemporary Hebrew entry in the local communal register,
personally entered the synagogue and stopped an incipient
attack on Jews by ordering the execution of thirteen ring-
leaders.[10]

Nor was Peter averse to making exceptions, especially in
favor of converted Jews. At least one Courland banker,
Lipman Levy, though a professing Jew, was not only allowed
to come to Moscow on business, but as the Court's fiscal
agent he was also able to play a considerable political role.
Other foreigners included Iberian New Christians (Marranos), like Peter's court jester, Ian Lacosta (Acosta), whose
biting satire helped the Emperor to expose to public ridicule
some of the boyars' "backward" mores. Of greater importance
were two other converts: Baron Peter Shafirov and Count
Anton Devier. Shafirov was baptized in his childhood by his
converted Polish-Jewish father who had settled in Moscow.
Because of his extraordinary linguistic ability and diplomatic
skill he rose quickly in the ranks of Peter's bureaucracy,

achieving the titles of baron and privy councillor. He also served as vice-chancellor and senator of the Empire, accompanied Peter on his journeys to the West, and was largely responsible for achieving, in 1711, an honorable peace with Turkey after the Turkish army had surrounded Peter and his outnumbered troops. Devier was a young Portuguese Jew living in Amsterdam when Peter arrived there on his first trip in 1698. He so impressed the Tsar that he was immediately taken into Peter's services after accepting Christianity. Before long he was given the responsible position of police commissioner in the new capital of St. Petersburg; he performed administrative wonders in helping build up the new metropolis.

Both these men, however, ran afoul of Prince Alexander Meshnikov, Peter's favorite, doubly influential because the Tsarina (later Catherine I) had been his maidservant and mistress before she married Peter. Shafirov appeared to Meshnikov not only as a dangerous rival, but also as a quarrelsome partner in a joint business venture at Archangel. After a brief trial the vice-chancellor was deprived of all his honors; only moments before his scheduled execution he was taken off the scaffold and sent to Siberia. Devier decided to marry Meshnikov's old-maid sister and finally achieved his aim by informing the Tsar that the lady was pregnant with his child. Before long Meshnikov found an opportunity to take his revenge. Devier, too, was deprived of all honors and exiled to Siberia, where he performed important administrative duties with his usual competence. After a few years a rapid turn in the wheel of fortune, characteristic of early eighteenth-century Russia, brought both men back to St. Petersburg. They were rehabilitated but, with their health ruined, they did not live long enough to enjoy their renewed influence. Independently, Meshnikov was now sent off to Siberia.[11]

Perhaps as in other countries such influential converts might have paved the way for the admission of professing Jews. But these promising beginnings were cut short under the brief, intolerant regimes of Catherine I, Peter II, and Anna Ivanovna (1725-40). In 1727, all Jews were formally banished from the country. Even one Zundel Hirsh, who had

contracted to supply silver for the Russian mint, had difficulties in securing delay until the completion of this trans-
action.[12] In the border district of Smolensk, long a battlefield
between Poland-Lithuania and Muscovy, a few Jews maintained a precarious foothold after its permanent incorporation
into the Muscovite Empire. However, when in the small
community of Sverovich one Baruch Leibov dared to erect
a synagogue across the street from a church and to influence
a retired naval captain, Alexander Voznitsin, to study the
Bible in the Jewish vein and, finally, to undergo formal conversion to Judaism, the ensuing outcry reached Anna's ears.
Both culprits were brought to St. Petersburg and condemned
to death. Their burning in a public square before a very
large crowd on July 15, 1738, sounded a permanent warning
against the possible heterodox implications of the admission
of other Jews to the Empire. In the following year the Senate
decreed the expulsion of all Jews from the Ukrainian and
White Russian territories annexed by Russia. Though postponed because of the then raging Russo-Turkish war, this
decree was executed in 1740, affecting 292 men and 281
women scattered through 130 manorial estates.

This exclusive policy was pursued with even greater vigor
by the new Tsarina, Elizabeth Petrovna (1741-62). Generally
a religious fanatic who also ordered the quiet demolition of
many mosques in the southern districts (she refrained from
publicizing this ukase only out of fear that it might provoke
reprisals by the Ottoman authorities against their Christian
subjects), she ordered, in 1742, that

> all Jews, male and female, of whatever occupation and
> standing shall, at the promulgation of this Our ukase, be
> immediately deported, together with all their property,
> from Our whole Empire, both from the Great Russian and
> Little Russian cities, villages, and hamlets. They shall
> henceforth not be admitted to Our Empire under any pre-
> text and for any purpose, unless they be willing to adopt
> Christianity of the Greek persuasion. Such baptized persons
> shall be allowed to live in Our Empire, but not to leave the
> country.

Elizabeth strictly adhered to this policy and, according to an
undoubtedly exaggerated Russian report of 1753, 35,000

Jews had been deported from Russia during the preceding decade. Even a Marrano physician, Antonio Sanchez, who had lived in St. Petersburg since 1731 and been in charge of the medical department of the army, was forced by the Empress in 1749 to leave his honorific post at the Academy of Science and to depart for Paris.[13]

Intervening developments in the industrial and commercial fields, to be sure, induced many enlightened Russians to abandon their traditional aversion to Jews. A number of petitions reached the Court, especially from merchants in the Ukraine and Riga, who felt that these restrictive policies played havoc with their international trade. They clamored for the readmission of Jewish merchants who otherwise were diverting much trade to Germany to the detriment of these border provinces. The Senate was sufficiently impressed to advocate such a readmission at least "to the border localities." But Elizabeth simply jotted down on the Senate report: "From enemies of Christ I wish neither gain nor profit."

❧ 2 ❧

Under Catherine II and Alexander I
1762–1825

So DEEP-ROOTED were the Russian majority's anti-Jewish prejudices that even Catherine II (1762-96), despite her own more rational attitude, had to proceed gingerly in the Jewish question. The problem came up during the first weeks of her regime when she was still uncertain of the legally questionable dethronement of her husband, Peter III. The Senate unanimously favored the admission of Jews. Yet remembering Elizabeth's sharp declaration, Catherine felt that, since she had become Tsarina for the defense of the Greek Orthodox faith and since she had to consider the wishes of a predominantly pious people and a powerful clergy, she could not approve such a far-reaching reversal of earlier policies. She could but slightly relax the existing prohibition and, through specific administrative measures, admit some Jews particularly to the newly conquered southern provinces which actually cried out for new settlers. By 1769 she was indeed ready formally to open the Neo-Russian territories to Jewish arrivals.

A new era began with the partitions of Poland in 1772, 1793, and 1795. Each annexation of Polish territory brought into the expanding Empire ever-larger masses of Jews. In 1795, these were joined by coreligionists inhabiting the duchy of Courland which, long under Polish overlordship, had been for some time a Russian satellite but now was directly incorporated into the imperial structure. The Neo-Russian territories, on the other hand, greatly enlarged in 1774 in the treaty of Kuchuk-Kinarji with the Ottoman Empire, embraced but few Jews. Only the Crimea included some centuries-old Karaite communities whose allegiance to Rabbanite Judaism was rather loose and who could, at the whim of the Russian authorities, be declared a separate sect with a political and legal status of its own. It was, indeed, to the interest of both the government and this relatively small sectarian minority that it be legally separated from the main body of the Jewish people, whose integration into the ethnoreligious structure of the Empire was to cause so much difficulty to the imperial authorities.

Complications arose immediately after the first partition of Poland. Catherine II and many of her advisers were sufficiently influenced by the spirit of French Enlightenment for her to invite, for example, Denis Diderot to come to St. Petersburg and complete the Great Encyclopedia in peace. Realistically, too, the traditional exclusion of Jews from the Russian Empire no longer made sense (in her letter to Diderot of 1773 Catherine mentioned, indeed, the residence of three or four Jews in her capital). So long as the Empire consisted principally of Russians with small "backward" minorities, whose speedy absorption by the Russian nation appeared assured, an ethnoreligious group of known perseverance and an ancient history could appear as a menace to homogeneity. Now, however, Catherine's dominions included millions of Poles, Lithuanians, Baltic Germans, and Tartars, whose faiths, Catholic, Lutheran, and Muslim, and well-established cultures could not be expected to be completely absorbed in the Russian language and Church.

Among these heterogeneous groups, in part inhabiting the economically most advanced provinces, Jews constituted at first but a relatively minor element, since the First Partition had brought only some 27,000 Jews under the scepter of the Tsarina. Western doctrines and Catherine's personal religious tolerance tended to moderate the imperial policies toward the Jewish minority, at least until it began clashing with some deep-rooted vested interests. Here, too, the methods of enlightened absolutism, as practiced in Prussia and Austria by Frederick the Great and Joseph II, promised effectively to mold the lives of this extraordinary, and hence somewhat difficult, minority according to the plans of the Empire's central authorities.

Not surprisingly, like most of their contemporaries in that

Age of Reason, Catherine and her immediate successors believed that human affairs could be regulated from above by
well-thought-out and well-intentioned plans without reference
to traditions and established institutions. It was not until 1803
that the levelheaded statesman, Mikhail Mikhailovich Speransky, argued for gradualness also in the treatment of Jews.
Although not yet the influential minister that he was to
become a few years later, Speransky insisted at a meeting of
the Committee for the Amelioration of the Jews that

> reforms enacted by state power are, for the most part,
> unstable; they are particularly ineffective when they run
> counter to centuries-old customs. It is preferable and safer,
> therefore, to propel the Jews toward perfection by opening
> to them new avenues for the pursuit of happiness, super-
> vising their activities from a distance, and removing ob-
> stacles from their path, but without the use of force. One
> ought not to establish new special agencies acting in their
> behalf but rather encourage their own fruitful pursuits. In
> short, as few restrictions and as much freedom as possible—
> these are the simple ingredients of an effective social
> order.[1]

Such ideas, anticipating the nineteenth century historical
schools of jurisprudence, were premature even in 1803. They
would have fallen on completely deaf ears in Catherine's
entourage two or three decades earlier.

JEWISH RIGHTS

At first the Empress saw no reason for singling out the
Jews for special legislation. In fact, after incorporating the
eastern provinces of Poland Lithuania in 1772, she issued a
manifesto welcoming all inhabitants (including Jews) as her
new subjects and promising them the continued exercise of
the rights they had enjoyed under the previous regimes and
equal treatment with the older Russian population. Persuaded
by the then dominant mercantilist theories that Jews could
help to develop industry and trade, the proclamation actually
urged them not to change their occupations of businessmen
and craftsmen. Before long they were invited to join the
respective three guilds of "merchants," or become "burghers,"

a category embracing most of the urban population, to which
by virtue of their occupations and financial strength they
would normally belong.

In subsequent years Jews were indeed allowed to participate fully in the public life of their municipalities. In her
general constitutional reform Catherine farsightedly tried to
decentralize the governmental machinery of her far-flung
Empire and to place more responsibility upon the self-governmental municipal bodies of two burgomasters and four
councillors each (in smaller townships, one burgomaster and
two councillors) and, in the countryside, upon the provincial
representations of landowners. At first Jews were admitted
to these municipal organs on a basis of equality. This was
indeed a revolutionary step, for nowhere else in Europe did
Jews enjoy such political rights, except in Tuscany, where at
about the same time Grand Duke Leopold (later Emperor
Leopold II) was also opening municipal offices to his Jewish
subjects.

As in many other phases of her administration, however,
Catherine found that there was a tremendous gap between
intention and fulfillment. In practice, the local burghers often
sabotaged the imperial decree relating to the Jewish franchise. More generally, their resistance led to the creation of
separate curias of Jewish and non-Jewish voters, whereby
Jews were deprived of all influence over the election of the
non-Jewish burgomasters and councillors. This separation
became doubly meaningful when a decree of 1786 reduced
the maximum number of Jewish councillors to one-third. Even
that provision was disregarded in practice, many municipalities having no Jewish councillors at all, while in a few others
Jews formed the majority of the Council. Nor was all this
truly significant. Despite Catherine's intentions the seat of
power remained with the bureaucracy. The fate of Jews, like
that of the rest of the population, depended far more on the
decisions, even whims, of local officials or at best of provincial
governors, than on that of any freely elected municipal or
guild councils. Thus a measure which might have been a
harbinger of a truly egalitarian treatment evaporated into thin
air.

Further complications were caused by the substantial num-

ber of Jews living in villages belonging to great Polish and
Lithuanian landlords where they were treated almost on a
par with the villeins. At the same time these landowners'
income to a very large extent depended on their Jewish
agents, who sold their surplus produce on markets in the
country or abroad, exercised their monopolistic rights of distilling liquor, sold it in taverns, and extended credit to the
farming population. Alcoholism being quite prevalent among
the peasant masses, this situation naturally led to much
friction between them and the Jewish innkeepers and moneylenders who, on their part, were often squeezed dry by the
landlords and the state's tax collectors. The government could
not shut its eyes to this evil heritage of Poland's anarchical
regime, especially since the peasantry in both the old and the
new provinces was in a state of more or less permanent
unrest. We must bear in mind that serfdom had been a relatively modern institution in Russia and that the peasants had
reconciled themselves to it mainly because the landowning
aristocracy had largely taken over the defense of the country.
That is why when, in 1762, Catherine freed the noble class
from military service, rumors began spreading among the
peasants that she had thereby also abolished the state of serfdom, a fact which the selfish landlords had concealed from
their dependent masses. Certainly, outbreaks like that led
by the Cossack pretender, Emilian I. Pugachev, in 1773-74,
which spread like wildfire through the Volga and Ural regions, served as a serious warning.

Matters came to a head after Catherine's death under the
weak regime of Paul I (1796-1801). In 1799, a severe famine
ravaged many western districts. To answer the grievances of
the suffering farmers, the government decided to consult the
assemblies of landlords in Minsk and other provinces. It may
have been well aware that the mismanagement of their
estates by those very landlords and the entire institution of
serfdom were mainly responsible for these catastrophic
shortages. Yet it had to place its reliance on the landed
aristocracy, the mainstay of its regime. Understandably, these
nobles did not blame themselves, but rather explained the
crop failures through natural and other causes, aggravated by
the Jewish innkeepers' exploitation of the peasants. Their

suggestions culminated in the ousting of Jews from the entire liquor industry and the handing over of all production and distribution thereof directly to the landlords or their appointees. Thus the village Jews, who had long suffered from their intermediate position between nobles and villeins and who, as far back as 1648-49, had paid for it a tremendous price in life and treasure during the Cossack massacres in the Ukrainian areas, now found themselves squeezed again between the millstones of aristocracy and peasantry.

INCIPIENT SEPARATION

Another cause of concern to the Russian regime was the traditional Jewish autonomy. From the days of the Babylonian Exile the Jews of the dispersion had developed a vast network of communal institutions of their own which provided not only for the religious needs of their members but also took care of such semisecular requirements as education, the judiciary, and social welfare. Under Polish rule, the *kahal*, as this communal structure was called, served also as a major tax collecting agency for the government. This all-embracing separatist institution appeared, as we shall see, to many Russian officials incompatible with the desired incorporation of Jews into the various estates to which they belonged by virtue of their occupations or financial standing. The more Catherine herself and her advisers were permeated with the ideas of Western Enlightenment, the more they resented this Jewish "state within the state."

Yet they saw no way of abolishing it entirely. Although little was publicly said about it, one could not overlook the substantial communal debts carried with them by the respective *kahals*. According to statistical data dating from prepartition Poland, it appears that the Jewish communities owed at that time the vast amount of 2,305,111 zlotys in capital and 196,478 zlotys in interest. Curiously, only some 900,000 were owed to Jews. The next largest group consisted of the clergy, whose claims of 842,777 zlotys in part dated back to the seventeenth century, and the nobles who appeared as creditors of amounts aggregating 737,468 zlotys.[2]

The abolition of the *kahal*, or even a substantial reduction of its authority, would have raised the specter of insolvency, or at least of a protracted forced liquidation of these debts which, for instance, even in more prosperous France engaged the attention of administrators and judges for decades after the Jewish emancipation. In Russia nobody seriously thought of such extreme measures, particularly since there, too, the Jewish communal organs could be put to good use in increasing the governmental revenue from the newly acquired Jewish population. These special contributions could be collected quite apart from the doubling of taxes due from Jewish members of the various estates which, perhaps in reminiscence of a similar twofold tax previously imposed upon Christian sectarians, was early instituted by Catherine and continued by her successors. The fiscal needs of the Empire thus combined with the desires of the Jewish people itself to maintain the old Jewish communal structure fairly intact.

Under these circumstances the government considered it wiser not to let the Jews spread out into the Empire's interior provinces. Complex as the situation already was in the West, it did not wish to complicate further the internal conditions in old Russia where Jews faced the perennial hostility of the population, further aggravated now by competitive business factors. The merchant class of Moscow went up in arms against the few newly arriving Jewish merchants who were able to undersell it by importing cheaper goods of higher quality. After a Moscow protest in 1790, the Tsarina determined to hold back the influx of Jews from the western provinces. In her decree of 1791, she provided that the rights extended to Jews as members of guilds of merchants and burghers related only to territories newly taken over by her. These included the Neo-Russian provinces which so badly needed new settlers that she even contemplated inviting German colonists from abroad. Here, as well as in her two other decrees of 1783 and 1794, Catherine thus laid the foundations for what was to be styled the Pale of Jewish Settlement which, as such, was injurious to Jewish status and, in the long run, was also detrimental to the best interests of the entire imperial population.

Beset by the complexities of this situation, the Russian regime embarked upon the usual outlet: the appointment of

investigating committees. Especially under Paul and during
the early years of Alexander I (1801-25) committees of ministers, for the most part presided over by the minister of
interior, Prince Victor P. Kochubey, went rather deeply into
the peculiarities of the Jewish position and collected all sorts
of opinions from informed, uninformed, and misinformed
officials, groups of landlords, and some Jews. Among the
outstanding opinions rendered was that by Ivan Grigorevich
Friesel, governor of the Lithuanian province. Of German
descent and imbued with the new ideas of the rights of men,
Friesel advocated a thoroughgoing reform of Jewish religious
and cultural, as well as economic life. Curiously, he was
seconded therein by some influential Jewish leaders such as
Nota Khaimovich Notkin who often visited St. Petersburg on
business. In a similar vein, reflective of the contemporary
debates of the Mendelssohnian circle in Prussia, ushering in
the Jewish enlightenment movement in Central Europe, were
also the memoranda written by two other Jewish merchants,
Abraham Peretz and Loeb Nikolaevich Nevakhovich. The
latter even published in 1803-1804 a pamphlet in both Russian and Hebrew under the characteristic title of "The Outcry
of the Daughter of Judah," the first Jewish apologetic work
in the Russian language. These voices were not representative
of Jewish majority opinion, however. Most communal elders
engaged in delaying tactics and usually advocated the postponement of any reforms for some twenty years.

Probably the most influential voice heard in the days of
Paul and again under Alexander I was that of Gabriel
Romanovich Derzhavin. Quite prominent as a Russian poet
of the ultrapatriotic school, Derzhavin was born and educated
in the Russian interior and probably had never seen a Jew
before he was dispatched by Paul to the western provinces
to review the Jewish situation (1799-1800). Here he consulted members of various classes, including Jesuit teachers.
He also received a memorandum from an "enlightened"
Jewish doctor, Elias Jacob Frank, who, during his earlier
Berlin studies, had absorbed much of the ideology then dominant in the progressive Jewish circles of the Prussian capital.
Finally, in 1800, Derzhavin submitted a report bearing the
characteristic title: "An Opinion on How to Avert the

Scarcity of Food in White Russia Through the Curbing of the Jews' Avaricious Occupations, Their Reformation and Other Matters."[3]

Derzhavin was convinced that, although the usefulness of the Jewish people to society at large was questionable, the Jews always managed somehow "to lord it over the nations among whom they lived." Yet he did not believe in their elimination from the country. With pietistic resignation he wrote:

> Since Providence, for the realization of some unknown purpose, has left this dangerous people on the face of the earth and has not destroyed it, the governments under whose rule it lives ought to tolerate it. It is also their duty to take care of them in such a manner that the Jews be useful to themselves and to society at large in whose midst they live.

To achieve this purpose Derzhavin proposed the division of the Jewish group into four classes—merchants, city burghers, rural burghers, and commoners—largely dependent on their occupations and the assessment of their property ranging from 50 to 1,000 rubles. He advocated the suppression of the *kahal* not only for the benefit of Jews but also as a defensive measure for the protection of Christianity. In its place there should be established purely religious institutions like the synagogues and the rabbinate, headed by a central organ which he called Sendarin (Sanhedrin). He also advocated restrictions of the Jewish franchise in municipal elections and specific economic disabilities. Nevertheless he was convinced that, if accepted, his proposals would make future generations remember Emperor Paul as a benefactor of Jews "who, as fanatic and stiff-necked enemies of the Christians, are destined by fate to remain eternally scattered."

Probably even without Paul's death, Derzhavin's proposals would not have been seriously considered in St. Petersburg. Although as minister of justice he was appointed by Alexander I to another Committee in 1803, his influence was not marked; it vanished altogether after his resignation from the ministry. On the other hand, the Committee felt the impact of Adam Czartoryski, both because of his strong personality and his intimate friendship with the Tsar. Czartoryski, a

Western-oriented statesman, was greatly influenced in turn by the debates which had taken place in Poland in connection with the great reforms undertaken, though not fulfilled, by the so-called Quadrennial Diet of 1788-92, and especially by the liberal proposals submitted at that time by the Polish publicists, Count Tadeusz Czacki and Mateusz Butrymowicz. The outcome of the deliberations of Alexander's Committee was a mixture of liberal theoretical postulates and highly restrictive practical measures.

Such a mixture greatly appealed to the tsar in the early "liberal" period of his reign, and he readily included many of the Committee's suggestions in the decree he issued on December 9, 1804, which may be considered Russia's first fundamental law regarding Jews.[4] This law upheld the admission of the Jews to municipal councils and general courts of justice while maintaining their *kahal* organization. The latter's elders now had to be elected every three years which would impede the theretofore customary semidictatorial perpetuation in office. Rabbis and communal elders (who had to continue raising the government taxes) were speedily to acquire the knowledge of either Russian, Polish, or German, in which languages Jews were soon to conduct all their business. All schools up to universities were to be open to Jewish students who, moreover, were to be safeguarded against any violation of their religious scruples. Secondary school pupils, as well as Jewish municipal councillors and travelers beyond the Pale, were to abandon their peculiar Jewish garb. Ironically, the Jews themselves argued that, because as a rule they wore beards, they would prefer to be clad in the Russian rather than the German attire. At the same time the Jewish communities were allowed to maintain their own schools, but these had to adopt the general curricula and use the general languages of instruction employed in public schools, replacing the methods theretofore in use in the old-type schools of rabbinic learning.

If these assimilatory measures were greeted at least by the small progressive minority of Jews with considerable elation, the other provisions of the statute caused general consternation. To cut short the perennial difficulties between Jews and peasants, the Jews were given the choice of either becoming farmers themselves, in which case they could settle not only in the eleven provinces (plus Courland) theretofore assigned to them but also in the more remote provinces of Astrakhan and the Caucasus, or else leaving the rural districts altogether. They were to be evacuated from the villages of the latter two provinces and of Little and New Russia within about two years (by January 1, 1807) and from the other rural areas one year thereafter.

We shall see that some Jews were indeed ready to start a new life in agriculture. But their leaders realized much better than the statesmen in St. Petersburg the enormous practical difficulties confronting such mass resettlement on the land. On the other hand, the cities offered few economic opportunities to the rural evacués. At the death of Catherine II in 1796, Russia's urban inhabitants were estimated at only 1,310,000 in a total population of some 36,000,000 (including 7,000,000 newly acquired subjects). The cities already included a large Jewish population having difficulties in eking out a meager existence. The addition of many thousands of displaced persons was bound to play havoc with the entire Jewish economic and social structure.

THE NAPOLEONIC WARS

Implementation of this drastic measure had to be suspended, however, largely because of unexpected developments on the international scene. Internally, too, confronted with the loss of their agents, many landlords submitted petitions arguing at least for the postponement of this threatened removal. Kochubey likewise saw the difficulties in transplanting no less than sixty thousand Jewish families, or more than three hundred thousand souls, into overcrowded urban areas.

The decisive factor, however, was Napoleon I's move to reconstitute the ancient Jewish Sanhedrin with the participation of world Jewry. As conceived by the Emperor of the French, delegates from all countries were to reestablish this supreme organ of the Jewish people which, discontinued since ancient times, could now serve again as the authoritative interpreter of Jewish religious law. Austria and Russia, embracing masses of Jewish subjects, took fright. The Russian government undoubtedly shared the fears expressed by Count Clemens Metternich, then Austrian ambassador in Paris, in his letter of October 23, 1806. Referring to Napoleon's preparations for an invasion of Central Europe, Metternich wrote: "There is no doubt that he will not fail to present himself as a liberator to the Christian people of Poland and as a messiah to its immense Jewish population."[5] The Russian government, too, became apprehensive that French sympathizers among the Russian Jews might adversely affect the prospective Russian military operations on the side of Austria.

Even before Russia's defeat in the "battle of the three emperors" at Austerlitz in December, 1806, Alexander decided to appoint a new committee to review the Jewish situation. In February, 1807, he dispatched Senator Ivan A. Alexeiev to the western provinces, euphemistically instructing him to ascertain to what extent "the military circumstances and the present condition of the border provinces as well as the economic ruin of the Jews, which is inevitable if their expulsion be enforced," make such resettlement difficult or impossible. Jewish deputies, especially Zundel Sonnenberg, a prominent businessman with intimate connections at court, also pressed hard for the suspension of these deportations. True, after concluding the alliance with Napoleon at Tilsit in 1807, Alexander's fears of French intervention receded and, prompted by his new instructions, some local authorities proceeded with the execution of the old order. The difficulties became so immediately manifest, however, that, after the uprooting of several thousand families, the government suspended all further deportations. They were, in fact, resumed only at the very end of Alexander's regime in 1824-25.[6]

Napoleon's invasion of Russia was, of course, merely postponed. In 1812, he finally embarked upon that fateful campaign which, after bringing his troops all the way to Moscow, ended with the disaster of his *Grande Armée* and spelled the beginning of the end of his meteoric career. To forestall Jewish cooperation with the invading armies—such cooperation was indeed expected on the part of the Poles (including some Polish Jews) craving liberation—the government initiated an anti-French propaganda among the Jewish masses.

It did not take at their face value the professions of loyalty by Jewish communities which, under both Catherine and Alexander, had actually ordered patriotic poems in Hebrew and German from the Berlin poet Naphtali Hirz Weisel (Wessely) for presentation to these monarchs on their visits to the western provinces (1780, 1801, etc.). At least one of these panegyrics was translated into German by Moses Mendelssohn himself.[7]

To persuade the population that it was better off under its Russian regime, the government now resumed the arguments already advanced after Austerlitz by the Holy Synod. To arouse Christian public opinion the Synod had pointed out that Napoleon had, during his Egyptian campaign, associated with the persecutors of Christianity and proclaimed himself a defender of Islam.

> To the greater shame of the Church he assembled in France Jewish synagogues, ordered to pay honor to the rabbis, and reestablished the great Jewish Synedrion, that same godless congregation which once dared to condemn to crucifixion our Lord and Saviour Jesus Christ. He now attempts to unite the Jews scattered by divine wrath over the whole world and to lead them to the overthrow of Christ's Church and to (O horrible impudence overstepping all his wickedness!) the proclamation of a false messiah in the person of Napoleon.

At the same time Jews were informed that, by convoking the Sanhedrin, Napoleon had wished to initiate far-reaching religious reforms in order to undermine the very foundations of Jewish Orthodoxy.[8]

Without such governmental pleading most Russian Jews proved loyal to the tsar. Apart from their fears of the French type of emancipation, with all the perils it involved for their traditional religious observance and their vested communal interests, Jews had had a long record of loyalty to their respective governments. Only under extreme provocation of a severe persecution did they occasionally waver. In Russia, in particular, they were told by their own leaders, then and later, that the tsar was really a benevolent ruler of all his subjects and that the repressive measures against the Jews originated either from the evil advice of Jew-baiting counsellors or from local officials acting without the tsar's knowledge. To the pro-Russian leaders belonged the outstanding Hasidic rabbi, Shneur Zalman of Ladi, who so strongly advocated unflinching allegiance to Russia that, upon the approach of the French armies, he had to flee for his life deep into Russia's interior. Another Hasidic rabbi, Israel the Maggid (Preacher) of Kozienice, punned on Napoleon's name, using the biblical phrase *napol tippol* (thou shalt surely fall, Esther 6:13). In practice, too, Jews, though not yet formally drafted into the army, performed many useful services for the Russian troops, first during their retreat and then at their triumphant return, through furnishing them necessary supplies and providing useful information about the movements of the French forces.

Alexander I realized the value of that loyalty. Harking back to his earlier liberalism, he became at times a spokesman for Jewish rights beyond Russia's frontiers. He lent a willing ear particularly to Sonnenberg and to another Jewish agent, Eliezer (Lazar) Dillon, who frequently appeared at headquarters before and during the Tsar's sojourn at the Congress of Vienna, the Vienna police speaking glibly of "Tsar Alexander's two court Jews." Among other matters, that Congress adopted a "Confederate Act" to serve as the constitution of the newly formed Germanic Confederation which included certain safeguards for Jewish rights previously enacted by the member states. Alexander felt that, as a signatory of the Treaty of Vienna, he had to help uphold the provisions of that Act. When after 1815 the growing German reaction led to the abrogation, by the free cities of Frankfort, Bremen, and Lübeck, of the rights which their Jewish inhabitants had attained during the French occupation, Russia's diplomatic agents joined those of Austria, Prussia, and England in reiteratedly protesting against this infringement of the Confederate constitution. More dramatically, Alexander I lent a willing ear to the British missionary, Lewis Way, who had visited him in St. Petersburg and who later, while the tsar was attending the Congress of Aix-la-Chapelle, submitted to him a memorandum advocating full emancipation of all European Jewry. Alexander ordered his Foreign Minister, Count Charles Nesselrode, to submit this memorandum to the other members of the Congress and to urge for it sympathetic consideration. This move proved both belated and abortive, however. In the growingly reactionary atmosphere of the early post-Napoleonic era the European statesmen were in no mood to hasten Jewish emancipation against a growingly hostile public opinion.[9]

Nor was that anti-Jewish mood limited to the western countries. In the patriotic fervor of 1812 the tsarist regime had to fall back on the old national-religious loyalties of the Russian people. Liberals like Speransky had to be discharged and replaced by inferior, but reliably Orthodox, counsellors. The tsar's new chief adviser, Admiral Alexander S. Shishkov, reminisced that he and the Tsar had often read together selections from the Hebrew prophets which seemed to fit particularly the crisis of the moment; both men allegedly shed "tears of overcharged emotion." At that time a newly founded Bible Society found such an echo in the population that it could not "satisfy the hunger of millions of our countrymen," according to the Society's president, Prince Alexander N. Golitsin. While this Bible-mindedness of Russian society helped stimulate certain sectarian trends and, by 1826, was found to be a danger to Russian Orthodoxy, the newly rising waves of religiosity and mysticism (one need but recall the tremendous influence exercised by the mystic ladies, Baroness Barbara Juliane Krüdener and Madame Catherine Tatarinov, upon the tsar himself) cut short whatever Western liberal tendencies had made themselves felt in Russian society and the court *camarilla* in Alexander's earlier days.

This general reactionary mood could accrue only to the disadvantage of Jews. Hostility toward them flared up on several occasions soon after the War of 1812. Golitsin, Alexander's lifelong friend, had been placed in 1810 in charge of the religious minorities, although he continued to serve as procurator of the Holy Synod, and as such was the leading lay executive of the Russian Orthodox Church. His and his associates' bent of mind clearly showed itself in a rather minor and unpublicized affair of 1814. During the summer of that year the thirteen-year-old daughter of Rabbi David Slutsky of the then rapidly growing Jewish community of

Kiev was kidnapped one Friday night from her home, held incommunicado from her parents for several months, converted to Christianity, and married off to a Christian husband. She succeeded in smuggling out a few notes to her parents, indicating her chagrin about the separation and her unwillingness to abandon Judaism. Once she made good an escape from her guardians, but was quickly overtaken. When the matter finally reached the Synod in St. Petersburg it decided that the conversion was perfectly legal. It apparently even instituted proceedings against the unhappy father for having "maligned" the local churchmen. We do not know from the extant archival documentation the ultimate outcome of that affair, but that there was an obvious miscarriage of justice seems beyond question. Golitsin must have taken a hand in these unfortunate proceedings, although three years later he was to uphold the right of the Jews to be heard through their own deputies.[10]

Even more threatening was the outcropping of Blood Accusations in Grodno in 1816 and Velizh in 1823. These allegations that Jews murdered a Christian (usually a young boy) in order to secure his blood for their Passover ritual, and other manifestations of popular animosity, which the government failed to counteract, were symbolic of the steady retrogression in the Empire's policies toward the Jews. This reaction was to reach its climax under Alexander's successor.[11]

☙ 3 ❧

Under Nicholas I and Alexander II

1825–1881

ALEXANDER I'S LATTER-DAY romanticism and his mystic leanings made him increasingly impatient with the Jewish resistance to conversionist efforts. Not only the Bible Society, but also a special Society of Israelitic Christians started with high hopes of converting Jews to Christianity. The results proved utterly disappointing, but the ensuing conflicts added fuel to the existing religious antagonisms. Foreign observers were easily misled. The French playwright, Jacques Ancelot wrote to his friend X. B. Saintines from St. Petersburg in June, 1826 that the ordinary Russian is religiously quite tolerant. "Jew, Muslim, Protestant or Catholic arouse no aversion on his part; he may complain about them, but he does not blame them and never persecutes them." This certainly was not true of the governmental circles during the regime of Nicholas I (1825-55).

Throughout the reign, the new tsar concentrated on fostering "Orthodoxy, Autocracy, and [Russian] Nationality," according to the well-known formula suggested by Count Sergei S. Uvarov, his minister of public enlightenment. Personally, too, Nicholas was well characterized by a leading Russian historian, Sergei M. Soloviev, as "a despot by nature, with an instinctive aversion for every movement and expression of individual freedom and independence. Nicholas loved only the soulless mass movement of soldiers under command." Although he had had little contact with Jews before ascending the throne—he had officially been second in line of succession and owed his elevation to the voluntary abdication of his elder brother Constantine—he showed his general prejudice on his visit to the western provinces in 1816, when he observed in his diary, "The ruin of the peasants in these provinces are the *Zhids*. . . . They are full-fledged leeches sucking up these unfortunate provinces to the point of exhaustion." But he added: "Surprisingly, however, in 1812 they were very loyal to us and assisted us in every possible way even at the risk of their lives."[1]

WIDESPREAD MISCONCEPTIONS

Nicholas' observation was characteristic of the then regnant opinion among the Russian intelligentsia. Its large segment of army officers usually came in contact only with Jewish innkeepers, agents, moneylenders or—spies. None of these represented the cream of Russian Jewry. Apart from occasional words of admiration for the beauty of Jewish women, we hear, therefore, only adverse comments on Jews.

This negative attitude prevailed also among the Decembrists who, during the brief pause between Alexander I and Nicholas I, staged the unsuccessful uprising of December, 1825. Although generally liberal-democratic, these revolutionaries envisaged little improvement in the status of Jews without speedy assimilation. Paul Pestel, intellectual spokesman of the southern section of the party, combined extreme Russian nationalism with his democratic ideals. Hence he saw the future of Russia only in terms of a homogeneous Russian nation which would completely absorb all national minorities including Jews. In his chief Decembrist treatise, *Russkaia Pravda* (Russian Truth), he advocated the abolition of Jewish autonomy and the complete integration of Russian Jewry. But he also contemplated the more desirable alternative of transplanting the Jews to an underpopulated area in Asia Minor and establishing there an independent Jewish state. Less extreme were the ideals voiced by the only Decembrist of Jewish descent, Grigorii Peretz who, about 1810, had submitted to conversion to Russian Orthodoxy together with his (then wealthy) father, Abraham Peretz, the tsar's "commercial councillor" in St. Petersburg. Grigorii, grandson of a Galician rabbi and of a distinguished Lithuanian talmudist-philanthropist, played but a minor role in the movement and, after its failure, spent but fourteen years in prison. The Russian Jewish masses, nevertheless, interpreted the conversion of the Peretz family as an additional warning against the pitfalls of Enlightenment. At the same time the predominantly assimilationist policies of the Decembrists, the sole vocal opposition group, confirmed the belief of the Jewish masses that their future lay only in the appeasement of the tsar and his officials.[2]

Russia's bureaucracy was always keenly sensitive to the changes in the central government. Most lower officials were not only generally underpaid (the vast majority even in the early twentieth century had to get along with monthly salaries equivalent to $10.00 or less), but were also removable at the discretion of their superiors. Hence they quickly sensed the winds of intolerance blowing from St. Petersburg. In the religious sphere the new mood lent greater credence to the old Blood Accusation. This perennial source of friction which, since the twelfth century, had embittered Judeo-Christian relations in many parts of Europe, reappeared in the newly acquired western provinces from the days of Catherine. However, the government discouraged the sporadic rumors. In 1817, Alexander I forbade the circulation of unfounded libels of this kind; the officials were to investigate possible murders without reference to the blood ritual.

On the occasion of a new Blood Accusation, however, in Velizh, Vitebsk province, in 1823 the local judiciary was given free rein to introduce this element which, under Nicholas, was blown up by the testimony of three local Christian women. At every successive hearing these witnesses elaborated their story and embellished it with incredible and intrinsically contradictory details. The affair drew ever wider circles and finally engaged the attention of the imperial Senate, the majority of which was ready to condemn the accused. In the meantime all synagogues in Velizh had been closed and the alleged culprits kept in prison. Only owing to the efforts of Admiral N. Mordinov, chairman of the Department of Civil and Spiritual Affairs in the Council of State, who happened to own estates in the vicinity of Velizh, the tissue of lies and phantasies woven by the imaginative witnesses was fully unraveled. In 1834, the department acquitted all accused Jews, offered them compensation for their unwarranted sufferings, and ordered their accusers deported to Siberia. The tsar approved this decision, but noted that, while in this particular case the Jews were clearly innocent, he was still convinced that, just as there existed criminal sects among Christians, Jews, too, probably embraced sectarians believing in the ritual value of Christian blood.

It is small wonder, then, that the ritual murder libel continued to flourish in Russian folklore. In 1844, Skripitsin, one of Nicholas' advisers on non-Christian faiths, submitted to the tsar an extensive memorandum buttressing that libel by spurious quotations from the Talmud and rabbinic literature, long known from anti-Semitic writings in Germany. This memorandum subsequently served as the basis for a two-volume work by Hippolyte Lutostanski, a Catholic priest defrocked because of many excesses and immoralities (among others he had allegedly raped a Jewish woman), who added further plagiarisms from other sources. At first Lutostanski merely intended to use that work for blackmail, offering not to publish it if the Moscow rabbi, Solomon Zalkind Minor (1827-1900) would pay him 500 rubles. But, upon the latter's refusal, he issued the volume in 1876, and followed it up three years later by a comprehensive two-volume work, *The Talmud and the Jews.*

Despite the repudiation of their contents and the revelation of the author's abysmal ignorance of rabbinic literature by such a distinguished Orientalist as Daniel Chwolson, a converted Jew, Lutostanski's works and similar other writings enjoyed a vogue among Russian anti-Semites to the end of the tsarist regime. This literary character assassination received additional nourishment from another ritual murder accusation in the small locality of Perwisi, near Sacheri in the Caucasus. To be sure, owing to the brilliant defense of two attorneys at the district court of Kutais (hence the designation of Kutais affair), all defendants were acquitted in 1879. But this outcome failed to pacify the contemporary anti-Jewish press and the few pseudoscholarly defenders of the ritual murder myth.

CANTONIST EXCESSES

Far more drastic, though less enduring, was Nicholas I's ukase relating to the so-called *Rekruchina*. Until 1827, Jews usually fulfilled their military duty by the payment of a special tax. Now Nicholas, who considered himself primarily a soldier, decided to force the Jews to serve in person. Remarkably, such extension, under discussion since 1800, was treated not as a privilege to be granted to Jews as part of their sharing in all citizens' rights and duties, but rather as a punitive measure to help reduce the size of the Jewish population, to make it pay up tax arrears, or else to force it to take up agricultural pursuits. Now Nicholas added another decisive motive. In a confidential memorandum he wrote that "the chief benefit to be derived from the drafting of Jews is the certainty that it will move them most effectively to change their religion." Although unfamiliar with this express statement, the Jewish community sensed the missionary zeal behind the new decree and, from the outset, repudiated it as a piece of calculated governmental oppression. A group of pietists in Starokonstantinov went so far as to address a bitter complaint against it to God and to assure its delivery handed it to a deceased man.

The main provisions were rather simple: At the age of eighteen a specified number of Jews were to be drafted for twenty-five years of service; they could be taken at the age of twelve for several years preparatory training added to that twenty-five year term. Like other subjects, Jews could still send substitutes, but in their case the substitutes had to be Jews, too. Certain categories, including rabbis, guild merchants, students, skilled artisans, and agricultural workers, as well as single sons and their families' sole breadwinners, were to be exempted, but otherwise the rotation was to affect all Jewish families beginning with the largest. A curious formula of an oath, apparently taken by many of these recruits in Hebrew as well as Russian, is still extant. The young soldier was made to swear that he would faithfully perform his duties and obey his superiors as if he fought for "the salvation of our own land and our holy Torah." After adding a statement that he had no mental reservations about his oath, the soldier concluded, "But if I should sin, either of my own will or persuaded by someone else, and violate the oath which I am taking today faithfully to serve in the army I, together with my family, shall be excommunicated in this world and the world to come, Amen."[3]

Administration of this draft was handed over to the Jewish communities themselves and soon became the source of endless internal friction. Most cumbersome was the following paragraph: "The community may at any time draft by verdict any Jew who is guilty of irregularity in the payment of taxes, or of vagrancy, or of any offense not tolerated in the community. If a Jew is thus enrolled by an order based on this statute, and is found eligible for service, the community shall be given a receipt to that effect and be credited with it on the following year's quota." Since most Jewish families knew what to expect, many youngsters of draft age fled to forests, mutilated their bodies so as to become physically ineligible, and resorted to all sorts of subterfuges to evade the draft. The communal authorities, implacably pressed to meet their quotas, often employed so-called *khappers* (kidnappers) who seized the required number of youths on streets or by invading private homes. These ruthless agents often used such illegal methods as forcibly depriving of their certificates young men occupationally exempted from the draft. Most tragically, they often seized children aged eight or nine (one allegedly aged five) and claimed that they were twelve years or over.

As a result, legions of small children were forced to march thousands of miles to reach their destination. Sometimes half the contingent died on the way. One need but cite the telling description by Alexander Herzen, who witnessed what he called "one of the most awful sights I have ever seen" in a small village of the province of Vyatka.

Pale, worn out, with frightened faces, they stood in thick, clumsy soldiers' overcoats, with stand-up collars, fixing helpless, pitiful eyes on the garrison soldiers, who were roughly getting them into ranks. The white lips, the blue rings under the eyes looked like fever or chill. And these sick children, without care or kindness, exposed to the icy wind that blows straight from the Arctic Ocean were going

to their graves. . . . Boys of twelve or thirteen might somehow have survived, but little fellows of eight or ten. . . .
No painting could reproduce the horror of that scene.[4]

On the march the process of Christianization began. All
means were considered justifiable, including flogging and
other tortures. "Get yourselves baptized, scoundrels, or else
I will flog you to death!" one commander roared. Estranged
from their communities, living as outcasts among hostile comrades, removed at a tender age from their families and
friends, a great many cantonists sooner or later submitted to
baptism. A few resisted and survived all tribulations. Others
preferred suicide to conversion. According to a widely circulated story (soon dramatized in a German poem, *Die beiden
Matrosen*), Nicholas was once reviewing his troops in Kazan
and the commander wanted to impress him with an improvised ceremony of mass baptism of the Jewish cantonists. Yet
the children, brought to the Volga to be baptized, by concerted action immersed themselves in the river and drowned.

We have no definite information about the total number
of Jewish victims of the *Rekruchina* while it lasted—from
1827 to 1856. According to some records, 26,279 were
drafted in 11 years. Another estimate mentions some 40,000
in the first 17 years. The total may indeed not have exceeded
60,000 in the entire 30-year period. The Jewish population,
which at that time may have averaged some 3,000,000, could
sustain such losses without serious interruption in its numerical expansion. However, their psychological impact was most
far-reaching and enduring. The class struggle, which had
existed in the East-European Jewish communities even before
the partitions of Poland, now assumed an unprecedented
sharpness, since the *kahal* authorities charged with the draft
were prone to favor members of the educated and wealthy
classes over the "vagrants" and "tax dodgers" mentioned in
the decree. Bribery of officials, including the kidnappers,
likewise tended to shift the burden of the draft on the shoul-
ders of the impoverished masses. The populace was never to
forget these injustices. A typical folksong bitterly complained:

> Tots from school they tear away
> And dress them up in soldier's gray.

> And our leaders, and our rabbis,
> Do naught but deepen the abyss.
> Rich Mr. Rockover has seven sons,
> Not a one a uniform dons;
> But poor widow Leah has an only child,
> And they hunt him down as if he were wild.
> It is right to draft the hard-working masses;
> Shoemakers or tailors—they're only asses!
> But the children of the idle rich
> Must carry on, without a hitch.[5]

Military service as a means of Christianization proved no more effective than Nicholas' similar efforts to suppress the sectarian deviations of the Dukhobory and Molokani. Forced into the army from 1826 on, these sworn pacifists performed all peaceful tasks but, regardless of tortures, refused to fire a shot. Finally, the Tsar, fearing to undermine the discipline of the other soldiers, dispersed these recalcitrant sectarians over the Caucasus (1839-41). Yet, rightly observes Hugh Y. Reyburn, "Nicholas found that to scatter burning coals among combustible material is not the best way to extinguish a fire."[6] The sectarians merely increased their religious propaganda in the new environment. Moreover, the drastic misuse of military service for penal servitude could only prove detrimental to the Russian army which, ever since Napoleonic days, had considered itself invincible. When, at the end of Nicholas' regime, it had to meet the crucial test of the Crimean War, the "degenerate" Western powers proved victorious. Learning the lesson, Alexander II speedily discontinued the cantonist system in 1856.

NEW CODE

Nor was Nicholas any more cognizant of the realities of the Jewish situation when he attempted to codify the laws governing the Jewish status. A passionate legalist, he considered codification a major task of government. He succeeded, by 1833, in publishing a major code of laws, the so-called *Polnoe sobranie zakonov rossiiskoi imperii* (Complete Collection of Laws of the Russian Empire) which served as a basis for all future tsarist collections. He followed it up by a new statute for Jews, published in 1835, after many years of deliberation by a special committee appointed by Alexander I in 1823. The Tsar's objective was to introduce order into the welter of often conflicting ordinances which had accumulated since the first fundamental Jewish statute of 1804 and to help eliminate the confusion, of which such an informed adviser as P. D. Kiselev was to complain. Without introducing major innovations the new statute defined more definitively the Pale of Jewish Settlement which thenceforth was to include the provinces of Grodno, Vilna, Volhynia, Podolia, Minsk, Ekaterinoslav, Bessarabia, Bialystok, Kiev (except for the city of Kiev), Kherson (without Nikolaev), Taurida (without Sevastopol), Moghilev and Vitebsk (without the villages), Chernigov and Poltava (without the fiscal and Cossack villages), and finally Courland and Livonia (Latvia). In addition there were the provinces of the autonomous Kingdom of Poland until its incorporation into the Empire in 1863. These boundaries remained more or less intact to the outbreak of the First World War.

The law provided further that Jews should not be allowed to settle anew in the villages along a fifty-verst, or some thirty-mile-wide strip along the western frontier, in order to prevent Jewish smuggling. The specter of illicit imports had already haunted Alexander's government which, in 1820, had induced the Vilna *kahal* to place smuggling from the neighboring provinces in Prussia under a religious ban. It did it despite its own efforts to outlaw bans within the Jewish community and despite the refusal of the Minsk community to follow Vilna's example. The Vilna excommunication, characteristically, became the subject of an extensive correspondence within the Prussian cabinet which feared that this measure might interfere with Prussia's exports to the Tsarist Empire.[7]

Evidently, the ban did not achieve its purpose and we hear no more about it under Nicholas who, in 1843, proceeded to the total elimination of Jews from the frontier districts. The ukase, uprooting scores of thousands of Jews from their old habitats, not only caused widespread consternation in the Russian Jewish community, but also reverberated through the European press. It even evoked an unpublicized intercession by the Rothschild family which, as early as 1822, had launched a huge Russian loan of £10,000,000, very helpful in that early period of reconstruction and currency stabilization after the Napoleonic wars.[8]

On the other hand, the comprehensive statute of 1835 definitely suspended further expulsions of Jews from villages to cities, acknowledging defeat of a measure futilely carried on for some three decades. The government had come to the conclusion that such expulsions had merely ruined the Jews without benefiting the peasants. The 1835 statute included prohibitions for Jewish males to marry under the age of eighteen, and females under that of sixteen. It renewed the old medieval restrictions of Jewish employment of Christian domestics and the erection of synagogues near churches. At the same time, it confirmed the Jewish franchise in municipal elections, except that it now demanded a reading knowledge of Russian from each Jewish councillor. A supplementary decree of 1836 restored the old limitation of Jewish council members to but one-third.[9]

Nicholas also introduced in 1836 a special censorship of Jewish books. Censorship had long seriously hampered all Russian intellectual creativity, but here an effort was made to review not only newly published books and pamphlets (no Jewish papers or magazines were as yet appearing in Russia), but also to subject the older Jewish letters to close surveillance. Those allegedly containing statements prejudicial to Christianity or to Jewish loyalty to the Crown were publicly burned, first in St. Petersburg and then in the provinces. In the exercise of its supervision the government had to rely mainly on ignorant converts and corrupt Christian censors. To what extent misinformation ran rampant even in the highest ministerial circles may be noted from the report by Daniel Chwolson that, in 1844, the minister of the interior had suggested to the tsar the suppression of a secret Jewish book called *Rambam* (a well-known abbreviation of Rabbi Moses ben Maimon or Maimonides) which allegedly ordered Jews to murder Christian children and drink their blood. Six years later the better informed minister of public enlightenment recommended the publication of the same Maimonidean Code, with a German translation, as a textbook to teach morality to Jewish children.[10] Needless to say, censorship, somewhat refined in the following years, impeded the free development of Jewish learning, especially since Jewish printing presses were allowed to function only in the two localities of Vilna and Kiev or Zhitomir.

EDUCATIONAL REFORM

Nicholas and his advisers soon realized that, in order to be effective, their stick would have to be combined with a carrot. In 1840, under the guidance of Sergei S. Uvarov, the minister of public enlightenment, a large-scale action was instituted to induce Jews to establish schools devoted to secular subjects taught in Russian. To be sure, admission to governmental schools had long been open to Jewish students, a privilege reiterated in the statute of 1835. However, these schools were so completely dominated by Christian ideology and, promises of safeguarding Jewish conscientious scruples to the contrary, so clearly served missionary purposes that they were long shunned by Jewish pupils. In 1835 there were only 11 Jews among Russia's 1,906 university students. More significantly, as late as 1840, the 80,017 pupils in primary and secondary schools embraced altogether 48 Jewish students. Now an effort was made to enlist the aid of the growingly vocal minority which preached "enlightenment" and rapprochement with Western culture and which had already begun founding, on its own, Jewish schools with a general curriculum.

One such school in Riga had invited a young German scholar, Dr. Max Lilienthal, to serve as its principal. Now Uvarov urged Lilienthal to propagate the establishment of such modern Jewish schools throughout the Pale. The young German scholar was duly impressed. In his letter of February 8, 1841, to Rabbi Isaac Loewi of Fürth, he described the cultural "backwardness" of the Russian Jews and added:

Yet all these fetters are to be removed. His Majesty, the Emperor, has favored the plan of the high-minded Minister of Education to emancipate the Jews. Two hundred schools are to be opened throughout the Empire, elementary, city and high schools. The young people who pass through these schools are to receive all the rights of citizenship

without trammel. This is a great and glorious thing, the
like of which our history has not yet produced; not a too
sudden deliverance from the bonds of the Middle Ages
without being able to make use of the freedom, as happened in France; nor a restless exertion and struggle
without obtaining the least advantages, as in Germany.
No, the exalted desire of the monarch is for education and
emancipation, for culture and the rights of man.

In another letter, requesting the distinguished Italian scholar,
Samuel David Luzzatto, for information about the rabbinical
seminary in Padua and about the availability of its graduates
for teaching posts in Russia, Lilienthal spoke of no less than
eight hundred new Jewish schools requiring teachers. Lilienthal's enthusiasm communicated itself even to Luzzatto, who
later was to assume a most reserved and critical attitude
toward Jewish emancipation. In his reply, the Italian scholar
assured Lilienthal of his perfect willingness to cooperate with
him, for "what could be a greater comfort to me than to see
the truly philanthropic and paternal zeal with which the
Russian government seeks the betterment of those Jews who
dwell in its dominion?" Even more enthusiastic were the
German Jewish leaders, Ludwig Philipson and Isaak Markus
Jost, who were in direct correspondence with Uvarov and
already compiled lists of Jewish candidates available for
teaching posts in the new Russian schools. More cautious
were Abraham Geiger and the Vienna rabbi, Isaac Noah
Mannheimer, and still more so the politically experienced
West-European leaders, Sir Moses Montefiore and Adolphe
Crémieux.[11]

For practical reasons it was far more important to persuade
the Russian Jews of the government's good will. Equipped
with official credentials Lilienthal traveled through the western provinces, trying to interest the Jewish communal leaders
in the new scheme. Most Jewish elders rightly suspected that
the government was pursuing a conversionist, rather than
enlightened, program (this was indeed the tenor of the secret
correspondence between Uvarov and the Tsar) and viewed
the whole undertaking as another attack on their accustomed
way of life. According to Lilienthal's reminiscences, the

leaders of the Vilna community, which he visited early in 1842, put to him the ominous question:

> Doctor, are you fully acquainted with the leading principles of our government? You are a stranger; do you know what you are undertaking? The course pursued against all denominations but the Greek proves clearly that the government intends to have but one Church in the whole Empire; that it has in view only its own future strength and greatness and not our own future prosperity. We are sorry to state that we put no confidence in the new measures proposed by the ministerial council, and that we look with gloomy forebodings into the future.

In retrospect, this reaction of the levelheaded, if politically untrained, traditionalists was far more realistic than the unbounded faith in the government's good intentions among the progressive minority.[12]

The Minsk elders advanced the remarkable argument that pious Jews, reared in their old traditions, were bearing up well under their inferior social and political status. But no sooner would their children attain general education and be deprived of the traditional solaces, they would doubly resent the discriminatory laws and practices and live an extremely unhappy life. Uvarov and his associates did not notice their inner inconsistency when they tried to force Western education upon the Jewish community, while discouraging most of their own people from attending secondary schools altogether. It was the same Uvarov who, on June 11, 1845, suggested that the fees in the *gymnasia* be increased "because in secondary schools and universities there is an evident increase of young men born in the lower orders, for whom higher education is useless; it is a superfluous luxury which takes them out of their original condition without profit to them or to the state." This restrictive policy was pursued particularly in the advanced western provinces. As a result, by 1852, 3,458 of 3,790 pupils attending the 33 western district schools were children of the nobility. A year later throughout Russia 80 percent of the *gymnasia* pupils were children of nobles or officials, 2.2 percent were the offspring of the noncelibatarian Orthodox clergy, while the rest of the population supplied only 17.8 percent—a decline of fully 10 percent (from 27.8) as compared with 1826. However, the Jewish school was to serve as an instrument of the desired integration of the Jews into Christian society, religiously as well as socially. This could be achieved only clandestinely. In his report of March 17, 1841, Uvarov himself wrote, "In directing the instruction in these schools against the influence of the Talmud, it is not necessary openly to proclaim this intention." Before long, however, Lilienthal realized that he was being duped by the government and departed for the United States, where he was to play a leading role in the nascent Jewish Reform movement.[13]

Practical difficulties were also staggering. To begin with, there were not enough qualified Jewish teachers for the projected schools. The old-fashioned *melamdim* long obstructed the entire undertaking. But a few attempted to pass the required examination in Russian and many of those who passed it secured the certificate by bribery, rather than knowledge. The Christian school principals, appointed by the government, were much more interested in their revenue than in the quality of instruction. Peter Marek rightly observes that these officials actually occupied two remunerative posts, "one in the service of the ministry of public enlightenment as official disseminators of culture, and the other in the employ of local Jewish communities as the most trusted and effective fighters against the educational policies of that very ministry."

Nevertheless, sustained by the growing desire of Jewish youth to secure general education, the program was making slow but perceptible progress. In 1847, the two rabbinical seminaries of Vilna and Zhitomir opened their gates to a small but eager band of Jewish students. Other Jewish "Crown schools" began enrolling more and more students. By 1857, their pupils reached the respectable figure of 3,293, and seven years later that of 5,711 (in addition to 1,561 Jews attending Russian schools) which, though still a small minority of the Jewish school population, laid the foundations for the subsequent large-scale entry of Jewish youth into the Western pursuits. Little did the government foresee that it was thus opening the gates for a youth which was later to furnish important recruits to the revolutionary movements.

This myopia of the authorities was doubly remarkable as, during that very period, they were discouraging peasant children from going beyond primary schools and, if possible, from attending schools altogether. It is but another illustration of the contradictory and confusing tsarist policies toward the Jewish subjects, based upon both misinformation and ill will.

Even foreign interventions proved completely futile. Sir Moses Montefiore, the distinguished British philanthropist and communal leader, who had submitted a memorandum on the Jewish question to the tsar on his brief visit to London in 1844, journeyed to Russia two years later, in order to help persuade the government of the need of more salutary reforms. As an important London banker and Nathan Meyer Rothschild's brother-in-law, he was courteously received by the tsar, had several conferences with Uvarov and other influential officials, visited many communities, and upon his return to England submitted a number of proposals to Nicholas—all to no effect. The Russian police, which kept him under close surveillance and reported all Jewish visitors he received, were irked by hearing Russia compared with Turkey as objects of his intervention. On the other hand, Sir Moses was startled by the Russian officials' constant harping on the backwardness of the Russian Jews, their excessive adherence to the Talmud, and even "that they starved themselves all the week in order to have candles and fish for the Sabbath." When the Rothschild firm tried to secure a residence permit in St. Petersburg for one of its agents, W. Davidson, the British ambassador, Lord Bloomfield, did not even dare to press the subject with the tsar during his visit of a few days to the Peterhof. On this occasion Nicholas told him, to cite his report of June 28, 1847, "that he [the tsar] had no great feeling for the Jews and was resolved not to change the law of Peter the Great or make any concessions in favour of Mr. Davidson or any person professing the same religion." Similarly negative were the results of a visit by a French Jew, Jacob Isaac Altaras who, in the same year, proposed to the tsarist authorities the resettlement of a number of Russian Jews in Algeria which, then under French suzerainty, was supposedly prepared to extend hospitable treatment to these newcomers. At first the Russians demanded from Altaras a per capita ransom for their exit permits. But anxious to get rid of some Jews, they offered to make a gratuitous exception from their general prohibition of emigration for Jewish families in groups of one hundred or more. Only young men of draft age were not to be allowed to leave. Yet Altaras left Russia without completing any arrangements and the entire scheme came to naught.[14]

Characteristically, during those very years tsarist law deprived even Jewish businessmen traveling abroad of their Russian citizenship if they failed to return within the term of one to two years stated in their passports. This law affected particularly Russian pilgrims to the Holy Land who, after a brief sojourn, found themselves in the position of stateless citizens, a situation fraught with great dangers under the unsettled conditions of the Ottoman Empire. Because of these uncertainties the Russian Jewish community of Jerusalem, led by its rabbi, Isaiah Burdaki, applied, in March, 1849, to the British consul for British protection under the then existing system of capitulations. According to Lt. Colonel Hugh Henry Rose, the British Consul-General in Beirut, he had been told by his Russian counterpart, C. Basily, "that it is possible that henceforward every year some two or three hundred Jews will leave Russia for ever for Palestine; but I perceive that Mr. Basily thinks and hopes that the whole Jewish population in Russia will eventually do the same." Whether or not formally approved by the Porte, this arrangement was largely acted upon by British consular officials for several decades.[15]

WHIFF OF LIBERALISM

A new epoch in Russian history, though far less in that of Russian Jewry, began with the accession to the throne of Alexander II (1855-81). Of a far more hesitant character, the new Tsar was willing to lend his ear to advisers who, under his father's regime, had ineffectually pleaded for reforms. By conviction he was a staunch conservative. Reading in a report the word "progress," he noted, "What is progress?" and forebade its further use in official documents. Yet the growing industrialization of Russia, which made free labor far more remunerative to factory owners, helped to force the government to proclaim, in 1861, the general emancipation of the peasants, earning for Alexander the designation of Tsar-Liberator. Many Jews shared the general enthusiasm which greeted the new regime; they hailed the emancipation decrees and looked forward to their own speedy liberation as well. A typical young scholar, Emanuel Borisovich Levin, who was to evince a lifelong concern for Jewish rights, submitted, in 1858, a memorandum to Alexander II on the subject of the "kidnappers" and the evils which had arisen from the cantonist system, now gone into discard. In another memorandum, addressed to the Jewish elders of St. Petersburg, Levin urged concerted action to secure full equality of rights for Jews.

Except for the abolition of the cantonist system, however, and the submission of Jews to the general draft laws, the removal of Jewish disabilities was quite slow. Probably more important than the few specific alleviations of Jewish status was the toning down of the government's conversionist policies. Religious instruction in the government schools, still obligatory, was now left to the discretion of the parents who, if they so desired, could engage private tutors for their children (1859). The tsar forbade the conversion of Jewish children under fourteen without the consent of their parents (1861). Such small chicaneries as the reduction of a Jewish criminal's penalty if, during the trial, he embraced Christianity, or the monetary gifts theretofore given to Jewish soldiers accepting baptism, were now stopped by the decrees of 1864-66. There also was a slight liberalization in the Jewish rights of settlement. Cities like Kiev which, though located within the Pale, were officially closed to Jews, were now opened at least to their upper classes. Other cities had to give up their residential restrictions of Jews to specific ghettos.

However, legislation aiming at ultimate Jewish equality was never adopted. True, it now found eloquent champions in the minister of interior, Count S. S. Lanskoi and the Governor-General of New Russia, Count Alexander G. Stroganov, and it began looming as an important public issue in the contemporary press and literature. Before long the Jews

found vigorous publicists of their own, such as Osip Rabinovich and Yoakhim Tarnopol, who demanded emancipation
not as a gift for good behavior but because of the inherent
rights of all men. "History has proved," Rabinovich wrote in
an editorial of his new journal, *Razsvet* (The Dawn), "that
our legal equality never depended on the level of our education, but rather on the political development of the nations
among whom we lived." He was, of course, not against the
quest for better education. But, as he claimed, "we should
strive after perfection out of pure love for the highest ideal
of perfection." He could readily point to the general progress
of Western education among the Jewish youth, which in those
years had begun entering the Russian secondary schools en
masse. From the small percentage of 1.25 in the secondary
school population in 1853, the ratio of Jewish male students
rose to 13.2 percent of the much larger enrollment twenty
years later.[16]

Nevertheless, the Tsar's chief advisers were still adhering
to the old doctrine that Jews should be granted equality only
after they had proved their usefulness to the country. The
Jewish Committee, headed by the jurist Count D. N. Bludov,
rejected the suggestions submitted by Lanskoi and Stroganov
and decided only in favor of a slow extension of Jewish rights
"in proportion to the spread of true enlightenment among
them, the transformation of their inner life, and their induc-
tion into useful occupations." The only difference from
Nicholas' approach was that, instead of emphasizing the harm
accruing to Russian society from the unproductive or "useless"
Jews, the stress was now laid on enlarging the rights of the
"useful" Jewish citizens. Accepting that governmental distinction, a group of leading Jews, headed by Joseph (Yozel,
Evzel) Günzburg (1812-78), petitioned the Tsar to permit
at least merchants of the First Guild, graduates of Russian
schools, and skilled artisans to move freely beyond the Pale.
These Jewish leaders were thus prepared to accept, at least
temporarily, the continued discrimination against the majority
of their people.

A turning point away from these semiliberal policies came
with the outbreak of the Polish insurrection of 1863. The
Poles now fraternized with the Jews, pledged them full

emancipation and, in return, received much support from them. True, the Polish nobility could not quite overcome its traditional feeling of superiority. We are told of a Jewish innkeeper who, at the risk of his life, hid a fleeing aristocrat in his cellar. When he brought the fugitive some food he was greeted with the shout: "Remove your hat, you dirty Jew!" Yet the ruling circles in St. Petersburg were frightened at the prospect of a Judeo-Polish alliance; doubly so, since the Empire was also threatened by the intervention of Napoleon III and other foreign Polonophiles. With considerable effort and much cruelty the Russian army suppressed the revolt and inflicted severe retribution on participants and onlookers alike. Contrary to the prediction of the Austrian Consul-General in Warsaw, Baron Lederer, that the Jews would utilize their intermediary position between the Russians and the Poles to wrest from the former some egalitarian legislation, this uprising made a lasting "anti-alien" impression upon Russia's governing circles. They felt that thenceforth they should rely only on the Russian Orthodox population to which the minorities should be assimilated as speedily as possible. While the main assimilatory pressures were now exerted on the Ukrainian and other Uniates, whose submission to the Pope had become doubly irksome as the Papacy had taken the side of the Polish rebels, and, to a lesser extent, on the Lutherans of the Baltic provinces, the new religio-ethnic intolerance necessarily affected the Jews as well.[17]

Anti-Jewish feelings were further intensified in official circles by the publication, in 1867-70, of essays and a book, the *Kniga Kahala* (The Book of the Kahal), by a converted Jew, Jacob Brafman. In this volume Brafman reproduced many excerpts from the minute book of the Minsk community from the years 1795-1803 which, torn out of context and considerably doctored by him, revealed a degree of Jewish xenophobia which seemed to bear out the old Jew-baiting accusations.[18]

The change in public opinion was equally noticeable. The leading Russian papers, including the *Novoe Vremia* (New Time), which before long became the Russian equivalent of the London *Times*, turned increasingly reactionary, particularly in Jewish affairs. There also were popular riots in

Odessa in 1871. Largely instigated by the Greek population
of that cosmopolitan harbor city (truly developed only under
Duke Armand Richelieu after 1803, Odessa embraced 17,000
Jews as early as 1857), these disturbances lasted for three
days without any police interference. Rather than blaming
the attackers who had beaten many Jews and looted stores
and apartments, some of the local Christian intelligentsia
placed the blame on Jewish "exploitation."

As a result of these changes in attitude, the interventions
of such influential Jewish leaders as Baron Horace Günzburg
(son of Joseph-Evzel, 1833-1909) had little effect. Minor
restrictions were added to the recruitment of Jews for the
army. The new municipal law of 1870 renewed the limitation of the Jews' membership on municipal councils to but
one-third and confirmed their ineligibility to the post of
burgomaster. Only the admission of Jewish students to secondary schools remained unrestricted, Alexander II himself
reminding the superintendent of schools in Odessa, who had
suggested some sort of *numerus clausus*, that but recently the
government itself had "sought to break down Jewish separatism by attracting them to Russian schools." Because of the
growing need, Jewish physicians were taken even into government service in the interior of Russia without a full-fledged
M.D. degree.[19]

Governmental hostility to Jews came to the fore also in
Russia's foreign affairs. After the conclusion of the Russo-
Turkish War in which some Jewish soldiers distinguished
themselves, Prince Alexander M. Gorchakov argued at the
Congress of Berlin of 1878 against including provisions for
Jewish equality in the treaties with Rumania and Serbia. He
contended that one must not compare the Jews of these
countries, or of Russia, with their Western European coreligionists who alone, because of their cultural and economic
attainments, merited equality. But all these unfriendly acts
were mere skirmishes presaging the major clashes which were
to come after the assassination of Alexander II in March,
1881.

❦ 4 ❦

Under Alexander III and Nicholas II

1881–1914

As in many other autocracies, the succession of a Russian ruler by his son often led to a reversal of previous policies. The general revolt of youth was reinforced here by the varying autocratic propensities of father and son or two brothers. Such reversals had been manifest in the transition from Alexander I's to Nicholas I's regime, and again from that of the latter to the reign of Alexander II. However, these reversals were neither sudden nor complete. The reactionary policies of Nicholas I had been well initiated during the last years of his father's reign. Similarly, ever since 1863 strong reactionary forces made themselves felt under Alexander II and they only came to fuller fruition on Alexander III's accession to the throne.

All pretenses at liberalism were now dropped. The new Tsar had long been deeply imbued with the old authoritarian ideals, especially by his mentor Constantin Petrovich Pobedonostsev, a former professor of the University of Moscow and now overprocurator of the Holy Synod. A well-trained jurist and logical thinker, Pobedonostsev was an unbending doctrinaire who considered the old ideals of Russian nationalism and Orthodoxy, the only safeguards for Russia's greatness. He and the Tsar did not hesitate to promote obscurantism among the peasant masses and to seek to suppress both religious dissent and the nationalist movements among the peoples of foreign stock. They did not realize that they were thus playing into the hands of the rising revolutionary parties, of which the successful assassination of Alexander II should have served them as a warning.

Pogroms and May Laws

As a matter of fact that assassination was used as an excuse for anti-Jewish legislation. Although the terrorists included only one Jewish woman, Hesia Helfman, whose contribution had consisted merely in providing shelter for her fellow conspirators, officially inspired rumors were spread that Jews had played a leading part in the revolutionary upheaval. The newly organized secret league of nobles (*Sviaschennaia Druzhina*) for the defense of the existing order, engaged in large-scale anti-Jewish propaganda. It stirred up sufficient resentment among the peasants to lead to bloody outbreaks in many communities, particularly in southern Russia.

Equivocal hints dropped by such officials as the anti-Semitic Governor General of Kiev, Alexander Romanovich Drenteln (seemingly a member of the *Druzhina*), persuaded would-be attackers that the Tsar wished to see the Jews suffer retribution. They disregarded such appeals for peace as were issued by Governor General P. D. Sviatopolk-Mirskii of Kharkov who pleaded that "only enemies of the Fatherland can sympathize with the disturbances and only thieves and robbers can hope to gain from street riots." As a result, a series of pogroms swept over the Ukraine and its neighboring provinces beginning with Elizavetgrad, a city of some 32,000 inhabitants (April 27, 1881). Next to Kiev or Berdichev the greatest sufferers were the hundreds of smaller settlements completely helpless to stave off the disorders. The local police and military forces reacted with painful slowness, whether because they were unprepared for this sudden epidemic of attacks, or because of the reluctance of their military and civil commanders to use force against their coreligionists in the defense of hated Jews. In most cases the authorities tolerated assaults and looting of Jewish quarters for two days before effectively intervening on the third day. Quite a few policemen and Cossacks mingled with the looters; they speedily vanished on the approach of troops. Only in the northwestern provinces did the authorities stop the disturbances at their very inception. As if to prove to the world that this was a spontaneous reaction of

the masses against their Jewish exploiters, the Russians rejoiced when, on Christmas day 1881, a similar outbreak
occurred in Warsaw, where but two decades earlier Jews
and Poles had marched together against their tsarist oppressors. Here, too, some Russians were the chief instigators;
one of the arrested, a former Russian colonel, was found in
possession of a detailed list of Jewish shops singled out for
pillage.[1]

Psychologically, the impact of these pogroms was even
greater than the physical and material damage. Russian
Jewry, and with it world opinion, awoke with a start at
the sight of this revival of what had long been considered
an extinct method of settling Judeo-Gentile controversies.
Even Eastern Europe had not been the scene of large-scale
massacres since the Cossack rebellion of 1648-50, except for
some local disturbances in White Russia in 1744 and under
the leadership of Gonta in 1768. That is why even the loss
of a few hundred lives and the great material damage (estimated in Kiev alone at 2,500,000 rubles), almost irreplace-
able for impoverished Russian Jewry, mattered less than the
feeling of insecurity which pervaded the entire community.
It was but partly mitigated by the Western expressions of
sympathy. On the other hand, the protest meetings in London and New York, the parliamentary debates in the American Congress and the British Parliament, as well as the
extensive reportage in the foreign press (for instance, a series
of articles anonymously published by Joseph Jacobs in the
London *Times*) could not fail to make some impression even
upon the most obdurate Russian leaders. Alexander may have
on occasion voiced utter disdain for the Western press. On
a visit to Marienbad in 1888, where he willy-nilly became
acquainted with some liberal Austro-Hungarian newspapers,
he complained that the press had fallen into the hands of
self-seeking journalists. "It is hard to imagine," he contended,
"a despotism more irresponsible and violent than the despotism of printed words." Yet even he admitted that the press
had become a great power in the world and he tried, at least
at home, to control it by an ever-stricter censorship, which
he reinforced by a decree of 1883. With respect to the
pogroms he was personally shocked and perplexed by the

bloody turn of events and, on one government report, he noted "Some one must have had a hand in inciting the people against Jews. A careful investigation of all such cases is imperative." Yet he deplored more the necessity for the government to prosecute some "patriotic" Greek-Orthodox assailants than the losses in Jewish lives and property.[2]

Rather than being fearful that, once the masses tasted blood, they might turn on their real oppressors (in the initial stages the authorities tried to place the blame for the disturbances on the nihilists), the tsarist regime decided to restrict more and more the rights of its Jewish subjects. To both foreign and domestic accusers it answered by echoing the expostulations offered by local officials, guilty of impassivity in checking the disturbances, that this was but a popular reaction to intolerable Jewish "exploitation." During a twenty-minute interview with a Jewish delegation, headed by Baron Horace Günzburg, Alexander himself declared, "On the souls of the Jews, too, a sin is burning; they are said to be guilty of exploiting the Christian population." And he added the query: "Why do they so gladly evade military service?" The government considered itself in duty bound, therefore, to devise legislative means to protect the populace.

At Court the influence of such relatively liberal advisers as Count Mikhail T. Loris-Melikov, the minister of interior, sharply declined. Alexander doubtless shared Pobedonostsev's opinion of Loris-Melikov, as defined in an anonymous memorandum which the overprocurator forwarded to the tsar on April 30, 1881. Here the minister's honesty was acknowledged, but he was characterized as "an extremely ambitious person, thirsting for power, a heartless egotist and of wholly oriental mentality and morality [the count was of Armenian origin]. . . . The count would make a good governor-general of the Caucasus but he does not understand Russia and the Russian people whose aspirations do not evoke any echo in his heart." Moreover, behind Loris-Melikov stood, in the memoralist's opinion, the Jewish terrorist, Grigorii Davidovich Goldenberg, who often outwitted the gullible minister. Curiously, at the time of the submission of that memorandum the overprocurator seemed unaware that Goldenberg had turned idealistic traitor, had repented and committed suicide nine months before. Loris-Melikov who, in 1880, had escaped assassination by Meir (Ippolit) Molodetskii, a recent convert to Christianity, was now removed in favor of Count Nikolai P. Ignatev, master of intrigue and confirmed reactionary. In his explanation of the massacres Ignatev wavered between the attribution of the bloodshed to nihilists and to Jewish "injurious influences" upon the masses. In his memorandum to the tsar of August 22, 1881, he declared that the cause of the pogroms, "so incompatible with the nature of the Russian people," was the rapid economic expansion of the Jews during the preceding regime.

> Having adopted strict measures [Ignatev added] to suppress the earlier disturbances and mob rule and to protect Jews against violence, the government feels justified in pursuing speedily an equally energetic course in order to remove the existing abnormal relations between the original inhabitants and the Jews. It must protect the Russian people against the Jews' injurious activities which, according to local reports, were responsible for the disorders.

This memorandum suggested the enactment of more restrictive laws.[3]

To initiate the new legislation the government, like its predecessors, started with a committee. This time the investigation was handed over to gubernatorial commissions organized in each of the fifteen provinces of the Pale (outside the Kingdom of Poland) in addition to that of Kharkov. Although each commission included two Jewish representatives appointed by the governors, all cards were from the outset stacked against them. In the very circular, sent out by Ignatev to the respective governors-general on August 25, 1881, the aim of these deliberations was defined as relating to "the harmful impact of the economic activity of Jews on the Christian population, their racial separatism, and religious fanaticism." Since some of the governors themselves were implicated in the disturbances, they had every reason to choose members sympathetic to Ignatev's point of view. Under the circumstances it is astonishing that five commissions, or nearly one-third, recommended the opening of the entire Empire to Jewish settlement as the only remedy of the existing shortcomings.

Needless to say, their advice was not taken. On the contrary, the government proceeded with great dispatch to issue on May 3, 1882, new "temporary rules," forbidding Jews to settle anew outside towns and hamlets and to carry on any business on Sundays and Christian holidays. In this formulation some of Ignatev's extreme demands were toned down and, if properly administered, the hardships of the "May Laws" for the Jewish people might have been mitigated. Strict observance of both Christian and Jewish holidays, to be sure, would have made Jewish business less competitive. But in many smaller towns Jews had little to fear from Christian competition; elsewhere they could purchase "protection" from the local police.

Corrupt Russian bureaucracy interpreted even more freely the clauses relating to new settlement. Sometimes it refused to readmit Jews to their old residences after an absence of but a few days (for instance, in order to attend synagogue services on high holidays in a neighboring city), declaring them to be "new settlers." On occasion it expelled Jews who merely changed their residence from one house to another in the same locality. Not surprisingly, these administrative persecutions, coming on top of the sanguinary persecutions by hooligans, convinced Russian Jewry that it was unwanted in its centuries-old habitat. It knew what was in the minds of an Ignatev and his ilk, whether or not it had heard Ignatev's hypocritical explanation offered in April, 1882, to the American chargé-d'affaires, "We have on the one hand 5,000,000 Jews, Russian subjects, clamoring to be freed from all special restraints, and we have on the other, 85,000,000 Russian subjects clamoring to have the 5,000,000 expelled from the Empire. What is to be done in such a case?"[4]

STIMULATED EXODUS

The temporary rules were supposed to be replaced by permanent legislation to be passed, as the legal custom demanded, by the Council of State. In February, 1883, Alexander III appointed a "High Commission for the Revision

of the Existing Laws relating to Jews" under the chairmanship of Count Constantine I. Pahlen, a former minister of
justice. The so-called Pahlen Commission reviewed thoroughly
the century-old legislation, the debates of the gubernatorial
commissions, and many other data. It took five years before
it completed its labors and submitted its proposals which,
because of their moderation, did not find favor with the Tsar
and his chief advisers. Unperturbedly, the administration
not only continued to enforce the May Laws, but superimposed upon them a number of further restrictions, among
them a *numerus clausus* for secondary schools and schools of
higher learning. Under the excuse that Jewish students were
"quick in joining the ranks of the revolutionary workers," a
quota of 10 percent was established, in 1887, for all such
schools within the Pale, 5 percent outside the Pale, and
3 percent in St. Petersburg and Moscow. This quota was
subsequently reduced to 7, 3, and 2 percent, respectively.
As a result, Jewish university students often had to overcome
serious legal and financial difficulties to obtain their higher
education in foreign universities. Upon their return to Russia,
such disgruntled foreign graduates were doubly likely to
disseminate the liberal doctrines current in the Western
lands.

In 1889, a decree restricted the admission of Jewish,
Muslim, and Karaite lawyers to the bar, requiring, in each
case, special permission of the minister of justice on the
recommendation of the presidents of local bar associations
or judicial institutions. While the few Muslim and Karaite
candidates had little difficulty in securing such permits,
Jewish applicants were regularly rejected for about fifteen
years and had to make their living through formally assisting
Christian colleagues and by other evasions. Even after admission, a Jewish lawyer could be subject to special chicaneries. According to an anecdote told in her Memoirs by
Countess Mariia E. Kleinmichel, General Cherevin, head of
the secret police under Alexander III, had pacified a lady
friend, who was losing a lawsuit to a party represented by
a Jewish attorney, by assuring her that he would deport
the Jewish lawyer to Siberia under some trumped-up political
charge. Although brought back before his appeal would

reach the higher authorities, the latter would in the meantime be prevented from pleading on the next day and thus lose his case. When the countess protested, Cherevin explained, "I cannot hold the scales impartially between intimate friends of mine and a dirty Jew who, if he is not guilty to-day, may have been yesterday, or will be tomorrow." The story has it that, during his absence of three months, the attorney not only lost his case but also his pregnant wife, who had been so frightened by her husband's arrest that she immediately miscarried and died.[5]

Chicaneries of that type, both legal and extralegal, multiplied from day to day. In another sensational move the government expelled the Jews from Moscow on the first day of the Jewish Passover of 1891. Only a small group of old settlers was allowed to remain, while the newly constructed beautiful synagogue was closed down and, ultimately, under constant governmental pressure, turned into a charitable institution. The authorities paid little heed to the plight of thousands of Christian workers who lost their employment in Jewish factories and commercial establishments (the important silk industry almost entirely suspended operations) and to the protests of Christian merchants and manufacturers in 1893.[6]

It became increasingly manifest that the government was trying to make the Jewish position in the Empire altogether untenable. Although generally emigration from Russia without an exit permit was strictly forbidden, the authorities placed few obstacles in the way of would-be Jewish emigrés who in ever swelling numbers fled across the border, particularly to the Galician frontier city of Brody, from where they expected to be rescued by their Western coreligionists. We shall see, in another connection, that the majority of these refugees found their way to Hamburg or Liverpool and were ultimately shipped to the United States and other countries. Needless to say, such mass emigration created considerable difficulties also in the countries of immigration. Notwithstanding the general reluctance of Western statesmen to interfere in the internal affairs of other lands, President Benjamin Harrison reported in his Third Annual Message to the Congress of the United States of December 9, 1891, that

> this Government has found occasion to express in a friendly spirit, but with much earnestness, to the Government of the Czar its serious concern because of the harsh measures now being enforced against the Hebrews in Russia. . . . It is estimated that over 1,000,000 will be forced from Russia within a few years. The Hebrew is never a beggar; he has always kept the law—life by toil—often under severe and oppressive civil restrictions. It is also true that no race, sect, or class has more fully cared for its own than the Hebrew race. But the sudden transfer of such a multitude under conditions that tend to strip them of their small accumulations and to depress their energies and courage is neither good for them nor for us.
>
> The banishment, whether by direct decree or by not less certain indirect methods, of so large a number of men and women is not a local question. A decree to leave one country is in the nature of things an order to enter another—some other. This consideration, as well as the suggestion of humanity, furnishes ample ground for the remonstrances which we have presented to Russia while our historic friendship for that Government cannot fail to give the assurance that our representations are those of a sincere wellwisher.

One million was a rather conservative figure. People were prepared to accept as true a statement allegedly made by Pobedonostsev to the Jewish publicist, Alexander O. Zederbaum, that the only solution for the Jewish question in Russia was that one-third should emigrate, one-third become Christianized, and one-third should perish.[7]

Such exodus of Jews seemed to be directed into more orderly channels after the organization, in 1891, of the Jewish Colonization Association by Baron Maurice de Hirsch. Confirmed anti-Semites like Pobedonostsev and Alexander III were not averse to dealing with Jewish big business. Even in St. Petersburg the great railroad builder Samuel Poliakov had free access to the overprocurator who, on several occasions, reported to the tsar Poliakov's schemes to secure for

Russia a foothold in railways being built in Turkey and Persia. The Russian government was still more inclined to maintain relations with such leading Jewish bankers abroad as Gerson, Bleichröder, Bismarck's trusted adviser. They were taken aback when, under the impact of the Russian pogroms, the Paris Rothschilds withdrew from a consortium negotiating a half-billion franc loan for the Tsarist Empire.

It was somewhat easier to deal with a genuine philanthropist like Baron de Hirsch before whom one did not have to conceal one's conviction of the desirability of Jewish mass departures from Russia. At his first attempt to help his Russian coreligionists De Hirsch offered to pour 50,000,000 francs into a scheme for establishing trade schools within Russia so as to train Russian Jewish youths for crafts and farm work. After having advanced 1,000,000 francs which was used for the training of Russian youths for the Orthodox priesthood, Hirsch withdrew his offer, when the government insisted that this amount be placed at its disposal without any strings attached. Undeterred, the Belgian banker continued the negotiations, but now asked for an arrangement to evacuate, as he hoped, fully 3,250,000 Jews from Russia over a period of twenty-five years, and to settle them in colonies overseas, particularly in Argentina. The latter location must have appealed to Pobedonostsev who had previously evinced interest in the spiritual welfare of several thousand Greek Orthodox settlers in Buenos Aires and its vicinity and repeated the observation of the minister of the navy that "these little known southern harbors might offer shelter to our navy in case of war." The government instructed, therefore, its local officials to extend full cooperation to Arnold White, a member of the British Parliament and a known champion of anti-alien laws there, who was twice sent by Hirsch to Russia to conduct the negotiations. Pobedonostsev personally gave him an autographed letter of introduction. However, as we shall see, for reasons beyond either Hirsch's or the tsar's control, this colonization scheme attained but meager results and the overwhelming mass of emigrés continued to flow in the direction of North America.[8]

Nor could the Jews count on the support of an enlightened public opinion. The great Russian writers of the interior had little personal familiarity with Jewish life, especially in the crowded western ghettos which they knew only from occasional visits. That is why most of their descriptions of Jewish characters are stereotyped and lifeless. They also readily shared the prejudices of their environment. The great masters—Pushkin, Lermontov, and even the better-informed Gogol—of the earlier decades in the nineteenth century knew only of such characters as Jewish poisoners, spies, and cowardly traitors.

Later in the century, particularly after the pogroms of 1881-82, the conscience of the people began bestirring itself. Even then some liberals were deterred from voicing loud protests against the pogromists. Many had grown to believe in the righteous instincts of the masses and looked with abhorrence on violent measures to be taken by the police against the "people." Yet the circle around the distinguished thinker, Vladimir S. Solovev, and the eminent novelist, Vladimir G. Korolenko, marshaled enough dignity and courage to voice sharp protests against massacres of innocent Jews. To be sure, Leo Tolstoy appended his signature to Solovev's petition to Alexander III only because, as he said, he had sufficient confidence in his friend that he could subscribe to anything that Solovev would write. When the philosopher finally assembled one hundred signatures of distinguished intellectual leaders it was suppressed by the government, together with his Foreword accompanied by a number of philosemitic letters attached to a booklet by his longtime friend, Rabbi Feivel Goetz. This fate was to befall also Solovev's efforts to persuade Pobedonostsev in 1892 to tone down the persecution of Christian sectarians. There is no evidence that the overprocurator ever answered that remarkable epistle, in which the writer frankly indicated his personal dislike of the recipient, who, unbeknown to him, had already unfavorably commented to Alexander III in 1888 on Solovev's influential work on *The Russian Idea*. In his novel *Yom Kippur*, Korolenko actually depicted sympathetically some Jewish characters. The pogrom in Nijni-Novgorod in 1882 made so strong an impression on the youthful bystander, Maxim Gorki, as to cause him to relate these happenings on the occasion of the later pogroms.[9]

Somewhat more equivocal was Anton Chekhov's attitude. A southerner like Korolenko, he had had much greater opportunities for observing Jewish life. Chekhov's Jewish characters vary with his changeable conservative and liberal views. But at least during the Dreyfus Affair of the 1890s he broke off with his long-time friend A. S. Suvorin because of the latter's outright anti-Semitic and anti-Dreyfusard stand. Even generally liberal Ivan S. Turgenev was but moderately friendly in his story *The Zhid*. Fiodor M. Dostoevsky, on his part, could not quite fit the Jew into his dream of a messianic Russian people. At best he came around to formulating the idea that Jews should be granted equality of rights, provided they would not thus become stronger than the native population, a condition which no one could guarantee in advance and which nullified the entire proposition. Next to these masters there was a growing host of lesser writers, for the most part rabidly anti-Semitic, who had the ear of the majority of the Russian readers. As against this wall of hatred, indifference, or at best sympathetic misunderstanding, the pleas advanced, as we shall see, in both fictional and publicist works by the growing number of Russo-Jewish writers passed largely unnoticed. Works by these apologists were, as a rule, read by Jews who needed no convincing. This situation began changing but slowly after the death of Alexander III in 1894.

THE LAST TSAR

Accession to the throne of Nicholas II (1894-1917) involved no immediate change in the governmental system or detailed policies. Although Pobedonostsev's personal influence declined somewhat, his spirit continued to dominate the thinking of the Tsar and his court *camarilla*, some members of which, supported by the reactionary Tsarina, attained an even greater influence. Quite early in his regime (January, 1895) Nicholas announced in a public address: "Let it be known by all . . . that the principle of autocracy will be maintained by me as firmly and unswervingly as by my lamented father."[10]

Nevertheless, some Jews seemed to detect harbingers of a

better future. Nicholas' declaration in his imperial manifesto that his sole aim was to seek "the happiness of all his loyal subjects" and the invitation extended to three rabbis to participate, at government expense, in the coronation ceremonies seemed promising gestures. The St. Petersburg community reciprocated by commissioning Mark Antokolski to produce a silver angel handing the crown to the new Tsar and donated it to Nicholas. However, the entrenched Russian bureaucracy successfully resisted any relaxation of pressures on the Jewish population. So conservative was, indeed, the prevailing trend in the first decade of the new reign that no substantially new policies were adopted, while the old screws of legal and administrative discrimination were turned more tightly. The only justification Pobedonostsev knew to offer to a Paris delegation of the Jewish Colonization Association in 1898 was that Jews were natively more gifted, better educated, and more aggressive than the average Russians and that, hence, the latter needed legal protection against being wholly dominated by them. This faked humility, already adumbrated by Dostoevsky, served as a ready excuse even for such a relatively liberal Minister of Interior as Prince Peter Dimitrevich Sviatopolk-Mirskii to do nothing during his short tenure of office (1904-1905).

Among the principal administrative restrictions was a further lowering of the *numerus clausus*. The aforementioned reduction of the Jewish quota to 3-7 percent, was now interpreted to refer to each particular department in the universities and colleges. Since Jews knew in advance that they would not secure government appointments in teaching or civil service, they naturally tended to select training for the liberal professions of medicine or law. According to the new interpretation, therefore, the total number of Jews in the academic enrollment was bound to fall below the general quota.

Governmental animus was directed particularly against the legal profession which enabled Jews not only to display their forensic talents, but also to use them in the defense of their coreligionists appearing at court. At times, the brilliant defense of Jewish defendants by Jewish attorneys and their role in uncovering the machinations behind anti-Jewish attacks proved extremely embarrassing to governmental officials. It is small wonder, then, that in 1897 a special committee deliberated the introduction of a new *numerus clausus* for Jews in the legal profession beyond the restrictions in admission to the bar enacted in 1889. No such law was issued; but the Jewish ratio in the legal profession constantly declined. Physicians, too, were now restricted to private practice and excluded from all government posts. Obviously, no clearer illustration of tsarist inconsistencies was required than the early drive under Nicholas I to force the Jewish youth to attend general schools, as contrasted with the persistent governmental efforts half a century later to discourage Jewish participation in the country's general educational system.[11]

Similarly old, but more intensive, was the enforcement of the settlement restrictions relating to Jews, although many more voices were now heard pointing to their adverse economic effects. A pamphlet on "The Effects of Antisemitism," published in 1897 by Professor N. Shmerkin, submitted detailed evidence about the fall of both state revenue and grain exports, especially of the finer grades, in those provinces outside the Pale from which Jews had been exiled since 1881. The allegedly high interest rates of 15 to 25 percent charged by Jews were raised by Christian usurers to 75 to 200 percent after the departure of these competitors. In 1895, the Cossacks of the Don, Terek, and Kuban regions successfully protested the contemplated expulsion of Jews, because the latter were the sole distributors of their produce. For similar reasons even the governor-general of the Caucasus persuaded the central authorities to revoke an impending decree of banishment of newly settled Jews from that area.[12]

In most other cases, however, the combination of bureaucratic inertia and bias prevailed. Time and again the police staged regular night raids on Jews found beyond the Pale, in rural districts, or even in such southwestern towns as Kiev. Whenever seized, sometimes in their night attire, such illegal residents, men, women, and children, were imprisoned or speedily deported. In some cities the police actually set for information concerning illicit settlers rewards twice as high as for the denunciation of hardened criminals. To add insult to injury, the Kiev police paid its large personnel mainly devoted to the detection of Jewish lawbreakers from the revenues of the Jewish meat tax. Going further back into the Middle Ages in his report to the Tsar of 1895, Pobedonostsev complained of the pernicious religious influence exerted by Jews upon their Christian household help. Of course, the overprocurator did not bother to submit full documentation for his sweeping accusation.

All these chicaneries added fuel to the resentment on the part of the Jewish masses and, without stopping their constant growth, merely increased their self-assertiveness and political consciousness. Economically, to be sure, the pauperization of Jews proceeded apace. According to an economist, A. Subbotin, the number of Jewish paupers increased by 27 per cent in the four years of 1894-98. In many communities fully 50 percent of the Jewish population depended on charity, particularly during the Passover week. The flight abroad likewise continued notwithstanding objections raised by some Jewish leaders who saw in it a sign of weakness or lack of patriotism.

These very assertions illustrated, on the other hand, the progressive integration of Jews into the political fabric of the Empire; more and more of them now believed that their ultimate future lay with political action which would force the government to grant full equality of rights to all citizens. This became, indeed, the heyday of newer Jewish ideologies and the formation of Jewish parties. We shall see that in 1897 were founded both the Jewish-Socialist *Bund* and the World Zionist Organization. True, the latter was led by such Westerners as Theodor Herzl and Max Nordau. But its chief source of manpower and much of its spiritual and ideological energy came from Russian Jewry. In addition there also were all sorts of combinations of Zionism and Socialism. Many other Jews preferred to join the general Russian parties, both liberal and socialist. The government reacted sharply to all these movements, regarding them as equally subversive of the established order. Even Zionism which, in its ultimate goal, was to contribute to the further evacuation of Jews from Russia was soon outlawed, because it unavoidably contributed to Jewish militancy against the prevailing oppression.

Aided by the government, the conservative groups went over to a counteroffensive. Through machinations of the secret service agents, especially one Peter Rachkovskii, a tale was concocted—out of an old French story and a German story—relating to an alleged Jewish conspiracy to take over the world. In essence, this story was prepared in 1895, but it was not published in Russia until it appeared in serial form in the reactionary newspaper *Znamia* (The Banner), edited by a well-known pogromist, P. A. Krushevan, in St. Petersburg (in nine successive issues of August and September, 1903). In 1905, this apocryphon was reprinted by the government press in Tsarskoe Selo, the imperial residence. It was appended to a book by an alleged "mystic saint," Sergei Nilus, entitled *The Great and Little: the Coming of the Antichrist and Satan's Rule on Earth,* as an illustration of the saint's predictions. By that time its origin was more or less forgotten and some circles began attributing the plot to the World Zionist Organization and its first Basel Congress of 1897. Another edition, under a different title, was published by another anti-Semite, G. Butmi, in 1906. This editor denied the specific connection with the Basel Congress, but insisted upon the origin of that conspiracy from an alliance between Herzl, the Bund, the Russian Masons, and the British Foreign Office. He wrote:

England, through its agents, the Russian Masons, is co-operating for the internal enslavement of Russia by the Jews, by Jewish Zionists, by means of stirring up internal sedition, paralyzing the potential resistance of Russia to the wiles of British foreign policy. The agreement on this subject between the Zionists and the Masons was apparently arrived at in 1900, at the initiative of Dr. Herzl, founder of modern Zionism. Thus Jewish Zionism, working in Russia under the protection of Russian Masons, is well-organized and spread throughout Russia by the treacherous agency of the British foreign policy, which is always inimical to Russia but friendly to the Jews.

Although this fabrication thus was semiofficially promoted and another version was published and widely distributed by the Army staff of the St. Petersburg Military Region, it did not play a major role in the history of Russian anti-Semitism. Only years later, under the impact of the revolutionary changes occasioned by the First World War, did this product of the Russian secret service attain its worldwide notoriety under the title of *The Protocols of the Elders of Zion.*[13]

New Pogroms

At the same time there was increased violence in both the governmental repression and popular attacks. The pogroms of 1881 were a mere prelude to the greater bloodshed which took place in 1903 and 1905. The chief organizers now were members of the *Soyuz ruskago naroda* (League of the Russian People), founded in 1904. This paramilitary group, forming cadres of one hundred men each, came to be known in popular parlance as "The Black Hundreds." They included much military personnel and were often led by generals like Eugene Bogdanovich. Next to Jewish "exploitation," the new rationale blamed the Jews for the strength of the subversive movements. After investigating on the spot the Kishinev pogroms of 1903, Michael Davitt came to the conclusion that they had been planned "with the passive connivance of the Chief of Police and the active encouragement of some of his officers." This contention was fully borne out by the personal investigation of Bessarabia's new governor-general, Prince Sergei Dmitriyevich Urussov, a fair-minded, though conservative, official.[14]

This time the tsar himself viewed with equanimity the crimes perpetrated on his Jewish subjects and actually encouraged them by occasional hints. His acceptance of an honorary membership in the League of the Russian People for himself and his son was tantamount to a public demonstration. According to a widely-believed story, Nicholas II was supposed to have said to a general holding an important post in southern Russia, "I had expected that a much greater number of Jews would perish." On another occasion the tsar allegedly reassured a pogromist leader, Count Konovnitsin, "I know that Russian courts are too severe toward the participants in the pogroms. [This assertion is clearly controverted by such a travesty of justice as occurred in the investigation of the Gomel pogrom by the Kiev Court of Appeals in 1904]. I give you My imperial word that I shall always lighten their sentences, on the application of the League of the Russian People, so dear to me." The Tsar had effective collaborators in several successive ministers of interior, particularly the overtly anti-Semitic Viacheslav Konstantinovich von Plehve (1902-1904). To a Jewish delegation from Odessa Plehve was supposed to have unabashedly declared, "We shall make your position in Russia so unbearable that the Jews will leave the country to the last man. The Jews constitute in southern Russia ninety, in the interior forty percent of all revolutionaries." This was, of course, a gross exaggeration; it was part of the government's campaign to discredit the revolutionary movement by identifying it with Jews. On the other hand, according to Prince Urussov, it sufficed for him to show to the Kishinev chief of police a telegram sent by Plehve in 1904 and ordering the maintenance of public order. The chief exclaimed: "Be at ease, your Excellency: there will not be any disturbance in Kishinev."[15]

Contemporaries realized that many of the incendiary leaflets had been printed in the official press of the Russian gendarmerie and distributed by these supposed upholders of public peace. In fact, this was the most significant innovation of the Russian regime which far exceeded anything known about anti-Jewish massacres during the "dark" Middle Ages, when governments, as a rule, had tried to fulfill their primary duty of preserving public order. If a medieval regime wished to get rid of its Jews, it proceeded with a formal decree of expulsion, a procedure recognized as lawful by both Jews and Gentiles. By methods, now introduced by the tsarist regime (and later greatly elaborated and refined by the Nazis), the government itself instigated public disorders.

In 1903, it was the Kishinev pogrom which made a tremendous impression in and outside of Russia. Instigated by a former petty official P. A. Krushevan, editor of the reactionary local newspaper, *Bessarbets* (heavily subsidized by the government), this pogrom affected a community of some 50,000 Jews living side by side with some 60,000 Christians. In two days (April 6-7/19-20) 45 Jews were slain, 86 were seriously wounded, and 500 less seriously hurt. More than 1,500 houses and shops were plundered or destroyed. This outbreak was followed by a somewhat lesser attack on the community of Gomel, which actually had a Jewish majority of 20,400 in the total population of 36,800. Undeterred by the ensuing universal outcry, a much larger wave of pogroms took place in 1905 in connection with the First Russian Revolution. This time some 660 Jewish communities were affected in the course of a single week (October 19-25/November 1-7). Among them was the community of Odessa which had by that time became one of the great intellectual centers of Russian Jewry. Of the 165,000 Jews residing in that city no less than 300 victims lost their lives, thousands more were wounded and crippled while 40,000 were economically ruined. In all, this pogrom wave cost the Russian Jews about 1,000 dead, 7,000–8,000 wounded (many of them permanently crippled) and property losses of 62,700,000 rubles (*ca.* $31,000,000).

In contrast, however, to many earlier massacres, the assailants now often encountered a determined Jewish self-defense. Taught by previous experiences, the Jewish youth, now politically far more sophisticated, organized itself in defensive detachments, which would have met the unorganized, often drunken, pogromists on more than even terms, were it not for the intervention of the Russian military. Rather than protecting the peaceful Jews against their bloodthirsty assailants, the troops often stood passively by until the Jewish self-defense appeared on the scene. At that moment it was greeted by a salvo from the Russian soldiers, some of whom, encouraged by their own commanders, actually participated in the murders and lootings. Subsequently, too, many a young Jew was dragged before the courts because of his part in the defense. At times these Jewish detachments were accused of having started the riots by attacking Christians. While most courts did not subscribe to such nonsense, many had gradually lost their judicial independence under the corrupt administration of the new Minister of Justice, I. G. Shcheglovitov, and proceeded against the defenders rather than the attackers.

In the meantime, there was a natural revulsion to these barbaric methods among some of Russia's intellectual leaders. Dostoevsky remained the staunch Russian nationalist and, for the most part, quite unfriendly to the Jews. But Tolstoy was forced by Kishinev to take a public stand. "The outrages at Kishinev," he declared, "are but the direct result of the propaganda of falsehood and violence which our Government conducts with such energy." True, like the upper classes generally, some intellectuals tried to wash their hands of any responsibility for these manifestations of mob hatred. But Maxim Gorki was not alone in contending that "cultivated society is no less guilty of the disgraceful and horrible deeds committed at Kishinev than the actual murderers and ravishers. Its members' guilt consists in the fact that not merely did they not protect the victims, but that they rejoiced over the murders."[16]

REVOLUTION AND REACTION

Such occasional expressions of sympathy inspired some leading Jews to believe that ultimately Russian society would extend to the Jewish minority its brotherly embrace. The majority, however, was increasingly convinced that it could rely only on its strength. This feeling was clearly expressed by a leading Jewish poet of the age, Simeon Samuel Frug (1860-1916), who had absorbed enough of Russian culture to contribute some distinguished poetry in the Russian language. But he also wrote beautiful Hebrew and Yiddish poems. One of these read:

> The wholly dead may patient wait,
> But there's a people sick and gray,
> Not wholly dead, not wholly living;
> Are saviors sent to such as they?

> No savior from without can come
> To those that live—and are enslaved.
> Their own Messiah they must be,
> And play the savior and the saved.[17]

Out of this recognition Jews not only organized their own self-defense but entered the broad stream of Russian politics, particularly during the Revolution of 1905. When, under the pressure of strikes and public demonstrations, Nicholas II finally issued, in October, 1905, a manifesto promising basic freedoms to the whole population, he passed over the Jewish question in silence. But the Jews were determined to use their newly won franchise to wrest from the government full equality of rights by constitutional means. In a "Declaration of Jewish Citizens" the six thousand signers wrote in 1905 with great dignity:

> We expect to secure civil equality not because it would make the Jews more useful citizens and benefit others. Nor do we look forward to equality as a reward for the blood our brothers are shedding on the Manchurian fields, just as their brothers had shed their blood in former wars. We do not even demand civil equality because of our centuries-old residence in lands which now form part of the Russian Empire. We demand civil equality and equal submission to general laws as men who, despite everything, are conscious of their human dignity and as conscientious citizens of a modern state. We do not expect these rights to be bestowed upon us as an act of grace and magnanimity or because of some political expediency, but as a matter of honor and justice.[18]

Jews actively participated in the elections to the First Duma (Parliament), voting wherever advisable for Jewish candidates and elsewhere throwing the weight of their ballots on the side of liberals and moderate labor leaders. The Jewish socialists, however, boycotted the election because they saw in it but a reactionary tool of pacification of the discontented masses and expected the ultimate solution of the Jewish question only from direct revolutionary action.

Despite this boycott the Jews succeeded in electing twelve of their own coreligionists to the Duma, including the distinguished leaders Maxim M. Vinaver, Shmarya Levin, and Leonty M. Bramson. Although the League for the Attainment of Jewish Rights which sought to unite the Jewish factions for common action was run by nationalistic Jews who would have preferred to see the formation of a Jewish bloc similar to the Polish bloc in parliament, the deputies themselves decided to join the two leading parties of the Cadets (Constitutional Democrats), a left of center liberal party, and the Trudoviki (Labor Party) still further to the left. The nine Jewish Cadets, though a small minority of the party's 179 deputies, made their influence felt beyond their numbers. Similarly, the three Jewish Labor members (out of ninety-four) often spoke up. Together the two parties formed a majority of the 476 deputies and, though refraining from calling the Duma a Constituent Assembly, planned to write a new egalitarian constitution. The plenary debates of May, 1906, raised the Jewish issue almost immediately. But the Octobrist conservatives urged slow motion, and persuaded the Duma to hand the matter over to a committee of thirty-three, including five Jews.

In the middle of the deliberations the news arrived of the Bialystok pogrom of June 14-16. After a number of outspoken addresses by both Jewish and non-Jewish deputies, including Prince Sergei D. Urussov, a former governor of Bessarabia and assistant minister of interior, who submitted a well-documented accusation of the regime partly based on his own experiences, the Duma elected an investigating committee of three deputies including a Jew, V. Jacobson, to institute an inquiry on the spot. The committee brought back a devastating report which made the following main points:

1. That there was no hatred of a national, religious, or economic character between the Jews and Christians in Bialystok.
2. That hostility to the Jews existed only among the police, who exerted themselves to promote ill-feeling in the army, by accusing the Jews of taking part in the movement of freedom.
3. That the pogrom was previously planned and prepared by the administration and that the local population was quite cognizant of these matters.

After a lengthy debate the Duma adopted, on July 20, a resolution reading:

That the only remedy for this situation unparalleled in the history of civilized countries, and the only means to prevent further pogroms, are to be found in an immediate judicial investigation and the punishment of all officials, high and subordinate, without regard to their position, who were responsible for the pogroms, and the dismissal of the Ministry.[19]

However, this resolution came too late to do any good. The Tsar, recovering from the revolutionary shock, disbanded the Duma. The liberal deputies, including all the twelve Jews, protested vigorously. At a meeting at Viborg, Finland, they urged the population to retaliate by passive resistance, such as refusing to pay taxes or submitting to the military draft. In reprisal, the government denounced all signers as traitors, condemned several to prison terms of three months, and withdrew their franchise. In the election to the Second Duma, therefore, these prominent leaders were not eligible and only four unknown Jewish deputies were elected. M. J. Herzenstein, a Cadet deputy of Jewish descent, and the Jewish deputy, G. Iollos, were assassinated by the Black Hundreds. By a coup d'état, the Tsar dismissed the Second Duma, too, and altered the basic electoral law, disfranchising a large majority of the population. As a result, the Third Duma was wholly dominated by the reactionary forces and, except for occasionally serving as a forum for Jewish and liberal, as well as Jew-baiting and reactionary, pronunciamentos, it was of little assistance to the Jewish cause. Its Jewish membership was reduced to two, to be raised to three in the Fourth Duma.

Parliamentary institutions thus proved of little avail to the Jewish minority. Tsarism resumed its cold war against its Jewish subjects with renewed vigor, though it was frightened enough by both the domestic and the world reaction not to continue with the hotter forms of warfare, the governmentally instigated pogroms. Nicholas II resisted any amelioration of Jewish status. He was abetted therein by the nobles who saw in any forward step a diminution of their own power. When in October, 1906, the reactionary Council of Ministers, presided over by Peter A. Stolypin, submitted to the Tsar modest proposals for the improvement of Jewish

status, Nicholas, after hesitating for two months, entered
the following characteristic note:

> Despite most convincing arguments in favor of adopting
> a positive decision in this matter, an inner voice keeps on
> insisting more and more that I do accept responsibility for
> it. . . . I know that you, too, believe that "A tsar's heart
> is in God's hand." Let it be so. For all laws established
> by me I bear a great responsibility before God, and I
> am ready to answer for this decision at any time.

Not surprisingly, the reaction assumed such force in the
following year that N. M. Friedman, one of the two Jewish
deputies in the Third Duma, could declare in February,
1910, "In the worst days for the Jews under Minister Plehve
there never existed so much cruelty and bestiality as is practiced today."[20]

Nor did the government hesitate to continue with its
literary incitation of one group of the population against
another, although it generally maintained a tight grip on all
publications through its vigorous censorship. In the decade
of 1905-16, on which we have some detailed data, it permitted the printing of 2,837 anti-Semitic books and pamphlets
with their distribution in 14,327,000 copies. The Tsar himself
contributed from his private purse no less than 12,239,000
rubles toward the dissemination of that scurrilous literature,
including the aforementioned prototypes of the *Protocols of
the Elders of Zion*.[21]

The government itself sufficiently believed in the myth of a
Jewish world conspiracy, a myth intimated as early as 1881-
83 by the famous Panslavist leader, Ivan Sergeevich Aksakov,
for Foreign Minister Count Vladimir Nikolaevich Lamsdorf
to submit to the Tsar a memorandum "on the anarchists"
(January, 1906). Partly guided by his wish to steer Russia's
foreign policies away from the dual alliance with France into
pro-German channels, he argued that the threat of the world
Jewish conspiracy could be averted only by Russia's concerted action with the German Empire and the Vatican.
He suggested that, in order to counteract the effort of the
Alliance Israélite Universelle with its "gigantic pecuniary
means" and its support "by the Masonic lodges of every
description," negotiations be begun with the Kaiser and the

Pope "for the purpose of organizing a vigilant supervision, and then also for an active joint struggle against the common foe of the Christian and monarchial order of Europe." The gullible Tsar noted on the memorandum, "Negotiations must be entered into immediately. I share entirely the opinions herein expressed."[22] Nevertheless calmer counsels prevailed and no action was taken. Since Lamsdorf's anti-French policy held out little promise of success against the Triple Alliance, he himself was dropped from the foreign ministry.

As a final coup Nicholas II and his advisers resorted to the time-honored method of blackening the Jewish name by a new Blood Accusation. Sporadic instances of the ritual murder libel made their appearance throughout the nineteenth century. The accusation of a Vilna barber, David Blonde, in 1900, led to a protracted trial, an appeal, and retrial, and ended in 1902 with his acquittal. Even the first unfavorable court sentence condemned Blonde only for an ordinary murder but did not impute to him any ritualistic motives. In contrast thereto the detection of the corpse of a thirteen-year-old Russian boy in Kiev in the vicinity of a Jewish factory in March, 1911, was blown up by the authorities into a *cause célèbre* through the ritual murder accusation of Mendel Beiliss, a minor employee in that factory. The trial conducted in Kiev in 1913 attracted worldwide attention. The Minister of Justice, I. G. Shcheglovitov, and his underlings marshaled a number of "experts" to prove the persistence of Jewish ritual murders, while the defense, led by the distinguished Jewish lawyer, Oscar O. Gruzenberg, produced the testimony of first-rate Oriental scholars like Paul Kokovtsev, against the very existence of such a ritual. A great many Russian and Western luminaries including Dmitrii Merezhkovskii, Leonid Andreev, Anatole France, Jean Jaurès, Gerhard Hauptmann, and Thomas Masaryk, likewise took up the cudgels against this revival of a dangerous folkloristic myth. More significantly, even the Kiev jury of unsophisticated peasants acquitted the defendant. This final defeat should have served tsarism as a warning that its extreme Judeophobia would not, as it had hoped, divert the attention of the masses from their genuine grievances to the Jewish scapegoat.[23]

5

Population and Migrations

IT WAS A SIGN of Russian Jewry's tremendous vitality that, despite all outside pressures and occasional losses in manpower brought about by pogroms, it steadily increased in numbers during the entire tsarist period. This was not only an absolute growth in population but, except for the last three decades which witnessed an extraordinary Jewish exodus from the Russian Empire, also relatively to the rest of the population. True, the statistical evidence for these statements is somewhat shaky. To begin with, the very estimates of the total Russian population, despite occasional governmental censuses or so-called "revisions," are far from reliable. In the Jewish case we often depend wholly on "guestimates." One can speak with some confidence of Russia's Jewish population for the first time after the census of 1897, only twenty years before the end of the tsarist regime. At that time the imperial population was estimated at 126,368,827, of whom 5,189,401 or 4.13 percent were Jews. Of course, the largest number was concentrated in the Pale of Settlement (including the ten provinces belonging to Congress Poland), whose total population numbered 42,352,-039 and included 4,874,636 or 11.46 percent Jews. Without Congress Poland, these figures were reduced by 9,401,097 and 1,316,576, respectively.[1]

RAPID GROWTH

The best estimates for the Jewish population after the Napoleonic Wars, when the area under tsarist domination had become fairly stabilized, show that in 1820 European Russia's total population (without the Caucasus) of some 46,000,000 (including some 3,000,000 in Poland) embraced approximately 1,600,000 Jews (about 400,000 in Poland). By 1851, the ninth official "revision" indicated (including the Caucasus) a total of 61,000,000 inhabitants, and a Jewish population of 2,400,000 (including 600,000 in Poland). By 1880 the general population increased to 86,000,000, the Jewish to about 4,000,000 (1,000,000 in Poland). This increase continued and, in 1910, reached 130,800,000 residents of Russia and more than 5,600,000 Jews. In short, in the six decades from 1820 to 1880, the Jews apparently increased by about 150 percent while the general population grew only by 87 percent. On the other hand, in the subsequent thirty years Jewry added only about 40 percent to its numbers, while Russia's general population climbed by 52 percent. The reason for this relative retardation is, of course, the tremendous rate of Jewish emigration which by far exceeded that of the non-Jewish peoples.[2]

Of equal interest are the internal shifts. Understandably, the Neo-Russian territories, first opened to Jews under Catherine II, showed the greatest ratio of growth. The Jewish percentage in the southwestern provinces, including Bessarabia, rose from 3 in 1844 to 7.4 in 1880 and to 8.9 in 1897. Sixteen years later, however, the ratio of Jewish settlers declined to 7.9 percent, although they increased in absolute numbers by almost 25 percent. In the entire period from 1844 to 1913 the general population of the area increased by 265 percent, the Jewish by 844 percent. In the older northwestern provinces Jewish growth in absolute numbers was actually larger, although its relative progress was much slower. In the fifty years from 1847 to 1897 Jewry increased there from 947,753 to 2,622,553 or by 177 percent. Yet compared with the rest of the population its ratio of 9.26 percent, which had interveningly grown to 16.88 percent in 1881, was reduced to 13.36 percent in 1897. This proportionate decline continued in the early years of the twentieth century when it was aggravated by incipient signs of biological retardation because of a declining Jewish birthrate. The Polish provinces showed slightly different trends, owing to the considerable immigration of so-called Litvaks from the northwestern provinces into Congress Poland. During the century of 1816-1913 the general population grew by 381 percent, the Jewish by 822 percent, the Jewish percentage rising from 7.8 to 14.97. Only the decade from 1880 to 1890 showed a temporary dip from 14.1 to 13.7 percent.

In contrast thereto the Jewish population density outside the Pale was very slight, except in the Baltic provinces of Courland (7.33 percent) and Livonia (2.24 percent), where Jews had lived in substantial numbers before the Russian occupation. Otherwise the province of St. Petersburg with its 21,270 Jews, forming 1.01 percent of the population, showed the largest concentration, owing to the presence of a substantial Jewish community in the capital. The second capital, Moscow, together with its province, had only 8,749 Jews or 0.36 percent. In toto, European Russia outside the Pale averaged in 1897 a Jewish population of only 0.34 percent, some provinces having as few as 0.03 percent.

Reasons for this extraordinary fertility of Russian Jewry are not far to seek. During the entire nineteenth century the overwhelmingly Orthodox majority of East-European Jews viewed God's blessing to Adam, "Be fruitful, and multiply, and replenish the earth" (Gen. 1:28), as a direct commandment. Early marriages were quite common; with them went large families. On his visit to the Jewish agricultural colonists in the province of Kherson in 1891, Arnold White learned "from the neighboring proprietors—Russians—who employed them, [that] they have no vice, unless early, improvident and fruitful marriages can be deemed a vice."

We have no exact statistics for the Jewish birthrate early in the nineteenth century, but it must have annually averaged some 40 births per 1,000 population. In this respect, to be sure, the difference between the Jews and their neighbors was not very substantial. Russia's general birthrate, particularly among the peasant masses, probably also averaged 4 percent of the population. Russian Jewry gained little by immigration even in the first decades of the century, when a number of Galician Jews, particularly scholars, educators, and writers, settled in the newly opened Neo-Russian areas. Unfriendly observers, including foreign visitors, spoke disparagingly of this influx. For example, Robert Lyall, who had spent a number of years in Russia, commented in his travel book, published in 1825, that Odessa had from the beginning become a place of refuge for the "worst members of society" from neighboring lands. Among the new arrivals were three hundred Jewish families, mostly from Galicia.[3] Nevertheless on balance Russian Jewry was probably losing more members through clandestine or overt emigration even before the latter assumed a mass character in the last three decades of the century. The Jews' relatively higher population increase must have depended, therefore, mainly on a generally lower mortality.

Once again we have no exact figures, but it is likely that Jews suffered somewhat less than their neighbors from the destructive forces of famines, pestilences, and wars. According to the historian Alexander Kornilov, the cholera epidemic of 1848 cost Russia about 3,000,000 lives. It was aggravated by the failure of crops and the ensuing famine, one of the numerous famines in Russia of the post-Napoleonic era (1820-21, 1833, 1839-40, 1843-46, and so forth). Another major cholera epidemic ravaged Russia in 1869, while a severe famine struck down hundreds of thousands of peasants as late as 1890-91. The Napoleonic Wars, too, seem to have accounted for a loss of some 1,500,000 Russian lives. The Jews suffered a great deal, too, during all these catastrophes, but their losses in manpower were somewhat mitigated by their higher cultural level and strong communal solidarity. Jewish communities, as a rule, strained all their resources to help coreligionists in need and probably relatively few died of full-fledged starvation. During the epidemics, too, the Jewish losses must have been minimized by communal aid and the ready availability of medical care in many localities.

Most decisive must have been the lower Jewish infant and child mortality. While even at the beginning of this century out of each thousand newly born peasant children some 450 died before the age of five, the figures for the Jewish community probably were for the same reasons very much smaller. Another factor was the great cohesiveness of the Jewish family, which traditionally went to extremes in saving the lives of its members, old and young. If that hypothesis

is correct, one can readily see that in each successive generation a much larger percentage of newly born Jewish children
survived into the age of reproduction.

On the other hand, losses occasioned by wars seem to have
affected more or less equally the general and the Jewish
population. Between 1815 and 1914 Russia enjoyed a relative period of prolonged peace, interrupted significantly only
by the Crimean War of 1853-56, the Russo-Turkish War of
1878, and the Russo-Japanese War of 1904-1905. In none of
these wars was the Pale of Jewish Settlement a major battlefield. But among combatants Jewish losses were probably as
high as those of their neighbors. It is a matter of record that,
when the results of the fairly reliable census of 1897 were
published, the Russian Jewish community heaved a sigh of
relief. For decades before the Jews had been accused of
shirking their military duties—there is no question that many
Jewish and non-Jewish young men successfully evaded their
civic obligation through bribery or other methods—and many
decrees were issued over the decades to prevent the allegedly
"excessive" Jewish evasions. One of them provided that
families, even remote relatives, be fined 300 rubles for each
"shirker," an amount which was often collected from the
poorest by the public auction of their meager household
goods. In 1901, it turned out that, while Jews amounted to
only 4.13 percent of the imperial population, the percentage
of their servicemen was 5.73. In other words, Jewish soldiers
and sailors, despite all the maltreatment they often suffered
from their superiors and comrades in the armed forces and
despite their religious scruples arising from the impossibility
of observing there the Sabbath and ritual food commandments, exceeded their population ratio by nearly 40 percent.
These facts, debated long before the census of 1897, were
fully borne out again by the established number of Jewish
combatants in the Russo-Japanese War.[4]

Of course, one must not lose sight of Jewish war losses of
their own kind: those occasioned by anti-Jewish massacres.
Ethically and psychologically, ten human victims of violence
are ten too many, but from the point of view of population
figures, the loss of several hundred or even a thousand mem-

bers did not seriously undermine the natural growth of a community numbering four or five million.

More important was another specifically Jewish source of demographic losses, namely conversion to Christianity. Notwithstanding the orthodoxy of the majority, quite a few Jews, whether in the armed forces, among the more easily assimilated intelligentsia, or in the group of straight careerists, joined the dominant faiths. An English visitor, Robert Pinkerton, was told by Archbishop Anatoli of Minsk that, in the two years between Pinkerton's visits, he had converted fifteen Jews of that city. According to the slightly exaggerating estimates of the Berlin missionary, J. de le Roi, no less than 84,536 Russian Jews found their way to the baptismal font during the nineteenth century. Nearly 70,000 of those joined the Greek Orthodox faith, while 12,000, primarily in Poland, became Roman Catholics.[5] However, the biological vitality of the Jewish people, undiminished during the entire nineteenth century, made up for all these losses, including even the largest drain of them all, the stream of emigration.

URBAN CONCENTRATION

Another important demographic feature was the growing Jewish concentration in large and medium-sized cities. The nineteenth century witnessed in Russia, though to a lesser extent than in Western or Central Europe, the gradual rise of large metropolitan areas. By 1884, there already were twelve cities of over 100,000 population in the Empire. Sixteen years later their number increased to sixteen. Next to the two capitals, the largest of these were Warsaw, Odessa, Lodz, Riga, Kiev, Kharkhov, Vilna, Ekaterinoslav, and Kishinev, each of which had a sizeable Jewish community. Odessa, Ekaterinoslav and Kiev, where Jews started to settle (or resettle) under Russian domination, showed the most substantial growth. The Odessa community embraced only 246 Jews in 1795; it grew to 17,000 in 1855, 138,915 in 1897, and 152,364 in 1904. Ekaterinoslav's Jewry rose from 320 in 1804 to 3,365 in 1857, 40,009 in 1897, and 69,012 in 1910. Kiev, which had long lost its medieval community, had 207 Jews in 1797, 3,013 in 1863, 31,801 in 1897, and 50,792 in 1910. Odessa thus became the largest Jewish settlement outside Poland, where Warsaw was speedily developing into the largest Jewish community in all of Europe (277,787 in 1908). Lodz, too, because of its extraordinary industrial expansion, witnessed the rise of its Jewish community from 2,775 in 1856 to 98,677 in 1897, to decline in the following eleven years to 88,201.

At the same time the older Jewish communities likewise grew substantially, if less rapidly. Vilna, which in the course of the nineteenth century achieved the honorific title of a "Lithuanian Jerusalem," grew from some 7,000 in 1797 to 23,050 in 1847, 63,996 in 1897, and 72,323 in 1910. Minsk increased from 2,716 in 1802 to 12,976 in 1847, 47,562 in 1897, but declined to 45,103 in 1910. In each of these cases the decline was due entirely to emigration.[6]

These figures assume even greater significance when one realizes that outside the Polish provinces the Pale embraced a nationally heterogenous population. Among the various nationalities inhabiting the northwestern and the southwestern provinces the Jews often constituted the majority, or at least the largest single group, of the urban population. More specifically, in 1897, 52 percent of the combined urban population of Lithuania and White Russia consisted of Jews. The next largest groups were those of Russians (18.2 percent), Poles (12.8 percent), while the White Russian native majority had a share of only 11.8 percent, the Lithuanians as little as 1.7 percent. In the Ukraine, to be sure, the Russians with 33.5 percent appear in the census as the largest urban group, followed by the Jews with 30 and the Ukrainians with 27 percent. But all these census figures were weighted in favor of the Russians, since undoubtedly many Ukrainians, White Russians, and Lithuanians listed themselves as Russians. Moreover, the "Russians" consisted chiefly of garrisoned soldiers, civil servants, teachers, occasional factory workers, technicians, and managers, in other words of frequently transient residents. Certainly, in all the urban centers of industry, commerce, education, and arts, Jews played a preponderant role. Their total contribution, therefore, to the Russian economy and culture, particularly in the most advanced western provinces, far exceeded their ratio in the total population.

Needless to say, these urban communities did not owe their extraordinary expansion to natural growth alone but also to the influx of settlers from the smaller towns and hamlets. Apart from taking full advantage of the opening of the Neo-Russian territories, Russo-Polish Jewry spoke of a "discovery of Volhynia," in the mid-nineteenth century. Although that province had belonged to pre-partition Poland and was densely populated by Jews even then, its growing sugar and other industries offered many new opportunities for Jewish entrepreneurs and workers. Hence Volhynia, which in 1847 embraced 174,457 Jews, witnessed their increase half a century later to 395,782, or by 127 percent. The agricultural colonization projects, too, drew some Jewish colonists, primarily to the Black Sea region.

Otherwise the Pale offered a permanent obstacle to internal Jewish migrations. Even the two capitals, which undoubtedly would have attracted a very substantial number of Jews, as they did after the Revolution of 1917, not only rigidly restricted their admission but also frequently saw the police stage raids on the few settlers who had secured entry in one way or another. Urbanization of the few Jews who managed to settle beyond the Pale was even greater than within it. Fully 82 percent of all Jews living in the province of St. Petersburg and 97 percent of all Jewish settlers in the Moscow province were concentrated in the two capitals. Similarly, Kharkov embraced more than 80 percent, Rostov-on-Don, nearly 75 percent of all Jewish residents in their provinces. Reinforced by climatic and economic factors, the law also sharply limited Jewish emigration even to the older Jewish settlements in the Caucasus or the Bokhara region reaching back to the early Middle Ages. While Russian peasants often found an outlet for their surplus population in Siberia (some 800,000 peasants settled there in the decade from 1886 to 1896 alone, and the annual rate of over 80,000 immigrants continued in the subsequent years as well), only few Jews could or would join that procession. That is why the census of 1897 revealed the presence of only 56,783 Jews in the Caucasus and 48,474 Jews in Siberia and Central Asia. It is small wonder, then, that as soon as the Neo-Russian territories began filling up and reaching a Jewish population ratio approximating that of the older provinces, Jews had to look for an additional *Lebensraum* elsewhere.

WESTWARD MIGRATION

Russo-Jewish emigration to other countries faced many obstacles, however. The tsarist system required that travelers carry with them governmental passports which were, as a rule, refused to would-be emigrés. Jews often had to resort to clandestine emigration even for religious pilgrimages to Palestine with the hope of ultimately being buried in its holy soil. Travelers provided with passports, we remember, lost their Russian citizenship after a brief absence and could not return to their native land.

Nevertheless, beginning with the 1840s the pressure became sufficiently great for substantial numbers of Jews to cross the frontiers to Germany and Austria. On German initiative Jewish leaders of Frankfort, Königsberg, London, and Paris submitted, in 1844, a petition to Tsar Nicholas I, asking that Jews be allowed to leave Russia without hindrance. Curiously, among the projected areas of Jewish settlement at that time, Texas loomed large; its German Settlement Association, headed by Prince Karl von Solms Braunsfeld, actually negotiated with Jewish representatives for the inclusion of Russian Jews in its projected colonization of European immigrants in that vast underdeveloped territory. Two years later Zacharias Frankel, a famed talmudic scholar, declared bluntly, "For the Russian Jews there is only one way out: to leave Russia and settle under a sky where the law recognizes human rights." His colleague, Ludwig Philippson, always prone to develop new schemes, suggested the establishment of a German Aid Association to organize the mass transplantation of Jews from Russia to a suitable new territory and to assist them in securing employment. Although premature at that time—such a *Hilfsverein* for East-European Jews under this very name was to be organized nearly sixty years later—it did indicate the concern of the Western Jews for the future of their Russian coreligionists languishing under the knout of Nicholas I and his underlings.

Out of the same concern, we recall, Jacob Isaac Altaras of Marseilles arrived in 1846 in St. Petersburg with his adventurous scheme of settling thousands of Russian Jews in French Algeria. The Russian government was inclined to go along, under the condition that the emigrés would lose their Russian citizenship upon crossing the frontier. François Guizot, the French minister of foreign affairs, however, vetoed the entire undertaking. "Do you mean to Judaize Algeria?" he allegedly asked Altaras.[7]

Nothing came out of these grandiose projects but there was a growing outflow of Russian Jewish individuals to Central and Western Europe, as well as the New World. During the first decades of the nineteenth century quite a few "Polish" synagogues were founded in America, indicating a swelling stream of immigration from Eastern Europe in general, for in the new lands outsiders paid little heed to the differences between Russian, Polish, Galician, or Rumanian subjects. Only a few decades later, when the emigration from these countries assumed a mass character, was it possible for the natives of these lands to separate themselves into special congregations and *Landsmannschaften,* according to their places of origin.

The turning point came during the great Russian famine and epidemic of 1868-69, from which Jews suffered along with their neighbors. At the same time economic conditions were constantly improving in the United States after the Civil War. News from relatives, previously settled in America was at times discouraging, but the pessimistic reports were far outnumbered by glowing descriptions from other expatriates. These high-strung expectations, which in Germany and Austria had reached a climax in the so-called On to America Movement of the revolutionary year 1848 and the early 1850s, now communicated themselves with even greater fervor to the Jews of Russia and Poland. Mary Antin, who came to the United States in 1891, reminisced about her youth in Plotsk, Russia:

"America" was in everybody's mouth. Businessmen talked
of it over their accounts; the market women made up their
quarrels that they might discuss it from stall to stall;
people who had relatives in the famous land went around
reading their letters for the enlightenment of less fortunate
folks, the one letter-carrier informed the public how many
letters arrived from America, and who were the recipients;
children played at emigrating. . . . A few persons—they
were a dressmaker's daughter, and a merchant with his
two sons—who had returned from America after a long
visit, happened to be endowed with extraordinary imagina-
tion (a faculty closely related to their knowledge of their
old countrymen's ignorance), and their descriptions of life
across the ocean, given daily, for some months, to eager
audiences, surpassed anything in the Arabian Nights.

Better informed, though no less prone to exaggerate, were
the readers of the Russian Jewish press which published
frequent dispatches from American Jewish correspondents.[8]

It was not altogether easy for reemigrants to return to
Russia. Those who had failed to fulfill their military duties
were arrested despite their American passports. Generally,
the problem of reciprocity in the treatment of American
Jewish citizens in the Tsarist Empire increasingly complicated
the relations between the two countries. The Russians took
the position that American Jews should not be treated more
favorably than native Jews, whereas the United States
claimed that there must be no discrimination between her
Jewish and non-Jewish citizens. Russia debated this issue also
with other countries whose Jewry enjoyed full equality of
rights, but it was only the United States which, after several
vain protests, took vigorous action. Under the pressure of
public opinion and fair unanimity in Congress, President Taft
in December, 1911, abrogated the commercial treaty with
Russia which had been in operation since 1832.[9]

Additional incentives to emigrate to America were given
by the lower rates for ocean travel, baits extended by commercial agents of shipping companies, the ability of earlier
arrivals to send more and more tickets to relatives, and
ideological postulates of the restratification of the Jewish
people from a predominantly mercantile class to one living
from "productive" occupations. All these factors were accel-

erated by the pogrom wave of 1881, the restrictive May Laws of 1882, and later ordinances. Psychologically, we recall, these physical and legislative attacks not only shook Russian Jewry, but also evoked a sympathetic echo among Western liberals. Various international Jewish relief organizations now fostered the emigration of Russian Jews to America or, in a lesser degree, to Palestine. True, good-will was not enough. The needs of the ever-swelling stream of emigrés transcended the resources of most relief groups, old and new, and often created much confusion, even resentment. Some American Jews viewed with alarm the possible deterioration of their own status as a result of the arrival of large groups of emigrés totally different in language and mores from the American population. As early as 1878, the American delegates to a Jewish World Conference warned their European colleagues against indiscriminate promotion of Jewish emigration to the United States. But as soon as the enormity of the Russian pogroms struck home opinion veered strongly toward helping the newcomers at all costs. Even then, however, the Alliance Israélite warned the other organizations that it feared "to provoke by our intervention, an emigration movement which, were it to assume too great dimensions, might entail difficulties so serious that even the united forces of Jewry would be unable to cope with them."[10]

On the other hand, an assembly of forty Jewish leaders in St. Petersburg, under the chairmanship of Baron Horace Günzburg, adopted, in April, 1882, a resolution rejecting "completely the thought of organizing emigration" because it was incompatible with "the historic rights of the Jews to their present fatherland." Among the Jewish youth, especially its new radical segment, the idea of fighting it out with the reactionary regime on the spot was constantly gaining ground. On their part some Orthodox leaders, such as Israel Meir Kahan, opposed emigration because they feared the ensuing neglect of Jewish rituals and customs among the expatriates in a new and strange world.

Nevertheless, emigration proceeded apace in ever-increasing numbers. The best estimates available show that during the entire half century of 1820 to 1870 only some 7,500 Russian and Polish Jews settled in the United States. During the decade of 1871 to 1880 the number of such arrivals suddenly rose to over 40,000. It increased again to some 135,000 in the following decade, to grow further to 279,811 from 1891 to 1900 and to 704,245 between 1901 and 1910. It continued at a high rate for four more years until the First World War shut almost all avenues for emigration from Eastern Europe. Needless to say, Jews were not the only ones to leave the Tsarist Empire for the United States. In fact, their ratio among Russian emigrés decreased from decade to decade, and from a majority of 63.3 percent in the 1880s declined to a minority of 44.1 percent between 1901 and 1910.[11] But while the tsar's other subjects often went to the United States only in order to accumulate savings and return to the old country, very few Jews repatriated themselves. In any case, Jews were the most conspicuous protagonists of that dramatic movement to friends and foes alike.

We have discussed at some length the emigration from Russia to the United States because that country received well over 70 percent of all Jewish expatriates and also because its egalitarian structure so sharply contrasted with the conditions at home. However, there was a simultaneous movement from Russia to Canada (in 1914 the annual peak of 11,252 East-European Jewish arrivals was reached), South Africa (during the first decade of the twentieth century there were 17,200 Jewish arrivals from Eastern Europe) and other British Empire countries. The British motherland herself became a major haven of refuge for some 120,000 Jewish immigrants in the four decades before World War I despite the anti-alien legislation which imposed severe restrictions.[12] Many Russian emigrés found their way to other West-European countries. Some of them, to be sure, originally planned to proceed to the United States but, largely because of lack of funds, had to remain at one of the way stations. If a number of these "transients" ultimately reached their final destination, a great many others found work and became adjusted to their respective environments.

One of the most fascinating phases of that migratory movement was Baron Maurice de Hirsch's large-scale attempt to colonize Russian Jews in such an underdeveloped country as

Argentina. Because of the bankruptcy of one of his firm's
debtors, Hirsch personally chanced to possess extensive tracts
of land there. He founded the Jewish Colonization Association in 1891, endowing it with the then enormous philanthropic donation of £ 2,000,000. Upon his death five years
later the Association received a bequest of an additional
£ 6,000,000. Its objectives were stated broadly in Article iii
of its charter:

> To assist and promote the emigration of Jews from any
> parts of Europe or Asia, and principally from countries
> in which they may for the time being be subjected to any
> special taxes or political or other disabilities, to any other
> parts of the world, and to form and establish colonies
> in various parts of North and South America and other
> countries for agricultural, commercial, and other purposes.

Obviously, the Russian Jews were foremost in the minds
of Hirsch and his Western associates. His representative, the
Englishman Arnold White, conducted lengthy negotiations
with the Russian ministers in St. Petersburg and obtained
from them pledges of active collaboration. Hirsch's scheme
was, as we recall, to remove on the average 125,000 Jews
annually during the following twenty-five years and thus to
reduce the biological pressure on them. He apparently over-
looked their dynamic natural increase which would have, to
some extent, nullified the effects of even such a mass exodus.
The American Minister to Russia, Charles Emory Smith, was
more correct in estimating in 1891 that at best 25,000 Russian
Jews could leave each year for Argentina; such emigration
would absorb only a fraction of their natural increase which
he estimated at 150,000 to 180,000. As it turned out even
25,000 Jews never arrived in Argentina in any single year.
The peaks of all East-European immigration to that country
were reached in 1906 and 1912, in each of which approximately 13,500 Jews settled there, most of them without the
support of the Jewish Colonization Association. Nonetheless
this gigantic undertaking of a philanthropic visionary made a
lasting impression upon both the Jewish and the non-Jewish
worlds.

❧ 6 ❧

Economic Transformations

WITH EVEN LESS PRECISION can one speak of the changes
in the economic structure of Russian Jewry during the nineteenth century. The general Russian statistics of that period
are largely based upon irregular reports by government
officials, men not only untrained in statistical work, but using
questionnaires lacking in uniformity even during the same
years and greatly differing from one "census" to another.
The results are therefore rarely comparable. Nor were Jews
or, for that matter, other citizens anxious to cooperate. If
the threat of military service (frequently used by the Russian
regime as a punitive measure) deterred many parents from
registering their children, the specter of excessive and arbitrary taxes made returns concerning one's occupation, income, and other economic data quite unreliable.

Nonetheless, the general contours of a major economic
revolution, which took place especially in the latter part of the
nineteenth century, emerge quite clearly from manifold detailed studies made by Russian scholars. Jews participated in
that general Russian, indeed European, revolution, beyond
their ratio in the population. In some respects they became
major victims of the new transformations, in others, their
often unconscious pioneers. While the economic structure of
Jews within the Russian Pale before World War I still bore
a remote resemblance to that of their ancestors a century
earlier, the minority, allowed to settle outside the Pale, had
undergone a total change.

After inheriting Poland's eastern provinces, the tsars found
many Jewish subjects settled in rural districts, but only

partially involved in agricultural pursuits. Many of them
were so-called *arendators* (lessees), a combination of innkeepers and landlords' agents. Apart from distilling and
selling liquor and accommodating transients, these small
rural entrepreneurs ran village stores, collected revenue
from farmers for their frequently absentee landlords, and
served as purchasing agents for Jewish grain merchants in
neighboring cities. On the side they cultivated small parcels
of land, had a few cows, goats, and chickens, and produced
vegetables and dairy products mainly for their own and their
employees' consumption. These factota played a necessary
role in the rural economy and, as later studies were to show,
enabled the farmers within the Pale to sell their produce at
considerably higher prices than were obtainable in Russia's
interior. In return, they supplied the farming population with
industrial articles imported from cities, sometimes from
foreign countries. These relationships were not always
amicable. Since the peasants were permanently exploited by
their landlords and the Jews often served as the latter's
operative agents, there was much anti-Jewish feeling, aggravated by religious animosities fanned by many priests,
Greek-Orthodox, Uniate, or Catholic.

Such Judeo-peasant tensions became a major preoccupation
of the Russian administration and served as a frequent excuse
for its discriminatory policies. In general, the controlling
feudal powers looked askance at too close relations between
the peasantry and its urban neighbors. In 1782, Catherine
II altogether forbade the town burghers to establish themselves in villages, "lest they exploit the peasants." If behind
this prohibition lurked the suspicion that urban settlers,
bringing with them "enlightened" ideas might help to undermine the established order, this dread was doubly justified,
the authorities believed, if Jews were the disseminators of
the new concepts. Overtly, the tsarist organs accused the
Jews not only of exploiting the peasants by usurious loans
and underhanded mercantile deals, but also of poisoning
them by selling them excessive quantities of liquor on credit.
With this accusation, repeated with endless variations, the
government felt justified to try to eliminate them from the
rural districts altogether.

On closer examination these imputations proved unfounded. As early as 1844, Ivan Funduklei, a non-Jewish statistician of the University of Kiev showed, after a close survey of a village community, that after the eviction of Jews both the prices and the consumption of liquor had gone up substantially. A government committee, appointed by Alexander II in 1870, reported that most complaints about drunkenness came from the Greater Russian provinces, fewer from the Ukrainian and Neo-Russian territories, and practically none from the western provinces densely inhabited by Jews. The fullest statistical material was assembled by the so-called Pahlen Commission in 1883-86. When carefully analyzed by scholars, including Ivan S. Blioch in a five-volume work devoted to a comparative study of the Great Russian, western, and Polish provinces, these data showed conclusively that there was far less alcoholism among the peasants within, than in the provinces adjacent to, the Pale. These and other studies also demonstrated that the western peasants (in part owing to the proximity of Jewish traders) were economically much better off than their opposite numbers outside the Pale.[1]

Agricultural Colonization

Nonetheless many progressive Jews themselves admitted that the Jewish economic stratification was unhealthy. Ever since the middle of the eighteenth century Western thinkers, both Jewish and non-Jewish, insisted on the necessity of making Jews more "productive." Under the influence of the physiocratic school of economics, in particular, which emphasized that only agriculture was genuinely productive, some leaders started preaching the return of Jews to the soil. Others combined that preachment with practical efforts of teaching Jews useful crafts, in order to divert them from their reputedly "parasitic" commercial occupations. The ideas which found a resounding echo during the grand debate on the Jewish question at the time of the Quadrennial Diet in Poland, also had representatives in Russia among Jews like Nathan Neta Notkin in 1797 and officials like G. R. Derzhavin from 1799 on. None of these advocates had in mind, of course, the occasional Jewish landlord who, like

Joshua Zeitlin, owned an estate with 910 "souls" on it. The number of such Jewish landowners constantly dwindled.[2]

Following the example set by Emperor Joseph II in Austria, Alexander I adopted the idea of colonizing Jews in the vast open spaces of New Russia. He and his advisers realized that, in order to be successful, such colonization would have to proceed by groups which, when transplanted into new village communities, could combine agricultural pursuits with the continued cultivation of their own religious and cultural mores. When, in 1806, the government assigned a tract of land of over 80,000 acres in the province of Kherson for young Jews physically fit and in possession of 100 rubles per family, a sufficient number of candidates responded for several such Jewish colonies to be founded. They had an initial population of some 600 families who gave their new settlements such picturesque names as *Sede Menuche* (*Sedeh Menuhah* or Field of Rest), and *Har Shefer* (Beautiful Mountain). Many more were willing to come. In the province of Vitebsk alone 867 families registered with the authorities, whose pecuniary means proved wholly inadequate, however, during that period of great fiscal stringency.

Not surprisingly, the settlers' enthusiasm cooled off in the face of stark realities. One of the earliest colonists reminisced later: "It took us four months until we dragged ourselves to Kremenchug. . . . Arriving on the spot, in a dismal land during a severe winter, we started to plough up the virgin land. . . . From time to time it occurred that we did not have the utensils to mill the grain, so we had to pound them with pestles in mortars and bake them with their hulls." Another *Sedeh Menuhah* colonist later recorded that, because of overexertion and the inhospitable climate, the colony lost two hundred members in the first three years. Complaints to the bureaucracy, submitted also by the German colonists, went unheeded. Some settlers speedily left and the news of their misadventures spread through the western ghettos. Under these circumstances it is truly remarkable that the Jewish colonies embraced in 1810 a population of 1,690 families, though not all living from tilling the soil.[3]

Another step forward was made when a great famine

struck the western provinces in 1821-22 and a number of Jews established themselves in new colonies with the reluctant aid of the government. A third wave followed in 1835 when Nicholas I issued a call to the pauperized western Jews to proceed to Siberia, whose cool climate was allegedly favorable to agricultural exploitation. The authorities set aside for this purpose over 40,000 acres in the vicinity of Omsk and Tversk. Unbelievable though it may seem, this governmental invitation was enthusiastically received by so many Jews, then in the throes of a great economic crisis, that the government feared an excessive Jewish influx into those distant areas. The Minister of Interior Bludov and General of the Gendarmerie Count Alexander K. Benckendorff argued that not only could a physically weak and undernourished population like the Jewish hardly survive the hardships of the long journey, but also that the moral standards of the local population, largely consisting of deported criminals, would not be improved by the settlement in its midst of an inferior class like the Jews.[4] Nicholas suddenly called off the undertaking in January, 1837, after several hundred Jews had already embarked on the journey to Asia at their own expense. These passengers were forcibly rerouted to the Black Sea region. In the early 1840s the movement continued with the arrival there of 5,619 Jews. It grew slowly until the reversal of the government policy in 1865.

Understandably, many colonists could not endure the hardships and departed. They did not have far to go because this was the period of tremendous growth of such industrial centers as Odessa, Elizavetgrad, and others. To be sure, the police tried to stem this unauthorized movement. It occasionally raided these cities and forcibly returned some colonists to their respective villages. On the other hand, it was the same bureaucracy which often made life in the colonies utterly miserable. Promises, however solemnly made, were easily broken. Because of inefficiency houses were not prepared in time for their occupants. Areas set aside for cultivation lacked water which, particularly in drought years, often had to be hauled from a great distance; seed allotted for planting usually arrived too late for sowing. These and other shortcomings had been pointed out in an early official survey of the Jewish colonies, presented to Benckendorff by a Colonel Ossigov who concluded his observations by saying, "One can, indeed, not blame the colonists if they deeply yearn to return to their earlier conditions in the cities, horrible as these were. For a man must be thoroughly demoralized to wish to live in this misery." Some Russian administrators abused their power. As Benckendorff himself observed, the chief administrator in the southern area, Colonel Demidov, forced the able-bodied men to earn money for him by working outside the colonies, while leaving in the latter only women and old men unable to perform the necessary agricultural chores.[5]

Nevertheless, on balance the Jewish rural population kept on increasing. True, there were intermittent declines, but in the long run the difficulties were overcome and the total number of inhabitants kept on growing, particularly in the 1840s and the 1850s. Here, too, government statistics are not reliable. As noted by two American officials, the government records for 1890 indicated the presence in the 17 Jewish colonies of the province of Ekaterinoslav of 574 families, consisting of 3,403 men and 3,772 women, together 7,175 souls. Such average families of over 12 and a preponderance of women in a colony appeared incredible at first glance. Closer examination showed, indeed, that fully 749 Jewish families lived there embracing only 2,744 men and 2,398 women, or 5,142 souls in all. This average of a little more than 6 persons per family and a male majority of about 54 percent were far more normal.[6] In any case, the colonies' long-range growth was undeniable. All along, moreover, they attracted an increasing number of individual settlers to their environs. It has been estimated that the total number of Jews living on land at the end of the governmentally supported colonization in 1865 amounted to some 33,000.

A complete reversal came when Alexander II's regime embarked on its forced pace of industrialization. It now prohibited altogether Jewish colonization on land and, in 1874, withdrew the land reserves previously set aside for this purpose. Alexander III went further. In his May Laws of 1882, he forbade the Jews altogether to acquire rural property. Nonetheless the momentum achieved in earlier years, as well as the economic pressures on Russian Jewry, stimulated further Jewish efforts in that direction and, by 1900, the Jewish agricultural population seems to have grown to some 100,000 persons. In Congress Poland, too, no less than seventy Jewish colonies were founded between 1817 and 1870, the Jewish agricultural population being estimated there at 28,391 as early as 1858.[7]

Apart from this quantitative increase of Jewish farmers there also was a constant improvement in the quality of their produce. The generation grown up in the colonies had fully adjusted itself to the new life and, with its intelligence and spirit of enterprise, succeeded in improving upon the methods employed by its neighbors. The new cultivation of tobacco in Bessarabia was predominantly in its hands. The French agricultural expert Tisserand who, in 1908, visited the Russian Jewish colonies in behalf of the Jewish Colonization Association, reported,

> It is impossible to find tobacco and maize plants more attractive than those which I have seen among the Jewish colonists of Dombroveni, reconstructed vineyards more remarkable than those of Resina, a nursery better arranged and better kept than that of Soroki, and cultivation more intelligently conceived than that of the agricultural school of Minsk. Everywhere the colonists show an excellent spirit and are open to agricultural progress. They thus avenge themselves for the strange imputation still weighing on them that they are unable to become farmers. As if industrious, intelligent, enterprising men could *a priori* be considered incapable of exercising the farming profession.[8]

At the same time, the steady removal of Jews from villages within the Pale, crowned by the May Laws of 1882 for Russia and 1891 for Congress Poland, more than outweighed the effects of the Jewish agricultural colonization. As before, therefore, Jewish economic endeavor was largely concentrated in urban occupations, particularly trade and industry.

CRAFTS

Our statistical evidence for the early Russo-Jewish economic structure is greatly complicated not only by the meagerness and unreliability of the extant data but also by their predominantly politicolegal, rather than economic orientation. Partial records of the Finance Ministry for the year 1818 indicate for the Ukrainian Jews an economic distribution of 86.5 percent in the two classes of merchants and burghers as against only 12.1 percent of craftsmen and their employees, and 1.4 percent of tillers of the soil. In the Lithuanian and White Russian provinces these percentages appear as 86.6, 10.8, and 2.6, respectively. Such computations, based on the legally significant registration in the prime urban categories of merchants and burghers (*meshchanie*) but paying no heed to the mass of unregistered persons, run sharply counter to whatever partial evidence has become available from archival researches in various parts of prepartition Poland.[9] While conditions may have undergone some minor changes during the first decades of the Russian regime, the Jewish economic structure remained essentially intact. These Polish studies invariably show a preponderance of Jews engaged in industrial occupations, including transportation, over the shopkeepers, merchants, and bankers.

In some areas the former class embraced fully 50 percent of the Jewish population. The following statistical table, representing the developments in the Kingdom of Poland in the course of the nineteenth century, is much more typical of the Jewish occupational distribution throughout the Tsarist Empire. The individual percentages, based upon incomplete censuses, are in themselves none too reliable; yet they offer the best available approximation of the prevailing trends.

Year	Commerce	Industry and Labor, including day laborers	Civil Service and Liberal Professions	Agriculture
1825	28.2	61.1	4.9	5.6
1843	21.6	67.8	2.6	4.8
1857	42.8	35.0	2.6	8.1
1897	39.04	46.7	4.38	2.33

We need not dwell in any detail on these categories.[10] Certainly, the high peaks reached in industry in 1843 and in agriculture in 1857 were owing more to inexact definitions, than to actual increases. But this table illustrates the general trends, best reflected in the census of 1897 which, as in the area of population, has furnished the relatively most dependable data.

A fuller understanding of these figures may be gained, however, only from a consideration of the qualitative distribution in the various branches of industry and to a lesser extent of commerce. Traditionally Jews were represented most fully in the clothing industry. In partial statistical records dating back to 1807 and covering the Jewish artisans in the provinces of Minsk, Kiev, and Ekaterinoslav, we find that the percentage of Jewish tailors, cobblers, and other clothing workers amounted to 69.7 percent of all Jewish artisans. Next in line were metal workers (6.8 percent), gold and silversmiths (6.1 percent), and barbers (4.1 percent). In contrast thereto the important building industry engaged only a tiny fraction of 2.6 percent of Jewish craftsmen. Probably these ratios can be generalized for most of the Pale of Settlement.

With the growth of Jewish population there also was an increasing proliferation of Jewish craftsmen, particularly in the traditional Jewish occupations. Usher Margulis has drawn some interesting comparisons between the neighboring provinces of Smolensk and Moghilev, Pskov and Vitebsk in 1861. In Smolensk and Pskov, both outside the Pale, one cobbler provided all the needs for the footwear of 280 and 494 persons, respectively; one tailor sufficed for 542 and 881, and one carpenter for 715 and 1,028 people, while one watchmaker took care of 4,498 and 4,495 inhabitants. In Moghilev (without Gomel, where the statistics are questionable) and Vitebsk (without Dinaburg-Dvinsk which, as a fortress, embraced a nontypical 30 percent population from the armed forces), these figures are: one cobbler for 127 and 200, one tailor for 70 and 210, one carpenter for 376 and 680, one watchmaker for 1,109 and 2,070 persons. As a result there was an increasingly sharp competition among the Jewish artisans. A would-be purchaser of material for a suit in Uman in 1810 found himself surrounded by five Jewish tailors, each trying to take his measurements and making exaggerated claims. This constant underbidding was but partially curtailed by the ever stricter regulations of the Jewish artisan guilds which tried to apportion customers to each craftsman, and otherwise to regulate their respective trades. None of these guilds were monopolistic, however, and, except for the right to employ apprentices, any non-member competed on an almost equal basis.[11]

As time went on there also emerged stronger non-Jewish competition. The growth of the urban population tended to bring about an increase of non-Jews active also in the branches of industry theretofore dominated by Jews. The sprawling metropolitan areas now had entire sections inhabited by non-Jews. Even more important was the growing competition from large-scale industry, whether based upon home work or concentrated in mechanized factories. It took time for the Jews to make the necessary adjustments from independent artisans to home workers or factory laborers. As a result there was a considerable drop both in the ratio of Jews engaged in their traditional occupations and in their average earnings, a decline not entirely compensated by the entry of many others into new branches of industry.

The story of Lodz which in the course of the nineteenth century grew into the major center of the textile industry for the whole Empire, may not be quite typical of the entire Pale of Settlement. Yet it tells a truly dramatic story, illustrative of the basic trends everywhere. In 1810, the Jewish tailors of Lodz successfully fought off the incursion of non-Jewish competitors. Fifteen years later we find the first 2 Christian tailors in the city. By 1862, the 41 Christian tailors almost equal the 49 Jews still engaged in that occupation. Similarly in 1821, all 8 Lodz bakers were Jews; in 1862 the 38 Christian bakers greatly outnumbered their 15 Jewish competitors. Perhaps the sharpest decline is noticeable in the distilling of liquor which, as we recall, had for so long been a target of attacks by both the government and non-Jewish public opinion. In 1820, Lodz still had 7 Jewish distilleries; a few years later, none. Part of that process of elimination was owing to the sharp opposition of Christian guilds which, though not quite as monopolistic as their medieval predecessors, were sufficiently powerful to promote the interests of their members at the expense of Jewish out-siders. In part, the Jews suffered from the competition of newly imported well-trained German craftsmen whose prod-ucts often were of better quality. The more untrained ex-pellees from villages were crowded into the ghettos of the Pale, the less good often became the quality of their products. Increased competition likewise led to the lowering of both prices and quality.

In some less dynamically developing areas the decline in Jewish craftsmanship and the number of craftsmen was less marked. The data for 1887 and 1898 show that in the provinces of Chernigov, Kiev, and Taurida there actually were substantial increases from 12.8, 12.0, and 15.1 to 15.5, 16.1 and 20.0 percent, respectively. But in the other, more congested areas of Jewish settlement, there was a definite decline, accelerated by emigration to other countries. On the other hand, resettlement of Jewish artisans in the interior of Russia was relatively slight. Although a special decree of 1865 opened up the vast expanses of Russia to Jewish crafts-men (in the Caucasus they had been allowed to function even earlier), their status as but temporary residents with no right to transmit these residential permits to their grown sons served as a major deterrent. Coinciding with the sus-pension of Jewish agricultural colonization, this decree was but a half-hearted attempt to attract some skilled Jewish workmen to Russia's interior as part of the governmental push toward industrialization. After three decades only some 2 percent of the Jewish artisan class lived beyond the Pale, particularly in the neighboring provinces of Smolensk and Pskov or the city of St. Petersburg. Administrative chicaneries made the life of Jewish artisans unbearable both inside and outside the Pale. According to an English visitor, E. B. Lanin, Jewish craftsmen were often forced to take examina-tions so construed that "even the most clever artisans have no hope of passing" them.[12]

Commerce

Neither were Jewish commercial enterprises immune from the destructive forces. Here, too, the combination of governmental and popular hostility with the inner weaknesses generated by the rapid population growth without the corresponding broadening of the economic basis undermined the traditional Jewish preponderance in commerce. Among the latter factors one might mention Russia's growing protectionism. In her effort to safeguard her home industries Russia, including Congress Poland, shut her gates for many imports by imposing upon them high customs duties. Jews who had been extremely active in the import and export business found their trade increasingly curtailed by these governmental policies. These restrictions were largely responsible for the decline in the number of visitors to the Leipzig fairs (in 1810 there had been 44 Christian and 296 Jewish visitors from Russia) and in the value of goods traded there.[13]

On the other hand, the Russian bureaucracy was both inefficient and corrupt. Since goods imported from Prussia and Austria were much cheaper, the tendency to evade the tariff by smuggling became irresistible. Count Frederick (Fryderyk Florian) Skarbek commented that "smuggling has been raised to the rank of a regular industry. A whole class of smugglers has arisen which, placed between the peasantry and the Jewish occupations, is engaged in an unceasing war with the frontier guards and the finance officials. At times these conflicts take on the form of overt mutiny." Another official observed that many peasants gave up agriculture in favor of smuggling. Many customs officials collaborated with the smugglers and placed all sorts of obstacles in the way of honest importers who wished to pay duties, rather than bribes. It is small wonder, then, that a survey conducted by the Ministry of Interior showed that, in 1844, 1,600,000 pounds of yarn entered Congress Poland in a legal, and 591,000 in an illegal fashion. Even more drastic was the importation of manufactured cotton goods of which, according to the same survey, only 57,000 pounds had entered legally, as against 2,000,000 pounds smuggled in.[14] From Congress Poland these wares were reexported to the rest of the Pale and to the interior of Russia, despite the existing customs frontier between these two sections of the Empire. Native Polish products likewise became objects of smuggling.

Since Jews were among the protagonists in this game, the government imposed various restrictions on their acquisition of rural land and houses in the vicinity of the Prussian and Austrian frontiers. It also persuaded the rabbis not to adjudicate litigations arising out of smuggling and, as we recall, even induced the Vilna rabbinate to issue in 1820 a ban on all smugglers, a ban which, some Prussian ministers feared, might greatly curtail the exports of Prussian manufactured goods. Finally, to stem this traffic completely, Nicholas I issued his aforementioned ukase of 1843, expelling all Jews residing within fifty versts (about 33 miles) from the frontier with Prussia and Austria; only owners of houses were to be allowed two years to dispose of them. "This order is to be executed without any excuses." Such drastic action, affecting thousands of innocent persons along with the guilty, caused a great outcry in the country and abroad, without in any way altering the basic discrepancy between Russia's insatiable demand for imported goods and the inefficient methods of restricting its satisfaction. The number of Jewish smugglers may have diminished but their places were taken by others, as is illustrated by the Warsaw statistics of arrested smugglers. From the high ratio of 83-96 percent in 1842-49, the proportion of Jewish defendants on this score declined to 37.4 percent in 1850 and to but 27.1 percent in 1851, or far less than the Jewish ratio in the mercantile population.[15]

More consciously anti-Jewish efforts curtailed the Jewish liquor trade. Ever increasing excise and license taxes, endless legislative vagaries, as well as the growing competition of non-Jewish distillers and innkeepers, reduced the Jewish share in this business to a minimum. To quote the Lodz experience again: in 1820 eight Jewish tavern keepers confronted three Christian competitors, ten years later the number of Jews was reduced to three, a number remaining constant till 1862, while the number of Christian saloon keepers had increased to sixty-four. In Berdichev the Jewish ratio among liquor dealers declined from 24.3 percent in 1789 to 6.3 percent sixty years later. At the same time some wealthy entrepreneurs were allowed to lease liquor concessions· extending over large areas which they usually operated through a hierarchy of subcontractors. One such concessionaire, Joseph (Yosip, Evzel) Günzburg (1812-78), created baron by the Grand Duke of Hesse-Darmstadt in 1874, paid the government in 1859-63 an annual rental of 3,777,440 rubles; two other Jews had contracts calling for rentals of 1,517,440 and 1,243,774 rubles, respectively.[16] While they often employed Jews, the relative number of Jews engaged in the liquor trade kept on declining. The growth of salt and tobacco monopolies likewise interfered the more harshly with these traditional branches of Jewish commerce, as the local authorities tried to favor Christian over Jewish licensees. Although a decree issued to this effect in 1824 had to be revoked in 1830 because not enough Christian applicants were available for the distribution of salt, in practice what had been an almost exclusively Jewish trade increasingly shifted into the hands of non-Jewish distributors.

The ratio of the Jewish mercantile class in the general Jewish population cannot easily be ascertained. Only a minority of Jewish businessmen was registered in the regular class of "merchants"; still fewer were entered under the First, Second, or Third Guild. The latter figures are, moreover, distorted by the fact that some Jews, though not really qualified, registered under one or another Guild and paid the respective fees merely to secure residential privileges outside the Pale or, at least, greater freedom in traveling there, as well as exemption from the military draft for their sons. Nevertheless a statistical account for 1852, compiled by Bernard Weinryb from three tables extracted by A. Yuditskii from a Kiev manuscript, is quite illuminating (see the next page). None of these figures reflect, however, the great mass of unregistered peddlers, agents, mercantile employees and others. Their individual transactions may have been extremely small, but in the aggregate their contribution to Russian commerce and their numerical strength within the Jewish population were very substantial. We have a graphic description of a small Jewish town by the contemporary Yiddish

Province	Jewish population	Jewish merchants (ratio of entire class)	Guild members			merchants	of each 1,000 Jews Guilds		
			I	II	III		I	II	III
Grodno	101,950	1,268 (96.1)	5	2	132	12.4	.05	.02	1.3
Kovno	98,641	458 (76.1)	6	6	125	4.6	.06	.06	1.27
Minsk	98,330	2,338 (88.2)	9	5	227	23.8	.09	.05	2.31
Vitebsk	57,766	1,397 (42.8)	6	5	141	24.2	.1	.1	2.44
Moghilev	99,088	2,672 (74.7)	4	5	276	27.0	.04	.05	2.79
Volhynia	190,804	7,648 (96.0)	8	12	696	40.0	.04	.06	3.65
Kiev	183,629	12,066 (82.4)	7	20	956	65.7	.04	.11	5.2
Kherson	45,241	704 (23.8)	10	15	679	15.6	.22	.33	15.0
Odessa district	12,657	2,928 (52.3)	10	20	450	231.46	.79	1.58	35.5
Poltava	23,971	2,627 (51.6)	1	2	215	109.6	.04	.08	8.97
Chernigov	28,919	1,704 (23.0)	2	2	111	58.9	.07	.07	3.85

novelist, Isaac Meier Dick, which includes the following paragraph:

> The hamlet looks dead during the whole week; it has the semblance of a gynocracy, that is a kingdom inhabited only by women. Men spend the week until Friday in the country, they wander from village to village and court to court with all sorts of notions, which they exchange there against flax, linseed, rabbit and calf skins, pig bristles and feathers. They sell all that to . . . the rich man of the community. In the hamlet itself remain only women, children, communal officials, students of the academy and a few *batlanim* [unemployed men].[17]

CAPITALIST PROGRESS

All these processes led to increasing pauperization of the Jewish masses by the middle of the nineteenth century. Not all Jews, however, took these blows calmly. Quite a few enterprising young men, sensing the spirit of the time, looked for novel outlets for their talents. The textile and clothing industries lent themselves particularly well to Jewish enterprise. Traditionally, the Jewish communities embraced, for socioreligious reasons, numerous tailors of their own. In independent Poland foundations were laid even for small Jewish factories employing a number of Jewish workers. The demand for such religious articles as prayer shawls in the growing Jewish population likewise stimulated the development *in nuce* of mass production methods. On its part, the Russian government, bent on the restratification of the Jewish masses, regarded, next to agricultural colonization, the establishment of factories as the most eminent means for retraining Jews for "productive" occupations. For this purpose it established, in 1809, a specific Jewish industrial school in Kremenchug, where 40 families of Jewish pupil-workers could be trained for industrial work in textile factories and serve as the hard core of a labor force to be used by factory owners in many communities. In the eight years of its existence this school taught the new trade to several hundred trainees (in 1810 their number amounted to 148 men) and also furnished employment to several master artisans serving as instructors.

Jewish entrepreneurs realized the new opportunities offered them by this governmental attitude, the generally growing Russian protectionism, and the rising internal demand for industrial products. Active individuals, like the Vilna merchant, Hillel Aronov Markevich, sought official aid in establishing several new factories. Although his application of 1813 to the Vilna Governor for a government loan to establish a textile mill was rejected, he continued to press the authorities for assistance in various industrial projects. In 1818, he petitioned for a six-year lease of two specified tracts of land in the vicinity of Vilna so that he might erect there (1) a factory for the production of artisan tools; (2) a paper mill; (3) an oil press; (4) a saw-mill along English patterns; (5) a brass factory; (6) a flour mill; and (7) a textile converting mill for the clothing factories. In this application he described his motivation as follows: "On the one hand, I feel the obligation to do my part for the benefit of my fellow citizens and, at the same time, contribute to the extent of my ability to the welfare of society as a whole. On the other hand, I should like thus to employ my considerable know-how and expertise." Markevich repeated his request to the finance minister two years later. But his petitions were constantly rejected because the authorities considered his resources insufficient for such an ambitious program and also because he had "his own profit, rather than that of society in mind." Nonetheless neither Markevich nor similar Jewish entrepreneurs abandoned their plans. By 1828, 75 Jewish textile mills were in operation in eight western provinces (40 in the province of Volhynia, 13 in Grodno, 10 in Moghilev). These factories employed among them 2,185 Jewish workers.[18]

From these small beginnings developed a major participation of Jewish entrepreneurs in Russia's industrial development. A remarkable illustration is offered by the Ukrainian sugar industry. As elsewhere in the Empire, where a sugar refinery had been established as early as 1719, sugar had long been produced largely by landlords who refined their own beets for local or, at best, district-wide consumption.

Israel Brodski, scion of a well-known rabbinic family—
Schor—but called Brodski because his father had come from
Brody, Galicia, entered that business in 1844, at the age
of twenty-one. At that time he arranged with one of the
Ukrainian landlords (in the district of Cherkasy) that, for
the substantial advance of 6,000 silver rubles, he was to
become an equal partner in the revenue from the sugar
refinery. Brodski was not satisfied with the traditional methods
of production. After surveying some mechanized refineries
in Germany, he imported the necessary machinery, together
with technicians to teach the local workers, and in the following years he built one refinery after another. Before
long he also established an effective sales organization. By
the 1870s and 1880s he had sixty agencies in all parts of
the Empire including the Caucasus, Siberia, and, shortly
thereafter, also in newly annexed Turkestan. From his new
headquarters in Odessa he and his sons successfully exported
great quantities of sugar to the Ottoman Empire, Persia,
and other countries. After his death in 1889 his sons, Lazar
and Leon, owned between them twenty-two major sugar
mills. Generally considered among the wealthiest Russian
Jews, they received high decorations from the Russian government and the Legion of Honor from France. The Brodski
example was effectively emulated by other Jewish entrepreneurs, including the families Zaitsev, Halperin, and
Balakhovsky. As early as 1872 an official report estimated,
probably with some exaggeration, that Jews controlled 25
percent of the entire sugar industry in the Ukraine. The
various joint-stock companies, which in the following decades
actively participated in the production and distribution of
sugar, were likewise often managed by Jewish directors and
large stockholders.[19]

It was in part owing to these Jewish sugar refiners that the
Russian sugar industry which, as late as 1880, did not supply
all the domestic needs, was able shortly thereafter to pile
up large export surpluses. According to government statistics
imports of sugar declined from 288,160 quintals (6.1 poods
each) in the quinquennium of 1888-93, to 7,642 quintals
in 1893-98. At the same time production increased by some
40 percent and exports shot up from 3,650,768 to 6,145,003

quintals. This increase was made possible in part by the lower prices which declined from 28.48 rubles in 1881-85 to 17.95 rubles in 1896-98. To be sure, much of that decrease was picked up in taxes which played an increasing role in Russia's imperial budget. Characteristically these prices were lowest in the Ukraine and considerably higher in Moscow and St. Petersburg.

Even more important for the Russian Empire was the entry of some Jews into the slowly developing railroad industry. Count Egor Kankrin, long-time minister of finance (1823-1844), was a spokesman for the conservative groups which feared that railways might "encourage frequent purposeless travel, thus fostering the restless spirit of our age." The progress was correspondingly slow. Apart from a short sixteen-mile line from St. Petersburg to the emperor's home in Tsarskoe Selo, opened in 1837, the first important line was that linking Vienna with Warsaw. Although it took that line nine years to be completed, as it also did that from Moscow to St. Petersburg (1839-48 and 1842-51, respectively), the state-appointed managers soon ran into great difficulties. The line was salvaged by a private joint-stock company, led by the Warsaw Jewish banker Herman Epstein, who owned more than 40 percent of the company's shares valued at 2,500,000 rubles. Almost immediately thereafter Epstein formed a new company to build the line from Warsaw to Bromberg in Silesia, while another entrepreneur, the convert, Leopold Kronenberg, was responsible for continuing the railway from Warsaw to Brest-Litovsk.

These Polish Jewish railway builders were overshadowed by their Russian compeers, particularly Joseph (Evzel) Günzburg, his son Horace, and Samuel Poliakov. Poliakov achieved the reputation of an efficient builder, when he succeeded in setting up the two partial lines from Kursk to Kharkov and from Kharkov to Taganrog, a distance of 763 versts (ca. 504 miles), in the record time of 22 months, whereas other lines required many years. The government had such confidence in his ability that, when in 1869 it decided to build an economically and strategically needed railroad from Voronezh to Rostov, the tsar accepted a proposal backed by only a minority of his cabinet to entrust its building to

Poliakov, although a rival Christian firm had underbid him by some 10 percent. Often aided by Jewish financiers in other countries, particularly the Pereire Brothers in Paris and Gerson Bleichröder in Berlin, Jewish builders were able to help greatly in the expansion of the Russian railway network which in the twenty years from 1856-76 grew from 982 to 17,418 versts.

These and other Jews were also active in developing the water transport on the great rivers of Russia, such as the Dnieper and the Volga. An earlier corporation controlling the Dnieper navigation proved very conservative and inefficient. It was followed by a second corporation, established by Jews in 1883. Within ten years the new group proved so successful that the former company was simply absorbed by its younger rival. Under the management of D. S. Margolin and other Jewish directors this combined company in 1911 owned 62 river steamboats and leased 16 others, which among them transported more than 70 percent of the cargo carried on that river. Under the direction of Grigorii Abramovich Poliak the water transport on the Volga and the Caspian Sea increased by leaps and bounds; it began to play an ever-increasing role in the transportation of crude oil and other oil products from the expanding Baku oilfields. Connected with water transport was also the growing business of marine insurance in which, like in other branches of the insurance business, Jews also excelled.[20]

Poliakov was not satisfied with his significant role in Russia's domestic transport system; he also cast covetous glances across the borders to the highly promising areas of the Ottoman Empire. Characteristically, the Jewish industrialist did not approach the regular ministries but contacted the Tsar through Constantine Pobedonostsev to whom he reported in 1886-87, that he had uncovered a joint Anglo-Austrian scheme to acquire the Balkan railway system and, by bringing it out into the open, had prevented its realization. He now asked for the government's support of a new Russian corporation which, together with some foreign bankers, would negotiate with the Porte. He also suggested that Russian capitalists be encouraged to build a railway in Persia. Alexander III, who apparently considered personal negotiations with a Jewish banker as below his dignity, noted on Pobedonostsev's report: "I am as embarrassed by this affair as you are, and do not know what decision to make."[21] In many other enterprises, nevertheless, Poliakov enjoyed the full cooperation of the Russian administration.

Russian oil fields, particularly in the Caucasus, likewise owed a great deal to Poliakov and other Russian-Jewish industrialists. Here, however, the international oil firms, particularly English and French, played an even greater role. Once again Jewish bankers and industrialists made excellent use of their personal connections with foreign coreligionists. In his negotiations with Pobedonostsev, Poliakov submitted a letter from his own son-in-law, James Hirsch, of the well-known German banking family. Baron Horace Günzburg had another Hirsch as a son-in-law. Since Russia had vast unexploited territories and natural resources, foreign capital was readily attracted, so long as its owners had confidence in the management of the new enterprises. The leading Jewish capitalists, personally known to their counterparts abroad, often inspired such confidence and loans were readily negotiated for investment.

In the oil industry Jews had first to overcome the legal obstacles connected with their residential rights around the Caucasian oilfields. As elsewhere, moreover, Russia's oil industry was extremely competitive and risky. There were extreme price swings dependent on the varying supply, which, in turn, depended on more or less successful drillings, as well as rapidly changing market conditions. These extremes are well illustrated by the prices of the 1890s. After a sharp price decline during the 1880s a quintal of crude oil could be acquired in June 1892 for 5.5 kopeks and one of petroleum for 27.5 kopeks, both priced far below the costs of production. By December, 1899, the price shot up to 1.05 rubles for the crude and 3.05 rubles for petroleum. Only industrialists with substantial cash resources could weather such crises. Nevertheless, beginning in a small way in the area of distribution of oil products, the Jewish firm of Dembo and Kagan expanded gradually in the 1870s and the 1880s, particularly through the disposal of by-products, which soon exceeded in monetary value the trade in kerosene itself. Before long, however, some Jews succeeded in penetrating also the production end of the industry. It was particularly the well-trained engineer, Arkadii Grigorevich Beilin, a doctor of philosophy of Berlin University, who made significant contributions to the improvement of the productive processes, the expansion of transport facilities, and the attraction of foreign, particularly Rothschild, capital to Baku and the other oilfields. It has been estimated that by the beginning of the twentieth century Jews controlled some 15-16 percent of the entire exploitation of oil, while their share in the kerosene refineries had risen to 44 percent. Despite residential restrictions, Jewish employees (many of them recruited through engineering fellowships established by Beilin) amounted in 1913 to 7.6 percent of all commercial and administrative employees engaged in the various firms producing and distributing oil products in Russia.[22]

As of old, many Jewish money traders, engaged not only in credit transactions but also in money exchange, holding deposits, and related activities, existed in almost all communities within the Pale. With the expansion of Russian industry and commerce and the transformation of the Russian economy into a money economy after the liberation of the peasants, the number of such local Jewish bankers increased considerably even in its ratio to the ever-growing Jewish population. Suffice it to cite the example of Berdichev, where in 1849-97 the proportion of money traders per 1,000 Jewish residents increased from 33 to 55. However, the main development now took place through corporate banking to which Jews contributed significantly also outside the Pale. Directorships of joint-stock banking companies often enabled Jews to establish their residences, especially in the two capitals. With the aid of coreligionists in other countries, leading Russo-Jewish bankers founded a large number of regional banks, some of which transferred their headquarters to St. Petersburg. These activities ranged far and wide and included the Moscow International Commercial Bank and several others controlled by the Poliakovs. An Austro-Jewish banker, A. I. Rothstein, who had been influential in the preparation of the Austrian banking laws of 1892, was invited by Sergei Y. Witte, Russia's outstanding finance minister, to help him in the monetary reforms then under way. In 1896, Rothstein organized the important Russo-Chinese Bank which, fourteen years later, merged with another bank into the large Russo-Asian Bank. These examples could readily be multiplied.

Expansion of Jewish and general banking was greatly hampered by government intervention and particularly its ever-changing regulations. No sooner was a comprehensive bank statute issued in 1862 when it had to be modified in 1870, 1879, 1883 and in later years. Next to the Bank of Russia and three other governmental institutions, moreover, private banking had to compete with 240 municipal banks, 116 mutual credit societies, 68 charitable loan banks and other public or semipublic establishments. In 1899, for which these statistics are given, there existed only 39 commercial banks which had to make up, through their 198 branches and their larger capital resources, for their inferiority in numbers. In addition, the Russian persecutions of Jews greatly interfered with the influx of foreign capital into the Tsarist Empire. The anti-Jewish riots of 1881-82 caused, according to a St. Petersburg paper, a lowering of the value of the Russian government bonds by 152,000,000 rubles. Western Jewish capitalists, such as the Rothschilds or the growingly important American firms, felt compunctions about extending loans to the Russian government. The importance of the Paris Rothschilds for the credit of the Russian Empire can hardly be overestimated. According to a recent computation, in the short period of 1889-93, Russia secured loans in the staggering amount of 3,390,000,000 francs from the French money market. By 1904, Russian bonds totaling 6,800,000,000 francs were in the hands of French investors. And yet, in 1906, Finance Minister Vladimir Nikolaevich Kokovtsev again tried to raise an additional loan of 800,000,000 francs, often employing unscrupulous inter-mediaries, such as an undercover agent, Raffalovich, who did not hesitate to bribe many Paris newspaper editors. The Paris Rothschilds also were under the pressure of the French government which could not view calmly the weakening of its major Russian ally. But the American Jacob H. Schiff, the senior partner of Kuhn, Loeb and Company, largely because of his intense Jewish loyalties, freely underwrote loans for the Japanese government during the Russo-Japanese war. But such compunctions were more readily overcome if the borrowing concerns were controlled by Russian Jews. Witte fully realized the importance of foreign Jewish finance capital for the development of Russia's economy and, largely for that reason, tried to exert a moderating influence on the tsarist policies concerning Jews.[23]

Jewish entry into liberal professions also made tremendous strides. Here, too, relations with the Jewish communities abroad proved helpful, especially after the enforcement of a *numerus clausus* at Russian universities. The introduction of that quota system itself testified to the growth of that class in the Jewish population. True, our statistical data are unclear and, apart from their general unreliability, cloud the issue by as a rule lumping the free professions together with civil service. In the latter the Jews were sharply discriminated against, except in so far as it related to employment by the Jewish communities themselves. Nor were Jewish professionals free of arbitrary decisions of the Russian administration. To some extent the government itself had fostered that transition from the old rabbinic to modern university studies by its promotion of Jewish "enlightenment" as well as by opening the areas of Russia's interior to Jewish professionals. Before long the two Russian capitals included a disproportionate number of Jewish lawyers, doctors, and other technicians, whose influence on the entire Jewish community of the Empire far exceeded their ratio in the population.

PAUPERIZATION OF THE MASSES

Such advances in the higher reaches of banking, industry, and the professions affected only a small minority of Jews. The masses, suffocating in the increasingly crowded ghettos within the Pale, sank ever more deeply into the mire of poverty. In Russia, as in other countries going through the early stages of modern capitalism, the rich grew richer while the poor became more and more indigent. In the Jewish case these trends were further aggravated by the existing legal restrictions on the Jews' residential and occupational rights, social ostracism and discriminatory taxation. These handicaps could much more readily be overcome by well-to-do businessmen and professionals, but the impoverished masses were exposed, partly for that very reason, to endless bureaucratic chicaneries, legal and extralegal. It has been estimated that in many communities up to 40 percent of the entire Jewish population consisted of families of so-called *Luftmenschen,* that is persons without any particular skills, capital, or specific occupations. These "breadwinners" of large families had to rely on occasional chores entrusted to them by relatives and friends; their income was unstable and, as a rule, quite inadequate. A Russian scholar, B. Miliutin, found already in 1849 that only 3 percent of the Jews possessed any capital at all, while the rest led a miserable existence. In the early 1860s partial studies made by other non-Jewish statisticians showed that, for instance, in the province of Kovno (Kaunas) it was quite common for several Jewish families to occupy a single room. In the province of Grodno a three- or four-room house sometimes accommodated as many as twelve families. "In most cases a pound of bread, a herring, and a few onions represent the daily fare of an entire family. . . . The average earning of a Jewish breadwinner amounts to 15 kopeks a day." The situation in the Ukraine was somewhat better but even there, according to a Russian landowner in the Kiev province, most Jews were poorer even than the peasants which, in view of the extreme poverty of the Ukrainian peasantry, was saying a great deal. More, the average Jew's income, whenever it came, was far less dependable than that of the peasant.[24]

Many of these descriptions date from the era of Alexander II's great reforms. Understandably, if the governmental policies toward Jews became somewhat less oppressive, the economic transformations created ever new difficulties for the Jewish population, hemmed in as it was both geographically and legally. The emancipation of the Russian peasantry, by pushing masses of liberated, but penniless and untrained, peasants into the hamlets and cities, created a large class of new competitors for the limited opportunities of making a living. Russia also suffered from recurrent depressions. Students of the Russian business cycle have shown that there was a decade-long depression beginning in 1858. After a short respite about 1870, there were new waves of depressions in 1873-76, in 1882-87 and in the early 1890s. Jewish occupations belonged to the most vulnerable in these periods, and unemployment grew among the Jewish masses by leaps and bounds.

Great impoverishment of the Jewish population is also evidenced by the statistics of Jewish charities, however incomplete. According to one record, indigent Jewish families increased in Russia from 85,183 in 1894 to 108,922 four years later. Even the latter figure is far from complete, since many towns had failed to report and a considerable number of "proud" poor, receiving secret support, did not appear in the records. Applicants for Passover charities reached in 1898 an average of 18.8 percent of the Jewish population, or some 7 percent of the total urban population of the Pale. Needless to say, all these charities lay heavily upon the Jewish communities and their philanthropic associations, the government contributing almost nothing. The burden was somewhat alleviated only by contributions from coreligionists abroad either through the large Jewish welfare organizations like the Jewish Colonization Association or the ORT (initials of the Russian equivalent of Organization for Rehabilitation and Training), or through private subsidies. In the years of mass emigration to the United States it was quite customary for many families to live largely on donations sent to them by relatives who had interveningly established themselves in their new countries of settlement.[25]

If anything, the vitality of Russian Jewry showed itself in its unconscious but, on the whole, acceptable method of adjustment to these untold miseries. Apart from embarking on large-scale emigration to less oppressive countries, the Jewish masses found an outlet for their energies in the new industries which were, in part, developed by their own leaders. The transition was not altogether easy. The numerous Jewish coachmen lost out in their competition with the railroads. Even Jewish artisans found that their respective skills in tailoring, shoemaking, or the food industry were of little avail in mechanized factories producing textiles, shoes, or food products. Jewish entrepreneurs, as well as

workers, had to pay a high price for the initial errors
accompanying this great transition. In Congress Poland and
other border provinces industrialization was promoted by the
factories built by German industrialists in order to avoid
the impact of tsarist protectionism. Lodz, in particular, developed into an important industrial center for the whole
Empire. But when this process extended into the interior
of Russia, where the region around Moscow became the
prime industrial center of the whole country, Jews found
themselves handicapped by residence restrictions.

Nevertheless the Jewish working classes were making
steady progress. Here and there they were aided by some
of their coreligionists who, for idealistic reasons, tried to
spread employment among their own people. One such
outstanding industrialist-philanthropist was Solomon Posner
who, as early as 1823, established a textile mill in Kuchary
in the province of Plotsk. The Brodskis in their sugar factories likewise preferentially employed Jewish personnel especially in executive positions. The Empire thus witnessed
the gradual rise of an industrial Jewish proletariat consisting
of both old-line employees of artisans and an ever-growing
number of regular factory workers. Needless to say, Jewish
laborers, together with the proletariat of other faiths, suffered
from the usual ills of the early industrial revolution, particularly the segment recruited from underpaid women and
children. We have no detailed statistics for Jews, but the
sex and age distribution among them probably did not differ
too greatly from that of the Russian workers.[26]

Recent statistical studies based on official records of the
Department of Commerce for 1887 have revealed the presence of 24.4 percent of women workers. Their ratio in the
textile mills of St. Petersburg in 1881 was 42.6 percent. More
startlingly, 9.2 percent of the half million laborers employed
by 3,316 enterprises surveyed in 1882-83, were juveniles
under fifteen. Some factories employed children aged ten.
Also the hours of labor, usually in excess of twelve daily, the
unsanitary working conditions in the factories, the instability
of employment, and the extremely low wages even for adult
males were very discouraging. According to a report sub-

mitted in 1896 to the Socialist International in London, the average Russian-Jewish worker often earned but 2-3 rubles a week for six days of 14-18 hours each. In the Jewish case additional complications arose from the wish of the pre-dominantly Orthodox workers to observe their Sabbath rest and from the mostly unfriendly attitude of their Christian fellow workers. It was also a far greater psychological strain on an artisan or petty shopkeeper to become a mere cog in a growingly inhuman industrial machine with unaccustomed forms of discipline, often aggravated by hostile and contemptuous Christian foremen. Nevertheless, the Jewish industrial proletariat was increasing from decade to decade, especially wherever it could form associations of its own, ultimately also a political party of its own, in which it found a more brotherly reception and fuller understanding of its cultural peculiarities.

Notwithstanding all these transformations the Jewish economic structure on the eve of the First World War still was relatively lopsided. The ratio of 2.33 percent of Jewish agriculturists supplied by the census of 1897 was, if anything, lower seventeen years later. It contrasted with the Russian population in which the farmers exceeded 90 percent of the total. Even within so-called urban occupations, the concentration of Jews in some, and their relative absence from others, made their economic stratification quite different from that of their neighbors. A Polish writer, quoting in 1914 the latest data supplied by the statistical annual of Congress Poland, pointed out that while in tailoring and shoemaking the proportion of Polish to Jewish workers was 40:56 percent and in transport 45:51.5 percent, in the lumber industry and carpentry the percentages were reversed to 73:17. The wool industry employed altogether some 40,000 Jews compared with 127,000 Poles and over 62,000 Germans. Jewish preponderance in commerce was more obvious. Dependent on its particular branches, the Jewish share still ranged from 80 to 95 percent despite the growth of a Polish bourgeoisie, stimulated by both government and public opinion, especially in the metropolitan areas of Warsaw and Lodz, as well as the presence of a fairly substantial number of both German and Russian merchants in the Polish cities. Similar conditions prevailed, on a somewhat lower scale, throughout the Pale.

In short, all the efforts at "productivization" of Russian Jewry, though enjoying the full support of Jewish leadership itself, were only successful to the extent of transferring Jews from one branch of industry or commerce to another, rather than in changing the entire economic structure of the Jewish people. This "abnormal" stratification aroused much antagonism among the non-Jewish majority and made the Jews doubly vulnerable to the successive catastrophies which befell them after 1914. But in the face of harsh economic realities little could have been achieved even by efforts of a much more powerful Jewish community than that which existed in Russia under an inimical government and hostile public opinion.

7

Communal Autonomy

IN THE EARLY STAGES of their economic struggles the
Russian Jews, like their ancestors in Poland, drew considerable strength from their communal solidarity. Russia had
inherited from Poland, and indirectly from medieval Germany, a strong and all-embracing communal organization
which to some extent minimized the external pressures. In
the economic sphere the *kahal* (the name, derived from the
Hebrew term for community, connoted the all-embracing
communal organization) exercised extraordinary jurisdiction
in balancing right against right and in helping the individual
Jews to fight their battle for survival. Small professional
groups, such as those of midwives or town musicians, were
completely regulated by the *kahal* which prescribed, for
example, the methods of performance and the fees of musicians serving at weddings. It also regulated the work of
teachers, communal scribes, and other professionals. In its
heyday it surveyed weights and measures and sought to
protect both the consumer and the producer by its general
supervision over prices and wages. It also tried to limit competition by invoking the medieval principle of *maarufia*, that
is, the specific connection between a customer and his supplier
which was not to be infringed upon by any outsider. Sometimes it went so far as to declare that connection hereditary.
Most importantly, the *kahal* tried to prevent undue Jewish
competition in relations with the outside world. According
to the old principle of *hazakah*, a title to land was acquired
only with the permission of the communal authorities. Such

licenses were often granted particularly in connection with the acquisition of real estate from Christians, so as to prevent Jewish would-be purchasers from unduly raising prices while bidding against one another. These responsibilities often involved the communal elders in extended litigation, but they served as an important line of defense for the Jewish community as a whole.[1]

Side by side with the central communal organization operated numerous voluntary associations which, though working under the general supervision of the communal council, enjoyed considerable leeway in their specialized fields of activity. In the economic sphere such functions were performed primarily by Jewish artisan guilds, whereas the far more competitive merchants, often individually belonging to general merchant guilds, saw little advantage in forming Jewish associations. Continuing the Polish traditions, the artisan guilds revealed the typically medieval interlocking of social and religious with the economic factors, many of them maintaining synagogues of their own and meeting a variety of social needs of their members. Like other guilds, they supervised the admission of apprentices and journeymen and often limited the number of master artisans, so as to restrict competition. Understandably, the journeymen, often thus held back in their professional advancement, occasionally formed associations of their own for the defense of their rights. When they tried in Minsk to hold independent religious services, however, the masters' guild invoked the aid of the *kahal* which forbade the journeymen to secede from the regular artisan synagogues. At the same time it ordered the guilds to adjust the journeymen's legitimate grievances. If, because of this socioreligious coloring of all such associations, Jews were not admitted to Christian guilds, this difficulty was minimized within the Pale by the fact that, in most areas, Jews constituted the majority of artisans, at least in the occupations extensively cultivated by them. On the whole, Christian artisans could, with equal justice, complain of discrimination by Jewish guilds in their nonadmission of Christian members.

Governmental Equivocation

Under Russian domination the Jewish communal bodies faced in many ways a novel and difficult situation. The authorities were at first more puzzled than disturbed by this unusual phenomenon. Russian society had long been divided into classes from the nobility down to villeins, and each individual could readily be subsumed under one or another of these established categories. Catherine II and her advisers doubtless glibly believed that they could simply incorporate the new Jewish subjects into these established groups. They soon realized with chagrin that the Jewish community was an entity of its own kind which could not easily be dissolved in the majority's corporate groupings.

More, for practical reasons the government found it advantageous to maintain that organization intact. Jews were better than average taxpayers and the revenue from them was most easily and inexpensively collected through their own communal organs. Particularly the so-called *korobka* (chest tax), originally an excise tax on ritually slaughtered meat but speedily extended to many other objects of mass consumption as well, and the candle tax could yield greater revenue for the Treasury, if they were rigidly supervised by the Jewish communities themselves.

Most of the *kahals,* moreover, had emerged from Polish domination with a public debt which could only be serviced by a continuously functioning communal body. Characteristically, their creditors often consisted principally of Catholic churches, monasteries, and nobles who considered such communal loans, even if bearing less than 10 percent interest, a fairly safe and enduring investment. Extant records of seventy communities, principally located in the provinces of Podolia and Volhynia, reveal that they owed 102,090 rubles on loans, in part contracted as far back as the seventeenth century. This was a fairly universal problem, common to both the East and the West. The Rhineland community of Worms, for instance, by 1800 owed six times more than the cumulative value of all its communal property. It took the wealthy communities of Alsace-Lorraine more than half a century after the French Revolution to liquidate in an orderly fashion the debts accumulated during the pre-Emancipation era.[2]

Occasionally the communities contested the claims of some debtors by pointing out that their past payments had covered both the principal and the interest at moderate rates. On the other hand, some creditors were more interested in their regular annual income than in the repayment of the principal. True, Russia's national debt was likewise increasing from decade to decade. But, unlike the Treasury, the Jewish communal organs could not print paper money and reiteratedly depreciate the currency in circulation, a process but partially checked by Count Egor Kankrin's and Witte's financial reforms of 1823, 1839-43, and 1893-99. The government could not afford, therefore, to undermine too radically the delicate structure of Jewish communal indebtedness without incurring great losses in its own revenue and ruining some influential Christian creditors.

On their part, the Jewish communities had to adjust themselves as best they could to the new governmental structure. In declining Poland the prevailing anarchy enabled each group to run its own affairs with relatively little interference. This system led to many internal abuses and particularly to excessive concentration of power in relatively few families, but there was little outside supervision and the Jewish community resembled indeed a sort of "state within the state." Now Catherine's enlightened absolutism tended to convert the Jewish community, too, into an agency of the state's totalitarian control. Under Nicholas I the manifold earlier attempts were consolidated in the generally discriminatory law of 1835, articles 67-68 of which demanded that the *kahal* be held responsible for the enforcement of governmental regulations among the Jews, as well as for the collection of taxes due to the Crown and the county treasuries. It also was to render annual accounts of its income and expenditures to both the municipal councils and the central Treasury. On assuming office, all Jewish elders were to take an oath of loyalty and to pledge themselves to execute faithfully all orders of the authorities, supply the quota of recruits, collect all state and communal taxes after assessing them justly among members, and generally to enforce obedience to law and order.

Not surprisingly, these extreme regulations broke down in execution and little change manifested itself immediately in the operation of Jewish communal bodies. Almost in despair, Nicholas and his associates embarked upon the radical enterprise of suppressing the traditional *kahal* altogether. In a decree promulgated on December 19, 1844, the tsar declared that "a separate Jewish administration need not exist and all *kahals* and their subsidiaries are hereby declared abolished. Their functions are to be assumed by the municipal councils and assemblies, each according to its competence." The decree further defined, in detail, the new prerogatives of the municipal councils and other organs, the substitute methods of collecting Jewish taxes, and the means of providing for the residual duties of the Jewish communities. Curiously, Jews had become so inured to governmental persecution that they took this new edict, too, in their stride. When Sir Moses Montefiore visited Russia two years later and transmitted to the tsarist ministers the main grievances of their Jewish population, he emphasized the civil disabilities much more than the restrictions legally imposed upon Jewish self-government. His informants must have felt that, with or without governmental cooperation, they could carry on more or less in their accustomed ways. The Russian official who complained to Max Lilienthal about the Jews' extreme tenacity in maintaining their communal life was quite right in asserting that a Polish rebellion could be suppressed with military force, but that the quiet Jewish obstinacy was being fought in vain.[3]

Not that the Jews consciously wished to oppose governmental regulations. Their old rabbinic law had taught them that the "law of the kingdom is law" and that even in litigations submitted to Jewish courts the existing governmental ordinances must be respected. The only qualification the rabbis had placed on this principle was that such laws must not be discriminatory but apply to all citizens alike. This principle was now reiterated by one of the outstanding talmudic leaders of the time, Rabbi Isaac ben Hayyim, head of the famed rabbinic academy of Volozhin.

In general, the Jewish masses and their leaders attributed all antagonistic governmental acts to the provincial authorities or to the tsar's advisers, rather than to the tsar himself. Sometimes they tried to outdo one another in professions of loyalty. We recall the patriotic poems recited by welcoming deputations in honor of Catherine, Alexander, and other monarchs. Catherine was sufficiently impressed by one such ceremony to mention it in one of her letters, and to stress that on that occasion Jews and Dominicans stood side by side. Beyond such verbal expressions of loyalty Jews demonstrated their allegiance to the Crown at such critical moments as the Napoleonic invasion of 1812, the Crimean War, and the Russo-Japanese War. In an interesting report to their communities about a conversation they had held with Alexander I, the Jewish deputies Eliezer (Lazar) Dillon and Yehudah Zundel Sonnenberg recorded the Emperor's promise to investigate Jewish grievances and urged their constituents sharply to combat Jewish smuggling, of which the Emperor had personally complained. "This is contrary to the teachings of our holy Torah," they added, "which orders us to observe carefully the emperor's commands."[4]

Nor did anyone raise the question whether synagogue audiences should continue reciting the traditional prayers for the welfare of their monarchs including even such anti-Jewish rulers as Nicholas I and Nicholas II. This custom caused some embarrassment to Galician Jews during the First World War. At that time the Austrian police discovered that many Galicians were using prayer books imported from Russia and containing these liturgical blessings with the full names of the tsar and his family. Since Russia was at that time an enemy country, a search was instituted throughout the Jewish communities so as to expunge the incriminating passages from these "subversive" prayer books.

Law Enforcement

Jews saw no conflict in loyalty when, cultivating their traditional mores, they paid little heed to the governmental efforts to subject them to the jurisdiction of general courts. In her first proclamation after the annexation of the Polish provinces, Catherine II promised to maintain the existing order and religious liberties of all inhabitants, including Jews. One article stated specifically: "The administration of law and justice among Jews shall continue to be entrusted to their present courts, though in the name and under the authority of Her Imperial Majesty."[5]

Within ten years, however, the Russian authorities started to retreat from this pledge and increasingly tried to subsume the Jews under the jurisdiction of the municipal and other courts. They were prompted not only by the general tendency of authoritarian regimes to control all facets of their subjects' life but also by the wish to channel the substantial judicial fees to the tsarist or municipal judges. The law of 1804, finally, tried to restrict the operation of Jewish tribunals to purely religious affairs and otherwise to treat them as mere courts of arbitration, if voluntarily accepted as such by the parties. But whatever their status in public law may have been, the Jews respected their own courts of justice and readily submitted themselves to their judgments even after the reiteration of these restrictive provisions in the edict of 1835 and the total abolition of the *kahal* in 1844.

As a rule, Jewish courts administered justice more efficiently and speedily than did the general courts. Having behind them centuries of experience and well-defined legal principles embodied in codes of law, commentaries and *responsa* by rabbis, all of which were intensively studied by the entire Jewish intelligentsia, their sentences usually met with the instantaneous approval of public opinion, often the very parties against whom judgment was issued. In his autobiography, the Hebrew writer, Abraham Jacob Paperna, maintained that in his native hamlet there was no Christian court and litigations were largely settled by the law of the fist. In contrast thereto,

in all monetary litigations, quarrels between husband and wife, or any other controversies they [Jews] usually repaired to the Jewish court which enjoyed the full confidence of the local Christians as well. Whenever the latter had a controversy with a Jew, they usually turned to the rabbi who, after listening to any plaintiff, immediately sent his beadle for the defendant who appeared almost instantaneously. Both parties placed on the table the judicial fee—both having to pay the same amount—and the proceedings began. Shortly thereafter the rabbi pronounced the sentence which, as a rule, the litigants accepted without demurrer or the help of court marshals.[6]

This somewhat idealized picture reproduces fairly well the informality of Jewish trials which, in financial and family matters, often followed the rules of equity and resulted in amicable settlements, rather than in sentences according to formal law. The official Russian machinery, on the contrary, moved very slowly and some cases were pending in various instances for years on end. It is small wonder, then, that according to an outstanding Russian expert, as late as the 1880s, many Christians repaired to Jewish courts even in litigations with other non-Jews.

Evidently there existed areas of conflict between these rival judicial systems. One of the most effective weapons of Jewish law enforcement consisted in the promulgation, or a mere threat, of a ban which readily forced any recalcitrant party to appear before the court or to accept its unfavorable judgment. Although because of centuries-long abuses the Jewish ban, like its Catholic counterpart, had lost some of its efficacy, the communal elders could still force a rebellious member to his knees by refusing him certain religious services, such as circumcision, rabbinical wedding, or the religious burial in consecrated ground. An excommunication also implied various forms of social ostracism. Jewish guilds, or the *kahal* behind them, could threaten any artisan with the loss of membership, or at least with his demotion from master artisan to journeyman. The tsarist government looked askance at the exercise of this power which it was unable to control. Time and again it ineffectually tried to outlaw bans but, since their promulgation rested with rabbis backed by a general assembly of members, even the suppression of the *kahal* in 1844 made little of a dent in the continued authority of Jewish courts over their coreligionists.

Conflicting interests of state and community came to the fore also when, in order to strengthen its supervision, the government encouraged informing among Jews, sometimes promising to turn over the ensuing fines to the informers. On the Jewish side, on the other hand, informing had long been considered a major crime, because it was likely to embroil not only a few individuals but, by the process of generalization, entire Jewish communities in serious difficulties with their neighbors and governments. In medieval Spain the Jewish courts had secured privileges of passing death sentences on informers who were considered guilty of high treason toward their community. This tradition was kept alive in the Polish and Russian communities, although executions became very infrequent and they were treated as murderous acts by the authorities. One such incident in the small Podolian town of Novo-Ushitsa in 1836 actually brought about sharp retribution. Two Jews for a long time played the game of receiving payments from the government for informing, and from the Jews for not informing, until the Jewish elders decided to get rid of the two blackmailers. Although the executions were carried out quietly and the local authorities were effectively bribed, the governor-general ordered a sharp investigation. After a trial before a military court, the majority of the eighty Jewish accomplices was sentenced to hard labor in Siberia, while most others had to run a gauntlet between five hundred soldiers; few of these survived the ordeal. The only person acquitted was the Hasidic leader, Rabbi Israel Friedmann of Ruzhin, who had fled to Austria, where he founded the subsequently famous Hasidic dynasty of Sadagóra, Bukovina.[7]

Even without this severe punishment, such drastic means of disposing of informers would hardly have continued in the subsequent decades. But here always was a source of conflict between the authorities which saw in informers welcome allies, and the communities which resented them as traitors. In any case, Jewish judicial autonomy began weakening in the latter part of the nineteenth century as part of the general decline in communal solidarity resulting from the newer social and ideological movements.

SOCIAL WELFARE

No opposition was evinced by the government to the ramified communal charities. In general the Russian Empire had to leave all philanthropic efforts to the initiative of private individuals or the churches. From time immemorial the Jewish community had concerned itself with the social welfare of its members in an even broader sense than do modern welfare states. Since charity was connected with religion, social welfare embraced moral, as much as physical, well-being. Not only did the community supervise, therefore, the morals of its members, exposing cases of rent gouging, excessive harshness by landlords toward tenants, or of illicit sex relations to public contumely, but it also tried to protect the good names of innocent persons. We even find communal minutes recording attestations for girls who had lost their virginity because of an accident or illness, lest they be subsequently accused of premarital intercourse. Charities were often delegated to special philanthropic associations. Like the professional guilds which, as a rule, also tried to assist their members in emergencies, these societies had had a rich history behind them, dating back to ancient and medieval times. Among them the burial society, the so-called *Hevra kadisha* (the holy association), carried the greatest prestige and wielded most power. At times, these societies were strong enough to defy the very *kahal*. Together with the rabbinate, they thus offered some checks and balances within the Jewish communal structure.

Much was left also to individual philanthropies, particularly to alms distributed among beggars. Mendicancy became indeed a major blemish on the Jewish, as well as on the general Russian, body politic, with the difference, however, that from time immemorial charity had so highly been stressed by rabbinic moralists and legislators that beggary lost much of its stigma. In his aforementioned autobiography Paperna observed that "the Jewish pauper does not ask for alms, as does his Christian counterpart standing before the door or near the window and bending down to the ground, but he brazenly enters the room and demands a gift as if it were his due. If he is refused, he becomes abusive and curses." Both on moral and practical grounds even impoverished families felt obligated to contribute their mite to both the communal and individual charities. Since the number of beggars increased by leaps and bounds and many families were unable to meet even their minimal demands, some communities began issuing scrip representing fractions of a kopek which enabled families to give something to all beggars at their doors. Much disturbance was caused by migratory beggars who moved from one hamlet to another and collected alms. The communities found themselves obliged to issue certificates to deserving mendicants who were then entitled to spend three days in one locality collecting alms before moving on to the next place. Such certificates were also given to the poor whom various householders had to entertain at Sabbath meals.

Above all, many communities erected a so-called *hekdesh,* a combination of hostelry and hospital, to accommodate both homeless visitors and sick persons. Such institutions were often maintained even by impoverished communities, unable to give them the necessary care. As a result they often degenerated into overcrowded unsanitary hovels which, rather than helping diseased persons, actually increased the dangers of infection. Understandably, these institutions, together with the whole system of beggary and other outworn methods of social welfare, were subjected to sharp criticisms by visitors from more advanced Western countries and by local Jewish reformers. The Minsk *hekdesh,* for instance, was thus described by a visiting English missionary, Robert Pinkerton:

> In the Jewish Hospital we saw forty-five young and old, of both sexes, seemingly without any classification of disease, placed in several small rooms; they certainly presented one of the most appalling scenes of wretchedness I ever witnessed; filth, rags and pestilential effluvia pervaded the whole place. A small apothecary's shop, with a kind of chapel, occupied one end of the building. The government contributed 16£ per annum towards its support; and the rest of the miserable pittance allowed to this lazarhouse is derived from the Jewish kahal and from private charity.

Similar harrowing descriptions are offered by the distinguished novelist, Shalom J. Abramovich (better known under' his pen name, Mendele Mokher Seforim), all of which made of the *hekdesh* a byword of opprobrium among the assailants of the traditional Jewish community life.[8]

CLASS STRUGGLE

As time went on the inner tensions in the community increased and greatly undermined Jewish solidarity. From the outset the Russian Jewish community had built-in elements of class struggle. Its predecessor, the Polish Jewish community of the eighteenth century, had suffered from the general dissolution of the Polish state and allowed certain anarchical elements to distort its traditional order. The growing inflation and, with it, the disproportionate indebtedness of the communities, together with Poland's arbitrary taxation system, had lent undue prominence to the communal plutocracy. Under Russian domination these conditions were, in some respects, further aggravated by the close alliance between the wealthy groups and the Russian bureaucracy. Russian law itself, by extending certain privileges to members of the merchant guilds and, to a lesser extent, to registered "burghers," injected a discriminatory factor into the communal relations as well. While the community still remained responsible for the total taxes imposed upon Jews of each district, its wealthiest members, belonging to the First Guild, were exempt from the head taxes and certain other imposts. To be sure, it appears that few of them completely shirked their communal responsibilities. Whether voluntarily, or under the pressure of public opinion and possible reprisals, they mostly assumed their share in the communal burdens. But such voluntary cooperation always injected an element of uncertainty and frequently lent the voices of such "volunteers" an undue weight in the determination of communal affairs.

Members of this class, moreover, were usually the entrenched leaders who, though formally elected by their respective constituencies, were little despots subject only in extreme cases to deposition by communal will. As a rule these communal tyrants entertained excellent relations with the Russian officials and, with the latter's aid, suppressed most opposing movements in the bud. We have a graphic description of such a small-time despot in the hamlet of Kamenets, Grodno province, from the pen of a reformist writer Yehezkel (Ezekiel) Kotik. Although such descriptions by a propagandist for reform must be partially discounted, the fact that the elder concerned, Aaron Leizer, was the writer's grandfather who left a strong imprint on the latter's childhood recollections, gives an inkling of what injustices could be perpetrated by a communal autocrat in the middle of the nineteenth century. It all began when some Jews succeeded in outbidding Aaron Leizer for a concession he had held from a neighboring landlord, at a time when he happened not to serve as "the elder of the month."

When my grandfather learned of it, he journeyed to the *ispravnik* [police official] and told him that he wished to become tax assessor. Thereupon the ispravnik arrived in Kamenets and took away the books and the seal from the tax assessor B. and handed them to my grandfather. Now grandfather went to work. In the first place, he sent attendants to seize the kitchen utensils, candlesticks, clocks, all that he could find, even bedding to which he had no right, in the houses of the opposition. To whom should grandfather listen? He had the ispravnik on his side. He also detected some old debts owed the community and he now demanded their payment at once. . . . There was great excitement in town and people quickly recognized that it was difficult to tangle with Aaron Leizer. . . . The outcome was that the group, which had intended to obtain the concession and which consisted, according to my grandfather's calculations, of seventy persons, had to take an oath in the Great Synagogue—all clad in praying shawls and holding scrolls of law in their arms, while the ram's horn was blown and candles were lighted—that they would commit no such injustice toward my grandfather. This was a most solemn oath. . . . The next day grandfather sent a letter to the ispravnik resigning from the post of tax assessor. The ispravnik, well informed about what was happening, gave his approval.[9]

On the other hand, in the predominantly tiny communities of the Russian Pale during the early decades after the partition of Poland, these communal elders had to reckon with the force of public opinion; otherwise they might have been boycotted by their own closest neighbors. Some of their acts could also be scrutinized by higher governmental authorities, if some aggrieved groups were aroused enough to invoke such outside assistance. We have, for example, the texts of such

applications to the minister of interior from Minsk and a small
Podolian community in 1852-53. One could also appeal to
the rabbinic authorities. Of course, the rabbis, like the rest
of the sprawling, if often grossly underpaid, communal
bureaucracy, usually were appointees of those very leaders
against whom they were asked to intervene. But there was
enough independence of mind, at least among the more
important members of the rabbinate, and they were sufficiently obedient to the postulates of rabbinic law which, as
always before, still embraced elements of what the Romans
called *fas* as well as *jus*, to adjudicate matters in accordance
with the principles of equity. More frequently, overt rebellion
against established communal authority was avoided by the
elders' own moderation. Some leaders, even if autocratic,
behaved like the benevolent despots of the Enlightenment era
who felt that everything should be done for the people, but
as little as possible by the people. Stories about communal
autocrats who sought to secure justice by humiliating certain
powerful but selfish individuals abound in the literature of
the age. Nonetheless members of the upper classes, mainly
consisting of the plutocracy, an aristocracy of rabbinic descent, and one of actual learning, felt as a rule closer kinship
for one another and, in case of conflict, sided with their own
class rather than with the majority.

Such conflicts became particularly frequent during Nicholas I's *rekrutchina*. No sooner did the edict appear in 1827,
than the entire community was plunged into mourning. Since
the administration of this barbarous recruitment system was
in part placed in the hands of the communal elders, however
reluctant, it was manifest that the lower classes would be the
main sufferers and some houses of Jewish elders in Minsk
and elsewhere were stoned. Though speedily repressed by
the government, these rebellious acts adumbrated the increasing chasm which this new law would create within the community. Having to deliver a certain quota of recruits—we
recall that that quota was set higher than the ratio of the
Jewish population—the elders had to choose what they considered lesser evils. The recruitment of underaged children,
for instance, at times sprang from the humane consideration
that boys of eighteen or twenty usually were already fathers

of families and that their forced enlistment would cause even greater hardships to more individuals. The law itself, moreover, exempted sons of merchants of the three guilds from all military service. It was not surprising when, from 1825 on, or two years before the enactment of the severe ukase, the number of Jews enrolled under these guilds increased by leaps and bounds. By paying a registration fee (the fee for membership in the third guild was rather moderate), Jews, like non-Jews, could thus secure exemption from military service for their children. Hence, for example, in the province of Kiev where Jews had outnumbered Christian commoners to but a minor extent, there now suddenly appeared on the rolls 42,910 Jews against 17,156 Christians, a disproportion which continued to 1845, or the entire period covered by the records. Communal leadership was also interested in saving young rabbis and rabbinical students, including children who showed special aptitude for rabbinic studies, because of the deep-rooted Jewish reverence for learning. At the same time uneducated children of illiterate parents could more readily be deceived by the various "kidnappers" who, by substantial *douceurs,* made them sign slips indicating their willingness to volunteer for armed service.

In general, the Russian administration treated these prospective servicemen almost on a par with criminals; they were often kept in chains until the respective draft boards examined their physical capabilities. Right at the beginning of this system a Kiev doctor, asked by the military authorities for the reasons of the high rate of mortality among the new recruits, replied:

> More than half of the 1,600 new cantonists brought together in 1828 had come from a considerable distance. According to the documents accompanying them, they were supposed to have been ten years of age but, since they were losing their first teeth, it was manifest that they could not be older than eight years. Unfortunately, no funds were available to return them to their parents in the distant localities. Hence the battalion was forced to keep them and to enter their ages according to the documents.[10]

Such frequent miscarriage of justice was blamed at home on the communal elders even if they happened not to be guilty. Ultimately, the government tightened its screws by decreeing that, for every recruit the community had failed to deliver, it was to be penalized by an increased quota of three recruits. Combining recruitment with fiscal administration, another edict provided that for every 2,000 rubles of tax arrears the community had to furnish an additional recruit without being released of its financial obligations. In short, caught between the Scylla of unrelenting government pressures and the Charybdis of an aroused communal membership, the communal leaders often acted like desperadoes and lost whatever prestige they had previously enjoyed among the masses. To many of them the formal abolition of the *kahal* in 1844 came as welcome relief from an impossible burden.

Nevertheless, the heritage of bitterness left behind by the recruiting laws, kept acute by the continued responsibility of the new semivoluntary associations for certain tax revenues, remained as a festering wound within the community. Combined with the rise of the new ideological movements, which undermined the traditional uniform Weltanschauung, these inner forces of distintegration augured badly for the future of the Jewish communal organization. Before long, an increasingly powerful chorus of voices demanded the replacement of the traditional communal organization by a novel form of a secularized and more democratically controlled "people's" community.

8

Religion and Culture

SURVIVAL OF THE Jewish people under the trying conditions of the tsarist regime was largely contingent on its adherence to its religious teachings which, for most of that period, dominated both the thinking and the practical way of life of the vast majority. These teachings, and the institutions giving them flesh and blood, had gradually evolved during more than two millennia of Jewish life in the Diaspora. In pre-partition Poland these forms of Jewish living had assumed a particular coloring; they were continued with undiminished vigor under the reign of the tsars. The relatively minor adjustments necessitated by the new environmental conditions were taken by the Jewish community in its stride. Ironically, the growing hostility of both the regime and the Russo-Polish public merely helped to reinforce the inner solidarity of the Jewish group and its attachment to its ancestral faith and mores. After a few decades, to be sure, there began emerging certain reformatory trends, expressed particularly in the so-called *haskalah* (Jewish Enlightenment) literature. But the fact that these trends received considerable support from the government for a while aroused suspicions among the Jewish masses. Anything that smacked of excessive rapprochement with the Gentile world was suspect as a path ultimately leading to apostasy from Judaism, a nexus which, indeed, underlay much of the government favoritism toward the reformatory movements.

Judaism of the old type was all-embracing in both its doctrine and its demands on daily observance. One needs but quote parts of the following appeal, issued in 1838 by the

Warsaw rabbinate in collaboration with several other communities. Its tenor was that, in order to appease the evident wrath of the Almighty, the Jewish communities ought to watch the more closely all phases of their members' behavior, a surveillance which the public was expected to welcome with great joy. They were to supervise most insistently:

(1) the *mezuzzot* (door-post scrolls) which are to be placed in every house on all doors, gates and other places requiring them. . . . The supervisor should check them every month in each city, particularly in places where there is suspicion that these *mezuzzot* might be stolen.

(2) the owners of bathhouses so that the water in the pools be sufficiently heated, for on cold days this matter may constitute a danger to life.

(3) the butcher shops, lest ritually permitted meats be sold in shops which also distribute non-kosher meats. . . .

(4) the removal of the sciatical vein so that it be accomplished without any residuum of doubt . . . for many butchers because of excessive greed sin on this score. Also to see to it that all meat be washed every three days according to Jewish law.

(5) in localities which have an 'erub (symbolically cordoned off areas for Sabbath use) to supervise their proper installation. Communities which do not have an 'erub should be urged to install it in a proper fashion. . . .

(9) to see to it that all stores be closed [on Fridays] at least half an hour before the time set for synagogue services so that there should be enough time to light the candles in full daylight.

(10) He who has the fear of God in his heart shall be careful to order his clothes from a reliable tailor who would not commit the severe transgression of *shaatnez* (mixing of wool and linen together). All should also be modest in their attire which is a good piece of advice for many reasons.

(11) Since many localities have toilets close to synagogues and prayer houses, and this is a great advantage for the population from both the standpoint of health and cleanliness during services, they should see to it

that these outhouses be kept clean and have doors in proper condition. They should also urge such localities which do not yet have them to install them. . . .

(15) It is highly appropriate to institute in every town a charitable chest for the poor who are ashamed of asking for their share for the expenses on Sabbaths and holidays. This charity is to be distributed every Friday morning.

(16) The teachers in each community should be careful in instructing pupils able to understand the laws of the *Shulhan Arukh* (code of laws) in some section of that code every day. Particularly in the laws relating to prayers, benedictions, ablutions of hands, the Sabbath, and other commandments which every Jew needs in order to know how to behave.

(17) Each community is to appoint supervisors for every wedding lest men and women dance together, God forbid. . . . Every man should also see to it that members of his family should not go on Sabbath and holidays to drink in taverns lest they become exuberant and careless.

(18) Every member is to supervise his family and personnel so that men not be alone with women and also that two unmarried boys not sleep in the same bed. . . .

This appeal is cited here at some length because it shows the range of religious supervision of the minutiae of daily living. Because of the public's general willingness to submit to such controls, the life of the individual Russian Jew was to some extent immunized from the effects of hostile governmental regulations and popular interference.[1]

SYNAGOGUE AND RABBINATE

Religious life centered around the synagogue and the school, as well as their main officials, the rabbis and teachers. Despite strong communal controls, much leeway was left to individuals and smaller groups in organizing their own places of worship. While "synagogues" consisted mainly of two types, the synagogue in the narrower sense (*bet ha-keneset*) and the prayer and study house (*bet ha-midrash*), there were many private and associational chapels where services were conducted in exactly the same fashion. Sometimes such lesser places of worship were organized for religious reasons, as during the protracted struggle between the new sect of *Hasidim* (Pietists) and *Mitnagdim* (their opponents). Since the former had introduced certain ritualistic innovations, it was but natural for them to hold prayerful assemblies employing these new rituals. Sometimes followers of a certain Hasidic leader were at variance with their counterparts of another Hasidic school and worshiped in separate quarters. Professional associations of craftsmen also often preferred to worship in synagogues of their own.

At times it sufficed for a wealthy member to quarrel with the leaders of a larger synagogue, or with the majority of its worshipers, for him to organize an independent group in his own home or rented quarters. Occasionally, the quest for synagogue honors, especially for being called to the recitation of the Scriptural lessons on Sabbaths and holidays, was potent enough to induce ambitious individuals to organize small congregations in which they could be more frequently summoned for such honorific assignments. Although all these institutions, major or minor, were subject to the general surveillance by the communal boards, they enjoyed considerable autonomy and revealed many variations which added much to the community's spiritual richness and afforded vast opportunities for the display of its creative talents.

The same local autonomy was also enjoyed by the rabbinate which in the two millennia of its evolution had undergone many transformations. The Russian rabbis, too, largely followed the patterns established in independent Poland, where, in 1764, the government had closed down the two central organizations of Polish and Lithuanian Jewry. Even more than before each community and its rabbi now had to rely on their own resources, only occasionally consulting with one another. Complete atomization was prevented only by the fact that, as before, an outstanding rabbinic authority, such as Elijah ben Solomon Gaon of Vilna (1720-97), enjoyed such a wide reputation for scholarship and saintliness that most communities accepted his judgments unquestioningly. Even he, however, ran up against considerable resistance in his own community of Vilna when he tried to outlaw the new Hasidic movement.

Other distinguished rabbis included Israel Lipkin, better known as Israel Salanter from his residence in Salant, near Kovno (1810-83), leader of a new ethical movement, and Isaac Elhanan Spector of Kovno (1817-96), both of whom played an outstanding role especially in the northwestern provinces. In many other parts of the Pale, too, rabbis were often approached by their colleagues to decide for them some ticklish problems in ritual or civil law. This was the highest form of recognition given to a rabbi, whose esteem rose with the number and geographic diffusion of his correspondents. If he received inquiries from other European countries or the United States, he thereby secured a seal of approval as an international leader. But apart from professional rabbis, holding office by communal appointment, many private citizens attained the same rank by virtue of their learning and saintly way of life. Salaried rabbis often bowed their heads in reverence before them and accepted their superior judgment. On the other hand, such flexibility and dependence on the more or less arbitrary judgment of a number of individual *cognoscenti* could also become a source of instability and give rise to many communal dissensions.[2]

Not surprisingly, this entire world of synagogue and rabbinate was alien to Russian officialdom which correctly sensed that much of Jewish "separatism" was protected by the ramparts of these two institutions. Before long the Russian autocracy tried, therefore, to seize full control of both. In its comprehensive law of 1835, it prescribed that only Jewish settlements of more than thirty families could maintain a prayer house of their own, and only such as embraced eighty families or more could also erect a synagogue. In larger cities Jews could maintain a prayer house for each thirty and a synagogue for each eighty families. Private chapels, even occasional services at private homes, required special governmental permits, unlicensed gatherings being subject to the huge fine of 1,000 rubles. (According to an official report of 1842, there were 604 synagogues and 2,340 prayer houses as well as 3,944 schools and 954 rabbis in Russia.) Each sanctuary, moreover, had to have an executive board to maintain decorum, regulate the income, appoint the personnel, as well as to submit annual reports to both the local police and the rabbi. At the same time the statute devoted fully seventeen articles to the rabbinate which was to be placed under much stricter governmental supervision. The rabbi was to keep vital statistics for the whole community, perform the necessary ceremonial functions at births, marriages, and burials, and above all see to it that all these activities be performed in full consonance with the existing Russian laws.[3]

One is readily reminded of Napoleon's equally autocratic reorganization of the French community in 1808, aimed at transforming it into a pliable organ of the authoritarian state. Napoleon could prove more successful, however, as French Jewry had partially deluded itself into seeing in the Emperor's grandiose gestures an element of the general emancipatory movement. It was this combination of emancipation with assimilation within a generally egalitarian society which had made possible that gradual weakening of Jewish communal bonds in Western Europe upon which Russian officialdom looked with such envy. It certainly could not be achieved in the Russian society with its rigid class distinctions and its sharp discrimination against Jews. In practice, therefore, the governmental effort to undermine Jewish communal self-government and to convert the rabbinate into a state agency failed miserably even after the abolition of the *kahal* in 1844 and the issuance of certain relatively minor amendments in 1850 and after.

The rabbis, whose spiritual function for the community was derived from their talmudic learning, their strict adherence to rabbinic law, their constant teaching and preaching of it in theory and practice, and their adjudication of ritualistic and civil controversies, were often completely inept to serve as governmental registrars, even if they had the desire to perform such major police functions for the state. In time, the government resorted to the appointment of official Crown rabbis, also salaried by the communities. In many cases, however, even such official rabbis served more as representatives of their communities before the authorities than as authoritarian leaders imposing the government's will upon them. That is why later in the century, quite a few patriotic

Jewish leaders, equipped with the knowledge of Russian and Western culture, accepted such official positions, without being condemned by their fellow Jews as police agents. Among them were such men as Rabbi A. I. Mase in Moscow, Dr. Judah Leb Kantor in Libau and Vilna, and Shemaryah Levin (1867-1935) in Grodno and Ekaterinoslav, later an outstanding Zionist leader, elected by the Jews themselves to the Russian Duma. The functions of these men were almost exclusively political and organizational, whereas their constituents' genuinely spiritual concerns were under the jurisdiction of their so-called deputies, the "spiritual rabbis," freely elected by the communities from among the learned talmudists.

EDUCATION

A similar variety of forms existed in the Jewish school system. Here even more leeway had to be given to private initiative for, according to Jewish tradition, the primary responsibility for educating the children rested with the parents, while each adult was to pursue his own program of self-education. At the same time the Jewish community, either through its central organs or through a variety of associations and committees, whether or not connected with the synagogue, saw to it that no male child should be deprived of the opportunity of acquiring at least a good elementary education. Girls did not have to study, but most of them were taught how to recite prayers, read Yiddish translations of the Bible, and so forth. The result was a sharp contrast between the Jews and their neighbors. To cite Abraham Jacob Paperna's somewhat romanticizing reminiscences, the situation of the small town of Kopyl, where he had grown up, was typical of the rest of the Pale: "There was no government or secular public school in Kopyl and the entire Christian population was illiterate. The Jews, on the other hand, had a plethora of schools, albeit of a special type, perhaps twenty in all. All Jewish boys aged four to thirteen were taught in *heders* (elementary schools). . . . Not infrequently a poor man sold his last candlestick or pillow to pay the teacher."

Undeniably, there was considerable anarchy in the system.

The teachers were often untrained for their jobs; some assumed their responsibilities only because they had failed in other callings. But there also were instructors, both gifted and devoted, who gave their pupils excellent schooling. The curriculum was quite limited. Even the Bible was not studied too intensively, the main emphasis being placed on the Talmud and rabbinics. Nor were the methods of instruction always on the level considered efficacious by contemporary pedagogues. The school facilities were often totally inadequate; a room in a ramshackle building with few sanitary provisions accommodated a score or more pupils of various ages and different stages of preparedness. Critics had a field day in describing these inadequacies. Typical of many harangues is the following correspondence from Vitebsk, written in 1894:

> Our Talmud Torahs are filthy rooms, crowded from nine in the morning until nine in the evening with pale, starved children. These remain in this contaminated atmosphere for twelve hours at a time and see only their bent, exhausted teachers. . . . Most of them are clad in rags; some of them are almost naked. . . . Their faces are pale and sickly, and their bodies are evidently not strong. In parties of twenty or thirty, and at times more, they all repeat some lesson aloud after their instructor. He who has not listened to the almost absurd commentaries of the ignorant *melammed* [teacher] can not even imagine how little the children gain from such instruction.[4]

Discounting the evident one-sideness of this portrayal, there is no question that the old school system offered many legitimate targets for critics whether recruited from the Jewish "enlightened" circles or from outsiders. Yet, backed by a millennial experience, the Jewish elementary school as a rule achieved its goals of giving good elementary training in Jewish subjects to the majority of children and preparing a substantial minority for more advanced studies after the age of thirteen. While we do not have solid statistical information concerning the enrolment in Jewish schools, it appears that, to the very end of the tsarist regime, a majority of Jewish school children attended such Jewish schools. According to one unreliable account, the Jewish schools in the Pale outside of Poland had an enrolment of 18,799 pupils in 1887. Only seven years later the number of enrolled pupils is given more accurately as 95,661, to rise further to 115,575 by 1911. Together with the ten Polish provinces the number in that year increased to 200,797. At the same time 126,976 Jews attended general schools in 1911, as against 29,526 in 1886. This marked a radical change from a century earlier, when almost all Jews went exclusively to Jewish schools, communal, associational, or private.[5]

Above the elementary *heder* stood the *yeshiva*, an academy attended by adolescent boys and young men, sometimes even after their marriage. Practically every distinguished rabbi tried to run a school of this type, formally or informally. His prestige rose with the number of advanced pupils he was able to train. The budgets of small academies were as a rule supported locally, the pupils being assigned to individual citizens for all meals on special "days" of each week. But there also were large national institutions; among them was that of Volozhin in the province of Vilna, founded in 1803 by Rabbi Hayyim, a pupil of Elijah Gaon, and another in Mir in the province of Minsk. Since these were national schools of higher learning, they felt entitled to send out messengers to collect donations from communities all over the Pale. Out of these gifts they were able to allot small weekly stipends of seventy-five kopeks to each of the pupils, while still assigning them to private homes on Sabbaths and holidays. The methods of financing for the most part proved inadequate and entailed great hardships for both faculties and students. Yet the majority of both accepted them without demurrer, feeling pride in their academies' intellectual achievements and simultaneously considering their own work the fulfillment of Judaism's supreme commandment.

This spirit animated also the unparalleled devotion of adults to continued self-education. In her interesting *Memoirs*, Pauline Wengeroff reminisced how her father, a busy and wealthy contractor, used to rise at four o'clock every morning so that he could devote several hours to talmudic studies before attending synagogue services and then going about his business. Apart from such individual efforts, there were group studies in the prayer houses which embraced a large part of the population. Even the sharp critic of communal life, Shalom J. Abramovich (Mendele Mokher Seforim), nostalgically reminisced how, during the intermission between the afternoon and evening services in the prayer houses, working men and others assembled at special tables where they were given instruction in one or another classic of rabbinic literature, including some ethical and homiletical works. Those qualified to do so studied the Talmud. Many adults organized special associations for the study of the Mishnah or Talmud; some tried to cover the entire Babylonian Talmud in a year by assigning a different segment of it to each member for daily study. Typical of this self-imposed discipline are the following provisions recorded in the minutes of the Grodno Mishnah Society: "A fine shall be imposed upon those who interrupt the study with idle chatter. Those finishing the reading of their chapter before the others shall nevertheless remain [in their places] until the Kaddish is recited, or else shall pay a fine."[6]

Such an extensive self-governing system of Jewish education was, understandably, a thorn in the flesh of Russian officialdom. On the one hand, it could not deny the right of parents to give their children religious education so long as the Jewish religion was tolerated in Russia. On the other hand, it viewed Jewish schools as the chief instruments of that Jewish separatism which it was trying to undermine. When in 1808, sixteen communities in the provinces of Vitebsk and Moghilev were asked why they did not establish secular schools, they replied succinctly that Jews neither wished to give their children secular education nor could they afford any additional burdens. This situation changed but slowly not only under governmental pressure, but also because of the growingly vocal demands for secular studies by the "enlightened" Jews themselves. Yet as late as 1840, we are told, only forty-eight Jews were enrolled in Russian primary and secondary schools, and but fifteen attended universities. This is the more remarkable as twenty years earlier the University of Vilna alone had, under the active sponsorship of Prince Adam Czartoryski, attracted some forty Jewish students in the course of two decades (1803-24). Only from the middle of the century did Jewish youth begin to flock into Russian secondary schools; the number of Jewish pupils then rose from 159 in 1853 to 2,362 in 1870.[7]

NEWER RELIGIOUS TRENDS

Education was but a reflection of the socioreligious and cultural conditions of Russian Jewry. In the first three decades of the nineteenth century it still was a fairly monolithic cultural group fully cherishing its traditional outlook. The largest inner division between *Hasidim* and *Mitnagdim*, inherited from the Polish regime, had lost much of its sharpness during the second and third generations of the Hasidic movement. Originating from the East-Galician and Podolian semirural communities, this semisectarian group shared, from its inception, some of the anti-intellectualism of the Eastern Churches. Although not quite condemning intellectual distinction as a sign of personal haughtiness before God, as did some of their Greek-Orthodox counterparts, the Hasidic leaders considered inner piety, ethical behavior, and semimystic communion with the Deity as a far closer expression of the fear and love of God than sheer immersion into the depth of rabbinic lore. Life of the Jewish masses under the Polish and the Russian dominations was full of suffering and sadness. Yet the Hasidic leaders, beginning with the founder of the movement, Israel ben Eliezer Baal Shem Tob (1700-1760), preached *joyous* exaltation of the Lord as the supreme form of worship. Apart from thus offering an anodyne to many miseries of daily existence, Hasidism, through its emphasis on ethical folktales and religious folksongs as well as the use of down-to-earth similes and parables, carried direct appeal to the folk psyche. Not only outright adherents of that movement, but also Ukrainian peasants wove legends around the mysterious personality of Rabbi Israel, who had left behind no written works but many dedicated disciples. These disciples carried the struggle into the Jewish communities and, despite the combined opposition of the entrenched communal bureaucracy, leading rabbis, and plutocrats, conquered most communities in the southern areas, and made considerable headway also in the northwestern provinces.

By the first half of the nineteenth century Hasidism's battle had largely been won. But with its victory also passed its truly heroic stage; it was followed by an almost total reconciliation of the new movement with the traditional rabbinic Orthodoxy. Whatever minor differences in theological doctrines may still have persisted—and these were, in part, the heritage of older debates among the devotees of the mystical and ethical literature of the pre-Hasidic age—Jewish religious practices were fairly uniform. Apart from some ritualistic minutiae relating to the examination of a slaughterer's knife or the hours allowable for divine service, the Hasidim fully subscribed to rabbinic law and observance. Now the negative aspects of Hasidism came much more clearly to the fore. Particularly the belief of many Hasidim in the hereditary charismatic powers of their leaders, the so-called *zaddikim* (righteous men), not only undermined the original egalitarian and democratic features of the movement, but also opened the gates to many abuses. There speedily emerged regular dynasties which, financially supported by their dedicated adherents, lived in palatial quarters with retinues of servants and displays of many luxuries. Ironically, rather than discouraging their poverty-stricken followers, this "conspicuous consumption" impressed the latter as a sign of divine grace and enhanced the leaders' prestige. In fact, dynastic allegiance often became so powerful that adherents of one family combated with even greater vigor the followers of another dynasty than they did their common enemies on the outside.

Among these long-lived dynasties stood out in the northwest the family of Shneur Zalman of Ladi, whose role during the Napoleonic invasion typified in some respects the political influence exerted by these new leaders. Shneur Zalman's grandson Mendel transferred his residence, in 1828, to Liubavichi which became the center of a special wing of the Hasidic movement. Like its founder, it cultivated cabalistic and rabbinic studies alongside the deep homiletical and ethical teachings characteristic of the movement as a whole. In the province of Kiev there arose the dynasty of the so-called Chernobil Hasidim founded by Menahem Nahum and his son Mordecai (Rabbi Motele). Another important founder of a dynasty, Israel ben Shalom Friedmann of Ruzhin (1797-1850), after having established a fine reputation throughout the Ukraine and Volhynia had, as we recall, to leave Russia and establish his residence in Austrian Sadagóra, whence he and his descendants held sway over thousands of followers in both empires until the First World War. In Russian Poland the outstanding dynasty was that established by the Warsaw leader Isaac (Itshe) Meier Alter in Góra Kalwaria.[8]

Independently influential were outstanding individuals such as Nahman ben Simhah of Bratslav or Levi Yitzhak of Berdichev, both of whom were remembered by a grateful posterity through a host of sayings and apothegms conveying profound lessons of Jewish thought and behavior. True, but few of these leaders still adhered to the old self-denial of the original founders. Certainly few of the new *zaddikim* emulated the example of Nahman of Bratslav who, in 1799, at the age of twenty-six, undertook a pilgrimage to the Holy Land at enormous personal sacrifice. Before starting out he wrote to his eldest daughter, "You will proceed to your future father-in-law, your next sister will become a servant, your little sister will probably be taken into some home out of pity, your mother will become a cook, and I shall dispose of all my household for traveling expenses." No such asceticism was expected from a grand seigneur like Israel Friedmann. Nevertheless, his followers and many outsiders believed in the sincerity of his declaration, "I am part and parcel of Israel's soul; if any Jew, be he at the end of the world, suffers pain, I feel it instantaneously." In another homily, Israel expatiated on the charismatic powers of a Hasidic leader, teaching:

> The true *zaddik* influences the material world, such as childbirth, health and livelihood, as well as the spiritual world, namely the spiritual well-being of all Israel, and particularly of his own followers. Even in the world to come all good stems from him. Every one must believe all this in complete faith. "Who is a fool? He who destroys what is given him." [Bab. Talmud, Hagigah 4a] refers to the man who loses his faith that all comes to him from the *zaddik*, thinking instead that he is able to secure it all by himself without the aid of the *zaddik*.[9]

Outsiders, however, including some rabbinic leaders, looked askance at such assertions and at the basic Hasidic belief in the chiefs' supernatural powers. But they made their peace with the movement and were prepared jointly to fight the rising waves of Enlightenment and assimilation.

Something like a compromise emerged in the so-called *Musar* (ethical) movement, founded by Israel Lipkin Salanter. Although an outstanding talmudist in his own right, Rabbi Israel increasingly preached the emphasis on ethics rather than learning, while repudiating Hasidism's antiintellectual and overexuberant features. In fact, his entire movement leaned toward asceticism, eliciting much opposition among other traditionalists who sought to uphold the long-accepted golden mean. This self-denying element of the *Musar* movement was ever more vigorously stressed by Israel's son and his later successors. Apart from founding first in Vilna and then in other communities special chapels for the cultivation of his brand of ethics (the so-called *Musar shtiblekh*), Rabbi Israel established a special academy of learning in Slobodka, in which intensive training in talmudic studies was combined with regular courses in ethical lore. Although he found many adherents and even patrons in Germany, the movement did not spread much beyond the Lithuanian and White-Russian provinces, where it penetrated even into the older academies and congregations. The impact of both Musar and Hasidism upon the masses of Russian Jewry is illustrated also by the numerous editions in which several older ethical and behavioral classics were now republished in Russia. Moses Hayyim Luzzatto's *Mesillat yesharim* (The Path of the Righteous) was in some respects a best-seller, reappearing in forty-three editions. It was followed closely by Abraham Danzig's *Hayye Adam* (Man's Life; a popular summary of Jewish observances) with forty-two editions, and by the medieval classic, *Hobot ha-lebabot* (Duties of the Heart) by Bahya ibn Pakuda, with thirty-six editions.[10]

JEWISH ENLIGHTENMENT

In contrast to this mass appeal of long-recognized Hebrew letters, many new creations, particularly if written by the "enlightened" critics of the existing order, had a hard struggle to penetrate an indifferent, often hostile public. The "enlight-ened" writers and their followers, the so-called *maskilim,* often made up by vociferousness for lack of popular acclaim. Most of them were, indeed, enthusiasts who had the sense of mission to spread enlightenment among their coreligionists; they took adversity and even outright persecution in their stride. An early pioneer in this field was Menasseh ben Porat, known as Illier from the town of Illya near Vilna (1767-1831). As a writer, Illier evinced more concern for the general sufferings of humanity than for the discords within the Jewish community. His booklet, *Pesher dabar* (Solution to a Problem), published in 1807, actually used moderate language and advocated reconciliation between the opposing camps. Yet even such a modest appeal was rejected by the entrenched Orthodoxy which succeeded in suppressing prac-tically all copies of that work so that in more recent years only one was found in the British Museum. A larger work was already in the press in Volhynia when a friend persuaded the printer to burn all the galleys together with the manu-script.[11]

Subsequent enlightened writings were far less restrained. The *Haskalah* movement, originating from the Mendels-sohnian circle in Berlin and Königsberg, had brought forth some outstanding scholars and writers in Galicia. Some of these aimed their shafts at Hasidism; among them Joseph Perl and Isaac Erter whose eloquent satirical works were widely read in Russia as well. The Galician influence spread also through a number of distinguished immigrants, including Basilius Stern (1798-1853), the director of the newly founded modern school in Odessa (later elevated to the rank of Russia's honorary citizen), and Simhah Pinsker (1801-64), an outstanding student of medieval sectarian movements. Some Russian visitors to Galicia also came under the influence of the leading nineteenth century Jewish philosopher, Nah-man Krochmal.

One of them, Isaac Baer Levinsohn (1788-1860), tried, in his *Te'udah be-Yisrael* (Learning in Israel), to furnish defi-nite answers to questions then agitating the minds of many young Jews, such as whether a pious Jew should devote him-self to the more modern study of the Hebrew language and grammar; whether he should learn foreign languages and secular sciences; whether such studies were useful altogether, and if so, were they not prejudicial to genuine piety? Of course, these were rhetorical questions and any reader knew from the outset the author's affirmative answers. While Levinsohn wrote in a heavy Hebrew style, his temperate approach found some acceptance even among the moderate Orthodox, in part because of the approval extended to some of his works by the tsarist administration. At times Levinsohn used his connections with the high officials as a subterfuge to overcome the resistance of the Orthodox to the printing of his books. On one occasion he actually invented the name of such an official. On the other hand, when he set out to defend some cherished Jewish traditions, particularly the Talmud which, because of denunciations by converts and Jewish extremists, was in ill-repute with the government, he lost much of the bureaucracy's sympathies. Similarly, when in 1834, he wrote his *Efes dammim* (Naught of Blood) in which, on the occasion of a Blood Accusation in Zaslav, Volhynia, he marshaled much rabbinic evidence against the ritual murder libel, his stock with the bureaucracy fell quite low. In any case, he was refused the governmental subsidy which his disease-ridden body badly needed. At the same time this book enjoyed great popularity among Jews and, in 1840 on the occasion of the Damascus Blood Accusation, which had created an international sensation and even elicited the intervention of several European powers, it was translated into English, while translations into Russian and German followed in 1883-84.[12]

Apart from the educational reforms the progressive circles, as well as Russian officialdom, were deeply concerned about the traditional Jewish costume which perpetuated Jewish "separatism." Such leading progressives as the scholars Mordecai Aaron Günzburg (1795-1846), Abraham Baer Gottlober (1811-99) and Samuel Joseph Fünn (1818-90), considered the special Jewish attire a main source of degradation of the Jewish communities. In an interesting memorandum, Gottlober argued that such special attire was limited to Eastern Europe, while in other countries Jews dressed like their neighbors; on their journeys even Polish and Russian

Jews dispensed with their Jewish costume. Historically, this attire was merely an adaptation of earlier Polish clothing which should now be definitely discarded.

> In the present nineteenth century spirit of the time [*Zeitgeist*], when most Israelites try to achieve rapprochement with the Christians and to accept European and Christian morals, we must consider the different attire as the first source of misfortune and prejudice. It alone is the strongest barrier separating Jews from Christians in social as well as religious life. . . . Indeed the majority of our coreligionists look forward with deep yearning to a new regulation concerning clothing.

When the government finally issued such an order in 1845, giving the Jewish communities a five-year period of grace after which the Jewish attire would be strictly prohibited, a group of Volhynian progressives, led by Gottlober, made a secret compact to appear in European clothing on the same day. To reinforce this determination Gottlober also wrote a satirical poem, most of which, however, remained unpublished.[13]

Among the younger enlightened Hebrew authors one may mention also the skillful writer and effective pedagogue, Kalman Schulman (1819-99), a popularizer in the field of science and history, whose works opened new vistas to many Hebrew readers theretofore trained only in the traditional rabbinic lore. His Hebrew rendition of Josephus, prepared from a German translation and also otherwise leaving much to be desired, received accolades even from some outstanding Orthodox rabbis. Deficiencies in accuracy were more than made up by his lucid and attractive style which, together with their novel content, converted his works into fascinating eye-openers for many of his contemporaries.

Most *maskilim*, however, turned into sharp critics of the existing community. Some became regular muckrakers, particularly with respect to Hasidism, to whose mystic and emotional beauties they were completely blind but whose institutional degeneration they described in all its lurid details. The critics included some outstanding builders of the new Hebrew style and literature. Even by writing a novel placed in the biblical age, Abraham Mapu (1808-67) made his purpose of contrasting the idyllic life of the ancient Israelitic people with the unsatisfactory present in Russia quite evident to the reader. His two novels, *Ahabat Siyyon* (The Love of Zion) and *Ashmat Shomeron* (Samaria's Guilt), which Joseph Klausner characterized as "the most romantic and the most permanent in the entire new literature," included characters and situations paralleling certain contemporary conditions. They enjoyed wide popularity, the former soon appearing also in German, English, and Yiddish translations. More overtly satirical was his *Ayit Sabua* (Speckled Bird of Prey; a Hebrew idiom for Tartuffe), in which Mapu derided contemporary Orthodox hypocrites.[14]

Towering above all his compeers was the poet, Yehudah Leib (Leon) Gordon (1830-92), who used his indubitable poetic gifts to spread the tenets of Enlightenment. Even his early biblical epics carried a contemporary message. Hailing the reforms under Tsar Alexander II, he wrote in 1863 his *"Awake My People!"* in which he coined the most representative watchwords of the whole movement. He exhorted his Jewish reader: "Be a man in the street and a Jew at home, a brother to thy [non-Jewish] countrymen and a [faithful] servant to thy king." But his lofty expectations remained unfulfilled. In 1872, he was given the opportunity to apply his doctrines in practice in his new capacity of Secretary both of the Society for the Promotion of Enlightenment among the Jews and of the steadily growing Jewish community of St. Petersburg. However, this career was cut short seven years later by a cabal of his Orthodox opponents with the local police which led to his and his wife's imprisonment and deportation for alleged subversive activities against the Russian regime. After a few months he was fully cleared and returned to the capital, but he was not restored to his former posts and had to earn his living as coeditor of the Hebrew periodical *Ha-Melits*. Nevertheless he continued to maintain friendly relations with Baron Horace Günzburg, the Society's president and chief financial patron, and he was greatly disturbed when one of the Günzburg enterprises experienced business reversals. Ultimately, the Russian government recognized Gordon's services for helping to Westernize his coreligionists by conferring upon him the rank of honorary citizen.

Nevertheless, disappointed by the general reaction in Russia and the slow progress of enlightenment among his own people, his mood became increasingly pessimistic, almost nihilistic. In his later years he saw little future for either Hebrew literature or the Jewish people at large. In a poem, "For Whom Do I Labor?" he expressed the belief that he probably was "the last of Zion's singers."[15]

Other influential Haskalah poets included the father and son, Adam (Abraham Dob Baer) ha-Kohen Lebensohn (1789-1878) and Micah Joseph Lebensohn (1828-52). Of the two the son was the more gifted poet, whose early death at the age of twenty-four evoked from the bereaved father a lamentation belonging to the most deeply felt pieces of the latter's poetic creativity. Gordon, too, commemorated the death of his young friend by a poetic cycle.

Enlightenment was not limited to Hebrew writers, however. There arose in Russia, Galicia, and Moldavia a series of Yiddish publicists and storytellers who, turning to best advantage a literary tradition several centuries old, were appealing more directly to the masses, including their feminine members, in a language accessible to them. When Mendel Lefin Satanover (1741-1819) published in 1817 his Yiddish translation of biblical Proverbs, he made a studious effort to avoid the theretofore prevalent Germanisms. He was followed by Israel Aksenfeld (1787-1866) who, though a busy notary in Odessa, became a prolific Yiddish writer. While but few of his novels and short stories were published, those which appeared reveal a keen insight into the realities of Russian Jewish life. His greatest difficulty consisted in having his works published. By decree of October 27, 1836, the Russian government closed all Hebrew printing presses except two which, for the following three decades, exercised a monopoly over all printing in Hebrew type. Those in Vilna and Zhitomir refused to accept Aksenfeld's works because the latter's sharp attacks on Hasidism and the existing communal institutions would naturally antagonize their main customers. Over more than twenty years, beginning in 1841, Aksenfeld bombarded the Russian Ministry of Public Enlightenment and the local Odessa officials with petitions seeking redress for this indirect censorship after the official Russian censor had expressed admiration for Aksenfeld's work. As a moderately prosperous notary public in Odessa, the writer was finally prepared to spread his works in lithograph form or to establish a printing press of his own—all without avail. The result was that before his death at the age of seventy-nine only two pieces appeared, followed by three more posthumous publications. Scores of other works have been lost. Nevertheless, recent students of Yiddish letters have discovered in his novel *Shterntikhel* (a feminine headgear) and other writings an inexhaustible source of information and insights into Jewish social life a century ago.[16]

Much better known in his day was Isaac Meier Dick (1814-93) who, though writing in a lower key, betrayed his genuine gifts as a storyteller. Having arranged with a publisher to submit a novelette every week, his literary output soared to more than four hundred items, some of which, despite their author's haste, were significant linguistic and esthetic contributions to Yiddish literature. Much less talented, though even more popular, was Nahum Meier Shaikevich (1849-1905), better known under his nom-de-plume, Shomer, who both in Russia and in the United States, where he settled in 1889, contributed much to the uplift of servant girls and uneducated workers. Like their Hebrew confreres, these Yiddish novelists injected new vigor into the sharp critique of the Russian Jewish community and furnished many a weapon for the class struggle by the rising Jewish industrial proletariat.

None of these authors approximated the genius of Shalom Jacob Abramovich or Mendele Mokher Seforim (*ca.* 1836-1917), rightly called the father of modern Yiddish letters. With a matchless sense of style in both Yiddish and Hebrew and a profound knowledge of the various aspects of Jewish life within the Pale, Mendele described it in a series of novels which have become classics in both literatures. His satire was always tempered with deep sympathy even for the weaknesses of downtrodden humanity. In his *Kliatshe* (The Old Mare), symbolic for the oppressed people, his *Massaot Binyamin ha-shelishi* (Travels of Benjamin the Third), a sort of *Don Quixote*, and other works, partially translated also into English, he became the most persuasive critic of his environment, because even the advocates of the established order found his general urbanity and humanity utterly disarming. At the same time Mendele felt called upon to write a popular work on science to spread its knowledge among the majority of his coreligionists, who read no other language but Hebrew or Yiddish.[17]

Even more important than their contributions to literature was the impact of these men on the gradual transformation of the ghetto community. While many of them were devoid of literary talents and often wrote in total disagreement with one another, theirs were the voices which articulated the unconscious strivings of a growing generation of Jews who sought ways out from the narrow confines of their traditional life. If they often opened gates, which they did not know how to close, their historic achievement was nonetheless very basic in helping to lead their people out of the ghetto to the vast outside world. In these efforts they were often supported by the government, not because it believed in the value of Haskalah letters but rather because it saw in them a method of breaking down the "separatism" of the Jewish community. Many officials hoped that the new movement might ultimately lead to the conversion and final absorption of the Jewish minority and thereby put an end to the ever troublesome Jewish question.

For this reason even Nicholas I's officials tried from the 1830s on to promote modern Jewish schools in which first the German, and later the Russian language, as well as secular subjects, would gradually outweigh the traditional rabbinic curriculum. Such modern schools were established in Odessa, Riga, and other communities. That of Riga, headed by the imported German teacher, Max Lilienthal, was but two years old when the government started to use the young pedagogue for the spread of its educational reforms among Jews. Most enlightened leaders were slow in perceiving the ultimate missionary aims of the government and basked in its much-cherished recognition. But before long they, like Lilienthal, realized the incongruity of siding with a government so oppressive as that of Nicholas I. It was easier for them to entertain great hopes during Alexander II's early liberal regime. Many *maskilim* helped the government to establish such new rabbinical schools as those of Zhitomir and Vilna, whose alumni, however, lacking true rabbinic training, could not possibly hope to obtain legitimate rabbinic posts. Many of them used, therefore, these schools merely as stepping-stones for admission to universities and a subsequent professional or business career, while to the Orthodox masses they appeared almost on a par with Christian missionaries. Ultimately, the government had to give up and to convert these theological institutions into teachers seminaries, whose pupils could secure positions at one or another "enlightened" primary or secondary school.[18]

For a while the government also tried to force the communities to appoint rabbis in command of a Western, preferably Russian, language and to authorize elementary instruction by teachers only after they secured a governmental license. These authoritarian measures broke down completely, however, under the passive resistance of the parents of school children and the large majorities of each community. Only belatedly did many of the Haskalah leaders themselves come to the realization, as had the spokesmen of European Enlightenment a century earlier, that rational schemes, however unimpeachably logical, could not, in a short span of time, transform a deeply rooted system of living. Hence came the despondency of such leaders as Gordon who, despairing of any quick rational solution, gave up all hope for the survival of their people.

Superficially no more successful was also the first experiment in Jewish journalism in the Russian language, the *Razsvet* (Dawn), a weekly, published in Odessa for one year (1860-61). Although directed by such able journalists and writers as Osip Rabinovich (1817-69), Lev Osipovich Levanda (1835-88) and, for a time, Yoakhim Tarnopol (1810-1900), this pioneering effort, addressed to both the small layer of a Jewish intelligentsia and the tiny segment of a sympathetic Russian public, appeared at first as a dismal failure. The difficulties were enormous. On the one hand, the effort to uncover many faults in the Jewish body politic and daily life antagonized numerous fearful readers who, even if they readily tolerated such criticisms in Hebrew or Yiddish letters, were apprehensive about their impact upon Russian public opinion if given wide circulation in the Russian language. On the other hand, in their attempt to defend the rights of Jews and to propagate ultimate equality, the editors had to run the gauntlet of official censorship, sometimes a double censorship from both the local Odessa office and the St. Petersburg headquarters. At the same time liberals of various shades of opinion, including some non-Jews, contributed regularly to the journal, whose editors expressed the hope that

> not belonging to the retrogrades, the extreme rationalists or the reactionaries, we dare hope that from these three categories a fourth will emerge which will have the final say. It will neither unconditionally destroy the old, nor unconditionally admire it in an effort to support it with all the brilliance of dialectics and sophisms. This will be the golden mean that will join what is reasonable in the past with what is necessary in the present.

Such a program was definitely premature in 1860-61, and the journal could not even marshal the minimum of 800 subscribers considered necessary to maintain it financially. The editors decided to suspend publication, since, as Rabinovich commented, "honorable death remained the only end for my journal." Yet the editors wrought better than they thought. Although they themselves referred to the pun that their *Dawn* had "lapsed into *eternity* instead of turning into *morning*," their magazine ushered in an era of Russian Jewish journalism which, in the remaining half century of tsarist rule, had many significant accomplishments to its credit.[19]

9

Ideological
and Partisan Strife

THE REGIME OF Alexander II, which gave the impression
that liberalism had come to Russia to stay, marked a turning
point in the history of its Jewish community. Until this time
Russian Jewry had been a fairly monolithic structure, notwithstanding the internal divisions between the Hasidim and
their "opponents," the "enlightened" and the old-fashioned.
Even some radical spokesmen of Enlightenment were con-
formists in their private life. Not until the days of Alexander
II do we hear of timid attempts at introducing Russian into
the synagogue proper. The adoption of vernacular sermons
had long been the touchstone of even moderate religious
reform in the West. In Russia the very spokesmen of Enlightenment knew little Russian and derived most of their
western culture through the medium of German. When they
founded their Society for the Promotion of Enlightenment
among the Jews, they considered as a principal part of its
program the publication of a Bible provided with both a
German translation in the Hebrew alphabet and Mendelssohn's commentary.

For the ordinary Russian Jews this emphasis upon German
made the entire Enlightenment doubly alien and artificial. It
made more sense to build bridges to the living Russian
language and culture. However, religious reform of the western type never gained ground in the Russian Jewish community. Essentially it was a postemancipatory phenomenon
when the Jews felt themselves to be more or less equal
citizens in the larger society, different from the majority only
through their faith. Russians of the Mosaic persuasion, such

as began emerging in the 1860s, were still a tiny minority and an obviously foreign growth on the body of Russian Jewry. Such individuals, moreover, were for the most part religious agnostics, prepared to abandon all traditional observance; they cared very little for what was happening within the synagogue precincts.

The sterility of the Enlightenment movement with its predominant negativistic emphases gradually became manifest to its devotees themselves. One of the first insiders to submit it to a sharp critique was Moses Leib Lilienblum (1843-1910), a brilliant, if unstable, writer who often changed his mind. From the outset he had come under the influence of Osias (Joshua Heschel) Schorr, the learned, radical Galician critic of the Talmud. Soon thereafter he felt the spell of the new Russian positivist philosophy, especially as expounded by the then popular writer, Dimitrii Pisarev. Many members of the new generation replaced the old idealism by a rather crude utilitarianism while pushing to even further extremes Enlightenment's superficial cosmopolitanism. In Lilienblum's case this was but a passing episode. He soon turned to Jewish nationalism and Zionism, of which he became an eloquent spokesman.[2]

FAMOUS CONVERTS

A different direction was taken by Abraham Uri (Arkadii Grigorevich) Kovner (1842-1909) who in his poverty-stricken home—his father was an elementary Hebrew teacher—had imbibed a deep hatred for the wealthy and learned members of his community. Personally unstable, prepared at the drop of a hat to abandon his wife and children, he joined the Haskalah movement almost immediately as its sharpest critic. In two volumes of essays entitled *Heker dabar* (Observations; 1865) and *Tseror perahim* (A Bouquet of Flowers; 1868), he submitted the contemporary Hebrew letters to a devastating critique. In his second book he vented his ire especially on Alexander Zederbaum (1816-93), editor of the Hebrew periodical *Ha-Melits*, who, upon Kovner's arrival in Odessa, had given him a good deal of work but who became frightened by the hostile reaction of many readers to the writer's

destructive criticisms. Kovner also came under the spell of
Pisarev's works and imitated the Russian's "demolition" of
Pushkin and Lermontov by a similar "debunking" of the
great Italian Hebrew scholar and poet, Samuel David
Luzzatto. In a letter to his fellow-writer, Paperna, this
"enfant terrible" of the Enlightenment literature prided himself on not being a Belinskii, that is, a writer interested in art
per se, but only in its utilitarian aspects. "This is the main
difference between us," he exclaimed, "you are an admirer
of beauty and the sublime, I of the mundane and the useful."
Not surprisingly, Kovner soon decided that he ought not to
waste his talents on a dead language like Hebrew. After
sending a copy of his "Bouquet" to Y. L. Gordon as his
"final" gift to Hebrew literature, he observed,

> Let our writers not imagine that they can create through
> Hebrew a living and enduring literature. This will never
> happen. Their task should much rather consist in using
> Hebrew and Yiddish to awaken in our youth a thirst for
> knowledge. But to still that thirst our youth will have to
> resort to the aid of European languages. Hebrew and
> Yiddish shall thus serve the Jewish reader as steps to the
> temple of living languages and only there will he perceive
> the true light.

His transition to Russian literature was hastened by Kovner's
rash criminal act when, employed in a minor office by the
Jewish banking house of Abraham Zak in St. Petersburg, he
forged a large check and tried to escape with that amount
and a newly married sickly wife to the United States. He
was caught and sent to Siberia, from where he returned to
St. Petersburg as a convert to Christianity and a fairly
prolific Russian publicist. But even in these later writings he
could and would not deny his deep attachment to the
Jewish people.[3]

Kovner's career is sketched here at somewhat greater
length because it was quite typical of a certain wing of
progressive Russian Jewish youth of the period, many of
whom likewise found their way to the baptismal font.
Among Kovner's contemporaries were such men as Yehudah
(Julian) Klaczko (1825-1906), who started in his native
Vilna as the son of an influential Jewish merchant and the

ardent poet of the glories of Zion, and wound up as a leading Catholic literary critic of Polish poetry and folklore.[4] Another convert, J. E. Salkinson (died in 1883), also born in Vilna as the son of a Hebrew poet and teacher, moved to Scotland where he served as a Presbyterian minister in Glasgow. He did not lose his love for Hebrew, however, and produced some of the best Hebrew translations of Shakespeare and Milton.

Ivan Stanislavovich Blioch (Jean Bloch, 1836-1901) became one of Russia's most distinguished economists and railroad builders. His five-volume work *Vliianie zhelieznikh dorog* (The Impact of Railways on Russia's Economic System), published in St. Petersburg in 1878, was speedily translated into French and Polish after having been awarded a gold medal at the Paris Exposition of that year. Another large six-volume work, published twenty years later, on future wars was translated into English, German, and French and seems to have stimulated Nicholas II to convoke the Hague Conference of 1899. Although a convert from his youth, Blioch left behind a testament which began, "My entire life I was a Jew and I die as a Jew." Similarly, Daniel Chwolson (1819-1911), a leading orientalist, never concealed his Jewish origin. Once asked whether he had undergone conversion out of conviction, he was supposed to have answered bluntly, "Yes, I was *convinced* that it was much better to live as a Christian professor than as an elementary Hebrew teacher." Throughout his life, Chwolson had many occasions to defend the Jews against accusations and calumnies. His works on Christ's Last Supper and the Blood Accusation were translated into German and enjoyed a European reputation. Among his orientalist studies several like the *Corpus inscriptionum hebraicarum*, his monographs on the Khazars, and the catalogue of his own large Hebrew library which included many incunabula represented significant contributions to Jewish learning. However, Abraham Eliyahu (Albert) Harkavy (1835-1919) was able to make even more significant contributions to Jewish scholarship while serving as custodian of the important Near-Eastern collections at the Imperial Library in St. Petersburg without giving up his Jewish faith.[5]

Among the other prominent converts was the physiologist, I. F. Tsion (Elie de Cyon, 1843-1912) who, while still a Jew, secured an award from the Academy of Sciences in Paris for an important physiological work. After his conversion his professorial career was cut short by his unpopularity with colleagues and students, whereupon he turned to diplomatic service. As an agent of the Russian Ministry of Finance he secured the first French loan for Russia and, in 1893, assisted in the conclusion of the Franco-Russian alliance. Considerable influence was also exerted by the convert Osip Notovich (1849-1914) who served for many years as the editor of the *Novoe Vremia* and founded the important political periodical, *Novosti* (News). Among the distinguished poets of Jewish descent was A. F. Fet, whose love lyrics written in his old age are described by the literary historian, Prince Dimitrii S. Mirsky as "among the most precious diamonds of our poetry." Unbeknown to many of his contemporaries, but fully realized by himself, was the fact that he was born to a Königsberg Jewish woman who had deserted her innkeeper husband while pregnant and run away with a Russian officer.[6]

Of international fame were the brothers Anton and Nicholas Rubinstein (1829-94 and 1835-81 respectively), both converted by their grandfather in their infancy. Even Pobedonostsev was Anton's great admirer. In trying to persuade Alexander III in 1886 to attend some concerts given by Rubinstein he wrote:

It is undeniable that today Rubinstein occupies the first place in the musical world and has no equal since the death of Wagner. According to unanimous opinion, no musician has ever demonstrated such a musical technique and such perfection in execution. His name is popular in Europe and America. Wherever he appears he receives the homage of the best representatives of music, art and literature. It is pleasant to contemplate that this artist of the first order belongs to Russia. By birth, education, social relations and family, his habits and way of life, Anton Rubinstein is a Russian and remains in Russia despite enticing offers from abroad.

(Rubinstein himself was less certain; he once complained to a friend: "The Russians consider me a German, the Germans—a Russian. Jews regard me as a Christian, the Christians—a Jew.") The Tsar did not require much urging, since already in the previous year he had attended the performance of Rubinstein's opera, *Neron*. Alexander also conferred upon the musician the title Excellency which evoked the following comment by Rubinstein to his mother: "I have a presentiment that I shall require this 'Excellenz' some day against the very powers which conferred it upon me. For all your baptism at Berdichev, we are Jews, you and I and sister Sophie." Perhaps because of this awareness of his Jewish descent, Rubinstein chose quite a few Old Testament topics for his musical compositions.[7]

POLITICAL STIRRINGS

At the same time Russia slowly opened her gates to professing Jews who achieved eminence in many fields, especially in law and medicine. Among the jurists one need but mention Herman Trachtenberg (1839-1895), who participated in the important judicial reforms of 1864 and, despite his faith, was appointed to an important post in the Ministry of Justice. Alexander Passover (1840-1910) achieved international fame through his numerous legal publications and the juridical periodicals he had founded. The number of Jewish doctors serving in the army was so large that, as early as the Russo-Turkish War of 1877-78, many received military decorations. An active public servant, like the physiologist Nicholas Bakst (1842-1904), was also an important contributor to contemporary scholarly journals. Irked by the unceasing attacks on Jews, Bakst published a collection entitled *Russkie liudi o Evreiakh* (Opinions of Russians about Jews). He was also instrumental, together with the banker Samuel Poliakov, in founding an organization for the promotion of crafts and agriculture among the Jews which later became known as the ORT.[8]

Bakst's booklet was typical of the concern of the Russian-speaking Jews for the opinion of their non-Jewish compatriots.

As before, the large masses of the Jewish population were much more fortified against anti-Semitic assaults than the more sensitive Russified intelligentsia which often greeted with excessive acclaim every favorable statement by a distinguished non-Jew. We recall that few of the eminent Russian writers were friendly to Jews. Fiodor M. Dostoevsky said many unkind words about Jews and Judaism, although in a private letter to Kovner of February, 1877, he asserted, "I am by no means, nor have I ever been, an enemy of the Jews." Leo N. Tolstoy, on the other hand, on one occasion sang a paean of praise of the Jewish people which, though included in a private letter, achieved wide circulation several years before his death in 1910. To quote only a few of the highlights of his answer to the query he had put to himself, What is a Jew?

> The Jew is that sacred being who has brought down from heaven the everlasting fire and has illumined with it the entire world. He is the religious source, spring and fountain out of which all the rest of the peoples have drawn their beliefs and their religions. The Jew is the pioneer of liberty. . . . The Jew is the pioneer of civilization. . . . The Jew is the emblem of civil and religious toleration. . . . The Jew is the emblem of eternity. . . . The Jew is everlasting as is eternity itself.

Even more outspoken in public was the distinguished philosopher, Vladimir Solovev. We recall his joining with other leading writers in protesting against the pogroms and the reactionary policies of the Russian regime. Such collective protests reappeared also in other periods of crisis, giving some comfort, at least, to the distressed Jewish intellectuals.[9]

Some brilliant young Jews, born in Alexander II's reform era, joined the Russian liberal movements. Particularly the great jurists, Maxim M. Vinaver (1862-1926), Henry (Genrikh) B. Sliozberg (1863-1937), and Oscar O. Gruzenberg (1866-1940), played an influential role in the development of the Cadet Party, while Leonty M. Bramson (1869-1941) became an important member of the farmer-labor *Trudoviki* Party. They persevered in their political activities despite severe discouragement on the part of the

Russian bureaucracy. Even a relatively liberal Prime Minister like Sergei Witte once complained to a Jewish delegation, consisting of Baron Horace Günzburg, Vinaver, and others, that "of late years the Jews have come to the fore as leaders of various political parties and advocates of the most extreme political ideas. Now, it is not your business to teach us. Leave that to Russians by birth and civil status and mind your own business." While the others allegedly acquiesced, Vinaver replied that in view of the forthcoming equality of all Russians it was indeed the business of the Jew to "offer every possible support to those Russians who were fighting for the political emancipation of the country." At the same time Vinaver and Sliozberg were very active in inner Jewish affairs, the former being the founder and presiding officer of the Jewish Historical-Ethnological Society, the League for the Attainment of Complete Equality, and other organizations. Gruzenberg achieved international fame as the defender of Beiliss against the ritual murder accusation. Bramson become a leader in Jewish social welfare, particularly through his untiring espousal of the ideals of Jewish self-help through the ORT and similar organizations.[10]

Some segments of the Jewish youth were attracted particularly to the Russian exponents of radical ideas. Once again it was a Jewish convert to Christianity, Nicholas Utin, who, as early as 1861, participated in a student demonstration and soon played a major role in the first *Zemlia i Volia* (Land and Freedom) organization. Having to flee Russia, he served as editor of Michael Bakunin's periodical in Geneva, although in the well-known conflict between Karl Marx and Bakunin he sided with Marx. There is no evidence that in his relations with Bakunin he was in any way influenced by the latter's occasional anti-Jewish remarks, such as that the Jews were sworn enemies of the Slavs. In Russia proper the majority of young Jewish radicals, whose number multiplied in the 1870s, was attracted by the ideas of the *Narodniki* and their slogan, "Go to the people." But instead of going to their own, the Jewish people, they preferred to join their non-Jewish compatriots in propagandizing their new ideals among the peasants. Most of them actually had little use for their own people; they saw in the Jew predominantly a petty bourgeois, the very artisan being as a rule the employer, and as such an exploiter of workers.

Later on Aaron Zundelevich, a leading revolutionary writer, reminisced about the 1870s: "For us Jewry as a national organism did not present a phenomenon worthy of support. Jewish nationalism, it seemed to us, had no *raison d'être*. Religion, that cementing force of Jewish unity, represented to us complete retrogression." Some of these early leaders, including Pavel Borisovich Akselrod (*ca.* 1848-1928) comforted themselves with the thought that the liberation of the Russian masses would automatically bring about also the freeing of Jews from tsarist bondage. Not even the Russian pogroms immediately affected this view. At the most, some of the Jewish radicals despairingly commented as did Lev Daitsch who wrote to Akselrod:

> A revolutionary can indeed give no practical answer now to the Jewish question. What should he do, for instance, in Balta where they beat Jews? Take their part? This would mean, as [the geographer] Jean Jacques Reclus stated, bringing down the wrath of peasants on the revolutionaries: 'Not enough they have murdered the Tsar but they also defend the *zhids!*' The revolutionaries thus find themselves on the horns of a dilemma; this is a simple cul-de-sac for both the Jews and the revolutionaries.

According to a plausible story, a Jewish *narodnik* joined the pogromists in Kiev to attack the wealthy Jews. But when he noted that the hooligans destroyed poverty-stricken Jewish homes, but spared rich Christian merchants and officials, he suffered a nervous breakdown.[11]

Curiously, many of these extremists were recruited from among the students of the Vilna rabbinical seminary and *Realgymnasium*. Having lost any real contact with the overwhelming majority of their people, they went all the way in their negativism. Ironically, this was the revenge the Jewish people took on the Russian regime for having forcibly implanted in it these alien educational institutions. A story told by the folk poet Eliakum Zunser has it that, in 1872, after the arrest of forty young Jewish "nihilists" in Vilna, Governor-General Potapov inquired of the leaders of the Jewish community why they had so many subversives in their midst. To which one of the Jewish representatives, Jacob Barutt (better known as R. Yankele Kovner) is supposed to have replied, "As long as we educated our children there were no Nihilists among us; but as soon as you took the education of our children into your hands they became so." According to Zunser, it was the tenor of this reply, transmitted by Potapov to St. Petersburg, which helped to bring about the closing of the two governmental seminaries.[12]

As a matter of record, however, the Jewish ratio among the *narodniki* did not exceed 4.4 percent in 1878, and declined to 4.1 percent two years later. This ratio roughly corresponded to the demographic strength of the Jewish community. In the subsequent decades the situation changed and, as more and more Jewish youth went through the Russian and foreign colleges and universities, their proportion grew even beyond their percentage in the urban population. They were far more attracted to the urban-centered Western type socialist movements, as exemplified by the "Land and Liberty" party, founded in 1876 by disillusioned *narodniki* and others, including the Jew, Mark Natanson. One of its offshoots was the more truly Marxist "Black Repartition" movement. Many of these latter-day revolutionaries may not have consciously sympathized with the sufferings of their own people, but they could not help subconsciously to seek release from their accumulated resentments by fighting the established order.[13]

Not that they were all welcomed with open arms in the radical camp. In trying to accomplish their main mission of teaching the Russian peasants both culture and socialism, they had to use all sorts of disguises, lest their Jewishness antagonize the listeners. Time and again these masks were unveiled and the preachers of universal brotherhood were rebuffed not only by unlettered peasants but, to some extent, also by their ideological comrades. Female revolutionaries often resorted to the simple expedient of marrying Russian Gentiles and converting themselves to Christianity.

THE "BUND"

Other Jewish socialists found such denial of their ancestry utterly unpalatable. Another pupil of the Vilna seminary, Aaron Samuel Liberman (1845-80), was perhaps less negativistically minded because, unlike most of his confreres, he grew up in a relatively "enlightened" household. His father, a modern Hebrew teacher, had instilled in him enough reverence for the Jewish tradition so that, although he rejected the Jewish religion, he remained a lifelong devotee of the Hebrew language. From the outset he, together with his friend Zundelevich, started propagating socialism among Jews. Fleeing before the police, Liberman had to leave Russia and spend many years in London, Berlin, and Vienna. In each of these capitals he tried to organize Jewish socialist clubs and actually issued a socialist periodical in Hebrew, the first publication of its kind. This periodical, of which only three small issues appeared in 1876, bore the programmatic title, *Ha-Emet* (The Truth), as explained in the prospectus, "Champions of justice are found among all peoples. Our· Jewish literature alone has lacked *emet* [truth]; for, since prophecy had ceased among the Jews, our writers have lost interest in the miseries and needs of our people." With all his sincerity Liberman was really a split personality, full of theoretical and practical inconsistencies. After his arrest in Vienna, he was asked in court about his religion; he proudly proclaimed: "I am a socialist." Yet when a socialist club, which he organized in London, was to hold a scheduled meeting on the Ninth of Ab (a fast day commemorating the destruction of the Jerusalem Temple), he suggested postponement with the somewhat disingenuous argument that "as long as the social revolution has not taken place, political freedom is of prime importance to every people." Hence the Jews may legitimately mourn the loss of their national independence eighteen centuries before. A generally unstable individual, Liberman ended as a suicide in Syracuse, New York, at the age of thirty-five.[14]

Like Liberman, Chaim Zhitlowsky (1865-1943) preached his socialism mainly to the Russian Jewish intelligentsia from abroad. First from Switzerland, and later from the United

States, he addressed himself in a number of Russian and Yiddish writings, effectively smuggled into the Tsarist Empire, to the thoughtful young Jews of his mother country, pressing a combination of socialist and national demands. His "A Jew to Jews," disseminated in 1892 in both languages, sounded the clarion call for national Jewish minority rights which, a quarter century later, were to receive basic international recognition in both the Soviet legislation and the Paris Peace Treaties. These ideas were more fully, and apparently in complete independence, developed by the middle-class publicist and historian, Simon M. Dubnov (1860-1941), particularly in a series of "Letters on Old and New Judaism," published in Russian in Dubnov's journal, *Voskhod,* in 1897-1906.[15]

Other Jewish socialists, particularly Arkady Kremer (1865-1935), were more practical and better organizers. Many of them belonged to the second generation of Jewish socialists who grew up in the era of Russian pogroms and tsarist reaction after 1881. It was much harder now to turn one's back on the downtrodden Jewish people, among whom, moreover, there had begun growing up a regular industrial proletariat. From the outset Kremer was a pragmatist. In his pamphlet, *Ob Agitatsii* (On Propaganda), written in 1893, he argued against the socialist propaganda couched in abstract Marxian terms. In his opinion the proletariat was to be brought to the concrete realization of its own plight and shown how the victory of socialism would benefit it directly. Needless to say, Kremer and his associates were far removed from purely practical trade unionism and the exclusive emphasis on the economic betterment of the working classes, although they were accused of such leanings by Lenin and others. His pragmatic approach also persuaded Kremer that agitation among Jewish workers had to be conducted in Yiddish, the only language they understood, and in terms approximating their daily experience.

Out of such considerations he and other Jewish socialists independently working in various communities decided to pool their resources and to found an all-embracing Jewish socialist organization. Thus originated the *Bund,* or The General Jewish Workers' League, established at a Vilna conference in 1897. Kremer who delivered the keynote address thus defined the program of the new organization:

> A general union of all Jewish socialist groups will have as its goal not only the struggle for general Russian political demands; it will also have the special task of defending the specific interest of the Jewish workers, carry on the struggle for their civic rights and, above all, combat the discriminatory anti-Jewish laws. That is because the Jewish workers suffer not only as workers but also as Jews, and we dare not and cannot remain indifferent at such a time.

This program found a resounding echo among the radical Jewish youth. It was completely in line with the thinking of Yuli Osipovich Martov (1873-1923), grandson of Alexander Zederbaum and an outstanding Jewish leader of general Russian socialism, particularly of its later Menshevik wing, who had delivered a speech along similar lines in 1895. In that stage of his career Martov had bluntly declared, "A working class content with the lot of an inferior nation, will not rise up against the lot of an inferior class. . . . The growth of national and class consciousness must go hand in hand."[16]

While Martov was moving away from this position in serving, together with Lenin, as editor of the *Iskra*, the Bund became increasingly nationalistic. At first it saw its main objective in the propagation of Marxian internationalism in the Yiddish medium, but after a few years of growing nationalist strife in the Russian Empire it began advocating Jewish national autonomy, along with that of the other national minorities. This programmatic change, which became manifest in 1903 and reached its full clarification during the Revolution of 1905, evoked a hostile reaction among the Russian socialists, including Lenin, who stubbornly denied the very existence of a Jewish nationality. Since the opposition based its main argument on the lack of a Jewish territorial concentration, the Bund was forced increasingly to stress the cultural foundations of Jewish nationalism.

Curiously, it was Vladimir Medem (1879-1923) who most clearly defined this part of the Bund ideology. Medem, whose father, an army doctor, had baptized all his children (stationed in Libau he first converted them to the Lutheran faith, but the youngest, Vladimir, grew up in the Greek-Orthodox religion), gradually found his way back to the Jewish people, although not to religious Judaism. Without making out of nationalism a fetish, he came to the conclusion, as he wrote in 1909, that "all attempts to combat nationalism through the old method of ignoring and hushing up the very facts of national differences and national characters have proved to be useless, mouldy and outworn." Medem and the Bund tried, therefore, to combine class struggle with recognition of national rights. They found a sufficient following in the Jewish proletariat to enlist some 40,000 members in their movement at a time (1906) when the major Russian Socialist Party counted no more than 150,000, and the Polish Socialist Party only 23,000 members. This became possible only after the Revolution when the socialists could more openly profess their credo. At the beginning of 1905, according to the *Large Russian Encyclopedia*, the whole Russian Party embraced only 8,400, contrasted with the Bund's 23,000 members. The Bund's strength was also recognized in international gatherings. At the Paris Congress of the Second International, the Russian delegation of twenty-nine representatives included twelve Bund delegates. When Russia's Social Democratic Party and Social Revolutionaries were assigned one vote each on the Central Committee, the former had to share this vote equally with the Bund. It was, therefore, of great importance that at its Sixth Convention, held in Zurich in October, 1905, when the revolutionary movement was reaching its crest, the Bund adopted a program demanding not only full civil and political emancipation for Russian Jewry but also

> National-cultural autonomy: to withdraw from the authority of the state and its local and territorial self-governing organs all functions associated with cultural affairs (education and the like) and to entrust them to the nation itself operating through separate institutions, central and local, elected by all members through a universal, equal, direct and secret vote.

The Bund basically adhered to this program also after its reunification with the Russian Socialist Party in 1906 and in the years of its general decline during the ensuing period of tsarist reaction.[17]

ZIONISM

In the dynamism of Russian Jewish society, the emergent socialist movement was not the only, in fact not even the most powerful, novel trend. Zionism not only increasingly became the dominant passion of the middle-class majority but it also penetrated deeply the plutocracy and the aristocracy of learning on the one hand, and the working classes on the other hand. The messianic ideal had long been the keynote of Jewish religion. Under one guise or another even the antireligious movements in nineteenth century Judaism were unable to cast off their messianic yearnings for an ultimate redemption of their people, or of mankind at large. The growing secularization of modern Jewry made the transition from religious messianism to political Zionism appear as but another link in that long chain of evolution. The rise of nationalism throughout Eastern Europe during the latter half of the nineteenth century and the Pan-Slavist preachment of the liberation of all Slavonic peoples exerted a considerable influence also on thinking young Jews. Not only the participants in the two Polish uprisings of 1831 and 1863, but many other Jews began asking why the liberation movements of the young nationalities should not apply to their own older people as well.

It is not surprising that Russian Jews living abroad reached a more mature understanding of the peculiar position of their people than did those who were swallowed up by the routine of their life within the Pale. It was no mere accident that Perets Smolenskin (1842-85), after settling in Vienna, became the most articulate spokesman of the new national movement. Austria was at that time, and for many decades thereafter, the main laboratory for national problems in Europe. In the neighboring Balkan Peninsula one people after another clamored for, and often achieved, national independence. From 1868, until his premature death in 1885, Smolenskin published in Vienna a distinguished Hebrew

periodical, *Ha-Shahar* (The Dawn), for which, with an un-
canny talent, he enlisted the collaboration of almost all
young and promising Hebrew writers. While still lacking
in clarity and subject to diverse interpretations, his ideas
significantly influenced his contemporaries across the border.
Above all he insisted upon the unity of the Jewish people,
based not on the usual criteria of territory, language, or
statehood, and not even on the binding force of Jewish law
and ritual, but rather on the somewhat vague, but to him
perfectly tangible "national spirit." In a series of programmatic essays, entitled "It Is Time to Plant" and published
in his periodical in 1875-77, he taught that "no matter what
his sins against religion may be, every Jew belongs to his
people so long as he does not betray it." In another im-
pressive work, *Am Olam* (The Eternal People), he argued
for the reconstruction of Jewish life in the socioeconomic, as
well as political sense. This designation was adopted by the
new movement which in the 1880s sought to transplant
thousands upon thousands of Russian Jews to the New World
and to settle tham on land.

To Smolenskin himself and to many of his associates this
solution appeared half-hearted. From the outset they felt,
together with such non-Russian thinkers as Rabbis Yehudah
Alkalai and Zvi Hirsch Kalischer, that only Palestine could
be for Jews the promised land of the future as it had been
in the past. The Russian pogroms of 1881 strongly reinforced
that trend. M. L. Lilienblum now toned down his positivist
rejection of the Jewish tradition and dedicated the rest of
his life to the struggle for the Zionist ideal. In his numerous
essays he penetratingly analyzed the position of the Jew
in the East-European world and found it wanting. Among
his fellow writers he appeared as a stark realist. He allegedly
once squelched an enthusiast who tried to assure him of his
readiness to sell his last shirt and to plough the Holy Land
with his nose, by simply asking, how much money could be
raised by such a sale and how many dunams of land could
be ploughed up with a nose. In a remarkable passage,
written in 1883, Lilienblum described the utterly contradictory, and hence essentially irrational, arguments underlying
the growth of anti-Semitism in Europe.

Opponents of nationalism see us as unflinching nationalists, with a national God and a national Torah; to the nationalists we are cosmopolitans, whose fatherland is wherever we prosper. Religious non-Jews consider us devoid of any faith, while freethinkers accuse us of being orthodox and believing in all sorts of nonsense. The liberals call us conservative and the conservatives denounce our liberalism. Some bureaucrats and writers view us as the promoters of anarchy, insurrection and revolt, whereas to anarchists we are capitalists and bearers of the biblical civilization, based, in their view, on slavery and parasitism. . . . Musicians like Richard Wagner charge us with destroying the beauty and purity of music. Even our virtues are turned into faults; "Few Jews are murderers," they explain, "because all Jews are cowards," which does not prevent them from accusing us of murdering Christian children.

Hence, Lilienblum concluded, the Jewish people ought to live its own natural life rather than pursue the unrewarding course of trying to appease outside opinion.[18]

Anti-Semitism which, in those very years, had become a potent force also in German and French letters and thereby achieved a certain respectability in Russian intellectual circles as well, was evoking different reactions among Jews. Some cringed and tried to obliterate the memory of their Jewish ancestry. Others, like the socialists and nihilists, believed that only a total revamping of the existing social order would solve the Jewish question, too. Still others, like Smolenskin and Lilienblum, drew the lesson that Jews must resort to self-help. The most influential spokesman of that idea was Leon Pinsker (1821-91), son of the distinguished scholar, Simhah Pinsker. As a busy physician, Pinsker had only occasionally participated in Odessa's Jewish communal undertakings. Under the shattering experience of the Russian pogroms, however, he published in 1882 his famous German essay, *Auto-Emanzipation*, in which he submitted anti-Semitism, so to say, to a clinical dissection. He roundly declared:

Judeophobia is a form of demonopathy, with the difference that the Jewish ghost has become known to the whole race of mankind, not only to some peoples, and that it is not disembodied like other ghosts. As a being of flesh and blood, it suffers the most excruciating pain from the wounds inflicted upon it by a timorous mob who imagine themselves threatened by it. Judeophobia is a psychic disorder. As such it is hereditary and, as a disease transmitted for two thousand years, it is incurable.

Since this malady of the Gentile nations was bound to last for the duration of Jewish life in the dispersion, he called for the "self-emancipation" of his people through its return to the land of its forefathers. As a practical man, he immediately proceeded with the organization of the "Lovers of Zion" movement whose headquarters he established in Odessa. He presided over that organization until the end of his life in 1891, during which time he and his associates succeeded in establishing a few new colonies in the Holy Land. Under their inspiration a number of youthful pioneers adopting as their watchword the battle-cry BILU (abbreviated from *Bet Iaakov lekhu ve-nelkha* or O, house of Jacob, come ye and let us go, Isa. 2:5), formed a first group in Kharkov in 1882 and proceeded to the Holy Land. These were very small beginnings, but they opened up a new era of Palestine colonization. They also increasingly served as the yeast which kept the Russian Jewish community in a permanent state of creative fermentation.[19]

A new impetus to the Zionist movement was given by Theodor Herzl and the foundation of the World Zionist Organization. Its first congress in Basel in 1897 was well attended by a delegation from Russia, despite the tsarist government's generally jaundiced view of any Jewish international activities. The official antipathy was but slightly mitigated six years later by Herzl's appearance in St. Petersburg and his negotiations with the Minister of Interior Viacheslav von Plehve. This dramatic visit with the man who was widely blamed for the Kishinev massacres caused much resentment, especially in the revolutionary circles. Yet bent upon promoting the scheme for Jewish emigration to Palestine under a Turkish charter, Herzl did not hesitate to invoke the aid of the Russian tsar. Unable to obtain an audience with Nicholas II, he negotiated with Plehve and Witte in terms which he defined in a memorandum to Plehve

after their first interview of August 8, 1903. Herzl asked the
minister's approval of the text of the following declaration
he was to read at the forthcoming Zionist Congress in Basel
and which was to sum up the tenor of these negotiations:

> I am authorized to declare that the Imperial Russian
> Government has the intention to support the Zionist move-
> ment. The Imperial Government proposes to intervene
> in our behalf with his Imperial Majesty the Sultan in order
> to secure a Charter of Colonization. In addition the Im-
> perial Government will place at the disposal of the Zionists
> conducting the emigration [to Palestine] certain amounts
> drawn from Jewish taxes. In order to prove the humani-
> tarian character of these measures, the Imperial Govern-
> ment proposes at the same time to enlarge in the near
> future the Pale of Jewish Settlement for those who do
> not wish to emigrate.

Plehve, who in his discussions with Herzl contended that,
rather than being an anti-Semite, he fondly remembered his
Jewish playmates during his family's sojourn in Warsaw when
he was five to sixteen years old, wished to avoid sharp denunciations by the Basel Congress of the government's role
at the Kishinev atrocities. On the other hand, the majority
of Russian Jews, despite the Bundist propaganda, hailed
Herzl as the great savior of their people.[20]
Nonetheless the practical outcome of these negotiations was
almost nil. Although the Russian administration was far from
disinclined to see a large-scale exodus of Jews from the
country—we recall its earlier support to Baron de Hirsch's
scheme of transplanting millions of Russian Jews to Latin
America—these talks proved no more fruitful than Herzl's
similar dramatic *pourparlers* with the sultan, Emperor Wil-
liam II, the Pope, and other leaders. When finally Great
Britain offered the Zionist Organization, through Colonial
Minister Joseph Chamberlain, the opportunity of colonizing
Jews in African Uganda, it was preeminently the opposition
of the Russian Zionists, led by the iron-willed Menahem
Mendel Ussishkin (1863-1941) and the youthful Chaim
Weizmann (1874-1952), which defeated the project. To the
Russian Zionists no country other than Palestine, hallowed

by a millennial tradition, could offer a genuine home for the Jewish people.[21]

Some radical Zionists had their eyes so firmly fixed upon the Holy Land that they were prepared to neglect the home-front. Negativistic toward the future of Jews in the dispersion, they considered the building of any permanent Jewish communal or cultural institutions in Russia a waste of national energies which would better be concentrated on the up-building of the Palestinian settlement. From the outset, however, one of the most influential Zionist thinkers combatted that idea. Asher Zvi Ginzberg (1856-1927), better known under his nom-de-plume of Ahad Ha-Am (One of the People), pleaded that Palestine, with its limited natural resources, could not even absorb the future increase in the world Jewish population. Hence the overwhelming majority of Jews would have to remain in their respective countries. Yet, he believed that a fairly strong Jewish community in Palestine, where it would not be subject to assimilatory pressure and could develop an independent modern culture of its own, could serve as a cultural center for the whole Jewish people. Such a program clearly involved a continuous building of Jewish culture in the dispersion as well. In a clear-cut argument against "The Negation of the Diaspora," then prevalent in certain Zionist circles (1909), he succinctly declared:

> The Jews as a people feel that they have the will and the strength to survive whatever may happen, without any ifs or ands. They cannot accept a theory which makes their survival conditional on their ceasing to be dispersed, because that theory implies that failure to end the dispersion would mean extinction, and extinction is an alternative that cannot be contemplated in any circumstances whatever.

At the same time he viewed the emancipation achieved by Western Jewry at the price of a high degree of assimilation as mere "slavery within freedom," perhaps an unconscious inversion of Alexander Herzen's well-known characterization of Nicholas I's regime as a period of external slavery and inner emancipation. This was, indeed, the tenor not only of his own brilliant essays, written in a fine Hebrew style, but also of the highly influential monthly, *Ha-Shiloah* (called after a slow-moving Palestinian river) which he founded in Odessa in 1896 and edited for six years. This organ served as the most important focus of Hebrew literary activity to the First World War.[22]

The difference between the cultural and political Zionists was not quite so sharp as it appeared to some contemporaries. Especially after Herzl's grandiose schemes to secure an internationally recognized Ottoman charter had proved unworkable, the Zionist Organization itself returned to the slower and more patient development of a vigorous Jewish settlement in Palestine. At the same time, within the Organization, the spokesmen of cultural Zionism, including Weizmann, played an increasing role. In Russia proper the struggle for Jewish rights became ever sharper. Partly under the pressure of public opinion, the Russian Zionists, like the Bundists, had to give up their aloofness from the domestic political struggles and to adopt, after a series of preliminary conferences during the stormy period of the First Revolution, the Helsingfors Platform of November, 1906, which included clearly defined postulates of national Jewish minority rights throughout the Empire. Suggesting free democratic elections of representatives to Jewish local, provincial, and national bodies, the convention demanded that these organs "possess the right to found, conduct and support all kinds of institutions which would serve the end of (1) national education, (2) national health, (3) mutual and labor aid, (4) emigration, and (5) matters of faith." Although realizing that Russian Jewry was internally divided between Hebraists and Yiddishists, the convention insisted upon the recognition of the rights of each nationality to use its own language also in official communications to and from governmental organs in all localities where its members exceeded a certain legally defined percentage of the population. These postulates remained the guide lines of domestic policies for the Russian Zionists during the following years of reaction, as well as during the First World War.[23]

Apart from these areas of agreement, the Russian Zionists also had many internal divisions. On the one hand, many socialists were attracted to the Zionist idea and hence could not share the Bund's anti-Zionist stand. Under the prompting of such influential socialist thinkers as Nachman Syrkin (1867-1924) and Ber Borochov (1881-1917), there gradually emerged a Zionist socialist wing, finally organized in 1906 under the name of Poale Zion (Zionist workers). The greatest difficulty, of course, consisted in reconciling Jewish nationalism, particularly of the Zionist variety, with Marxist internationalism. In an essay on the "Anti-Zionist Front," published in 1911, Borochov emphasized that "within Jewry the chief struggle is not between the proletariat and the bourgeoisie, or between the urban and agrarian population, but between Zionists and *Galut* [Diaspora] champions of all classes." The Poale Zion believed, therefore, that Jewish workers must ally themselves, on the one hand, with the Zionist World Organization and, on the other hand, with the Socialist International. They thus followed the program enunciated as early as 1901 by Syrkin in his "Call to Jewish Youth." Here Syrkin declared that the Jewish question could be solved only along the following lines: "(1) Social-democratic movements must be joined in those countries where the Jewish masses live; (2) a Jewish socialist commonwealth must be founded in Palestine and the neighboring lands; (3) Jewish clericalism must be fought through its replacement by a socialist, nationalist ideal." This policy was pursued with fair consistency except that the anticlerical propaganda was gradually toned down. There were splinter movements, too, such as those of the Socialist Zionists (S.S.) party who admitted the *raison d'être* of a Jewish nationality, but accepted the Territorialist ideology à la Israel Zangwill, postulating Jewish colonization of any territory which could serve as a Jewish homeland. There also was a "Seymist" party of non-Marxian socialists. Independently, Aaron David Gordon (1856-1922), taking over some ideas from the early Russian socialists and Tolstoy, soon propagated a new brand of Zionist socialism which was to replace the class struggle by the idea of mutual love and devotion to "a religion of labor." Moving personally to Palestine, Gordon, through example, as well as through the preachment of his brand of national socialism in his magazine, *Ha-Poel ha-sair* (Young

Worker), succeeded in raising a large number of disciples and
in significantly influencing the growth of the Palestinian
settlement.[24]

On its part Orthodoxy long remained opposed to both
socialism and Zionism. From the point of view of mass
following it still had behind it the majority of Russian Jewry.
But averse to political struggles, it remained largely inarticulate. Most of the Orthodox bitterly resented not only the
secularization of Jewish life preached by both socialists and
Zionists, but they also long viewed any political action, and
particularly one directed against the established regime, as a
serious danger to Jewish survival. Typical of that attitude
is a proclamation issued by a Minsk rabbi in 1902, when the
news of a Jew's assault on the governor of Vilna reached
him. He wrote

> A shudder passes over us when we hear the terrible story
> of what happened in the theater. How do we Jews, who
> are likened to a little worm—the worm of Jacob—come to
> get messed up in such matters? How do we Jews, who,
> according to all sense and reason, are always obligated
> to pray for the well-being of the sovereign power, without
> which we would long since have been swallowed alive—
> how do we Jews dare to climb up to such high places and
> meddle in politics? Oh, beware, Jewish children! Look well
> at what you are doing! God only knows what you may
> bring upon our unfortunate nation, upon yourselves, and
> upon your families. Our people always were proud of one
> thing—that they never had any rebels among them; and
> now you desire to wipe out this virtue, too. We hope you
> will think well about all this and you will not wish to place
> in jeopardy the happiness of our whole nation, your own
> fate, and the fate of your parents and families.

Zionism, in particular, appeared to many Orthodox as the
betrayal of the genuine messianic idea which believed in the
redemption of the people only after the advent of the supernatural Messiah.

However, there soon emerged within Orthodoxy itself a
group which accepted the temporary solution of a politically
secured Jewish state. As we recall, such rabbis as Alkalai
and Kalischer belonged to the earliest exponents of the Love

of Zion movement in its pre-Herzlian stage. In Russia the outstanding spokesman of Zionism before Pinsker was the Orthodox rabbi, Samuel Mohilever (1824-98). By 1902, that is but five years after the first Basel Congress, efforts were made by a number of Russian leaders to organize an Orthodox wing within the Zionist movement. These efforts led to the development, in the following years, of the so-called Mizrahi Organization, under the chairmanship of Rabbi Isaac Jacob Reines of Lida (1839-1915). This faction, seeking to attain the Zionist aims on the basis of the Jewish religious tradition or, as its motto has it, "the Land of Israel for the people of Israel based on the Torah of Israel," has ever since played a great role in the destinies of the Zionist movement and in the development of the Jewish settlement in Palestine.[25]

Perhaps this very formation of an Orthodox group within Zionism stimulated the anti-Zionist Orthodox to independent political activity. The initiative, to be sure, came from Germany. Many Orthodox rabbis, including some Hasidic leaders, joined Jacob Rosenheim of Frankfort in organizing a worldwide countermovement under the name of Agudath Israel. A constituent meeting in Katowice, held in 1912 with the participation of a large delegation of Russian rabbis and laymen, proclaimed to the world that Jewish life could be organized only on the basis of the Jewish religious tradition. It also aimed "to represent Orthodox Jewry as a whole before the outside world and to defend the Torah and its adherents against attacks." While little time was left before the outbreak of the First World War to develop this new organization, it injected an additional factor into the checkered political picture of Russian Jewry.[26]

LITERARY RENAISSANCE

Unavoidably, the new ideologies also penetrated the national literature in both Hebrew and Yiddish. Jewish nationalism of the late nineteenth century, as the earlier ones in Germany, Poland, or Italy, was then entering its heroic stage. Like the other European movements, led by Herder, Mickiewicz or Mazzini, the new Jewish national sentiment generated a cultural renaissance which found its outlets in great poetic and prose creations. This became, indeed, the golden age of modern Hebrew and Yiddish letters. Just as Jewish life had become more diversified and the cultural attainments of individual Jews more heterogenous and multi-colored, so did the creative literature of the age reflect the much greater vitality and abundant richness of Jewish thought. The rather shallow rationalist critique of the Jewish past, characteristic of the Enlightenment era, now gave way to a new appreciation of the rich heritage of the Jewish spirit in its manifold manifestations. At the same time there were strong literary echoes of the new appreciation of labor as the mainspring of social creativity. Nor was the gate shut to rebels and heterodox seekers of new truths.

Some of these novel attitudes came to the fore in the work of Chaim Nachman Bialik (1873-1934), a native of a small Volhynian town, who achieved eminence as a poet while living in Odessa. After the First World War he was allowed, through Maxim Gorki's intervention, to leave the Soviet Union and settle in Palestine. A great master of language and a bard who expressed his generation's innermost feelings, he raised Hebrew poetry to a level of attainment unsurpassed since the Spanish poets of the eleventh and twelfth centuries, whose works he now toiled to recover for the benefit of the twentieth century Hebrew public. Unlike his immediate "enlightened" predecessors, Bialik stood in reverence before rabbinic learning. His poem *Ha-Matmid* (The Talmud Student) became a classic of Hebrew letters because it erected a monument to the poor, industrious student who found in his devotion to talmudic studies some basic answers to the riddles of his life. Other well-known classics were his *Be-Ir ha-haregah* (In the City of Slaughter) and *Megillat esh* (The Scroll of Fire) in which he lent immortal expression to his people's mourning over its dead during the Russian pogroms. Certainly, the traditional "lachrymose conception of Jewish history" nowhere found a more eloquent expression. At the same time he wrote some of the most touching verses on the sanctity of labor.[27]

A different type of romanticism permeated the often paradoxical stories and learned works of Micah Joseph

Berdichevski (Bin Gorion, 1865-1921). This semi-Nietz-schean admirer of individual strength and exalter of such historic heroes as Cecil Rhodes, had a tender heart for the teachings of Hasidism and for the extraordinary piety of some Hasidic leaders. He who, in some respects, placed the Old Testament nature cults above the ethical monotheism of Moses, nevertheless spent a lifetime in collecting and reinterpreting biblical and rabbinic legends (mostly under the pseudonym of M. J. Bin Gorion). More consistently "pagan" was another outstanding poet of the Hebrew Renaissance, Saul Tchernichovski (1875-1943). After a stint in Germany, Tchernichovski returned to Russia to serve as a practicing physician in small Russian villages. Unlike Bialik and Berdichevski, he had but slight roots in the Orthodox Jewish tradition: his training was largely Western and his ideals were taken from world literature, of which he was an outstanding translator. Not undeservedly he was called the "Greek" in Hebrew letters, a designation borne out by such poems as "Before the Statue of Apollo" or "Sonnets of a Pagan." He also published fine Hebrew translations from Homer and Plato. Yet in moments of crisis his deep moorings in the Jewish past came to the fore. In reaction to anti-Jewish massacres he once wrote in his "This Be Our Re-venge,"

We are small.
We shall not rise up against you,
To cleave pregnant women with axes
(As you do); nor shall we set fire
To your roofs over your heads, and with iron bars
We shall not shatter the skulls of babes!
Not until with your brute hand you have uprooted,
Not until with your contaminated palms you have erased
  altogether
The image of God stamped upon us,
The tokens of ancient nobility of spirit,
And of descent from princely generations.[28]

A similar revulsion took place in Yiddish literature, par-ticularly in its greatest writers such as Isaac Leib Peretz (1852-1915) and Sholem Aleikhem (pseudonym for Solomon Rabinovich; 1859-1916) who, together with Mendele, have rightly been considered the chief stars in the firmament of modern Yiddish letters. Peretz was not an ivory-tower thinker. As a lawyer for some ten years in his native Zamość and subsequently as a secretary of the Jewish community of Warsaw, he had many opportunities to observe Jewish life in action. Although he had been writing in Russian, Polish, and Hebrew before he found his way to Yiddish literature (in fact, he and Sholem Aleikhem usually corresponded in Hebrew), and although he was an almost total agnostic, he came under the spell of Hasidism. The drama, *Di goldene Kait* (The Golden Chain), which he himself considered the best of his works, was in many ways an apotheosis of that mystical movement. So was his most popular story, "And Even Beyond," extolling the extraordinary charity of a Hasidic rabbi. But Peretz's versatile pen turned out many other short stories in which a variety of Jewish types was described with masterly characterization and unmatched beauty of expression. For instance, he depicts how Bontshe Shveig, meek and unassuming in life, is ultimately recognized in Heaven in his truly tragic grandeur.[29]

Sholem Aleikhem has charmed readers for three generations with his humorous and melancholy presentation of "average" Russo-Jewish types. Although through marriage and inheritance he came into a large fortune at the age of twenty-six (he lost his money rather quickly), he rarely depicted wealthy Jews with any degree of sympathy. His Tevye der Milkhiker (Tobias the Dairyman) has become a byword for a type of uneducated Jew full of malapropisms, but attractive through his deep sentimentality and milk of human kindness. His Menahem Mendel is the incurable dreamer who pursues his quixotic career without any loss of hope or dignity. Described with vivid humor, these and similar other characters in his stories and plays have acquainted the Western world with the daily life of the Russian ghetto, as had no other works. Descriptive of his life's work is the epitaph Sholem Aleikhem had prepared for his own tombstone before his death in New York in 1916.

> Here lies an ordinary Jew
> Who wrote in Yiddish, it is true;

And for wives, and plain folk rather,
He was a humorist, an author
Poking fun at all and sundry;
At the world he thumbed his nose.
The world went on swimmingly
While he, alas, took all the blows
And at the time his public rose
Laughing, clapping, and making merry
He would suffer, only God knows,
Secretly—so none was wary.[30]

Needless to say, next to these giants, there was a whole array of talented Hebrew and Yiddish writers who testified to the great internal diversity, as well as virility and creative vigor, of the Russian community at the turn of the century.

So did the incipient Yiddish theater. Going back to early modern Purim plays which, in their artistic crudity and directness if not in their theme and purpose, reminded one of the medieval mystery and passion plays, and to groups of singers enlivening Jewish weddings and other festive occasions, a Yiddish theater gradually emerged in 1878. Curiously, it was called into being by a Russian Jewish playwright and director, Abraham Goldfaden (1840-1908), with a predominantly Russian cast for a predominantly Russian audience—on Rumanian soil. This ironic situation arose in the wake of the Russo-Turkish War which turned northern Moldavia, particularly the city of Jassy, into a base of operations for the Russian military forces and their suppliers. Jassy had attracted a sufficiently large Russian colony at that time for one of the publicists, who later turned theatrical entrepreneur, to publish for it a Russian magazine. In 1879, Goldfaden who, like many leading literary and communal figures of the period, had been a graduate of the Zhitomir Seminary, returned to Russia. He and his troupe transferred their headquarters to Odessa, but they also visited Moscow and various cities throughout the Pale. Despite their utter lack of training and the popular, rather than artistic vehicles they had at their disposal, Goldfaden's and other troupes attracted wide and enthusiastic audiences for both their dramas and their operas. [31]

Temporarily, to be sure, the Russian Jewish theater was

stifled by a governmental prohibition of Yiddish public performances, issued, as a result of an Orthodox denunciation, by
the reactionary Minister of Interior Count Dmitrii A. Tolstoi
on August 17, 1883. Although obviously illegal, this ukase
was confirmed, on appeal, by the Senate in 1904 and recon-
firmed by the Ministry of Interior in 1906 and 1909, despite
the freedoms guaranteed by the Constitution of 1905. Nevertheless, the movement once set in motion could not be denied.
Under the guise of performing "German" plays a number of
theatrical groups, with the connivance of local police officials,
pursued their ever more creative, if precarious, careers.

The greatest flowering of this branch of Jewish art, however, though carried on for the most part by Russian personnel, came on American soil, until the 1917 abrogation
of the government prohibition formally reopened the gates
of Jewish theaters in Russia. On both sides of the Atlantic
Ocean, memorable plays, like that by Peretz and many
more by the prolific playwrights, Jacob Gordin (1853-1909),
Perets Hirschbein (1880-1948) who had established in 1908
a Jewish art theater in Odessa, and David Pinski (1872-
1959), all performed with extraordinary devotion to art by
an array of distinguished actors like Boris Tomashevski, Jacob
Adler, and their feminine counterparts, raised the Yiddish
theater almost overnight to the level of the best of the
European theatrical arts. What the distinguished German
historian Karl Lamprecht wrote about his impressions at the
New York Yiddish theater in 1904 was equally true of similar
achievements of the Russian-Jewish theatrical arts on their
native soil. Lamprecht compared his New York experience
to his visit to the Cologne Cathedral or the ruins of Paestum
and concluded: "I now realize what the ancient Hellenic
drama must have been so long as they played it with such
religious consecration."[32]

Such was the great *élan vital* and creativity of the five
million Jews of Russia when the country entered the titanic
conflict of World War I.

❧ 10 ❧

The First World War

AT THE OUTBREAK of the First World War in August, 1914 Russian Jewry found itself directly involved, as Russians and as Jews. Not since 1812 had the Pale been invaded by a foreign enemy. Unlike that Napoleonic campaign, however, which was of short duration and largely limited to a few existing roads in the direction of Moscow, the War of the twentieth century lasted for several years and extended over fronts of hundreds of miles. The devastation of the theaters of war was incomparably greater; it was further aggravated by a conscious scorched-earth policy pursued by the retreating Russian armies in supposed emulation of their ancestors a century earlier. Moreover, Jews now were made to serve in the Russian armed forces to the full extent of their able-bodied manpower. It has been estimated that the six hundred thousand Jews who wore Russian uniforms between 1914 and 1917 exceeded their ratio in the Empire's population. This high percentage was doubly significant as, beginning with the summer of 1915, the majority of the Jewish population (including that of Congress Poland) was withdrawn by the German occupation from later Russian drafts. Yet such repeated statistical proofs of loyalty during the War failed to silence the anti-Semitic accusations of alleged Jewish shirking which ultimately induced Count Alexis Tolstoi to institute a formal investigation.

Jewish willingness to offer sacrifices for the Russian mother country was the more remarkable, as the Russian administration for a long time unflinchingly pursued its old discriminatory policies. The press reported cases of Jewish soldiers who had distinguished themselves in the Russo-Japanese War and had thereby earned residence permits in the interior of Russia. When they were now again drafted for active service their families were ordered to leave, since the fathers had departed. Soldiers wounded on the battlefield were often taken into hospitals in the interior, but upon their discharge, were told to return immediately to the Pale. Yet just as in the dark years of Nicholas I's regime so did the Russian Jewish soldiers now fulfill their duty. What an editorialist (Colonel Peter S. Lebedev?) of the army organ, *Russkii Invalid,* had written in 1858, was doubly true during the World War.

> How can the Army slander the Jew, when tens of thousands of Jews are serving in the ranks and performing honestly and faithfully their duty to the Tsar and the Fatherland? Were not the ramparts of Fort Sebastopol colored with the blood of Jewish, as well as Russian soldiers, of Jewish soldiers who fought in the many battles for that stronghold even against their coreligionists in the enemy ranks? Let us be worthy of our century, let us denounce the unfortunate custom in our literature to mock and disdain the Jew.[1]

MASS EVACUATION

From the outset the approach of the Russian High Command toward Jews left much to be desired. True, since Russia was allied with Britain and France, she tried to spread news about the inner rapprochement between the various segments of her population. Undoubtedly stimulated by the idea of the *Burgfrieden* so eminently serving the purposes of the German war machine, the Russian foreign propaganda eloquently depicted an alleged fraternization between Jews and known anti-Semites. According to one story circulated abroad, the deputy, B. M. Purishkevich, a notorious leader of the anti-Semitic Black Hundreds who in 1911 had personally ordered the printing and wide dissemination of leaflets inciting to pogroms, visited a synagogue, kissed the scroll of law and, amidst copious tears, embraced the rabbi. In fact, however, anti-Semitic accusations were given free rein even under the strict war censorship.

At the beginning of the War the Commander-in-Chief, Grand Duke Nicholas Nikolaevich, though a member of the League of the Russian People, issued an appeal to the Poles, promising the unification of their country under the tsar's scepter with full civil and national rights. By implication Jews, too, expected to benefit from the new liberal trend in Russian policies. One can imagine how great the disappointment was when the news of sharp anti-Jewish actions began arriving from Galicia, most of which was overrun by Russian troops in the first three months. General N. J. Ivanov, the commander of the Russian troops occupying Lwow and, after a prolonged siege, the fortress of Przemyśl, behaved as if that territory had always belonged to Russia and been only temporarily estranged from it. The large Ruthenian population of the country, in its overwhelming majority Uniate, was simply declared to be part of the Russian people and told that Greek Orthodoxy was its proper religion. The Uniate Metropolitan, Count Andrew Szeptycki, was deported to Russia.

Jews were treated with even greater cruelty. Since most of them were loyal Austrian citizens, they were constantly suspected by the Russians of espionage for the Austrian army. Many individuals were imprisoned and executed. Quite apart from the usual atrocities committed by conquering armies on the civilian population, sharp measures were adopted in many localities against the entire Jewish population. Typical of many such military ordinances was one issued by the local commander, Prince Lobanov Rostovskii, during the occupation of the city of Kolomea in southeastern Galicia, and another promulgated by Nicholas Nikolaevich himself and sent to the respective military commands. The former read:

> I announce to the entire Israelitic population of the city of Kolomea that, if in the environs of the localities of Delatyn, Kolomea and Sniatyn the railroad, the telegraph or telephone services are damaged in the slightest there will be imposed a large contribution on the entire Jewish population of the city of Kolomea. Should that contribution not be paid within three days, the entire Jewish population of the city will be expelled from the territories occupied by our troops.

The Grand Duke's circular letter began:

> Our experience during this War has clearly revealed the hostile attitude of the Jewish population, particularly of Galicia and the Bukovina. As soon as there occurs some substantial change in the locations and movements of our troops, and whenever we temporarily evacuate one or another district, the enemy, because of the intervention of Jews, adopts cruel measures against the loyal non-Jewish population. In order to protect the population faithful to us from the reprisals by the enemy and to safeguard our troops against the treason which the Jews employ along the entire front, the Supreme Commander of the Russian armed forces considers it necessary that Jews be banished as soon as the enemy retreats. It is necessary to take hostages from among the rich or well-to-do and other persons holding important positions. One must also seize the most influential rabbis of the respective communities and to deport them all as prisoners to the interior of our country. (At first to the province of Kiev, where they are to be held in concentration camps.)[2]

This policy of mass evacuation soon began to be practised also on Russian territory at the approach of German and Austrian troops. As early as March, 1915, the Russian military authorities began with their large-scale expulsions of Jews from the border provinces of Poland, Kovno, and Courland. Particularly during the great Austro-German offensive of May through September, 1915, which ended not only in the recapture of most of Galicia and the Bukovina but also in the occupation of vast Russian territories from the vicinity of Riga down to the Rumanian border, forcible evacuation of Jews assumed enormous proportions. These moves were officially justified by alleged Jewish spying for Germany, although whenever courts had a chance to probe the accusations, they usually turned out, as in a famous case in Kuzhi, Kovno province, to be completely groundless. Many Poles were involved in that anti-Jewish spy-hunt, in part because they thus wished to divert the attention from their own often disloyal attitude toward their tsarist oppressors. Alleged widespread pro-German spying also offered defeated Russian commanders a ready excuse for their campaign failures.

True, Jews were not the only evacués. Apart from voluntary refugees, many other inhabitants of these border areas were forced to leave their residences, for the most part within twenty-four hours. The result was that an incomplete registration of the refugees being cared for in the territory still under Russian control showed that there were 2,700,000 such unfortunates in December, 1915, and 3,300,000 five months later. But Jews were both more suspect and more easily forced out from their concentrated habitations in cities. It has been estimated that more than 600,000 Jews were thus uprooted. Only because of the lightning speed of the Austro-German invasion which overtook some two-thirds of these exiles, were many of them able to return to their homes. This ebb and flow also caused extensive economic damage. A subsequent survey showed that only some 5 percent of the evacués were enabled to take along with them their movable possessions; 22 percent were removed with such speed that they had to leave everything behind; the rest salvaged varying parts of their holdings. In all, these refugees, voluntary as well as forced, sustained losses estimated at $350,000,000 to $400,000,000—a huge amount, indeed, in view of the dollar's still high purchasing power.

Nevertheless, the community of Vilna, for instance, found itself forced to accommodate thousands of evacués from the provinces of Kovno, Grodno, and Suwalki in the summer of 1915, before its own turn came to be occupied by the Germans. Jewish refugees had to be sheltered not only in private homes and various public institutions but also in synagogues and prayer houses. The food shortage was equally lamentable. The Russian railroads, unable fully to cope with peacetime transportation, broke down completely when they were faced with the tremendous logistic problems of the Russian fronts. Hence local shortages developed even before there was a large-scale famine. National competition, for instance, between the Vilna Poles, White Russians, and Jews for the purchase of whatever food could be brought in from the countryside, aggravated an already existing state of tension between these various minority groups. Trying to exonerate the people and to place the entire blame on the government, Maxim Gorki wrote in 1929:

In 1915, the most shameful anti-Jewish propaganda was started in the army; all Jews in Poland and Galicia were declared the spies and enemies of Russia. A disgusting pogrom broke out in Molodechno. It has been established that this Jew-baiting originated at headquarters, and, of course, it could not but contribute to the disintegration of the army, in which there were about half a million Jews. The people, enraged and blinded by want, were unable to detect their true enemy. If the authorities sanctioned the killing and robbery of Jews—why not kill and rob them?[3]

GERMAN OCCUPATION

By the end of 1915, most of the Pale had come under German domination. Those Jews who had hoped that the new masters would bring alleviation of their distress were quickly disillusioned. The German High Command, led by the later notorious anti-Semite, General Erich von Ludendorff, started out with a proclamation to its "dear Jews" in which high-sounding promises were made for their liberation from the Russian yoke.[4]

In practice, the German army pursued its usual policy of exploiting the local population including the Jews not only for the benefit of the occupying forces, but also for that of the German homeland. As the British blockade became increasingly effective and shortages of food and raw materials began to throttle the German war effort at home, the German commanders in the occupied areas ruthlessly seized foodstuffs, gold, silver, and other metals which could be used in German armament factories. Synagogues, like churches, were deprived of their candlesticks and other objects of worship accumulated over generations.

None of this was specifically anti-Jewish. The German authorities soon began issuing their official proclamations in Yiddish, as well as in German, Polish, and Lithuanian. They also allowed many refugees, previously concentrated in a few large cities, to return to their homes or to seek shelter in hamlets and villages where the food supply was somewhat more ample. For a while they even enabled some Jews to emigrate to the United States, then still neutral. It is estimated that 2,500 such emigrés departed from Russia in 1915-16. But as the American attitude toward Germany became increasingly hostile, the German military authorities suspended all further emigration to the United States. The total of some twenty-two thousand refugees found, for instance, in Vilna at the time of the German entry in 1915 was reduced by these manifold measures to but one thousand, fifteen months later.

Orderly bread rations likewise mitigated some hardships of the lower classes who could not afford black-market prices. But the situation was going from bad to worse and, by the end of 1916, many Jewish communities throughout the occupied area had to extend charitable support to more than half of their members. They were able to do so only because the newly organized American Jewish Joint Distribution Committee found ways and means of getting some materials through to both sides of the Russo-German front. As a result some city councils withdrew all support from destitute Jews under the excuse that they were getting sufficient help from their American coreligionists.

In time the Germans set in motion a westward movement of the Jewish population. Since the War placed increasing demands upon German manpower and since almost all able-bodied young men were sent out to the man-devouring fronts, there was increasing demand for laborers in the factories at home. More and more Jews, as well as non-Jews, were therefore drafted for labor battalions to serve either in an auxiliary capacity in the occupied zone or to replenish the working class in Germany itself. In the course of the War some seventy thousand Jews were more or less forcibly transferred to Germany, swelling the number of foreign-born Jews in that country and thus serving as additional targets for German anti-Semites, particularly during the 1920s.[5]

In the meantime, however, Jews, whose Yiddish language was more readily understandable to the Germans than any Slavonic tongue, and who, upon arrival in Germany could expect a more brotherly reception from the German Jewish communities, were preferred objects of this disguised manhunt. At the same time, such "favoritism" on the part of the occupation forces served to embitter still more the always tense relations between the Jews and their neighbors. The decree of the German authorities of September 17, 1915, which ordered the opening of schools with a Polish language of instruction for Polish children, and with German as the language to be used in the case of German and Jewish children, raised the specter of "Germanization" of Poland and added fuel to the existing resentments. Understandably, most Jews preferred the employment of either Hebrew or Yiddish in their own schools, and this clause had to be altered in October, 1916.

As the War progressed, Jewish sufferings kept growing; they affected even the mortality figures. True, the cholera epidemic, raging in western Russia earlier in 1915, was successfully stamped out by the German forces, for their own sake, by November of that year. But because of malnutrition and overcrowded quarters in Warsaw (which at one time accommodated 80,000 Jewish refugees), Vilna and other major centers, Jews were decimated by recurrent attacks of typhoid. The result was that, for instance, in Vilna, where before 1914 the annual Jewish death rate had ranged from 20.4 to 22.6 per 1,000 inhabitants, it increased to 34.4 in March, 1916, 41.5 in December, 1916, and 68.2, in 1917. In March, 1917, it reached the staggering total of 97.5 per 1,000. At the same time the number of births dwindled from 1,502 in 1913 to 489 in 1917. Similar conditions prevailed also in other occupied territories. On the Russian side of the front, too, the Jewish birthrate declined sharply while mortality went up and up. In Elizavetgrad, where symptoms of biological retardation had become noticeable before the War, the Jewish increase in population, as a result of the excess of natality over mortality, was reduced from 201 in 1913 to 164 in 1914 and 77 in 1915. This surplus turned into a deficit of 87-88 souls each in the subsequent two years.[6]

Undaunted, the Jews pursued their religious and cultural life with increased zest since the German military administration was much less restrictive than had been Russian officialdom. The Jewish parties were now free to build their educational institutions in accordance with their respective ideologies. The Zionists laid the foundations for a school system with the modern Hebrew language of instruction, which was later to develop into the noteworthy *Tarbut* structure in newly reconstituted Poland. The Bund, on the other hand, established the first secular schools with the Yiddish language of instruction which were later also to develop into the important CISHO school system in Poland. The Jewish theater, too, now coming out into the open, attracted major talents and, before long, the so-called Vilna Troupe achieved great renown for its high artistic accomplishments.

In Russia's Interior

On the other side of the front the much-reduced Pale of Settlement could no longer accommodate the large numbers of Jews. Their very evacuation, though inspired by suspicions of Jewish loyalty or temporary military exigencies, contributed to breaking down the historic barriers. Many evacués had to be transplanted into the interior of Russia and, for instance, the city of Saratov attracted an important new Jewish settlement. Jewish soldiers, too, were sent for training to various localities beyond the Pale. Willy-nilly the Russian administration had to relax the old residence restrictions, allowing by decree of August 4, 1915, the Jewish war sufferers to move into the interior of Russia, with some specific exceptions which betrayed the usual lack of logical consistency. Not surprisingly, it widely publicized this decree in the Western countries as a part of its War propaganda, naturally omitting to mention that this was but a temporary relaxation for the duration of the War only. In its general liberalization of admissions to schools the Jewish quota was substantially enlarged. Particularly Jews connected with the War effort were allowed to register beyond their usual allotment. As a result the University of St. Petersburg admitted, in 1915, some 600 Jews who helped swell its total enrolment from an average of 1,900 in the preceding three years to 2,600.[7]

However, the total relief was not as great as one might have expected. Bureaucratic chicaneries often made life very difficult for many newcomers. In Saratov even long-established artisans and guild members, who had theretofore pursued their callings on the basis of pertinent passports, were now told that, since passports were no longer being issued under the terms of the August decree, they were not allowed to work in these restricted occupations. Although the movement out of the Pale was greatly stimulated by the Revolutions of 1917, the Central Committee for the Relief of Jewish War Sufferers (EKOPO) found only 211,691 such Jewish residents in the interior. Yet many Russian peasants and city dwellers now had their first opportunity to become acquainted with living Jews, rather than with their distorted image presented by Jew-baiting preachers and officials. To some extent this breakdown of the Pale seemed to presage the possible coming of better times, although during the great retreat of 1915 the demoralized soldiery often committed untold brutalities on the civilian populations, and especially on its helpless Jewish segment behind the front.[8]

News of these atrocities and the generally arbitrary and cruel behavior of the Russian military commanders could not escape the attention of the Russian political leaders and the intelligentsia in the two capitals. The Duma, rather than losing in power because of the increased centralized controls characteristic of war emergencies, now gained in prestige. In the Jewish question, to be sure, even the Progressive Bloc, consisting of Cadets, Octobrists, and Right Nationalists, was fearful of arousing the internal antagonisms and proceeded at a snail's pace in demanding the removal of Jewish disabilities. Nonetheless it now became possible for Alexander F. Kerensky and N. M. Friedman to investigate the alleged high treason committed by the Jewish inhabitants of Kuzhi, "in Courland," which the High Command had widely publicized as a warning to all Russian armies. Seconded by Friedman, Kerensky announced to the Duma, "I declare now from this rostrum that I personally went to the town of Kuzhi to verify the accusation . . . and I feel it my duty to reiterate that this is but an ignominious slander. There was no such case, and under local conditions there could be none." Beyond that incident the Committee on Interpellations, representing all major parties, reported out (and thus gave an indirect sign of approval) an inquiry concerning the illegal acts committed by the armed forces and the bureaucracy against Jews. This interpellation of August 30, 1915, singled out eleven major illustrations of serious misbehavior and asked: "If the illegal acts of the authorities are known to the indicated individuals, what steps were taken by them towards the punishment of the guilty and the prevention of similar breaches of law in the future?"⁹

The Duma also dared to voice the growing grievances of the entire population against the confusingly arbitrary actions of the ever more chaotic Administration, particularly when the Tsarina and Rasputin began exercising their inordinate control over the ministries during Nicholas II's frequent absences at the front. The replacement of Generalissimo Nicholas Nikolaevich by the Tsar himself in August, 1915, merely helped to undermine further the dynasty's prestige because of its obviously inept efforts to stem the German advance and its equally clear mismanagement of the domestic economy. Apart from its organizational shortcomings, the Administration showed itself totally incapable of mitigating the ever sharpening contrasts between the war profiteers and the hungry masses.

On the other hand, as early as 1915 some of Russia's leading intellectuals felt obliged to publish "An Appeal for the Jews" in which they stressed the evil effects of the governmental discrimination against Jews. Although in connection with the partial removal of the barriers of the Pale there also was some relaxation of the *numerus clausus* and other educational restrictions, these intellectuals argued that, owing to the War, Jewish students could no longer repair to schools abroad while the home institutions continued to limit their admission to a small number. Wives and children of wounded soldiers were not permitted to visit their husbands and fathers in hospitals beyond the Pale.

Russian Jews have rendered honest service in all domains left open to them. They have given ample proof of their sincere desire to offer utmost sacrifices for their country. Hence, the curtailment of their civic rights is not only a crying injustice but also a condition injurious to the best interests of the state. The Russian Empire can and must derive its sustenance only from the union of all its nationalities. Only when Russia will accord its citizens equal rights will its power become indestructible. Fellow Russians! Remember that the Russian Jew has no other

fatherland than Russia and that nothing is more precious
to a man than his native soil. You must realize that the
welfare and strength of Russia is inseparable from the
welfare and freedom of all its constituent nationalities.

Among the signers were such internationally famous writers
and scholars as Leonid Andreev, Maxim Gorki, Alexander
Kerensky, Dmitry Merezhkovsky, A. Rimsky-Korsakoff, Mikhail Rostovtsev, Mikhail Ivanovich Tugan-Baranovsky, M.
Fedorov, and many others. The deep sense of guilt animating
these intellectuals found a vivid expression in Andreev's
rhetorical exclamation: "All powerlessness, if it is unable to
prevent a crime—becomes complicity; and this was the result:
personally guiltless of any offence against my brother, I have
become in the eyes of all those unconcerned and those of my
brother himself, a Cain." Even the rather stodgy State Council had to listen to a less eloquent but well-reasoned address
by Baron R. R. Rosen, former Russian ambassador to the
United States, who among other matters pointed out the
dangers to Russia's war effort emanating from the disapproval
by foreign public opinion. Discussing the general effectiveness
of the German propaganda, Rosen added:

> It is inconceivable that the framers of our policy should
> fail to realize that the propaganda directed against us,
> conducted under official auspices and equipped with the
> amplest resources, will scarcely cause our own interests
> and the interests of our Allies one-tenth of the harm which
> is caused to these interests by our attitude towards the
> Jewish population of Russia and our systematic violation
> of the legal conscience of the Finnish population—an
> attitude which smacks of the dark times of medievalism.[10]

In short, the feeling was constantly gaining ground that, once
the War would be over, the Russian constitutional system
would have to be rebuilt from its foundations and that Jewish
equality would be an indispensable ingredient of that reconstruction.

Nor were protests from abroad effective. England and
France were embarrassed by the news of Russian atrocities
toward Jews, especially since British diplomacy made strenuous efforts to draw the United States into the war against

Germany. In its American propaganda Britain often encountered the argument, at times advanced by Germanophile American Jews, that its ally, Russia, was much more barbarous than Germany for she committed atrocities against her own citizens, while the German armies only mistreated conquered populations. At first Britain tried to whitewash the Russian military. It was aided and abetted by its Petrograd envoys, civil and military, some of whom were personally anti-Jewish. They merely transmitted to London official handouts from the Russian Ministry of Foreign Affairs or High Command. Only when a collection of documents assembled by a Jewish committee in Petrograd, under the leadership of Vinaver and Dubnow, reached London via Stockholm and when another such collection was brought by the revolutionary, A. Shliapnikov, to New York in 1916, did the British give more serious consideration to Lucien Wolf's reiterated petitions for intervention in Russia in favor of both Jewish equality and a modicum of national self-government. However, this was a touchy situation among Allies. By the time the British diplomats bestirred themselves to effective action, Russian anarchy and the February Revolution of 1917 rendered all verbal intervention quite meaningless.[11]

Nor can one attribute, as is sometimes done, these anarchical conditions, including the misfortunes of Russian Jewry, to the evil influence of the notorious Rasputin and his henchmen at the tsarina's court. True, some of Rasputin's followers may have felt like his erstwhile friend, the monk Iliodor, who once exclaimed: "In the last resort the world would be safe from ruin only by the holy Russian people and not by accursed advocates, journalists, and all the rest of the Jews!" There also were in Rasputin's entourage a number of corrupt and mercenary agents, including one Manasevich-Manuilov, son of a Jewish merchant, then employed at the Ministry of Interior. However, at least on one occasion Rasputin himself is supposed to have scolded the wife of a Russian factory owner who had asked him blandly why he had not driven the Jews out of Russia. The mystic courtier is supposed to have replied: "*You* should be ashamed to talk like that. The Jews are as good people as we are. I am sure that each of you knows an honest Jew even if he is only a dentist!"[12]

With its accustomed vigor and pliability, Russian Jewry undertook an ambitious program of self-help. On both sides of the front Jewish communities had from the outset organized a Central Relief Committee to take care of both the local indigent and the waves of refugees and deportees. Known under the abbreviation EKOPO (*Evreiskii komitet pomoshtchi* or Central Committee for the Relief of Jewish Sufferers), this organization from its headquarters in Petrograd did all it could to stimulate the local relief activities. In the relatively brief period of its operations it disbursed some 50,000,000 rubles.

Politically, too, the Jewish leaders were quite active in defending Jewish rights, as well as in preparing for the hopefully approaching day of complete Jewish emancipation. The Jewish organizations formed a Political Committee in the capital which, consisting of their representatives and the elected Jewish Duma deputies, courageously took up the cudgels for its coreligionists. As early as 1915, it suggested to the communities to submit to the prime minister a joint petition inquiring about the government's plans for the postwar reconstruction of Jewish status. Governmental terror was too deeply ingrained, however, in the hearts of most local communities, for their elders to speak openly and unequivocally. The majority refused to sign this petition and none was presented.

Nonetheless the agitation for equality of rights now assumed new dimensions. But while the majority still entertained hopes that, upon the cessation of hostilities, the tsar himself would grant the Jews their well-merited rights, a growing radical minority looked for a revolutionary upheaval as the only means of salvation.

✤ 11 ✤

Era of Revolutions

1917–1923

WITH THE MAJORITY of the Russian people and the subject nationalities, Jews welcomed with joy the so-called February (March) Revolution of 1917. The government, first headed by Prince George E. Lvov and later by Alexander F. Kerensky, promised to introduce into Russia Western democatic institutions, based upon equality of all citizens and basic freedoms for both individuals and groups. On March 21 (April 3), 1917, a short time after the Tsar's abdication, the Provisional Government published a decree removing all disabilities stemming from differences of race or religion and thus declaring Jews equal citizens of the Empire.

All organized Jewish-parties, bent on securing also national autonomy for their people, decided to convoke an all-Russian, democratically elected, Jewish Congress. A committee, embracing the various parties and charged with the preparation of the election, appealed to the Jewish communities:

> Citizens, Jews! The Jewish people in Russia now faces an event which has no parallel in Jewish history for two thousand years. Not only has the Jew as an individual, as a citizen, acquired equality of rights—which has also happened in other countries—but the Jewish nation looks forward to the possibility of securing national rights. Never and nowhere have the Jews lived through such a serious, responsible moment as the present—responsible to the present and the future generations.

This rhetoric was followed by a seven-point program to be submitted to the Congress; its first two paragraphs again stressed the principle of national self-determination and the legal safeguards for the Jewish national minority.[1] The election was indeed held by direct, secret, and proportionate ballot in the autumn of 1917. Owing, however, to the grave internal disturbances, the inroads of the German armies during the summer of 1917 and, finally, the successful Communist Revolution of October (November), the Congress never met.

COMMUNIST UPSURGE

The second stage of the revolution, headed by Lenin, opened a new chapter in Jewish, as well as in world history. From the outset, there was considerable equivocation in the communist attitude toward the Jewish question. The presence of many Jews in the top echelon of the Communist Party made it appear to outsiders that the new regime would reform the Jewish status in a spirit acceptable to the Jewish people. In fact, anti-Semites in and outside Russia glibly equated communism with the alleged Jewish world conspiracy. They could easily point out that the first president of the Central Committee of the Party was Jacob Sverdlov, a Lithuanian Jew, that this Committee included four other Jews in its total membership of twenty-one, and that the long-time president of the Third International was Grigorii Evseevich Zinoviev (Apfelbaum). Among the leading diplomats of the period was A. A. Yoffe, Russia's chief delegate at the Brest-Litovsk Peace Conference and subsequently ambassador in Berlin. Yoffe unabashedly used his diplomatic immunity to spread communist propaganda in Germany, then in a desperate mood because of its defeat in the First World War. Later Maxim Litvinov (Wallach) helped in various capacities to reassert the position of the Soviet Union as one of the great world powers. A Galician Jew, Karl Radek (Sobelsohn), helped reorganize the Russian press and laid the foundations for communism's highly effective world-wide propaganda. From the scholarly point of view it was N. Riazanov (David Borisovich Goldenbach) who, as head of the new Marx-Engels Institute in Moscow, became the outstanding historian of the Marxist movement, editor of the chief classics of the Marxist school, and in many ways founder of the new Russian historiography. Above all these men towered Leon Trotsky (Leo Davidovich Bronstein), second only to Lenin in the leadership of the Revolution. As commander-in-chief and minister of war he reorganized the Russian army and successfully defended the new regime in many battles against its foreign and domestic enemies.[2]

The preponderance of Jews in the early communist leadership, which may have irritated even some of these leaders themselves,[3] is not at all surprising when one realizes how long the Bolshevik party had been an outlawed, underground movement with a number of eminent leaders but a relatively small following among the masses. Many Jewish intellectuals were attracted to its professed international ideals, as well as to its socialist radicalism which promised to put an end to the tsarist oppression. Perhaps in subconscious retaliation for the many years of suffering at the hands of the Russian police, a disproportionate number of Jews joined the new Bolshevik secret service. At least when the *Pravda* in December 1937 published a list of 407 officials of that service decorated on the twentieth anniversary of its existence, forty-two names, or some 11 percent, were identified as Jewish. The impression these facts made upon the ordinary Russian is rightly stressed by Leonard Schapiro: "For the most prominent and colourful figure after Lenin was Trotsky, in Petrograd the dominant and hated figure was Zinoviev, while anyone who had the misfortune to fall into the hands of the *Cheka* stood a very good chance of finding himself confronted with, and possibly shot by, a Jewish investigator."[4]

To the casual observer the intrinsically Russian, rather than international, mainsprings of the Bolshevist ideology and practice were far less apparent. Nor did he know, as a rule, that the attachment to Judaism of these Jewish communists was nil. At best some, like Litvinov, classified themselves as members of the Jewish nationality. Most others followed Trotsky's example in considering themselves nothing but Russians and believing that even the Russian nationality would ultimately give way to some sort of international culture. In his autobiography, Trotsky greatly played down his Jewish upbringing and antecedents. In many cases this revulsion from the Jewish past bordered on outright self-hatred and greatly contributed to the Revolution's destructive methods in dealing with the established Jewish institutions. Of course, to outsiders, particularly anti-Semites, such self-denial availed very little. When, for example, Zinoviev debated socialist issues with a leading anti-Bolshevik, Leon Martov, the German Jew-baiter, Count Ernst zu Reventlow, underscored Zinoviev's Jewish name Apfelbaum, but he failed to inform his readers that Martov's name had been Zederbaum.

A closer examination of the record showed that this numerical preponderance in the leadership did not reflect the actual Jewish participation in the rank and file of the Party. Our information for the early years after the Revolution is incomplete. But data made available for the period of 1922-30 showed that Jewish membership was gradually declining from 5.2 percent in 1922 to 4.3 percent in 1927, and 3.8 percent in 1930, although among the Komsomol youth the decline was somewhat less precipitous: from 4.6, to 4.4 and 4.1 percent respectively. Moreover, even if this median percentage of 4.5 in the Party membership exceeded by some 150 percent the Jewish ratio of 1.8 percent in the Soviet population, this disproportion was characteristic of many non-Russian nationalities, including the Poles and Latvians, the latter actually surpassing their population strength by some 1,100 percent. Even Ukrainians and White-Russians, who, in their own lands lagged in membership by more than one-third behind their ratio in the population, exceeded that ratio by 233 percent and 873 percent while living as minorities in each other's republics. The leadership of all parties, moreover, had to be largely recruited from the urban population, since the large majority of the peasantry was completely illiterate. Among the city dwellers only 2.25 percent of Jews had joined the Communist Party in 1927, while non-Jews had a share of 3.24 percent.[5] As time went on, the leadership, as well as the lower echelons, were gradually filled by non-Jews (Sverdlov, for instance, was replaced by Mikhail I. Kalinin) and, as we shall see, most of the early Jewish leaders died a violent death at the hand of their fellow communists.

Estrangement from their own people by the majority of Jewish communists helped to set the course of the revolutionary regime's policies in a direction running counter to the wishes of the Jewish majority. In the long run, this divergence carried in itself elements of great tragedy. Lenin, too, had long misread the overt signs of the Jews' national will. On principle, as well as for tactical reasons, he had demanded, as early as October, 1903, that the Bund give up its "separatism" and join the ranks of the Russian Socialist Party. At that time he wrote in the *Iskra* that the idea of a Jewish "nationality"

> is definitely reactionary not only when expounded by its consistent advocates (the Zionists), but likewise on the lips of those who try to combine it with the ideas of Social Democracy (the Bundists). This idea of a Jewish nationality runs counter to the interests of the Jewish proletariat for it fosters among them, directly or indirectly, a spirit hostile to assimilation, the spirit of the "ghetto."

More generally, he insisted, in a much-quoted passage, that "a nation must have a territory on which to develop, and, in our time at least, until a world confederation has extended this basis, a nation must have a common language." He adhered to this point of view (long held by the Bundists themselves but abandoned at the turn of the century) in his other essays written in the following decade.[6]

NATIONAL MINORITY RIGHTS

Upon coming to power, however, Lenin realized that there was almost complete unanimity among the Russian Jews of that time that they must be treated as a national minority. Realist that he was, he did not mind reversing his previous stand and including the Jews in the new Declaration of the Rights of Nationalities, issued by the Council of People's Commissars on November 15, 1917, but a few days after he had achieved power. This declaration promised to all nationalities equality and free self-determination, including the right of secession. The latter privilege was, of course, quite meaningless in the case of the dispersed Jews. But they must have greatly appreciated the pledge of the government to guarantee: "3. the removal of every and any national and national religious privilege and restriction; 4. the free development of the national minorities and ethnographic groups living within the confines of Russia." Hopes rose very high that, for the first time, Russian Jewry would be in a position to control its own religio-cultural and educational affairs.

Such hopes seemed to be fully confirmed by the reproduction, in the *Pravda* of 1922, of an interview Lenin gave to a Jewish correspondent of the *Manchester Guardian* and the London *Observer*. Here the Soviet leader assured this foreign correspondent that the experience of the preceding five years had fully convinced the Soviet government that the only way to eliminate nationalist strife was to offer maximum satisfaction to the aspirations of all nationalities. True, keener observers could have noted even then a discrepancy between the theory and the practice. Certainly, Simeon Dimanshtain, who soon was to assume the official leadership of the Russo-Jewish community, could clearly remember his own activities as minister of labor in the Lithuanian government during the short span of Soviet rule there in 1917-19. Whatever pledges for the evolution of the national Lithuanian culture may have been made by the new rulers, they themselves, Dimanshtain included, preferred to use the Russian language in their mutual exchanges. But these deviations from the rules could be dismissed as matters of simple habit and the Jewish community, like the other minorities, could confidently expect to be able to develop an autonomous cultural life of its own, unhindered, indeed aided and abetted by the regime.[7]

Careful readers of the subsequent governmental pronunciamentos must have noticed, however, that these pledges of national rights were aimed less at granting to groups of citizens complete freedom to develop their national cultures than at their more effective indoctrination in the new Weltanschauung. A few years later (in 1923) the nationalities were bluntly informed by the influential Commissar for Public

Enlightenment, Anatolii V. Lunacharskii, that education must refrain from teaching history in a way stimulating the children's national pride. "For I do not know what kind of thing is a healthy love for one's fatherland." More, Joseph Stalin who, even before his rise to supreme power, was the Party's chief theorist of the Marxist doctrine of nationalism, consistently preached that national minority rights, like nationalism in general, were to serve only as a temporary measure for the prevention of national strife during the era of upbuilding of a socialist society. Just as the concentration of state power through a dictatorship of the proletariat was intended merely to pave the way for the ultimate "withering away" of the state, as Marx taught, so was the promotion of national cultures to be but an intermediate link toward the ultimate submersion of all nationalities in a world nation. In his famous address to the Sixteenth Congress of the Communist Party of 1930, Stalin made it clear that "the flourishing of cultures, national in form and socialist in content, in the conditions of a proletarian dictatorship in one country, for the *purpose* of their fusion into one common socialist culture, common both in form and in content, with one common tongue, . . . in this lies the dialectical quality of the Leninist way of treating the question of national cultures."[8]

Vague as these formulations must have appeared even to trained Marxists—Lunacharskii's version was soon to be totally reversed in the crucible of the Second World War when the Russian regime had to appeal to the inbred patriotism of the masses—Jewish leaders could nevertheless entertain some hopes about developing their own culture. Few anticipated the hostile reaction to traditional Jewish culture on the part not only of those communist leaders who had severed all connections with Judaism, but also of those who were entrusted by the new government with the erection of the Jewish "sections" (*yevsektsiias*) in the various local governmental bodies. These sections were headed by a Jewish department in the Commissariat of Nationalities of the Council of Commissars. Perhaps the venom with which the Jewish communists approached all traditional institutions and the parties which had theretofore determined the course of

Jewish communal life may, in part, be explained by the bitterness long generated within the community by the divisive policies of the tsarist regime, its fiscal administration, and the cantonist system.

At any rate, no sooner did they attain power than the Jewish communists persuaded the government to outlaw all existing Jewish parties, especially the Zionist organizations. Under Nicholas II the Zionist movement had become the most potent force in Jewish public life despite the necessity of long operating underground. By 1918, when it was out in the open, it embraced no less than 1,200 local Zionist groups with some 300,000 members. But now the Second Conference of the Jewish Communist Sections in Moscow adopted, in June 1919, the following resolution:

> The Zionist party plays a counter-revolutionary role. It is responsible for strengthening, among the backward Jewish masses, the influence of clericalism and nationalist attitudes. In this way the class self-determination of the Jewish toiling masses is undermined and the penetration of communist ideas in their midst seriously hindered. Owing to its Palestine policy, the Zionist Party serves as an instrument of united imperialism which combats the proletarian revolution. In consideration of all these circumstances, the Conference requests the Central Bureau to propose to the pertinent authorities the promulgation of a decree suspending all activities of the Zionist Party in the economic, political and cultural spheres. The communal organs, which are the mainstay of all reactionary forces within the Jewish people, must be suppressed.

A little later (July 1, 1920) a secret circular of the Central Political Police argued that, since Zionism was well received in Western countries and nowhere persecuted, it must *eo ipso* be inimical to the Soviet Union. The government the more readily followed suit as Lenin had, as far back as February, 1903, attacked the Zionist "fable about anti-Semitism being eternal." It speedily outlawed the movement under severe sanctions, arrested some three thousand Zionist leaders, and deported many to Siberia's political labor camps.[9]

With the general Zionists were also outlawed the smaller groups of Labor Zionists, Young Zionists, and similar organizations. The other recognized Jewish groups, such as the People's Party (Folkisten) and the Bund, shared the same fate. In the totalitarian structure of the new regime there was no room for diversity of political organizations. All had to fit into the one mold of the communist-controlled Jewish Commissariat and its subdivisions.

YEVSEKTSIIA

Not surprisingly, the organizers of the Jewish Commissariat had difficulties in recruiting the necessary personnel. This is admitted by its first leaders, Samuel Agurskii and Simeon Dimanshtain. It all began when, on January 18, 1918, six Jewish communists met and asked for the appointment of Dimanshtain as a Jewish commissar. Appointed two days later, the new commissar presided on January 21 over a poorly attended public meeting which included some hecklers from the Bund and other parties. He was greeted by such epithets as "Jewish bureaucrat" and "Jewish *pristav* [petty police official]." The opposition aimed its shaft especially at Dimanshtain's avowed program *not* to promote specific Jewish interests. "As internationalists we do not pursue any special national tasks but only proletarian programs." Similarly hostile was the reaction of the Jewish press which, to quote Dimanshtain's recollections, "greeted the commissariat with venom in its mouth."[10]

The commissariat's first major step was, indeed, illuminating. The first meeting of the thirteen regional sections theretofore established, held on October 20, 1918, consisted of thirty-one communists and thirty-three hand-picked "impartial" delegates. It passed a resolution, succinctly stating that "all institutions hitherto operating in the Jewish quarter, like the 'communities' and the rest have no longer any place in our life. . . . All such institutions and establishments are harmful to the essential interests of the broad Jewish masses which they lull by saccharine songs of alleged Jewish democratism. The Jewish worker relies upon the victory of the proletariat during the October Revolution. He takes the power into his own hands and declares the dictatorship of the proletariat within Jewish society." In the spirit of this resolution the government soon began liquidating all existing Jewish institutions. In June, 1919, the Jewish communal organizations were abolished by a decree signed by both Agurskii and Stalin. In justification they wrote that around these organizations were grouped the enemies of the working class and the October Revolution and that the former's policies and educational work nurtured an antiproletarian spirit among their members. Included in the general expropriation of all communal possessions were the real estate and funds held by such national organizations as the EKOPO, the ORT, and OZE, an important health organization.[11]

In practice, to be sure, many difficulties emerged. In one nationalized Jewish home for the aged, for example, the administration had at one time only pork at its disposal. The predominantly Orthodox inmates not only refused such ritualistically prohibited meats but also all other foods which had come in contact with them. As a result, rumor spread throughout town that the old men and women received from the Revolution the blessings of starvation, rather thàn liberation. Always conscious of such propaganda effects, the Jewish commissars organized a central "Committee of Jewish Associations" (IDGESKOM) in July 1920, to which they admitted a number of old-time social workers. But this effort to placate public opinion failed, for the latter soon found out that their views were totally disregarded by the communist majority. They resigned six months later, rendering the Committee itself quite meaningless. It was formally abolished in 1924.

Most important were the anti-Judaistic policies of both the government and the Jewish commissariat. Convinced that all religion was but an "opiate" for the masses, Lenin and his associates had long proclaimed their opposition to any theistic faith. In an essay on "Socialism and Religion," written in December, 1905, Lenin had proclaimed, "Our propaganda necessarily includes the propaganda of atheism." When he came to power, the breach with the existing religious bodies was accelerated by the unyielding attitude of Tikhon, the official head of the Russian-Orthodox Church. Without wishing to enter a regular *Kulturkampf* à la Bismarck, the communists nevertheless managed to expropriate churches and synagogues with all their possessions, though allowing their members to form private religious congregations maintaining their own religious personnel. However, instruction in religion to children below eighteen outside their homes was strictly prohibited.[12]

Religious officials were treated as "declassed" members of society, which involved sharp discrimination in securing housing, always extremely limited, in food rations and jobs, as well as in the admission of their children to schools. Rabbis and other synagogue officials were placed on a par with the other ministers of religion and suffered the more severely, since they did not have behind them the backing of a nation-wide, still fairly well organized Church. Individually, they also suffered much from the general anti-Jewish feelings and public derision. True, we have no statistics of rabbis executed or otherwise slain during the Revolution, while we are told that no less than 32 bishops, 1,560 priests, and more than 7,000 monks and nuns suffered death at the hand of executioners or terrorists. The rabbinic class, too, suffered many losses, but these were largely the result of pogroms which, as we shall see, accompanied the revolutionary upheaval, especially in the Ukraine.

On the other hand, most synagogues were closed by decree. For instance, Kremenchug, embracing a community of 40,000 Jews, had before the Revolution a central synagogue and thirty-six lesser sanctuaries. Suddenly, during the Passover holidays, the worshipers arriving at the central synagogue found its gate closed. In general, Jewish communists were among the most vociferous objectors to religion; one of them, Emelian Yaroslavskii, served as president of the Russian Godless Society which, with full governmental support, spread atheistic propaganda throughout the country. In 1932 the Society had a membership of 5,500,000. The constitutional situation was well-expressed by a later decree of 1929, also included in the constitution of 1936, Art. 124, which stated: "Freedom for the conduct of religious worship and freedom for antireligious propaganda is recognized for all citizens." It clearly meant that one could not propagate religion in any form, but every one was perfectly free to spread antireligious propaganda with every means at his disposal. The program of the Communist Party went further. Issued in repeated new editions, it expressed the hope that the realization of its endeavors

> will result in the complete withering away of religious prejudice. The Party strives towards a complete destruction of the relation between the exploiting class and the organization of religious propaganda, thus effecting the actual liberation of the toiling mass from religious prejudice, and towards organizing a most extensive scientific, educational and antireligious propaganda.

At the same time the Party warned its members not to insult the believers' feelings, "since that would only lead to the strengthening of religious fanaticism."[13]

Such antireligious measures affected the Jews even more severely than their non-Jewish neighbors. To begin with, religion had for two millennia been the mainstay of Jewish life. With all the previous progress of secularization within Russian Jewry and the rise of its secularized national movements, it was still open to question whether any Jewish community could long survive without its religious moorings. In practice, too, the large majority of Russian Jews still were ritualistically observant and few envisaged a full Jewish life without religious ceremonies. Most Russian Jewish children had been attending religious schools; some of the numerous hamlets inhabited by Jews had no other schools, Jewish or non-Jewish. Aggravating these difficulties was the raging ideological battle between Yiddishists and Hebraists about the primacy of their respective languages in Jewish cultural life. Now the Jewish communists, and following them the government, denounced Hebrew as the language of the Jewish bourgeoisie, religion, and Zionism, and, hence, as an instrument of counterrevolution. If, for a while, certain manifestations of Hebrew culture were still allowed, its leading spokesmen increasingly realized that they were fighting a losing battle. Within a few years the Hebrew language and literature were largely confined to a few classrooms at universities, where they were taught as part of the ancient dead cultures of the Near East. Remembering with deep bitterness these efforts which proved quite useless against the overwhelming totalitarian pressures, the Hebrew poet

Elisha Rudin wrote a sort of epitaph for this dying culture in his native land, the "land of prison":

> On rivers of sorrow they stifled our song
> The song of Zion, crystalline and bright,
> Made old and young alike forget our tongue,
> Snuffed out its sparkles of splendor and light.
>
> On rivers of sorrow our tongue was slain,
> How can I ever forget my shame?
> The cup of our sufferings, the honor's stain,
> All that I swallowed in the sorrow's name.[14]

To the argument that Judaism without religion, Hebrew and its messianic ideal, whether in its old religious or its modern Zionist garb, could not long survive, most Jewish communists replied that assimilation was indeed a desirable goal. While the government soon adopted the policy of settling some Jews in areas where they could form a majority and thus be granted autonomous status (the vicissitudes of Jewish agricultural colonization will be described in a later chapter), the official Jewish leaders became increasingly convinced that, outside such autonomous regions, Jews would sooner, rather than later, be totally assimilated. This point of view was clearly enunciated by a leading spokesman of the Party at the Sixth (and last) All-Union Conference of the Jewish Sections which met in Moscow in December, 1926. Maria Y. Frumkina, known briefly as Ester, declared:

> Very likely the process of assimilation will engulf all the national minorities scattered in the cities. . . . Considering the probability of such assimilation, we must, by our approach, indoctrinate the Jewish workers and leaders not to judge each particular activity from the standpoint of national self-preservation, but rather from that of its usefulness to socialist reconstruction.[15]

Assimilation was greatly aided by the dislocations caused by the Revolution and Civil War. Many Jews, uprooted from their original habitats in the Ukraine or White Russia, drifted into Moscow, Leningrad, and other major cities, where they often found little organized Jewish community life and formed early associations with the uprooted masses of other nationalities. In fact, the rate of intermarriage was steadily climbing, reaching within a few years some 25 percent of Jewish marriages in the interior of Russia. On a visit to the Soviet Union in the 1930s the present writer was told that Jewish husbands were often preferred by Christian girls because they had a reputation of "not being drunkards and not beating their wives." True, in the United States with its separation of state and Church, mixed marriages have not necessarily resulted in the loss of the Jewish mate to his community. At times, the gains through conversion to Judaism have balanced the losses entailed by the conversion of the Jewish partner to Christianity. But in Europe, including Russia, a powerful tradition of many generations held true even in the avowedly atheistic environment of the Soviet Union that mixed marriages would, as a rule, lead at least to the raising of non-Jewish offspring.

ANTI-SEMITISM

Assimilation might have progressed much more rapidly were it not for various anti-Jewish manifestations. Despite the public fraternization betwen the Soviet's ethnic and religious groups, anti-Semitism began rearing its ugly head again soon after the establishment of the Soviet Union. These animosities caused concern not only to Jews. Apart from their running counter to the basic socialist ideology, Lenin and his associates sensed in them a great danger to the Revolution itself, especially since the early disproportionate share of Jewish leadership in the Communist Party was being used to excellent advantage by the anti-Soviet propagandists in and outside the country. Certainly, the temporary successes of the Ukranian armies fighting the Soviet troops were in part accountable to the stirring up of the deep anti-Jewish prejudice of the Ukrainian peasants by the anti-communist generals Pavel Skoropadski, Simeon Petliura and their henchmen.

For all these reasons the Council of People's Commissars decided to take stern measures against any form of anti-Semitic propaganda. In an announcement published in *Izvestia* on July 27, 1918 (August 9, 1918), the Council argued that in its pogromist agitation the bourgeois counter-revolution was merely making use of an old and tried tsarist weapon.

> The Council of People's Commissars declares that the anti-Semitic movement and pogroms against the Jews are fatal to the interests of the workers' and peasants' revolution and calls upon the toiling people of Socialist Russia to fight this evil with all the means at their disposal.
>
> National hostility weakens the ranks of our revolutionaries, disrupts the united front of the toilers without distinctions of nationality and helps only our enemies.
>
> The Council of People's Commissars instructs all Soviet deputies to take uncompromising measures to tear the anti-Semitic movement out by the roots. Pogromists and pogrom-agitators are to be placed outside the law.

Although the latter phrase was rather vague, it was the only item which put some "teeth" into the declaration. Ironically, we have later testimony that while Sverdlov, the Jew, prepared the main text of the declaration, Lenin personally added the final paragraph in red ink. He took the anti-Semitic menace so seriously that, in the vein of that declaration, he also broadcast on March 31, 1919, an appeal to the peoples of the Soviet Union and saw to it that it be recorded and replayed on subsequent occasions. However, this address, though vastly publicized abroad, was not published in the Soviet Union until after Lenin's death; it was first included in the second edition of his *Works* in 1932.[16]

Yet as soon as the Civil War and, with it, the danger of anti-Semitic complications for the Red Army were over, the governmental anxiety was greatly allayed. In its execution, therefore, the outlawry of anti-Semitism, which was announced with much fanfare in Western democratic countries —Russia was, indeed, the only country to place anti-Semitism outside the law, a measure in vain attempted later before the League of Nations—left much to be desired. As a matter of fact, the "Statute of Crimes Against the State" of February 25, 1927, subsequently incorporated in the Criminal Code, included only a general provision against arousing national enmities. Even the earlier regular "Collection of Laws and

Government Ordinances" and the Criminal Code of 1922 failed to mention specifically either this declaration or anti-Semitism in general. More significantly, the courts treated offenders quite mildly. A detailed review of prosecutions on this score in the province of Moscow in 1927-28, published by the Commissariat of Justice, showed that altogether 38 cases were handled during the entire year. Of the 70 defendants 10 were acquitted, 3 received a public reprimand, 30 were fined, and 12 were sentenced to compulsory labor, which at that time meant that they continued working at their regular jobs and merely forfeited up to 25 percent of their wages. Only 14 were condemned to prison terms, although their crimes included cases of "assault and battery" or "hooliganism," committed against Jewish fellow-workers. Russian society had indeed traveled a long distance since the first year of the Revolution when Maxim Gorki had voiced the prevailing opinion among the Russian intelligentsia:

> The emancipation of the Jews is one of the finest achievements of our Revolution. By granting to Jews the same rights as to Russians, we have erased from our conscience a shameful and bloody stain.
>
> There is no reason why we should be especially proud of what we have done. For one thing, the Jewish community has fought for political freedom in Russia with much more honesty and energy than many Russians. For another thing, the Jews have produced considerably fewer renegades and provocateurs. We should therefore not regard ourselves as "benefactors of the Jews," for we have no right to such a claim.
>
> By liberating the Jews of the Pale of Settlement from their shackles of slavery that constituted our shame, we have made it possible for our homeland to make use of the energies of people who know how to work better than ourselves; and each of us knows perfectly well that we need people who know how to work.[17]

For many Jews this reemergence of age-old hostility, doubly significant as it had found strong reverberations in Russia's interior where few people had ever met a Jew

before, appeared as a startling confirmation of Zionist predictions that anti-Jewish feeling would persevere in the
dispersion under any social order. As usual, such outright
hostility helped to cement internal Jewish unity, anti-Semitism
thus involuntarily mitigating the assimilatory pressures on the
Jewish minority.

UKRAINIAN POGROMS

At first the Jews had to pay a very high price for these
"benefits" of anti-Semitism. The first four turbulent years
of the Russian Revolution, which were filled with foreign
and civil wars and total instability (Trotsky spoke at that
time of the government leaving it to the "élan of the masses"
to shape the new realities of Soviet life) also witnessed the
renewal of pogroms against Jews in a degree far exceeding
anything known in tsarist days. The main seat of these disturbances, as in the earlier pogrom waves, was the Ukraine
which, now more than ever before, had become the main
center of Russian Jewish life. Its more than one and a half
million Jews, who before the War had constituted 66.8
percent of the Jewish population in the area remaining under
Soviet domination, diminished somewhat to 58.7 percent in
the census of 1926. Yet what took place in the Ukraine
was of decisive importance to all Soviet Jewry.

In 1917-20 the Ukraine became a major battleground for
ideologies and rivaling nationalisms. The growing Ukrainian
national movement had been sharply repressed by the tsarist
regime, but it received much encouragement from Austria
and Germany. Now leaders of that movement, including
socialists, seized the opportunity for building an autonomous,
if not sovereign, Ukrainian state. Combined with this national
uprising was a social revolution of the downtrodden peasantry. At the outbreak of the Revolution 83 percent of the
entire Ukrainian population was illiterate, considerably exceeding even the high general average of 76 percent for the
whole Tsarist Empire. Most significantly, the ruling groups
in the country were members of non-Ukrainian nationalities,
particularly Russians, Poles, and Jews. From these three
nationalities were recruited the big landowners, industrialists,

and government officials, as well as almost the entire urban population, including the majority of proletarians.

Among the non-Ukrainians, the Jews had least reason to oppose Ukrainian nationalism. Many Jewish leaders, both bourgeois and socialist, viewed the prospect of a Ukrainian state, particularly if federated with other Russian republics, with great sympathy. From the outset the Jews were promised not only equality of rights but also full autonomy. As early as July 1, 1917, while still under the Kerensky regime in Petrograd, the Ukrainian Central Council (*Rada*) appointed three vice-secretaries in charge of Russian, Jewish, and Polish affairs. More definitely the decree, issued on January 9, 1918, provided in its very first article that "each of the nations living within the boundaries of the Ukrainian People's Republic has the right to national-personal autonomy, that is to independent organization of its national life through the organs of a national association, the authority of which extends over all its members within the confines of the Ukrainian People's Republic. None of the nations can ever be deprived, or be restricted in the exercise, of this right." At the same time the vice-secretariats were raised to the rank of ministries. Arnold Margolin, a distinguished Kiev lawyer and for a time Ukrainian deputy minister of foreign affairs, could assert with some justice in May, 1919, that the Ukrainian Parliament had granted Jews more rights than had ever been given them in any other European country.[18]

Little did Margolin and his associates realize how quickly these promises would be swept away in the crucible of the Civil War, and that the successive armies in power would pay little attention not only to Jewish equality and autonomy but even to the very basic safeguards for Jewish life, limb, and property. In its quest for unexpected freedom, the Ukrainian peasantry knew few restraints. Often proceeding to direct action against its oppressive landlords and bureaucrats, it also attacked, with even greater venom, the Jews whom it held responsible for much of that oppression.

At the same time the Russian minority, especially the Old Guard, tried, along its well-trodden paths, to divert that popular animosity to the Jewish scapegoat. As early as September, 1917, the reactionary groups issued a proclamation, "Russian people, awake from your sleep! A short time ago the sun shone and the Russian tsar used to visit Kiev. Now you find Jews everywhere! Let us throw off that yoke, we can no longer bear it! They will destroy the Fatherland. Down with the Jews! Russian people, unite! Bring the tsar back to us." During the many ups and downs which characterized the Ukrainian Revolution these reactionary forces succeeded in April, 1918, in seizing for a while the reins of government under Hetman Skoropadski. They immediately revoked the January decree and tried fully to restore the *ancien régime*, including the old Jewish disabilities. Their rule did not last long enough to carry out this program, but their point of view was at least partially adopted by the anti-Soviet army led by General Anton I. Denikin and, to a lesser extent, also by the counterrevolutionary armies headed by Generals Alexander V. Kolchak and Peter N. Wrangel. When, in the summer of 1919, Denikin conquered almost the entire Ukraine, the Jews felt deeply threatened.[19]

As it turned out Jews were even more seriously endangered by the armies led by the Ukrainian nationalists under the socialist Simeon Petliura, who practically lost all control over his armed forces, bent upon slaughter and pillage of Jews. The atmosphere in April 1919 is well described by the novelist, Nikolai Ostrovskii. To a neighbor's question as to who occupied the town on that day, the reply is given: "Let's wait a bit and see; if they start pillaging the Jews, we shall know it's Petliura's men." As later observed by Salomon Goldelmann, formerly a member of the Ukrainian cabinet,

> The complete dependence of the High Command on the will of the officers' corps and the soldiery caused it simply to fear publicly to stand up against the pogromist mood in the army. It had no courage to punish the officers and commanders responsible for the bloodshed of Jews. The High Command was afraid to lose thereby its control over the army. In this fashion the authority of the Ukrainian High Command and that of Petliura, as unbelievable as it may seem, rested upon their sufferance of the destruction of the Jewish people.

According to a fairly authentic report, Petliura himself was
supposed to have said, "It is a pity that pogroms take place,
but they uphold the discipline in the army."[20]

Compared with these two groups, the Red Army could
almost appear as a savior. True, in its initial Ukrainian
campaigns it, too, was guilty of shedding Jewish blood. It
has been shown that no less than 106 excesses were committed by Red Army units in the Ukraine, although the
majority of these were staged by former members of the
Ukrainian or Denikin bands which went over to the communist side. The puzzlement of the average Ukrainian Jew
in the face of this hostility from all sides is well described
by the distinguished Russo-Jewish novelist, Isaac Babel. He
puts into the mouth of his *Gedali*, an unsophisticated Jewish
sympathizer with the Communist Revolution, the significant
query: "The Pole was shooting my kind, sir, because he is—
the Counter-Revolution; you shoot because you are—the
Revolution. . . . The Revolution is a good deed, done by
good men. But good men do not kill."[21]

Before long, however, the Red Army High Command
took steps to suppress such pogromist proclivities of its underlings and it succeeded in reestablishing army discipline. With
the progressive consolidation of Soviet power in the interior
of Russia and its effective struggle against both the counterrevolutionary armies and Poland, peace and order were also
restored in the gradually reoccupied southern territories.
Ukrainian Jewry, too, now began achieving a new sense of
security which it had lost ever since the departure of the
German troops from the Ukraine at the end of 1918.

The upshot was that, according to fairly reliable statistical
accounts prepared in the 1920s, some 30 pogroms and 50
lesser riots ravaged the Ukrainian communities in the course
of 1918. Thereafter, in a constant crescendo, the monthly toll
of 24 pogroms and 27 lesser riots in January, 1919, increased to 120 pogroms and 28 lesser riots in May, and
reached the record of 127 pogroms and 32 lesser riots in
August, 1919. In all, the year 1919 witnessed 685 major
and 249 minor attacks on Jews. The number began diminishing in the course of 1920, whose total of 142 major and 36
minor assaults did not greatly exceed the attacks of August,

1919 alone. In the first few months of 1921 the storm blew itself out completely. The direct loss of Jewish lives was enormous, easily exceeding 30,000 slain. Together with those who later died prematurely from wounds, contagious and other illnesses contracted during these disturbances, the number may well have reached 150,000, or some 10 percent of the whole Jewish population. The massacres thus left in their wake some 100,000 new widows and 200,000 orphans over and above the multitude of war widows and orphans. In addition there was raping of Jewish women and a wholesale destruction of Jewish property, communal as well as private. No less than 28 percent of all Ukrainian Jewish houses were said to have been burned, and 10 percent abandoned by their owners. Ukrainian Jewry would not have recovered from these blows in many years, even if it had not simultaneously faced the great challenges of the new revolutionary order.[22]

Curiously, the very Jews who had effectively fought off pogromists during the tsarist regime, were now prevented by their socialist leaders from employing these tactics. Anticipating the difficulties, some old-time Zionist and religious leaders demanded the organization of a Jewish self-defense from among the Jewish combatants returning from the front. But the socialist leadership, now in control, vetoed this suggestion because it considered it unwise, as well as unpatriotic, to form separate Jewish units. In Odessa, where these counsels were disregarded and a small Jewish force of six hundred men was organized, that combat-ready, well-trained and fairly well-equipped detachment succeeded in staving off all serious attacks during the two turbulent years.

Next to the Ukraine it was White Russian Jewry which suffered much from the pogromist bands such as those led by Bulak Balakhovich, as well as from the invading Polish armies. But its losses were far less severe and its communities could regain their equilibrium much sooner. Upon the withdrawal of the German army of occupation in November, 1918, there was no White Russian nationalist leadership capable of assuming control. The reentering Red Army was welcomed by the urban population then "in the hands of soviets dominated by Russian and Jewish parties, inclined by seven months of German occupation to be sympathetic to the communists." Nevertheless here, too, the Soviet troops found the major centers of Jewish life in a state of abject poverty and total disarray.[23]

It is small wonder that this traumatic experience left a permanent imprint on both the Yiddish and the Russian letters of the following decade or two. With the usual time lag several years passed before the great creativity of the White Russian and, to a lesser extent, the Ukrainian Yiddish writers was focused on the tragedy which had befallen their communities at the beginning of the Revolutionary era. Perhaps the most permanent expression of the Russians' sense of compassion toward the victims of the massacres was lent a dozen years later by the distinguished writer Nikolai Ostrovskii in his extraordinary novel *Kak zakalialas stal* (How the Steel Was Tempered), published in 1932-34. From another angle, Alexander A. Fadeev extolled Jewish heroism in the struggle against the counterrevolutionary army led by General Kolchak, a struggle in which he had himself participated and been twice wounded. In his oft-quoted novel *Razgrom* (The Debacle), written in 1925-26, the novelist depicts in graphic detail the battles fought on the distant Siberian steppes by an outnumbered Red Army detachment led by a Jew, Levinson. So outstanding, indeed, is the role of this Jewish military leader that some foreign translators renamed the novel *Levinson*. In those years, indeed, it looked as if full-fledged Jewish emancipation would become a reality.[24]

❧ 12 ❧

Interwar Consolidation

1924–1939

In 1921, the Soviet Union finally reached a certain measure of stability. After the secession of Poland, Finland, and the Baltic States and the inclusion of the Ukraine, its western frontiers became clearly defined and lasted until the outbreak of the Second World War. What remained still covered an area of almost one-sixth of the globe. Its stabilized regime, though subject to frequent changes in policy and methods, now began rebuilding the country's shattered economic life, particularly through the promulgation of the New Economic Policy (NEP) in March 1921.

The Jewish minority, too, began adjusting itself to the new situation. Its catastrophic economic position, to be sure, was officially accentuated when its majority of petty businessmen and artisans was declared socially undesirable. Even its so-called industrial proletariat consisted to a large extent of petty craftsmen, "bourgeois" in outlook, if proletarian by income. Since at least one-third of the entire Jewish popula tion was thus destined to sink into the mire of "declassed" persons, everyone conceded the need of heroic measures aim-ing at the restratification of the people through internal migration, agricultural colonization, and retraining for "use-ful" occupations. By reopening limited opportunities for private enterprise, therefore, the NEP helped create a transi-tional period for that necessary readjustment.

Simultaneously the new regime initiated a reorganization of Jewish public life to replace the now outworn patterns of the old Jewish community. It certainly was not aided therein by the aforementioned dichotomy between the small minority of Jewish communists and the large majority of Zionists, members of religious groups, and the Bund. Most Jewish members of the Party, moreover, tended to lose all interest in Jewish affairs and to identify themselves more and more with the broader streams of Russian life. It became incumbent, therefore, on the dwindling number of Jewishly interested communist leaders, largely generals without an army, to devise the means for such communal reconstruction.

NEW COMMUNITY

As a recognized national minority Jews were entitled to their own municipal soviets in towns and villages where they formed a majority of the population. None of the large cities fell into this category. But a great many hamlets in the Ukraine and White Russia and quite a few villages there and in the areas of Jewish agricultural colonization qualified for Jewish councils. In many other localities they, together with other minorities, could form mixed soviets. In all these cases Yiddish was declared to be at least one of the official languages.

Not surprisingly, the largest concentration of Jewish soviets was in the Ukraine. In 1925, 38 of the 250 non-Ukrainian soviets in the Ukrainian Soviet Republic were Jewish, equally divided between town and village. In the subsequent rapid growth until 1932, they reached the peak of 168 Jewish soviets (113 in villages and 55 in hamlets). White Russia, on the other hand, handled its national divisions differently. According to Yakov Kantor, the chief student of the Soviet-Jewish national organs, White Russia's program "concentrated not on setting up [separate] national districts, but rather on revamping the entire governmental, cooperative and social machinery so as to serve equally all the principal nationalities." As a result, there were relatively few minority soviets, the Jewish councils but slowly increasing from 7 in 1924, to 27 in 1931; among them, only 4 were located in villages. At the same time the White Russian regime fostered for a time the use of Yiddish on all governmental levels. With greater difficulty Jews established soviets of their own also in the

large Russian Republic. Only its western province of Smolensk had enough Jewish enclaves to justify a few such
autonomous councils. At the peak in 1930 there were 11
mixed and 1 purely Jewish soviets among the 26 non-Russian
soviets in the province.[1]

From the outset it became manifest, however, that these
autonomous organs were not intended to promote the interests of the Jewish community, but rather to serve as organs
for the diffusion of the new teachings of Marx-Leninism
among the Jews. Once again the difficulties were greater here
than in the case of other national minorities, for a larger
proportion of the new Jewish intellectual élite trained in the
communist Weltanschauung preferred to leave its small home
towns and to settle in Moscow. Hence many local Jewish
soviets, still rigidly excluding their seasoned old-time leaders,
even if they happened to sympathize with the new regime,
had to get along with untrained, second-rate personnel enjoying little prestige among their own people.

This shortcoming came to the fore also in the newly
organized Jewish courts, which at first were relatively more
numerous than those of other national minorities. From the
beginning the Party's intention was to teach Jews to repair
to such courts, rather than to their age-old rabbinic tribunals.
During the tsarist regime, as we recall, the latter, whether
employing formal talmudic law or, as was more frequently
the case, relying on principles of equity, were much more
efficient and judicious than the Russian courts. To wean away
the Jews from this ingrained habit, the Soviet Jewish courts
used Yiddish in all their proceedings and likewise tried to
employ common sense, rather than strict legal standards. By
1931, the Ukraine possessed 46 such Jewish judicial divisions,
White Russia, 10 and the Russian Republic, surprisingly,
fully 11. To cite Kantor again, these courts had "eliminated
the rabbinic administration of justice, formerly so common
in the Jewish *shtetl,* and had thus emancipated large groups
of the poor people from the influence of their class enemy."
Of course, these class objectives did not escape the attention
of the Jewish public and helped undermine its confidence in
these organs of indoctrination, rather than judicial impartial-

ity. Nevertheless, at their peak in the early 1930s the Jewish soviets and courts gave a semblance of a flowering Jewish autonomous community.[2]

Jewish, or mixed Jewish and non-Jewish, soviets affected, however, but a small minority of Jews. Even at their greatest Ukrainian concentration only some 14 percent of the Jewish population were represented in these councils. In White Russia, because of the peculiar multinational structure of the republic, their representation was quite minimal. What really mattered, therefore, was the participation of Jews in the general elections to municipal, regional, and national organs.

Here the original Jewish economic structure appeared as a serious drawback. The Constitution of the Soviet Union of December, 1922, basically repeating a text adopted in the original fundamental law of the Russian Republic of 1918, provided that only workers and peasants, that is persons performing "useful" work for society without employing other workers, could enjoy the full franchise. While the exclusion of policemen and security agents of the old regime affected Jews but little, the denial of franchise to all ministers of religion, landlords, entrepreneurs employing other workers, moneylenders, innkeepers, petty shopkeepers, agents, and persons without clear means of support, disqualified a large mass of Jews. In many communities within the old Pale the ratio of declassed Jews even in 1926-27, or some ten years after the Revolution, ranged as high as 45 percent. Children of such persons, even after gaining maturity, were still disqualified so long as they were living with their parents, or were financially dependent on them. Such disfranchisement went far beyond political life; it involved exclusion from labor unions and clubs, even loss of these victims' share in the food rations. It also impeded their means of earning a livelihood and of enjoying a modicum of social prestige.

Not until 1927 was there any major relaxation in these stringent laws. A decree of January 28, 1927, allowed exceptions to be made in drawing up lists of voters. Perhaps it was the result of this decree, or of a widespread practice which preceded it, that in 1926-27 there was a sudden drop from 44.6 percent to 29.1 percent in the number of disfranchised Jews in the Ukraine, although the proportion of such Jews in the larger Ukrainian cities was still very high. It certainly exceeded by far the Jewish ratio of 5.43 percent in the whole, and of 22.77 percent in the urban population of the Republic. Further modifications came in 1929-30, which enabled many small artisans, homeworkers, and unemployed persons to enjoy the franchise because, the legislator argued, they had been prevented from doing productive work by the discriminatory legislation of the Tsarist Empire. Also all Jews who had reached their majority after 1924 and lived from their own productive labor could now qualify. Further concessions were made to those Jews who had fought during the Civil War on the Soviet side, orphans left behind by pogrom victims, and other limited categories, except former merchants of the first or second guild or religious personnel. Finally, those Jews who, as we shall see, were willing to engage in agricultural labors in the colonies assigned to them in the Crimea or Biro-Bidzhan were forgiven for their past "unproductive" activities and granted electoral rights together with their associated privileges. The most sweeping enactment of this type was issued in November, 1930, in part stating:

> Among the persons allowed to be registered at labor exchanges are also those belonging to nationalities which under tsarism had been limited in their residential rights and their work opportunities, in so far as they [now] belong to the proletarian population of cities and hamlets, or are engaged in handicrafts, and do not exploit wage labor either by themselves or through their families.

In this fashion, the Soviet leaders felt, they could partially right the historic wrong committed on the Jewish people during generations of tsarist oppression. These concessions were reinforced by the Administration's actual need of employing more usefully the energies of a large and intelligent population, especially after 1928, when the First Five Year Plan had begun creating serious shortages of labor.[3]

FORCED PACE

Such socioeconomic integration of Jews into the Soviet fabric did not necessarily entail the promotion of their national identity. While still pursuing, on the whole, a favorable policy toward national minorities, the Soviet regime found that the Jews were in many ways an exception to the rule. Stalin, who by that time had become the undisputed autocrat of the Union, had stated his position very clearly in an early article on "Marxism and the National Question," written in 1912. Although, owing to Stalin's antecedents, this brochure focused on the problem of the Asian minorities, it reflected his basic views, even if he subsequently modified them in some details. Here he defined a nation as "a community of language, territory, economic life, psychological agreement (national character) which, historically created and enduring, expresses itself in the community of culture." He made it further clear that, if only one of these characteristics was missing, such a community did not merit the designation of a nation. He thus sharply repudiated the more subjective approach to national problems developed by the Austrian socialists, which reflected the different situation in the Habsburg Empire and which was far more akin to the Jewish nationalist ideologies.[4]

Jews certainly neither had a territory of their own, nor could they be considered a single economic entity. On the other hand, most of them were persuaded that they had a common national character and also a national language of their own. To be sure, the use of Yiddish was gradually declining, partly because of the migration of many Jews from the former Pale to the interior of Russia, and partly because the new generation preferred to speak Russian. As a result, the percentage of Jews considering Yiddish as their daily language (*Umgangsprakh*) had declined from some 95 percent in 1913 to 73 percent thirteen years later. Nevertheless, the national sentiment among the Jewish masses was still sufficiently strong to cause the government to disregard this irregularity, at least for a time.

One of the first victims of this anomalous situation was the Jewish national commissariat and its regional and local dependencies. At its inception this commissariat had to take over the numerous Jewish communal institutions in the field of social welfare and education. But as hospitals and other organs of social welfare, even schools, began to be administered mainly on a territorial basis by the local and regional soviets, the personnel of the Jewish commissariats found itself out of work. Hence, as early as 1920, the special Jewish Commissariat was downgraded to a mere Jewish department in the general People's Commissariat for National Affairs. Under its guidance the local commissariats still performed the important ideological function of displacing the traditional Jewish parties. But this task, too, proceeded smoothly under the totalitarian regime and it was completed within a few years. By 1923, the Jewish department could be reduced, therefore, to a single official and maintained more for appearances' sake than for actual work.

Liquidation of the old Jewish parties also removed the main *raison d'être* of the Jewish sections of the Party. By 1921, even many of the old Bundists and Left Labor Zionists had been absorbed by the dominant party, whereas all the other pre-Revolutionary ideologies were silenced or driven underground. Externally, the Jewish sections still carried on and, in 1924-26, they still met in All-Russian Conferences of Jewish Sections. These offered a sounding board for the few leading communists still interested in Jewish questions. But it became ever clearer that these meetings had outlived their usefulness, and none was convoked after December, 1926. Finally, the local Jewish sections were dissolved in 1930, as explained in the 1932 edition of the *Large Russian Encyclopedia:* "In order to overcome once and for all the nationalist tendencies still observable in the activity of the Jewish sections, the latter had been reorganized into a Jewish Bureau, according to a decision of the Central Committee of the Communist Party of the Soviet Union. In January, 1930, the Jewish sections were liquidated at the center, as well as locally."[5]

Although such a statement in the *Encyclopedia* could not have appeared without governmental approval, it did not necessarily represent a clearly defined governmental policy. Evidently, the much-harassed top leadership of the Soviet Union, if it thought at all of the Jewish question, had not yet reached any final decision. Certainly, the so-called President of the Union, Mikhail I. Kalinin, though more a figurehead than a real power in Soviet councils, still enjoyed sufficient prestige within and outside the Union, for his reiterated pronunciamentos to carry some weight. In a much-quoted speech he delivered on November 17, 1926, at the Congress of the OZET (in Yiddish, GEZERD), the Organization for Settlement of Jewish Toilers on Land, he declared:

> I believe that the drive for settlement on land animating a large part of the Jewish people's intelligentsia and still larger layers of the Jewish poverty-stricken masses, arises primarily from economic necessity and the desire to secure in one way or another a sound economic basis. But if we view this problem ideologically from the national standpoint, I consider it at least possible that behind this drive is concealed a powerful, unconscious mass manifestation: the wish to maintain one's nationality. To me this trend appears as one of the forms of national self-preservation. As a reaction to assimilation and national erosion which threaten all small peoples deprived of the opportunities for national evolution, the Jewish people has developed the instinct of self-preservation, of the struggle to maintain its national identity. . . . The Soviet government, rather than hindering it, helps this, as any other, nationality with all the means at its disposal (and these are far from ample) to achieve these economic goals and the amelioration of the well-being of the Jewish poverty-stricken masses, in the full realization of the importance which such action possesses for the Jewish nationality. . . . The Jewish people now faces the great task of preserving its nationality. For this purpose a large segment of the Jewish population must transform itself into a compact farming population, numbering at least several hundred thousand souls.

True, between 1926, when these words were spoken, and 1932 when the *Encyclopedia* article appeared, there was considerable deterioration of Jewish status and some weakening in both the national drive within the Jewish community and its recognition on the part of the government. Yet Kalinin's words did represent at least one wing of opinion within Soviet leadership, which found expression particularly in the new Biro-Bidzhan project.[6]

BIRO-BIDZHAN

The conception of a Biro-Bidzhan settlement was highly imaginative and by far transcended the mere scheme of agri-

cultural colonization, such as had long been under way in the
European parts of the Union. Devised in 1927 by Jewish
communists concentrated around the new welfare organization, the so-called KOMZET, it clearly aimed at the national
sentiment of the Jewish masses within and outside the Soviet
Union. True, adhering to his own ideology, Simeon Dimanshtain warned, at the very inception of the scheme (March 30,
1928), that "we need a compact Jewish settlement not for
any kind of nationalist purposes, from which we are far
removed, but for the sake of concrete goals which are connected with the general upbuilding of socialism in our country. Under healthier cultural and economic conditions the
Jewish masses will be transformed into competent and
exemplary builders of the new socialist life. Toward this goal
we ought to work energetically while combating all nationalist
tendencies." The KOMZET leaders, without contradicting
him publicly, effectively used nationalist arguments in their
appeals to Jews in Russia and still more to those abroad.
They hoped to undermine the still powerful Zionist sentiment
among the Jewish masses by proposing an alternate Jewish
homeland in the Far East. While condemning Zionism as a
tool of British imperialism, this new effort was presented as a
means of both helping to meet the great economic need of
Jewish restratification and to normalize Jewish life as that of
a territorially rooted nationality, similar to the other nationalities of the Union.[7]

Coming to the somewhat startling conclusion that European
Russia, including the region around the Azov Sea, no longer
had enough space for the development of a Jewish autonomous republic, the KOMZET leaders drew attention to the
availability of vast open spaces in the Far East. They selected
the large undeveloped region at the confluence of the rivers
of Bira and Bidzhan which, covering an area of the size of
Connecticut and Massachusetts combined, appeared to be
eminently suitable for their purpose. Its greatest advantage
was that the Jewish settlers would not have to displace any
native population (in contrast to Zionism which superimposed
Jewish rule upon a large Arab population in Palestine), for
there only were some thirty thousand inhabitants in that

entire district. Soviet propagandists made considerable use of this contrast.

> That is why [wrote M. Seme in December, 1934] we have in Palestine mutual pogroms between Jews and Arabs, Arab delegations appearing before the English High Commissioner against Jews, and Jewish delegations arguing against the Arabs. At the first assembly in the Jewish autonomous region, [on the contrary,] we had delegates of workers in collective farms from among all the peoples of the Soviet Union and we thus [generated] a new wave of international brotherhood. For this reason Zionism is a basis for counterrevolution and reaction among Jews, a meeting place for all their black fascist and clerical elements, whereas around the Jewish autonomous region are centered all the sympathies of the progressive and revolutionary elements in the Jewish masses of capitalist lands.[8]

It apparently required little effort to persuade the government of the worthwhileness of that project. Not only were the propagandistic advantages, particularly among foreign Jews quite obvious, and not only could this undertaking attract financial aid from American Jewish welfare organizations— we shall see how tremendous were the funds spent by the American Agro-Joint on the Jewish agricultural colonization in Soviet Europe—but it would also help to develop the large natural resources of the Far-Eastern region for the benefit of the whole Union. There were also weighty international considerations. In the late 1920s the Union became apprehensive of the growing stream of immigration from across the Chinese border. Overpopulated China had been sending waves of emigrés to all neighboring lands and there was real danger that they would also take over the underpopulated regions of eastern Siberia. Immigration from Korea further deepened these fears.

Before long, it also became clear that a successful Jewish colonization of Biro-Bidzhan would help to reduce the menace of Japanese expansion into the Soviet Far East. As the international situation deteriorated, particularly after the Japanese invasion of Manchuria in 1931, the strategic needs of the Far-Eastern provinces became doubly manifest. The

Soviet Union had to maintain a fairly large army in the provinces adjoining the Pacific coast. Remembering the causes of Russia's defeat in the Russo-Japanese War thirty years earlier and cognizant of the logistic difficulties of supplying its army with food and ammunition from the industrial and agricultural bases in European Russia, the Soviet government considered it doubly imperative to build up nearby agricultural and industrial centers which would, to some extent, resolve that logistic dilemma.

Once again Dimanshtain was most outspoken. In 1934, he declared: "To every conscious participant in the upbuilding of socialism it is as clear as day that it is important for our entire Soviet Union to protect our Far East against any outside intervention. One of the main elements in this undertaking is the necessity to settle that region as densely as possible with reliable, persevering elements. The stronger we are in the Far East, the more remote becomes the danger of war." On the other hand, it was precisely this danger of becoming involved in a Far-Eastern war that discouraged some Russian Jews from proceeding to Biro-Bidzhan and many charitable individuals abroad from extending it their financial support. To appease such compunctions of American Jews, Lord Dudley Marley, vice-chairman of the House of Lords and chairman of the World Committee to Aid Victims of German Nazism, declared that, "speaking as a member of the British General Staff and as one who has been all his life a soldier, I can tell you that no General Staff would ever dream of attacking Biro-Bidzhan, because it would be a sheer waste of time. I should think that Biro-Bidzhan would be about the safest place in the world in case of war, because it is entirely self-contained and, if it were cut off, it could live comfortably on its own produce."[9]

More fundamental difficulties consisted in the region's natural conditions unfavorable to speedy mass settlement, its great distance from European Russia, and, especially, the completely haphazard methods of its colonization. The fierce climate itself, with extremes of cold and heat in winter and summer, would have discouraged all but the hardiest pioneers. But the absence of roads and housing made any development scheme doubly arduous and slow-moving. From the beginning, moreover, the project was bedeviled by poor planning and inadequate financing.

Though the colonization scheme was to start in 1929, some Jews were sent by the Committee a year before, without any reasonable provisions at the receiving end. I. Sudarskii, who in his Yiddish monograph on Biro-Bidzhan offered apologies for the 1928 mistake by arguing that without it the scheme would have been delayed by a year, conceded quite a few other administrative errors. The initial selection of localities, often at a great distance from the Trans-Siberian railroad and almost wholly inaccessible by road or waterway, made the transportation of vitally needed building and agricultural supplies extremely arduous. An expert commission of ICOR, an organization subsidized and provided with personnel from the United States, though generally laudatory about the basic potential of Biro-Bidzhan, admitted that "there are many difficult problems to be solved before the land in its present condition could be transformed into fertile fields." At the same time Sudarskii cited highly optimistic meteorological reports, comparing average monthly temperatures and the average rainfall in Biro-Bidzhan's Birfeld with those of Kharkov, forgetting that averages mean little to a population afflicted by violent extremes. Similarly, he tried to show statistically that a small segment of the Biro-Bidzhan soil had yielded in the years 1909-17, 55 poods (*ca.* 36 pounds each) of summer corn, 59 poods of summer wheat, and 63 poods of oats per hectar. This production more or less equaled the 59.5 poods produced in the Ukrainian breadbasket, and considerably exceeded the average of 54.2 poods of the entire Soviet Union during 1925.[10]

Such optimistic calculations were clearly controverted by the realities, however. At the end of 1929, the local situation had become so desperate that a sympathetic Soviet writer, Viktor Fink, who accompanied the ICOR mission to the Far East, described for the Soviet public the dismal conditions at the Tikhonkaia railway terminal from where the colonists were to spread out to their respective settlements. Originally, new arrivals were to stay there only three days, but since the projected settlements were not yet prepared to receive inhabitants, nor were there roads to reach them, the colonists lived, indiscriminately crowded, in some improvised and unsanitary barracks for several months. It is small wonder, then, that many of the new arrivals returned home, although they found it extremely difficult to secure money for the two-week long trek to western Russia. Those unable to secure transportation, looked for employment in the somewhat closer cities of Khabarovsk and Vladivostok. In toto, we are told, of the 950 Jewish arrivals of 1928, 600 departed. In 1929, 1,875 arrived, 1,125 left. The respective figures for the following years are: in 1930, 2,560:1,000; 1931, 3,250:725; 1932-33, 11,000:8,000. Thus only the years 1930-31 witnessed a proportionately larger increase. In other years more than two-thirds of the immigrants departed. During the entire six-year period the ratio was 19,635:11,450. Although the ensuing slow growth sufficiently satisfied the government for it to proclaim, in May, 1934, that the area was to become a Jewish autonomous region, the Jewish settlers, far from becoming a majority, hardly reached one-fifth of the population. Their immigration had, in fact, attracted also an influx of many non-Jews, a larger percentage of whom remained in the country.[11]

Undeterred, the KOMZET leaders proceeded with their colonization scheme. Despite many disappointments, they believed in 1932 in the feasibility of carrying out a highly ambitious Second Five-Year Plan. In a brochure published by the New York ICOR in that year, A. Kantorovich proposed the adoption of a long-range plan not only to develop Biro-Bidzhan's agricultural resources but also to lay the foundations for big industry. While the cultivated area was to increase from 35,000 to 230,000 hectars in 1937, a number of factories were to be established for the exploitation of the vast forests, the production of building materials and so forth. The lumber industry could, in the author's opinion, annually cut and process 2,500,000 cubic meters of lumber, while the building industry was to establish no less than 18 new large state factories with an investment of 30,000,000 rubles. These and other improvements were supposed to support by 1937 a population of three hundred thousand souls (five times the number of the inhabitants in 1932), of whom more than

55 percent were to consist of gainfully employed persons.[12]

Characteristically, none of the planners seemed to evince concern about the availability of immigrant manpower. Although this Second Five-Year cycle coincided with the world-wide economic depression from 1929 on and the rise of Hitlerism in Central Europe and although millions of Jews in Germany, Poland, and the neighboring lands desperately looked for outlets for emigration, the Soviet Union was reluctant to admit such refugees, even if they were willing to proceed to Biro-Bidzhan. It was but a sop to foreign public opinion that the Central Council of the OZET (GEZERD) adopted in 1934 a resolution reading: "We consider it advantageous to bring from abroad certain contingents of qualified Jewish workers in deficit occupations [that is, where shortages of labor exist], taking into consideration the drive of Jewish workers in capitalist countries to take an active part in the socialist upbuilding of the Jewish autonomous region." Rumors soon spread, particularly in the United States, Britain, and France which, then slowly recovering from the Great Depression, were deeply concerned about the multitudes of refugees knocking at their doors, that Biro-Bidzhan was being prepared for large-scale colonization of Polish Jews. According to releases, distributed in 1936 by the American Committee for the Settlement of Jews in Biro-Bidzhan (Ambijan), "100,000 Jews in Poland have signified their desire to emigrate to Biro-Bidzhan." This clearly was but a propaganda and fund-raising gimmick. In fact, but a tiny trickle of communist stalwarts was admitted to the Soviet Union and practically none to Biro-Bidzhan.[13]

NATIONALIST OVERTONES

Contemporaries explained this Soviet reluctance by general xenophobia and the government's apprehension, lest these foreigners draw unfavorable comparisons between the standards of life and cultural amenities of the Soviet Union and the Western lands. Such comparisons, spread by word of mouth, might indeed have counteracted the rose-colored propaganda dinned into the Soviet citizens by newspapers and radio. But there also were deeper causes. Behind the international Marxist veneer, Bolshevism had always concealed much of its national Russian heritage. Its victory over the more truly internationalist Mensheviks was in part owing to these hidden nationalist mainsprings. In the 1930s came, indeed, a major turn in the general, as well as in the Jewish, policies of the Union. The rising tide of Nazism in Germany, the fulminations of Hitler and his associates against "Jewish" communism, and the spread of virulent anti-Semitic propaganda in all countries—all revived in Russia the memories of the First World War and the German invasion. The leaders realized that sooner or later there would come a showdown in which the weaknesses of the Soviet Union might become glaringly apparent. How uncertain even the intellectual Russian leaders had become was shown on the example of the distinguished historian Eugene Tarlé who had to make a complete *volte face* in the course of a single year (1937-38). While in his earlier treatment of the Napoleonic invasion of Russia in 1812 Tarlé had readily admitted that quite a few peasants had welcomed the French invaders, he had to reverse himself completely in the following year and to extol the patriotic behavior of the peasant masses during the great national war of the last century. Generally, historians of the modern period had to steer their course between the Scylla of historic determinism which traced all great historic transformations to basic socioeconomic factors and the Charybdis of the "cult of personality," according to which the impact of a hero like Stalin deeply influenced the historic evolution.[14]

Almost at once a new emphasis was placed upon Russian nationalism and patriotism, as opposed to the previous stress on Marxian internationalism. The revival of the worship of great national heroes like Dmitrii Donskoi and Alexander Nevskii, who had previously rated but slight mention in history textbooks, was symbolic of the new attitude. When in 1938, the Moscow youth ardently applauded the motion picture *Alexander Nevskii, Pravda* intoned: "They did it because the Russian nation is imbued with flaming patriotism and had been imbued with it throughout her history." Such rhetoric did not necessarily adumbrate a reversion to the old intolerance toward national minorities. Yet this return to prerevolutionary loyalties appeared doubly threatening as, for other reasons as well, the Russian nationality was constantly gaining ground at the expense of the smaller nationalities. The successive Five-Year Plans brought large masses of workers from various parts of the Union to old and new industrial centers, predominantly Russian in character, almost automatically inducing the assimilation of these stray groups to the Russian culture. As an efficient melting-pot the Red Army, too, served as an agency of unconscious Russification. The census of 1939 showed that the Russian nationality, which in 1926 had but a slight preponderance of less than 53 percent, had risen in the intervening thirteen years to 58.6 percent, and could look forward within a relatively short time to outnumbering all the other nationalities by two to one.[15]

This evolution was particularly dangerous to Jews, deprived of the solid territorial moorings of most other nationalities and with more and more of their members leaving their concentrated settlements in the Ukraine and White Russia for the great political and industrial centers of the interior. Anti-Semitism, too, had begun to raise its ugly head more or less publicly; the contagion emanating from Germany could no more be kept out of the Russian territories now, than had been possible during the rise of German literary anti-Semitism in the 1870s. The government's attitude continued unchanged. In an interview with a foreign correspondent in 1931, Stalin styled anti-Semitism a survival of ancient cannibalism. Although such statements may have been made for foreign consumption and were rarely reproduced in the Russian press, they did reflect a certain basic feeling in Party circles that anti-Jewish prejudice could only serve as a divisive and, hence, destructive force.

In practice, however, the police and court reprisals for anti-Semitic utterances and deeds continued to be very mild. In his aforementioned speech to the OZET of 1926, Kalinin tried to account for the disturbing phenomenon of the Russian intelligentsia's anti-Jewish feeling, in contrast to its alleged absence among workers and peasants, by the large influx of Jewish public servants and other professionals into Moscow which created ill-will among their Russian competitors. At the same time he considered this influx "of colossal importance" to the Jewish people. Asked why there were so many Jews in Moscow he answered: "If I were an old rabbi whose soul yearns for the Jewish nation, I would curse all Jews going to Moscow to accept Soviet positions, for they are lost to the Jewish nation. In Moscow Jewish blood mingles with Russian blood and the second or, at the most, the third generation converts itself into regular Russifiers." Much as Kalinin exaggerated the impact of intermarriage, his reference to the old rabbi was greeted with sympathetic laughter by the assembled Jewish communists. This particular audience, to be sure, also followed Kalinin's argument that, for reasons of both the spreading anti-Semitic prejudice and the preservation of the Jewish nationality, large-scale agricultural colonization in concentrated Jewish settlements had become doubly imperative. Foreign communist sympathizers, however, such as the German author Joseph Roth and the Austrian Otto Heller, drew the more logical conclusion that such policies in the long run spelled the end of the Jewish people. Roth wrote with enthusiasm:

> If the Jewish question is solved in Russia, it will be half solved in all countries (there are hardly any Jewish emigrés from Russia, but rather Jewish immigrants into the country). The religiosity of the masses decreases rapidly, the stronger barriers of religion are falling down, while the weaker ones of nationalism can hardly replace them. If this evolution continues, the era of Zionism as well as of anti-Semitism will be over . . ., perhaps also that of Judaism. Some will welcome this development, others will regret it. But everyone must view with respect the spectacle of one people being freed from the shame of suffering, and another being released from that of maltreating; of the persecuted being liberated from pain and the persecutor from the curse which is worse than pain. This is the great achievement of the Russian Revolution.

This statement was quoted with elation by Otto Heller, whose theme song was the forthcoming "decline of Judaism," although rather inconsistently he also extolled the Russo-Jewish agricultural colonization, particularly in Biro-Bidzhan. But

had not, as early as 1919, even a dedicated White Russian
Yiddish poet, Kloinimus, praised highly the total break of his
generation with its past? He himself had declaimed:

> I burned to ashes songs of old
> Long chanted in serfdom's day,
> Tore to pieces the ancient hold
> Of a past, left far away.[16]

Understandably, these major transformations in Russian
thinking ultimately affected also the developments in Biro-
Bidzhan. With the Japanese in occupation of Manchuria and
the Germans knocking at the western frontiers, the Russian
leaders were in a hurry to prepare their army for the dreaded
two-front war. Biro-Bidzhan was no longer viewed as a
primarily humanitarian, or at most domestically useful,
scheme of helping to restratify the Jewish masses, but as an
urgent strategic plan to help maintain an independent Far-
Eastern force. That is why the leaders now embarked upon
a more indiscriminate colonization of that Far-Eastern province, welcoming non-Jews on a par with Jews. They actually
preferred settlers with a previous agricultural or industrial
training who could more speedily develop the local resources.
Instead of appealing to declassed persons to seek social and
economic rehabilitation through that difficult type of pioneering, the government now turned to gainfully employed Jewish
artisans and farmers to proceed to the Far East as a matter
of patriotic duty.

In 1934, Dimanshtain claimed that the task of converting
the Jewish masses to productive work had already been
accomplished. Therefore, "a great proportion of the new
settlers in Biro-Bidzhan consists of workers or artisans recruited [by government agencies] to go there in order to
assume specific tasks." The colonization leaders raised their
sights and hoped to bring 9,000 Jews to that region in 1934,
3,500 families or some 14,000 persons in 1935, and 5,000
families or some 20,000 persons in 1936. The number was to
be halved in 1937, but altogether some 50,000 Jews were to
be settled during those four years. Actually, the number of
new arrivals fell far behind that figure and, while we do not
have exact data on the number of reemigrants, the total

increase in the Jewish population since 1933 was relatively slight. According to the *Emes* of June 3, 1937, the entire Jewish population of Biro-Bidzhan amounted only to some 18,000 or 23.8 percent of the total population of 76,500.[17]

In short, it became quite manifest that this high-sounding scheme which was to outshine the Zionist experiment of Palestine, was an almost total failure. Concurrently with the *Emes* report, appeared that of the British Royal Commission, headed by William R. W. Lord Peel, which for the first time officially suggested the partition of Palestine into an Arab and a Jewish state. Over and above the declining economic strains on Russian Jewry which now found greater employment opportunities in the rapidly expanding industrial centers in European Russia, there was, of course, the basic difference between the tremendous emotional appeal of the Holy Land to Jewish youth everywhere—in the early years of the Revolution even the Soviets tolerated the training of young Jewish *Halutsim* (Pioneers) for the redemption of that ancestral land—and the rather artificial scheme of building a Jewish home in a remote Far-Eastern territory, whose very name Biro-Bidzhan had to be especially invented for this purpose.[18]

Between 1937 and the outbreak of the Second World War the progress of the Biro-Bidzhan colonization was severely impeded by the great purges throughout Russia which victimized also many leaders of that project on the spot, as well as in European Russia (among them Dimanshtain, Alexander Chemeriskii, Frumkina). Unwittingly, Jews became major objects of that wholesale liquidation of the old leadership. Even in the preceding years the number of Jews in the Communist Party, in the sprawling bureaucracy, and in the Red Army officers' corps was steadily declining proportionately, if not in absolute figures. As education became more widespread and more and more Russians became available for public service (in some respects membership in the Party could also be considered such), the ratio of Jews steadily declined. We recall that between 1925 and 1930 that ratio had dropped from 5.2 percent to 3.8 percent. Compared with the Jews' percentage of 1.8 in the total population and their much higher educational level, these figures certainly were not excessive. Similarly, in the Red Army Jews had their normal ratio of 1.8 percent among the soldiers, but 4.4 percent among the officers, particularly in the medical corps, in the administration, and among the "political commissars." Only in general government service, which in the Soviet Union included all educational posts, in banks, and in most other businesses, did the Jewish proportion reach 8.6 percent in 1929.[19]

In the 1930s there was considerable retrogression also in this area. Our information concerning membership in the Communist Party is no longer as detailed as that in the preceding decade. We shall see that even the percentage of Jews in the professions declined. Most illuminating are the statistics of Jews elected in 1938 to the Supreme Soviets of the respective republics. Since such elections were based on single-party tickets, their selection was quite deliberate and centralized. While in the Russian Republic the percentage of Jewish members was 4.1 or almost five times the Jewish ratio in the population (0.9 percent), in the Ukraine only two Jews were elected out of a total membership of 304. This tiny percentage of 0.7, or but one-seventh of the population strength of 4.9 percent, can be explained only by the Party's conscious appeasement of the Ukrainian majority which was now reverting to its anti-Semitic atavisms. This disproportion becomes doubly evident when one realizes that, for instance, the Supreme Soviet of the distant republic of Tadzhikistan embraced fully eleven Jews, or 3.9 percent of its membership, as against their tiny ratio of but 0.3 percent in the population. Evidently, in this and other Asiatic republics there neither existed any anti-Semitic heritage nor perhaps any conscious differentiation between Russian-speaking Jews and other Russians.[20]

More spectacularly, the great purges of 1936-1938 removed the most prominent names among the Jewish leaders of the Communist Party. After the defeat of Trotsky in his contest with Stalin for succession to Lenin, there still remained a great many "old" Bolsheviki in the highest echelons of Party and government. Now the heads of Zinoviev and Kamenev rolled in the dust, Radek was sent into exile, and many others simply disappeared, with or without trial. At the time when Marshal M. N. Tukhachevskii was being tried for conspiring

with the Germans, the Jewish general, Jan Gamarnik, chief
of the Political Administration of the Army, committed suicide. Otherwise he would undoubtedly have joined the nine
other fellow members of the Central Committee of the Party
who were executed, or his thirty-six other colleagues (out of
a total of seventy-one) who simply disappeared. Even two
years later, at the Eighteenth Party Congress of 1939, Gamarnik's successor as head of the Army's Political Administration, L. Mekhlis, spoke of "The Gamarnik-Bulin gang of
spies" who had allegedly done their greatest damage by
appointing traitors to the high levels of the officers' corps.
No less than fifteen thousand Red Army officers were apparently liquidated, greatly contributing to the undermining of
the morale and the organizational strength of the armed
forces at their approaching emergency. These dramatic trials
were highly publicized in the country and abroad, but thousands of lesser officials and Party leaders were executed or
banished to Siberia, unsung and even unmentioned, except in
the closest circles of relatives and friends.[21]

Since in the intervening two decades there had grown up
a new generation of Party leaders and executives, the condemned were easily replaced by persons in whom Stalin
placed greater trust. At the top of the Party structure and
the Council of Commissars there remained only one Jew,
Lazar M. Kaganovich, probably spared from the purge by his
family relationship to the Russian dictator. All of which did
not prevent the German propagandists from still shouting
from the housetops about "Jewish" Bolshevism and from
citing, in constant reiteration, the older, long superseded,
data. If the earlier rise of a number of Jewish politicians and
agitators, for the most part completely estranged from their
people, to positions of leadership in the Party and government, had bestowed few benefits upon Russian Jewry at
large, their sudden elimination as "traitors" to the cause could
only cast aspersion on the trustworthiness of the whole
people. It merely added fuel to, and furnished a convenient
cloak for, the growing anti-Semitic resentments among both
the intelligentsia and the masses.

❧ 13 ❧

Socioeconomic Reconstruction

IN THE FIRST twenty-two years of the Soviet regime the Jewish population underwent great changes, not so much in numbers as in its diffusion through the country. Our information is limited to results of censuses which, from the outset, contained considerable margins of error. The very definition of "Jew" was largely based upon the personal declaration of each individual telling the enumerator to which nationality he belonged. We know that, like Trotsky, many Russified Jews, particularly if living outside the original Pale of Settlement, considered themselves members of the Russian nationality, even if many neighbors still regarded them as Jews.

For the sake of comparison, moreover, the data assembled in 1897 by the last fairly acceptable tsarist census had to be reworked to cover the areas which, after 1921, emerged as definitive parts of the Soviet Union. This task was mainly performed by ORT officials, whose inadequate facilities necessarily left a considerable residuum of doubt. An official Soviet census, attempted in 1920, was never carried through because of the unsettled conditions in many areas. We thus have to rely largely on the census of 1926, which has, indeed, been examined rather carefully by scholars in the Soviet Union and abroad. The next census of 1939 was soon beclouded by the Second World War, although Soviet scholars still had a chance partially to work up its results before the German invasion of June, 1941.

BIOLOGICAL SLOWDOWN

A comparison between the three censuses of 1897, 1926, and 1939 shows that the Ukrainian segment of Soviet Jewry was constantly shrinking. From two-thirds (66.8 percent) in 1897, it declined to but slightly more than half (50.8 percent) forty-two years later. However, in absolute figures it diminished only by about 100,000 persons between 1897 and 1926, and by another 41,000 in the subsequent thirteen years. On the other hand, the Russian Republic (including the tiny Kazakh and Kirghiz communities) more than quadrupled in these forty-two years (from 209,000 to 969,000). In 1939, this Republic embraced 32.1 percent of all Soviet Jewry, overtaking White Russia, whose percentage had dwindled from 18.8 percent to 12.4 percent. Between them these three republics still embraced 95.3 percent of all Jews in the Union. In comparison, however, with the Union's general population, the Jewish percentage had dropped sharply from 2.4 percent in 1897, to 1.82 percent in 1926, and to 1.78 percent in 1939.[1]

The explanation for all these changes is not difficult to find. In the seventeen years before the First World War the tremendous emigration to the Western Hemisphere and other lands drained away a much larger percentage of Russian Jews than non-Jews. During the First World War Jews, living close to the battlefields, sustained greater losses than Russia's population as a whole. This was especially true during the Civil War of 1918-21 when pogroms took, as we recall, a toll of over 100,000 Jewish lives in addition to their generally increased mortality caused by the disturbed conditions in the exposed areas.

More significant was, therefore, the decline of the Jewish ratio in the peacetime years of 1926-39, when the Union's total population increased by some 16 percent, while the Jews added only some 13 percent to their numbers. In part, this retardation resulted from their decidedly lower birthrate. Even between 1897 and 1926 the Jewish birthrate had fallen from 35.9 to 24.6 per 1,000 inhabitants, whereas among the non-Jews the decline from 50.2 to 43.3 per 1,000 was far more moderate. True, Jewish mortality was also much lower; in 1926, it was only 9.1 per 1,000, leaving an excess of births over deaths of 15.5 per 1,000. But the non-Jews had an excess of 23.3 per 1,000. These trends seem to have continued in the following thirteen years. Although exact data are not available, it is very unlikely that mortality should have gone much below the 9.1 figure of 1926, whereas natality probably declined further, particularly in view of the growing ratio of the Jewish urban population. Unfortunately, the figures are not absolutely comparable, because the census of 1897 recognized three categories of cities, hamlets, and rural districts, whereas the two Soviet censuses assigned the "hamlets" to either the urban or the rural category. According to the 1897 census, of the total Jewish population in the larger area of the Pale 48.84 percent lived in cities, 33.05 percent in hamlets, and 18.11 percent in rural districts. By 1926, the urban population embraced 82.4 percent, while the rural Jewish population amounted to only 17.6 percent. Since in 1926 this classification included many inhabitants of the *shtetls*, formerly listed as hamlets, this reduction is doubly meaningful. This process of urbanization continued in the subsequent thirteen years, reaching a ratio of 87 percent of urban, as against 13 percent of rural Jews. All this despite the progress of the agricultural colonization, including that of Biro-Bidzhan. At the same time the Jewish percentage in the entire urban population, then in a period of rapid expansion, was actually declining. Even in the Russian Republic, despite the great influx of Jews from the western areas, the ratio of Jewish urbanites fell from 3.1 percent to 2.2 percent between the two censuses of 1926 and 1939. In both the Ukraine and White Russia that percentage was almost halved (it declined from 22.7 to 11.7 and from 40.2 to 23.9, respectively). In the whole Union the Jews now constituted only 4.7 percent of the urban population, as against 8.2 percent thirteen years earlier.[2]

Nonetheless, there occurred in those very years a most significant shift of the Jewish masses to the large cities, particularly in Russia's interior. While Odessa, with its 153,194 Jews, still retained even in 1926 its preeminent position, it had grown in the preceding three decades by only 10 percent.

On the other hand, Moscow's Jewry grew from 8,095 in 1897 to 131,244; that of Leningrad (St. Petersburg) from 16,944 to 84,480; that of Kiev from 32,093 to 140,256; and that of Kharkov from 11,013 to 81,138. This process continued thereafter with considerable acceleration. Unofficial estimates ranked the Jewish community of some 400,000 Jews in Moscow in 1939 as the largest community not only in the Union but in all of Europe. Leningrad with 250,000 Jews likewise belonged to the largest metropolitan concentrations of European Jewry. Understandably, in such capitals the birthrate tended to sink, as it did elsewhere in that period, while intermarriage and other assimilatory factors operated with redoubled strength. The same was true in a different way in those new industrial centers created by the operation of the Five-Year Plans. Magnitogorsk in the Ural Mountains, for instance, embraced a community of forty thousand Jews, all of them new arrivals in a strange environment and with relatively few contacts with one another. This feeling of isolation was doubtless responsible for the partial failure of the directed emigration of trained young Jewish workers to the Ural region. At the beginning of the systematic planning in 1928-29 only 538 of 1,220 young apprentices assigned to the planned schools actually reached their destinations, and but 350 remained.[3]

At the same time the Soviet Union was confronted by the problem of Oriental Jews who had lived in the Asiatic areas almost from the dawn of their recorded history; certainly, since the early centuries of the Christian era. In the Republic of Uzbekistan, which included the old Jewish community of Bukhara, there still were thirty-eight thousand Jews in 1926, the majority of them of Oriental origin. For many centuries they had valiantly fought against assimilation by the environmental cultures. They developed their own Tadzhik dialect of the Persian language, were for the most part deeply religious, and intensely attached to Hebrew culture. Now they were told that they had to live without their religious tradition, use Tadzhik rather than Hebrew as their national language, and adjust their economic pursuits to the new demands. According to the communist economist Yurii Larin, an official investigation in 1928 had shown in what abysmal conditions some of these Asiatic Jews (often wrongly equated with the Caucasian Mountain Jews) lived, particularly when they left their old habitats. We are told that "when they arrived in Derbend, they dug holes in the ground which they covered above against rain. In these holes these people still live after ten years. . . . One can easily guess their high ratios of mortality and disease."[4] However, these were deep-rooted cultural traits of the ancient Jewry inhabiting the Iranian Plateau and its environs. They appeared equally shocking to the Israeli immigration authorities when the mass influx from those regions came in recent years. But the acclimatization of these Oriental groups in Israel proceeded at a much faster rate.

Another interesting demographic phenomenon was the disproportionate excess of women over men in the Jewish population. If in 1926, 1,115 women were counted for every 1,000 Jewish men, in contrast to a ratio of 1,069:1,000 in the general population, one could still explain it by the greater losses sustained by males during the First World War and the subsequent pogroms. But that disproportion still continued in 1939 when the Jewish ratio was 1,102:1,000, although this time the general ratio had inexplicably increased to 1,087:1,000. One of the reasons undoubtedly was that men more readily left their old habitations and moved into the interior of European and Asiatic Russia, where some failed to register altogether or to identify themselves as Jews. This fact is illustrated by the greater preponderance of women in the Ukraine and White Russia than in the other republics. Here the plethora of female members among Jews actually increased between the two censuses. It amounted to 1,140 and 1,122 in 1926, respectively, and rose to 1,160 and 1,139 thirteen years later. On the other hand, in the Russian Republic as well as in Uzbekistan the two sexes by 1939 had become almost fully balanced at 1,013 or 1,001:1,000. Only in the Turkmen Republic did both censuses reveal a deficiency of Jewish women of 819 or 844 per thousand men. A similar disproportion existed, in 1939, also in the rural districts throughout the Union. Both phenomena doubtless resulted from a preponderance of male immigration.[5]

"Productivization"

Most complicated and often involving great personal and family tragedies was the painful process of economic restratification. Apart from being ruined by wars and pogroms, the Jewish communities now faced the task of transferring the majority of their members from "unproductive" to "useful" occupations. The economic structure of prewar Russian Jewry is well illustrated by the results of the census of 1897. We recall that, roughly speaking, the gainfully employed Jewish population was divided into three major categories: (1) artisans, home workers, and factory workers numbering together 46.7 percent; (2) merchants, petty shopkeepers, commercial agents, and others, 39.4 percent; (3) all the rest, including 2.33 percent of farmers and 4.38 percent of professionals and civil servants. In addition there were a host of unemployed or persons without a steady occupation.

First to be declared unwanted was the commercial class. This transition was not only difficult for themselves but also for the Ukrainian and White Russian Republics where, as in the rest of the Pale, Jews had constituted fully 72.8 percent of that entire class. That percentage diminished during the wars and pogroms because many Jews had died or escaped either to the east or west. In 1921, the NEP temporarily reopened some of these occupations, but the pressures, especially on the small businessmen, remained in full force. The taxes imposed upon them usually were quite ruinous. One case revealed by the official investigation of June and July, 1925, in the district of Proskurov, which had severely suffered during the pogroms, showed that, while the entire stock of merchandise owned by a poor storekeeper was valued at 17 rubles, his taxes amounted to 40 rubles. Unable to pay, he was condemned to a six-month prison term. Other persecutions by tax collectors were illustrated in the small town of Saratov when forty-five persons were summoned to a court seventeen miles away for alleged tax arrears ranging from 9 to 30 kopeks. It is small wonder, then, that "the population compares the methods of collecting special debts and taxes with the activities of the bandits of 1920." The result was that many Jews pursued their trade clandestinely and in defiance of the law. Naturally, if caught in illicit trade, including black marketeering or foreign exchange transactions, all of which highly flourished in that era of great scarcities and tremendous depreciation of the ruble, they were severely punished. The frequency of such trials merely added to the zest of the prosecutors and increased the ill-feeling of the population toward Jews. That is why the census figures of 1926 counting only 125,000, or 11.8 (13.3 in the Ukraine alone) percent of all gainfully employed Jews as belonging to the commercial class, are undoubtedly an understatement. Many of those classified as pursuing "indefinite occupations" and totaling 7.3 percent, doubtless included commercially active persons. Nevertheless the days of the legitimate private merchant, Jewish and non-Jewish, were numbered. According to the economist Genrikh I. Neiman, private retail trade was reduced from its still dominant position of 57.7 percent of all trade in 1923-24, to but 5.6 percent in 1930, to be almost wholly suppressed from 1931 on.[6]

Apart from its economic consequences, the persistence of the Jewish merchant, whether during the NEP period or later, also created much ill-feeling among the non-Jews. Even after the independent trader had submitted to socialization and become a business agent in a state or cooperative commercial enterprise he, if a Jew, became the focus of many grievances of the dissatisfied population. As late as 1935, Jews may have occupied more desirable positions in the socially controlled Ukrainian trade than the Ukrainians, but they were far outstripped by the Russians. Yet in many areas a NEP-man had become synonymous with a Jew and he was so treated in some of the belles lettres of the period. When he later served mainly as employee in a state wholesale establishment or a retail store during the prevailing periods of scarcity, he was accused by the resentful consumers of diverting the scarce merchandise for his own or his friends' benefit. It made little difference that the vast majority of the former Jewish shopkeepers were themselves in a more or less permanent state of starvation. What a Jewish agronomist said at a convention of Jewish farmers in Minsk in January, 1928, about the conditions in the small Jewish communities was doubly valid for the preceding years. He contended that the population of these Jewish hamlets was dying of hunger three times daily, and that its only foodstuff consisted of potatoes.[7]

Nor were artisans clearly separated from traders. Not only had they traditionally engaged in a variety of commercial transactions, such as buying raw materials and selling their own finished products in the market, but some had now found the going extremely difficult and tried to supplement their income by one or another form of trading, mostly clandestine. However, even without such subterfuges the whole artisan class was at first condemned by the communist leadership as "exploiters." This was especially true, since many of them employed apprentices and journeymen; in other words, by definition they lived from the labor of others. But not even craftsmen working only with the aid of their own families escaped the wrath of the impatient reformers.

As a result, the whole class faced enormous difficulties in securing raw materials or credit from the governmentally controlled suppliers and was also subject to excessive taxation. The general trend was to force artisans into cooperatives which were given much more favored treatment by the officials and thus could produce wares both of higher quality and at lesser prices. This favoritism is well illustrated in White Russia, where in 1926 only 5 percent of all craftsmen had joined cooperatives, which were allotted fully 80 percent of all available raw materials. However, this solution which seemed so easily acceptable in theory had many adverse practical effects. In a pathetic description of the economic conditions in the small town of Molcv, which appeared in the Moscow *Emes* of February 1, 1923, the correspondent, S. Margolin, wrote:

> In order to evade the strict regulations, some craftsmen tried at the beginning to form cooperatives [*artels*] and to work by themselves without engaging the assistance of any workers. . . . During the season members of these cooperatives have worked beyond their strength, labored twelve hours or more daily, only in order to produce without the aid of outside workers.

To end these evasive methods of the artisans trying to get along without workers, the district office of the professional associations tried to impose the law of an eight-hour day also upon the artisans themselves, and resolved that no craftsman should be allowed to work after 6 P.M. It was thought that in this way the artisans would be forced to maintain hired labor and, with its aid, keep up the production on its previous levels. But all these means did not save the situation. The artisans preferred to curtail production or even to liquidate it completely, rather than hire workers. . . .

In general the organization of production in our time is connected with so many difficulties that everyone finds it more profitable to trade in merchandise, rather than to produce. The result is that the majority of artisans and workers in Molev spend more of their time in the market place than in the factory. There one can find workers, specialists in various branches, and particularly former leather workers. In short, speculation increases at the expense of production.

Similar complaints were also heard from other smaller and larger cities, except that in Odessa a correspondent mentioned a new practice of entrepreneurs distributing work among many home workers, who labored at their homes under difficult and unsanitary conditions from fifteen to eighteen hours a day. In the shoemaking branch alone there existed six hundred such workers. Outwardly, of course, these laborers could be classified as independent artisans working on their own account. In the very capital, according to one plaintiff, the Second State Candy Factory found itself overstocked with products and sent out its best workers to sell them in the market. The *Emes* correspondent described this situation under the sensational title, "A Factory which Produces Agents."[8]

Quality had also suffered from the generally unsettled conditions during the wars and pogroms which had depleted the available well-trained manpower and opened the road for the entry of substandard producers. The new legislation which discriminated against entrepreneurs employing outside labor affected deeply the very training process of skilled artisans. It has been estimated that in 1897, the approximately 259,000 Jewish artisans consisted of about 50 percent of master artisans and another 50 percent of outside assistants and apprentices. By 1926, the number of such employees had shrunk to 15 percent (even that largely because their dismissal had become very difficult) and in some areas they practically disappeared. For example, in 1924, the city of Minsk had 664 Jewish craftsmen, but only 7 apprentices. According to the census of 1926, there were in all of the Ukraine 126,462 Jews living from crafts, or 20.6 percent of all gainfully employed Jews. Of these only a small minority of 9,471 (or some 7.5 percent) employed outside help, whereas some 80,000 worked by themselves, while 21,000 others worked together with some 16,000 members of their families. Evidently, the propaganda against the exploiters of labor, combined with the fear of sinking into the status of declassed persons, made the vast majority of Jewish craftsmen wary of engaging the services of even apprentices or journeymen. Understandably, this failure to train qualified apprentices resulted in a general deterioration of all crafts, individual or cooperative, because they fell into the hands of many self-taught and ill-equipped persons.[9]

Such perseverance of Jewish craftsmen was facilitated by communal self-help. From time immemorial the Jewish communities have tried to aid their distressed members by extending charitable loans through societies organized by public bodies. From the days, especially, of the Jewish Colonization Association's widespread social welfare activities in Tsarist Russia the Jewish communities had inherited a system of charitable loan banks which were very helpful to Jewish artisans. Even in 1926, the former area of the Pale still had some 300 such institutions embracing 85,000 members. Although now they were dependent on loans from the state banks and their own future was quite dismal—they were to be speedily liquidated by the government—they helped for a time to maintain the hold of Jews on the small private industries. In that year, according to some estimates, 85 percent of all private producers of clothing and 75 percent of all shoemakers in the Ukraine and White Russia were Jews. However, one establishment after another was closed; many individuals found their licenses either revoked or not renewed.

Before long most members had to join the industrial proletariat in state factories. Yet as late as 1941, it is estimated
that some 14 percent of Soviet Jewry (at that time aug-
mented from the annexed Polish and Baltic provinces) were
still making a living from some craft or other.[10]

When one considers that a great many Jews in the remaining occupations also found themselves in the position of
economic undesirables, one may readily gauge the extent
of the economic catastrophe which engulfed Russian Jewry.
Certainly, not only the former wealthy groups of bankers,
industrial entrepreneurs, and landlords, but also the numerous
religious officials and teachers who had formed the élite of
the earlier generations, now found themselves deprived of
the simplest means of earning a living. Because for them the
transition was so sudden and because psychologically they
were least prepared to face the hardships of the dispossessed,
they would have suffered severely, even if the law had not
specifically singled them out for sharply discriminatory treatment as "declassed" persons.

INDUSTRY AND PROFESSIONS

It was a sign of the tremendous vitality of Soviet Jewry
that, rather than throwing up its hands in despair, it energetically set about the task of reconstructing its shattered
economic basis of subsistence. The immediate remedy was to
join industrial labor which was now not only given the
opportunity to earn a fairly decent livelihood, but also
became the kingpin of the new society. Of course, there had
been quite a few Jewish factory workers also in prewar
Russia. In 1897, the Pale of Settlement had already included
46,300 Jewish factory workers among the 547,300 Jews
classified as "workers" in the census. Although the important
industrial centers of Lodz and Bialystok, with their thousands
of Jewish workers in textile and other factories, had now
been lost to the Soviet Union, a substantial percentage of that
Jewish industrial proletariat still remained, particularly in
the Ukraine and White Russia. While the other categories
of "workers," in which the original census included craftsmen
and their employees as well, was gradually diminishing,

factory labor was speedily increasing even before the First Five-Year Plan of 1928. According to the 1926 census, the number of Jewish factory workers had risen in the Ukraine to 40,149, in White Russia to 10,639, in the city of Moscow to 3,768, and in Leningrad to 3,692. In the latter two cities the Jewish factory workers exceeded in number all other categories of workers among Jews. Together with the still tolerated craftsmen and homeworkers this "working class" included, according to the census of 1926, 34.3 percent of all gainfully employed Jews.[11]

Of some interest is also the occupational distribution of these various categories of workers. Not surprisingly, most of them still pursued the old trades in one or another branch of the clothing industry. Nearly one-third of all Jewish workers in the Ukraine (31.7 percent) were engaged in the needle and allied trades. To these one must add textile workers (including weavers and dyers) of 4.7 percent, and leather and fur workers (including cobblers and furriers) of 18.3 percent. In White Russia the percentages were somewhat similar (24.6, 4.0 and 27.2 percent respectively), while in Moscow the respective ratios considerably differed (23.8 percent, 13.6 percent, and 6.3 percent), as they did in Leningrad (30.4 percent, 8.0 percent, and 8.7 percent). The textile workers were, of course, primarily factory hands. On the whole, Jews constituted a very high percentage of all workers in these fields. In White Russia they were fully 72.3 percent of all clothing industry workers; 74.3 and 65.5 percent of all textile, leather and fur workers. Nor was this their highest percentage; it was exceeded by that of the Jewish printers who, not very numerous as a class, totaled 88 percent of all White Russian, and 75.4 percent of all Ukrainian printers. Other important branches of industry with more than average Jewish concentration included the food and metal-working industries, although here, and still more so in the building and lumber industries, Jews often lagged behind their ratio in the urban population.[12]

After 1926, the process of industrialization, which had become the cynosure of all eyes, finally began opening new opportunities for Jewish workers as well. While the available data do not clearly distinguish between wage and salary earners, there was a tremendous leap forward in both categories. Jointly the two groups increased from 394,000 in 1926, to 562,000 in 1930, 787,000 in 1931 and more than 1,100,000 in 1935. The percentage of manual workers in these years rose from 38.8 percent to 40.4 percent, 43.5 percent, and may have ultimately exceeded 50 percent of these totals.

If by the time of the census of 1939 the percentage of manual laborers had declined to 43 percent, out of a total of nearly 1,500,000 Jewish wage and salary earners, this was owing to the increase of Jews endowed with higher technical skills, including many who started as manual laborers and worked their way up to managerial or semimanagerial positions. Although no longer quite so easy as in the early, anarchical stages of the Revolution, when councils of workers often seized factories and appointed some members to serve as managers regardless of their lack of technical qualifications, such rise from the ranks continued throughout the years. On the other hand, managers often found themselves in the unenviable position of being blamed for all failures to live up to some preconceived, sometimes wholly unrealistic, plans. The great labor turnover and absenteeism must also have caused many a sleepless night to bewildered managers. In the early 1930s, the average tenure of a factory worker had sunk to but four months, to rise gradually to a little more than a year from 1934 on. Incidentally, this extreme mobility of workers, which has plagued the Soviet economy to the present day, also places many additional question marks before any Russo-Jewish industrial statistics of that period. Yet, for whatever validity this estimate may have, according to Lev Zinger, the only Soviet Jewish student able partially to analyze the results of the 1939 census, fully 71.2 percent of all gainfully employed Jews belonged to the two categories of wage and salary earners. Together with the other governmentally approved activities in agriculture (5.8 percent), cooperative crafts (16.1 percent) and professions, Jews were thus absorbed in approved economic processes, completely eliminating the original disproportion of "unproductive" Jews.[13]

Equally noteworthy was the qualitative change in the types

of employment. According to Lev Zinger, Ukrainian Jewish miners who, in 1926, amounted to only 0.1 percent of the Jewish wage earners, rose to 3.3 percent by 1936, although they had first to overcome deep-rooted anti-Jewish prejudices of non-Jewish fellow workers graphically described in a play by Peretz Markish and a novel by H. Orland published in 1933. Metal workers doubled in that period from 14.1 to 28.3 percent; chemists increased from 0.8 to 2.8 percent, and so forth. This huge increase was made possible by the rapid progress of industrialization under the two Five-Year plans. Overcoming the sharp declines during the early years after the Revolution, the Soviet Union produced in 1937 three times as much oil and steel, four times as much coal, and twenty-five times as much machinery as in 1913. A number of Jewish names also began appearing among the Stakhanovite workers in various industries. One Avrom Blidman distinguished himself as a longshoreman. In the Moscow Stalin Automobile Works one Perlshtain succeeded, in 1938, in fulfilling his norm three times over. Summarizing these transformations within a mere decade Zinger writes:

> The large absolute increase in the number of workers of the Jewish nationality; their heightened specific weight; their migrations from the hamlets and cities of the former Pale to the central industrial regions of the Soviet Union; the numerical growth of Jewish workers in the leading branches of the socialist industry—all this has demanded that the entire class of Jewish laborers should, within an extremely short period, be catalyzed in the socialist industrial cauldron, should free itself from all petty bourgeois, religious, nationalistic prejudices, and should organically be integrated into the general multinational workers' family.

This staggering task was accomplished, moreover, despite the difficulties generated by prejudiced Gentile workers, "through daily educational work in an international vein" which was conducted in every factory and plant. While one may dismiss such propagandistic rhetoric, the factual substratum of Zinger's assertions reflects at least a modicum of reality.[14]

In the category of salaried personnel were now included

also the majority of what corresponded to liberal professions and communal employees before the Revolution. It has been estimated that, in 1897, there were some 1,500 writers and artists, 4,500 doctors and other medical personnel, 10,000 religious functionaries, 16,000 teachers, and so forth. In the following twenty years before the Revolution there was a great onrush of Jews to colleges and universities, both domestic and foreign, and the number of Jewish professionals increased very greatly. Regrettably, no exact statistics are available for 1917. But it is generally known that, while the Revolution was antagonistic to religious personnel and the legal profession, it sharply increased the demand for doctors, teachers, and government officials of all kinds. The discouragement of the legal profession by the new society did not prevent, however, certain invidious comparisons between the number of functioning Jewish and non-Jewish lawyers. Such complaints were muted under the Soviet regime but came into the open during the German occupation. A Ukrainian newspaper complained, in March, 1942, that of the 250 lawyers practising in Kharkov only 35 were non-Jews.[15]

Reference has already been made to the considerable percentage of Jews in government employ in the early years after the Revolution and their subsequent gradual decline in relative, with a simultaneous increase in absolute, figures. With the progress of socialization more and more occupations fell under the category of government service, including even personnel active in creative arts, whose livelihood now depended on state stipends. Factories and banks were socialized and their managerial class belonged to the upper ranks of salaried workers. An interesting statistical account for the Ukraine and White Russia in the mid-1930s showed that the percentage of Jews in managerial capacity was as high as 20.7 and 24.5 percent, respectively. In addition there was a category of so-called "experts" who amounted to 35.0 and 31.7 percent. Further information of interest is offered by the following breakdown:

engineers, architects and builders	25,000
medium technical personnel	60,000
agronomists and other agricultural experts	2,000

scientic workers (university professors, etc.)	7,000
teachers in primary and secondary schools	46,000
cultural workers (journalists, librarians, etc.)	30,000
artists	17,000
physicians	21,000
other medical personnel	31,000
bookkeepers and accountants	125,000

In other words, according to Zinger from whom these data are culled, there was a two- to five-fold increase in these categories between 1926 and 1939. In short, the estimate given, in 1941, by the Institute for Jewish Affairs in New York may not be too far from the truth. According to this estimate, Soviet Jewry included 1,400,000 gainfully employed persons, of whom no less than 450,000 or 32.2 percent were government employees (this category embraced, of course, the workers in state commercial and industrial enterprises), while 250,000 or 17.8 percent pursued liberal professions. It thus appears that fully one-half of the whole Jewish population in the Soviet Union was concentrated in these two occupational strata.[16]

In all these areas, there was a particularly noticeable increase in the participation of Jewish women, many of whom reached the higher managerial and other influential positions. As a rule, Jewish women progressed much more rapidly than their non-Jewish opposite numbers. For instance, the percentage of women occupying leading positions in the White Russian banking institutions in 1936-37 was 15.4 percent; among the Jews their ratio exceeded 25 percent. In the Ukraine women experts amounted to only 11 percent, among Jews, over 26 percent. This emancipation of the women, as well as the growing recognition of the value of a well-educated citizenry for both the economy and society, was reiteratedly emphasized by Stalin, particularly in his address to the Eighteenth Congress of the Communist Party of 1939. Jews were merely following their age-old inclinations, as well as responding to inescapable economic needs, when they made effective use of the new opportunities for acquiring higher education.

AGRICULTURAL ADVANCES

Another revolution in Soviet Jewish life occurred at first through the growth of the Jewish agricultural population. Ever since the beginning of the nineteenth century Jewish colonies had accommodated a substantial number of Jewish farmers, in addition to many individual Jewish tillers of the soil scattered through many provinces of the Pale. But the First World War, and still more the Civil War and the pogroms, had ruined a great many Jewish homesteads, particularly in the province of Ekaterinoslav, where two Jewish settlements had been totally uprooted with the loss of a thousand lives. Other colonies also suffered severely. Their decline was accelerated by the famine of 1921 which forced many farmers to seek employment in cities. In all, the Ekaterinoslav province, which in 1913 had embraced 10,622 Jewish farmers, saw their number dwindle to 4,263 in the following nine years. Even in 1924, after slow recuperation, these colonies reached only some 68 percent of their prewar population. Equally catastrophic was the elimination of livestock. The number of horses was reduced by 94 percent in 1913-22, slowly to recover to 28 percent of their prewar strength two years later.[17]

For a while the reentry of Jews into agriculture proceeded without any plan. Nor was it restricted to the former centers of Jewish colonization. From the outset the famished Jewish masses in the Ukraine and White Russia seized the opportunity of securing some of the land which had become available for distribution from the confiscated estates of landowners and churches. It was perfectly natural for families to obtain from the authorities the allotment of a small parcel of land in the vicinity of their own residences. While individual applicants were usually given only lots of about eleven acres, collectives were assigned as much as twenty-three acres per member family. But it was not difficult for several Jewish families to get together and form a collective.

In this respect Jews were treated exceptionally well. According to general rules, only actual tillers of the soil were entitled to a share in the land distribution. Yet, since Jews had been discriminated against during the tsarist regime (we recall the May Laws of 1882), they did not have to meet that qualification. This was indeed the tenor of decrees, issued in the summer of 1924 by both the Ukrainian and White Russian authorities, which provided: "During the distribution of the reserve areas of the Republic the requests of individual Jews and Jewish collectives are to be satisfied in the same measure as those of the local population, although the former have not been engaged heretofore in tilling the soil." This privilege aroused considerable resentment among the Ukrainian and White Russian peasants, since the confiscated estates had not sufficed to still their own inveterate land hunger. As a result, moreover, of the general insecurity and economic instability confronting the urban population no less than eight million persons had left the cities for the countryside in 1917-20. Hence the average distribution of land in most Soviet provinces ranged only from one to five quarters of an acre per person. It is small wonder, then, that the Jewish recipients often encountered much ill-will on the part of their neighbors.[18]

Yet starvation in the cities was so great that 22,857 Jewish families, or 112,161 persons, willing to be colonized registered during January and February of 1925 in nineteen western provinces. Up to that year some 6,500 Jewish families had acquired and cultivated land in excess of 122,000 acres. All this was done through self-help, with very little propaganda on the part of the Jewish communist leaders and with little direct support from the government. Some encouragement, both financial and professional, was extended to the new settlers only by the old Jewish social welfare organization, the ORT, which received most of its funds from abroad.

This relatively successful popular initiative inspired the Jewish leaders to conceive a major plan to help solve the complicated problem of the "declassed" Jews while simultaneously increasing the flow of badly needed foreign exchange into the country. On August 29, 1924, they organized an official committee, known as KOMZET (Committee for the Settlement of Jewish Toilers on Land). Headed by a high-ranking non-Jewish commissar, Peter G. Smidovich, this Committee was assisted by a Jewish association pursuing the same purpose, called OZET (Society for the Settlement of Jewish Toilers on Land) and was primarily devoted to propaganda and fund raising.

After extensive deliberations, the Committee selected certain areas in both the Ukraine and the Crimea for concentrated Jewish colonization. In the Ukraine, where the nucleus of old Jewish colonies could easily be expanded, the three districts around Kherson, Zaporozhe, and Krivorog held out considerable promise for a sufficient concentration of Jewish settlements so that they speedily qualified for the designation of "Jewish administrative regions." To emphasize their indebtedness to the Revolution, the Kherson region was renamed Kalinindorf in 1927. Two years later the Zaporozhe area was called the October Region (with its chief settlement in Novo-Zlatopol), while in 1930 the Krivorog region became known as Stalindorf. In all these administrative regions the Jews formed an absolute majority, ranging from 70 percent in the Zaporozhe to 73 percent in Stalindorf and 86 percent in Kalinindorf. But they had close non-Jewish neighbors in large numbers. In this way the KOMZET evidently tried to prevent these administrative regions from becoming wholly Jewish. Otherwise, they feared, the compact settlements might arouse in the colonists those very aspirations for separate national existence which, though postulated by President Kalinin in his aforementioned speech of 1926, they found completely unpalatable.

Central Crimea seemed, both because of its natural resources and its crying need for population, an even more promising area for Jewish colonization. Here the main project was named after its initiator Larin who, with considerable optimism, projected the establishment of a Jewish region of about 1,350,000 acres to accommodate 220,000 Jews. He later raised this estimate to 400,000 persons. Although by 1928 the Crimean project faced the competition of Biro-Bidzhan, it was decided to pursue both projects independently. In 1931, this new Jewish administrative region, with its chief settlement in Fraidorf, embraced some 610,000 acres, of which more than 57 percent were assigned to Jewish colonization. The rest had to be shared with a cosmopolitan group of Russians, Ukrainians, and Germans which, in the aggregate, amounted to 40 percent of the population.

Devoid as it was of any major ideological appeal, except for meeting the old watchword of "productivization," Jewish colonization made excellent progress in the first few years. The Jewish communist leaders made it perfectly clear that, unlike their Zionist counterparts, they did not pursue any nationalist aims. Most outspoken in this respect was the chief of the OZET, Yurii M. Larin, who wrote:

> If the purpose of the creation of Jewish agricultural settlements in the Soviet Union were to consist exclusively in the initiation of small national units in order to perpetuate the Jewish people as such, it would not warrant the moving of a finger for such work because of the total absence of any historical prospects for success. . . . We do not believe that every people must exist forever as a national unit; we believe, on the contrary, that ultimately all peoples will be fused together into one people.

With such an ideology it is not at all surprising that, at the Conference of Marxist Agrarian Political Scientists in December, 1929, he proposed drastic measures against the so-called *kulaks* (rural plutocrats), including confiscations, deportations, and forced labor. Larin paid no attention whatsoever to the ill-will which such statements were bound to create among influential segments of the peasantry not only against him personally, but also against him as a Jew and leader of a Jewish organization.[19]

This exclusively socialist, rather than nationalist, emphasis did not prevent these very politicians from extolling the virtues of the Soviet remaking the very character of its Jewish people. After describing how the previously downtrodden, physically weak and ever nervous and agitated average Russian Jew had become an upstanding, calm, and self-assured citizen, particularly in Biro-Bidzhan, N. L. Semashko, writing under Dimanshtain's aegis, claimed that "nothing of that kind had happened or could happen anywhere else in the world, not even in the fraudulent, Zionist Palestine, for the chauvinist narrow-mindedness and the capitalist exploitation continues to weaken and cripple the working Jew in Palestine."

In practice, nevertheless, the official colonizers stressed the selection of colonists without regular occupations. They tried to retain the "productive" Jews, including artisans, in their old settlements for the benefit of the Soviet economy. During the first years, to be sure, the New Economic Policy which had driven many artisans into mercantile endeavors, did not favor the departure of merchants and other "unproductive" groups. According to a 1924 report in the *Emes*, a majority of 72.8 percent of the colonists actually consisted of former farmers, artisans and workers. The conditions changed totally under the First Five-Year Plan which began absorbing the craftsmen and workers into large-scale industry while increasingly dispossessing the mercantile class. In the early 1930s, therefore, the Crimean colonists included only 7.8 percent of former farmers, primarily those who had tilled suburban plots assigned to them during the early revolutionary years, and 11.3 percent of former workers. The large majority now came from the "unproductive" classes of petty shopkeepers, agents, and similar groups.[20]

Governmental support was imperative at every stage. Only the government could allot land (in 1925-27 it set aside 259,917 desiatins or some 650,000 acres for this purpose), superficially clear it, and provide transportation. But substantial funds were needed for housing, agricultural machinery, cattle, and other necessities; also to maintain the settlers from the time of their arrival to the harvesting of their first crops. If the colonists planted vineyards and orchards, for which the Crimean climate was particularly suitable, the waiting period naturally was much longer. For all these needs the government could extend only limited credit, so that most of the money had to come from foreign Jewish welfare organizations. Next to the ORT and the ICA, long active on the Russian scene, now appeared the most important factor, the American Jewish Joint Distribution Committee, working through its specialized subsidiary, the Agro-Joint. The latter's field work was entrusted to a trained American agronomist, Dr. Joseph Rosen. According to a tabulation compiled by Arthur Ruppin who, as a leading executive in the Jewish colonization of Palestine, had much personal experience but also a certain bias in this matter, the government's outright contributions rose from 400,000 rubles in 1924-25, to 1,515,000 in 1927-28, and to 2,600,000 in 1928-29. Credits extended by Russian sources to the colonists rose in these years from 303,500 to 600,000 and 1,000,000 rubles, respectively. At the same time the foreign Jewish organizations, particularly the Agro-Joint, raised their contributions from 1,851,475 rubles in 1923-24, to 7,140,221 in 1927-28, to fall off to 3,782,000 a year later. In toto, the Russian contributions (including credits) during that first five-year period amounted to 9,072,500, contrasted with a foreign share of 20,447,840 rubles. This disproportion is doubly remarkable, as the Agro-Joint was operating in the Soviet Union without the backing of the American government which had not yet recognized the Soviet regime and entertained no diplomatic relations with it. Equally astonishing is the fact that the Agro-Joint's backers, mainly recruited from the wealthy classes, were discouraged in their humanitarian endeavors by neither the Soviets' avowed aim of fostering the world revolution nor by the no less outspoken Jewish segment of the Communist Party at home.[21]

The decline of foreign contributions in 1928-29 doubtless reflected the growing disillusionment of donors and experts. True, despite great initial difficulties, the number of Jewish farmers was constantly increasing. While the 1926 census counted only 155,400 Jews in the peasant category, the OZET claimed that, in 1928, their number had reached almost 220,000. In 1931, the three categories of Jewish farmers were listed in the following order: 21,870 families cultivating some 1,460,000 acres lived in organized colonies outside Biro-Bidzhan; 9,700 families continued to till almost 300,000 acres in the old-time Jewish colonies; 20,340 families still clung to their suburban land totaling a little more than 300,000 acres. If these figures are correct, 51,910 families, or approximately 250,000 souls, derived their livelihood from farming in European Russia. This ratio of some 9 percent of the Jewish population was unmatched elsewhere, except among the Jews of Carpatho-Ruthenia, then under Czechoslovak domination, and in the rapidly expanding Zionist colonization of Palestine. If continued, this movement might indeed have revolutionized the Jewish economic structure, a doubly remarkable feat as it would have reversed the general modern historic trend from the village to the city. Such a reversal, long preached by nationalistic Jewish leaders, had nowhere else been attained in any substantial degree.[22]

Nor was it really attained in the Soviet Union which, in the 1930s, witnessed a major retrogression. While none of the schemes was formally abandoned, many were allowed to wither away gradually. Doubtless the most important single reason was the progressive industrialization of the Soviet Union during its first two Five-Year Plans which had drawn a multitude of farmers into the industrial centers. We have seen how actively Jewish workers and intelligentsia participated in the upbuilding of the Russian industries during the 1930s. The gradual absorption of the former declassed persons into the economic stream dried up the major source of manpower for the colonization schemes. The failure of agricultural crops, particularly during the great famine of 1932, discouraged Jewish colonists, especially in the more recently established settlements devoid of reserves from earlier years. The disillusionment of the foreign welfare workers and the attrition of the financial contributions from abroad also played a role.

As a result, by 1939, there probably remained less than 25,000 families or 175,000 persons still qualifying for the designation of a Jewish agricultural population. Notwithstanding the glaring fanfare over more than a decade, Biro-Bidzhan's 3,000 families were not only outnumbered by the 5,000 living in the Crimea and the 8,500 in the three administrative regions of the Ukraine, but also by the 7,000 estimated to have continued tilling the soil in scattered collective farms in the western republics. In short, the share of Jewish farmers had thus dropped back to little more than the 6 percent counted in the census of 1926.

On the other hand, the intervening peaceful years enabled the more recent agricultural population to take deeper roots in the soil and to increase its agricultural production, both quantitatively and qualitatively. Some Jewish farmers again started winning prizes at agricultural displays. For instance, at the All-Union Agricultural Exhibition of 1939-40, there appeared no less than two hundred Jewish collective farmers from the Ukrainian regions. One of them won the honor prize, another a small gold medal, eight others small silver medals, and so forth. Ironically, some of the greatest progress was made in the breeding of pigs. In the Kalinindorf region, for instance, during a year and a half in 1935-36 the number of horned cattle rose from 3,363 to 4,223; that of horses from 1,715 to 2,091. In contrast thereto, the respective figures for porkers are 1,990 and 4,798, or an increase of almost 150 percent.[23]

Were it not for a similar upsurge in the breeding of sheep, one might almost have assumed that these Jewish farmers had done it out of spite for their religious tradition. In fact, however, they merely followed the dictates both of their economic necessities and of the Party. It was precisely in those years of 1939-40 that the entire governmental apparatus was making strenuous efforts to force the collective farmers to increase their production to meet certain very high goals. On May 27, 1939, it was provided that any collective farmer who had not fulfilled the required minimum of 60-100 working days a year should be expelled and his property confiscated. Similarly, the previous maximum of 9.6 hours of work during the harvest season was replaced in 1940 by the requirement to start at five or six in the morning and to continue until sunset. Jewish farmers could no more escape that pressure than did their non-Jewish neighbors.

❦ 14 ❦

Cultural Attrition

IF IN THE SOCIOECONOMIC SPHERE Soviet Jewry showed a remarkable degree of pliability and creative adjustment, its cultural achievements proved inadequate to meet the new challenge. True, one could argue that the general cultural level among Jews had not declined and that they merely exchanged their traditional Jewish for new Russian cultural values. Certainly, if there had been little illiteracy in the pre-Revolutionary community, there was even less of it two decades after the Revolution. Women, in particular, whose cultural advance was retarded in the traditional Jewish educational system, were now given full intellectual opportunities. However, any specific Jewish cultural identity was greatly diluted and by 1939 Jewry as such was in a state of intellectual stagnation.

Moreover, the socioeconomic adjustments consisted primarily in the Jews abandoning their traditional middle-men's pursuits in favor of industrial labor, agriculture, and civil service. They thus merely fulfilled the wishes voiced by their own leaders in Russia and elsewhere for two centuries. In the cultural sphere, on the other hand, assimilation to the cultures of the environment was desired only by a small minority of Jews. True, enlightened leaders viewed a modicum of assimilation as an historic necessity. But even the progressive East-European thinkers regarded it as mainly a means of modernizing their national culture. Now, however, under the instigation of the Jewish communists with their deep-rooted hatred for the basic traditional Jewish values in religion, Hebrew, and Zionism, the Russian government and society turned quite hostile to the preservation of any of these traditional moorings of Jewish culture.

YIDDISH SCHOOLS

Invoking the fact that Yiddish had been the spoken language of some 97 percent of Russian Jews back in 1897, the new regime now elevated it to the rank of a national language, the official language of the Jewish national minority. The new Soviet-Jewish school, intended to serve that national minority, had to use Yiddish as its language of instruction. There was some conflict in this matter with the Bukharan and other Asiatic Jews, the old-time Krimchaks, and others who had never spoken Yiddish. The aforementioned substitution of the Tadzhik Jewish dialect for Hebrew in Bukharan-Jewish schools elicited immediate protests. After all, unlike Yiddish, Tadzhik had practically no cultural history of its own and no worthwhile literature to replace the Hebrew letters as a proper medium for education. Remarkably, the local Turkestan communists sharply opposed the introduction of either Tadzhik or Yiddish, as was propagated by the local branch of the *yevsektsiia*. In a joint meeting of the Tashkent Jewish Professional Association and the Fourth Section of the Russian Communist Party of September 14, 1919, the 323 members present adopted a sharp resolution against the introduction of the Farsi or Tadzhik language into the local Jewish schools. They demanded that the pertinent decree be immediately revoked and that Hebrew become the language of instruction; "otherwise not one pupil will be sent to school. We find it necessary to warn in this connection that no manner of force will stifle in us the desire to educate our children in the Hebrew language as we demand." This extraordinary insistence of a communist group prevailed for a time, but ultimately Hebrew instruction had to give way to that offered in Russian and Turkmen schools which before long were attended by the large majority of Jewish children.[1]

Jewish communist leadership ran roughshod over all such protests. Its purpose was, in fact, not so much the preservation of Jewish culture through the medium of Yiddish or

Tadzhik, but rather the use of these linguistic media for the indoctrination of both children and adults in the communist principles and world outlook. Summarizing the achievements of Soviet Jewish education during the first fifteen years after the Revolution, a communist educator, Judah Dardak, contended:

> Assisted by all means at the government's disposal, the school won one victory after another. First, the Sabbath day of rest was abolished. Secondly, all books with a nationalist coloring were removed. These steps enabled the school to raise the level of instruction and to include anti-religious and international subject matter in its curriculum. Work in school follows the general program of the People's Commissariat for Education. The very concept of "Jewish history" is alien to the school. Any general course in the history of the class struggles may include sections describing the struggle of Jewish artisans against their employers and of Jewish workers against the Jewish or any other bourgeoisie. All subjects are taught in the [pupils'] mother tongue [Yiddish] and a special course in Yiddish literature is also given.[2]

Naturally, the first victim of this new trend was the old-type religious *heder* and *yeshivah*, the primary, secondary, and schools of higher learning, developed by the Jewish community over a period of two thousand years. True, despite their outlawry they found enough devotees among teachers and parents to maintain themselves for many years. The main organ of the Jewish communists, the Moscow newspaper, *Emes*, admitted that, as late as 1927, many such schools still operated in smaller towns. In the Ukraine only some 60 percent of the Jewish school population at that time attended either the general or the Yiddish public schools (in a ratio of 51:49 percent), the rest largely consisting of pupils of the traditional types of religious teachers. Elsewhere, however, the latter were speedily losing ground. In White Russia more than 87 percent of Jewish school-children between 8 and 14 years of age went to public schools, also almost one-half (47.3 percent) to schools with the Yiddish language of instruction. There also existed Yiddish secondary schools, but not such of higher learning. While some of the major universities in Moscow, Kiev, Kharkov, and Minsk maintained sectors for Yiddish studies, these were intended only for students specializing in these fields. In all, during 1927, fully 111,377 Jewish pupils were registered in Yiddish schools, as against 180,420 in general public schools. This ratio of 38.2:61.8 percent was sufficiently high for many Jewishly interested communists in the Union and abroad to contrast it with the situation in Western Europe and America, where the vast majority of Jewish children attended non-Jewish schools.[3]

In fact, however, the Yiddish school differed from the general Soviet school in form, rather than in substance. The basic curriculum was the same, except that the Yiddish language and literature constituted one of the required subjects. Even in the selection of Yiddish literary creations, communist rather than Jewish criteria were employed. If among the great literary figures Sholem Aleikhem and Mendele were paid particular attention, this preference was in part owing to their satirical descriptions of the ghetto community which could be used as a foil for contrast with the achievements of Soviet society.

Indoctrination offered by the Yiddish school was considered so valuable that, according to Yakov Kantor's testimony, the authorities forced Jewish children in many localities to attend that school even if their parents preferred a school with another language of instruction. Of course, in some smaller localities in the Ukraine, White Russia, and the Jewish agricultural colonies, where Jews formed the majority of the population, there often was no alternative. In contrast thereto in the Russian Republic, which included the large Jewish communities of Moscow and Leningrad, fully 97 percent of the entire Jewish school population was registered in government schools (there was practically no *heder* or *yeshivah* available there), including some 8 percent who attended Yiddish schools. These were about equally divided between the twenty-one so-called "primary" four-year schools, and the somewhat more advanced eight seven-year schools functioning in the entire republic in 1926-27. Even in the western republics there was a difference between the major cities and smaller localities. In Odessa, for example, where the Jewish minority amounted to 36.4 percent of the population, only 9 percent of all pupils enrolled in Yiddish schools. In Kharkov the discrepancy was even greater: with a population ratio of 19.4 percent, that of pupils in Yiddish schools was but 2.9 percent.[4]

The statistics for the large cities are given only for 1933, and no reliable data are available for the later prewar years. But there is no question about the progressive diminution of enrolment in the Yiddish schools during that period. From the outset the Jewish school system had to contend with a severe shortage of well-trained teachers in both pedagogy and Jewish subjects. From replies to a questionnaire circulated among the White Russian Yiddish teachers in 1925, it appears that only some 14 percent had received any pedagogic training whatsoever. The majority was also so blatantly ignorant of Jewish lore as to give rise to frequent complaints in the Yiddish papers. These deficiencies could not be made up by the newly improvised seven Jewish teachers' seminaries and several university sectors, with their maximum of three hundred graduates a year. Using data scattered over many publications, Jacob Lestchinsky estimated that in the Ukraine enrolment in Yiddish schools had dropped from 94,872 in 1930-31, to 73,412 four years later. The relative decline was even greater: from 46.6 to 32.5 percent. In White Russia, where the registration in such schools had reached the peak of 36,650 pupils in 1932, it shrank to approximately 30,000 in the subsequent five years. This deterioration of the Yiddish school system continued unabated. Even many functioning schools found themselves doomed when their first grades were discontinued because of insufficient enrolment. School boards often tended to merge the Yiddish with the Ukrainian or White Russian schools, while leaving Yiddish as a subject in the curriculum, which really meant that the Yiddish school was abolished. In all, according to Lestchinsky's estimates, in 1940, altogether 85,000-90,000 children attended schools with the Yiddish language of instruction (including 3,000 in Biro-Bidzhan). This decline was doubly significant as it coincided with the general rapid increase in the school enrolment throughout the Union, which Stalin praised in his address to the Eighteenth Congress of the Communist Party in 1939. It was in part owing to the mobility of the population and the transfer of increasing numbers of Jews from the western republics to the interior of Russia. In part, however, it was the result of progressive assimilation, whether voluntary or under the pressure of the growing Russian, Ukrainian and other nationalisms in reaction to the ever tenser world situation.[5]

All along the Jewish enrolment in schools of higher learning increased by leaps and bounds; it rose from 9.4 percent under tsarist oppression to 16 percent in 1926-27. That even here Jews preferred certain branches of study over others is not at all surprising. In White Russia and the Ukraine they constituted no less than 46.6 and 44.8 percent, respectively, of all students attending medical schools. In the Russian Republic, too, their ratio of 11.2 percent of all medical students was wholly out of proportion to their population strength. Next to medicine the most popular subjects were economics (47.8, 32.1, and 18 percent, respectively, in the three republics); industry and technology (no data for White Russia, but 31.9 and 14.6 percent in the two other republics), teaching and art. Curiously, agronomy and related subjects, which played such a tremendous role in the propaganda for Jewish restratification, attracted far fewer students (12.4, 8.0, 3.9 percent). After 1927, the general enrolment in schools of higher learning so greatly increased that the Jewish percentage in most branches of learning decreased substantially. According to Zinger, in 1938, Jews formed only 13 percent of the student bodies at universities and colleges and 5 percent in technical schools. But in absolute numbers, as well as in its ratio to the total Jewish population, Jewish enrolment was still growing rapidly.[6]

HEBREW PUBLICATIONS

Other cultural media, too, claimed much of the government's attention. Books, pamphlets, and periodicals now appeared in ever greater profusion, largely from the governmental-owned printing presses and publishing firms. The theater, both in Russian and in the minority languages, also received much greater government support. The Yiddish press, literature, and stage now also achieved a circulation or attendance undreamed of before.

During the first unsettled years of the Revolution the will of the people still favored Hebrew publications which had suffered greatly during the First World War. The afore-mentioned outlawry of any publication in Hebrew letters within the military zone had extended over the entire Pale of Jewish Settlement and beyond. But as soon as the demo-cratic republic was established in 1917, Hebrew writers and publishers made use of the new freedom of the press and issued a substantial number of Hebrew periodicals and books. Characteristically, Moscow, though not yet the official capital of Russia, became, next to Odessa, the greatest center of Hebrew culture. This was owing to the residence there of many Hebrew poets, writers, and scholars, as well as of wealthy Jewish patrons, especially the Hillel Zlatopolsky-Shoshana Persitz family and Abraham Stybel, who lavished much of their rapidly growing wealth on fostering Hebrew-language publications.

Beginning in July, 1917, a Hebrew daily *Ha-Am* (The People) began appearing in Moscow despite the paucity of Hebrew readers in the capital and the difficulties of com-munication with the· provinces. The number of subscribers never exceeded fifteen thousand, not enough· to maintain a daily paper. Nevertheless, after a brief interruption during the October Revolution, the journal resumed publication, first as a weekly and then again as a daily. Its days were numbered, however, especially since it was overtly critical of the new regime. On December 7, 1917, Benzion Katz fearlessly wrote in his editorial: "The Russian Revolution surpasses in its savagery all the negative features of the French Revolution. . . . We have only one hope that the reign of this new Inquisition will not last very long." The newspaper had to suspend publication in June, 1918, while its personnel looked for avenues of emigration.

It was far easier to publish annuals, quarterlies, and other collections. Some of these materials had been available before the War but could not be published owing to the tsarist re-strictions. An excellent collection, styled *Keneset* (Assembly)

and edited by Chaim Nachman Bialik, had been ready for
the printer in 1915. The important periodical *Reshumot*
(Sketches), devoted to folklore and ethnography, had actually been set up in the same year. But neither saw the light
of day until 1917. As a bibliographical curiosity, a volume
on the history of the Lovers of Zion movement appeared
in print with the title page bearing the date of 1914, while
the wrapper gave the real year of 1919. Probably the most
important of these periodical publications was the *Hatekufah,*
a quarterly established by Stybel, of which the first three
volumes of some 700 pages each appeared in Moscow in
1918. Published in an attractive format, it gathered around
it the chief Hebrew literary talents. Unlike most of the other
publications, this quarterly survived its suspension by the
communist regime; together with its sponsor, it emigrated
to Warsaw where it continued to be published, if less frequently, during most of the interwar period. The yearbook
Keneset, on the other hand, which, after a lapse of many
years began reappearing in Palestine, was but a spiritual heir
to Bialik's original collection.[7]

In regard to Hebrew books, Odessa retained its primacy
for a time. True, at first publication of Hebrew works was
extremely difficult. In a pathetic letter of September, 1917,
Bialik tried to explain to David Frischman the reasons why
his publishing firm, the *Moriah,* was unable to carry out its
original program: "The price of paper is two rubles a pound
instead of ten kopecks. Good printing font is not available,
nor are workers or Hebrew printing presses. There simply
is nothing here, and who is able to work under such conditions?" Eight months later he still commented that "the printing of a Hebrew book is more difficult than the parting of
the Black Sea." Nevertheless, according to Y. Slutski's recent,
probably incomplete, tabulation, 119 Hebrew works were
published there in 1917-19, out of a total of 188 titles in all
of Russia. Moscow was second with 25 publications, closely
followed by Kiev with 18.[8]

However, Odessa's preponderance stemmed mainly from
textbooks and children's literature, the growth of which was
truly phenomenal. During the early Revolutionary years the
Zionist intelligentsia energetically set out to erect a modern

school system with the Hebrew language of instruction. A society, *Tarbut* (Culture), founded early in 1917, immediately undertook to establish a number of Hebrew elementary schools, to be followed by secondary schools and other educational institutions. Its career was cut short by the suppression of Hebrew instruction by the Jewish communists, but it survived outside the Union, celebrating great victories even under the unfriendly regime of interwar Poland. It was most effective in the new Republic of Lithuania where the majority of the Jewish school population attended *Tarbut* schools. But as long as it lasted in the Soviet Union, the *Tarbut* society made strenuous efforts to supply the new schools with both trained teaching personnel and textbooks. No lesser a person than Bialik participated in this popularizing effort, he himself authoring ten thin pamphlets intended for children. So sanguine were these Hebrew leaders of the future of their educational system that one of their major efforts, particularly sponsored by the Stybel publishing firm, consisted of a gigantic program of translations into Hebrew of the great classics of world literature. Remarkably, they assumed that their reading public also required translations of the great Russian authors; no less than three volumes by Tolstoy appeared in a Hebrew rendition during that short-lived flowering of the Hebrew book after the Revolution.

All these enthusiastic efforts came to naught in 1919 when, with the outlawry of Zionism and "clericalism," also came the suppression of the Hebrew book. All Hebrew presses were speedily nationalized and converted to the use of Yiddish publications serving communist aims. The distinguished Hebrew writers now lost their means of subsistence and were deprived of all opportunities for creative work. Only some of them were fortunate enough to join Bialik who, in 1921, had obtained the permission for himself and a group of associates to emigrate to Palestine.[9]

Remarkably, the old-type rabbinic literature which, for a time, lagged far behind, proved somewhat more enduring. Before the War its publications (including ethical and Hasidic writings) far exceeded in both numbers and readership the other Hebrew or Yiddish letters. However, most of the publishing firms specializing in this branch were concentrated in Warsaw and Vilna, now lost to the Soviet Union. Probably the existing supply at least of the older classics and handbooks accumulated in synagogues and private libraries still was sufficiently large. Later when the needs of the ever dwindling Orthodox population could no longer be satisfied, zealous men found ways and means to publish some such books, long after the more modern Hebrew letters had been outlawed.

Making use of the small freedoms granted by the New Economic Policy, some enterprising small-town publishers succeeded in distributing many liturgical works (needed in both synagogues and Orthodox homes), calendars and such. Jacob Ginzburg of Bobruisk was resourceful enough to secure from the reluctant communist authorities not only the necessary permits but also the more difficult allotment of printing paper. One of his stratagems was to establish printing presses in several localities, including Plotsk, Minsk, and Poltava, so as to require less paper for each press. The *Komsomolskaia Pravda* of April 10, 1928, commented, with a sigh bordering on admiration, on Ginzburg's success in distributing no less than 100,000 copies of Hebrew liturgical works in the single year of 1927-28. "He has at his disposal alert booksellers who deliver his books directly to the houses of believers. No agent of our publishing firms is able to compete with them in their talent to distribute books." The Hebrew calendars published by these small firms almost became best-sellers; that for 1927-28 allegedly sold in 75,000 copies. However, all such "alarmist" reports of the communist press, though testifying to the continued vitality of the Jewish and other religions in the Soviet Union after a decade of Godless propaganda, could not gloss over the constant attrition of the traditional institutions. In another issue (of June 22, 1928) the same *Komsomolskaia Pravda* described the "disquieting" religious situation in Kiev and, among other matters, reported that "lately an underhand, hidden Jewish khedera [doubtless referring to the traditional Jewish school, the *heder*] has begun to be widely spread; also so-called 'Tribunals of the Rabbis'; here dozens of Jewish children are being influenced in a certain direction; here also the 'faith-

ful' seek protection, advice, and help!" But, in the long run,
that feverish activity, whether overt or clandestine, led
only to a dead-end street: in the 1930s practically no Hebrew
works of any kind were allowed to appear in the Soviet
Union.[10]

YIDDISH LETTERS AND THEATER

Output of Yiddish letters was incomparably larger. From
the outset the Jewish communist leaders felt the need of
supplying the Yiddish-speaking public with books and periodicals in their own language. Moreover, since the state took
pride in its lavish support of culture, the publishing firms
did not have to calculate sales and profit possibilities. Authors, too, were assured of their governmental stipends
regardless of the number of copies sold. Those whose sales
reached high figures, often going into hundreds of thousands,
received additional royalties which frequently placed them in
the category of best-paid officials. While such vast distribution was usually attained only in Russian or Ukrainian, the
sales of some Yiddish books also exceeded anything known in
the West. In this respect the Soviet Yiddish writers could
claim primacy over their confreres in the two other great
centers of Yiddish culture, Poland and the United States.

Regrettably, the various statistical accounts of Yiddish
books published in the Soviet Union are neither complete nor
fully comparable. The relatively best data are offered for the
years 1932-35 by N. Rubinshtain in annual bibliographical
surveys. But published under state auspices in Minsk, they,
too, had to omit books interveningly condemned by the Party
as exponents of "Trotzkyite and counterrevolutionary propaganda." The constant quantitative rise in titles, sizes of books,
and their aggregate circulation came to a halt in 1932-33;
it was followed by a steady decline. According to these data,
the 1928 total of 238 Yiddish books published in 1,368 sheets
(of 16 pages each) with an aggregate circulation of 875,000,
rose four years later to 653 titles, 3,087 sheets, and 2,558,585
circulation. In 1933, titles reached the record figure of 668,
but we are not told about their sizes or circulation. The
reversal came suddenly when in 1934 there appeared only

348 titles in 2,424 sheets and with a circulation of 1,551,880 copies. Compared with other languages, moreover, the Yiddish output became disproportionately small. In the Ukraine the 426 Yiddish titles, published in 1934-36 and distributed in 1,983,695 copies, amounted to only 3.1 percent of all titles and less than 1 percent of the general circulation, while Jews still numbered more than 5 percent of the population.[11]

As in many other fields, the Yiddish publications were often concentrated in large publishing firms. The single publishing house *Emes* in Moscow could boast of producing, in the five-year period of 1933-37, no less than 852 Yiddish titles with a circulation of 6,240,925. A breakdown in the subject matter of these publications by years and fields is truly illuminating. In the first place it illustrates the sharp decline of antireligious propaganda. In that entire five-year period the *Emes* published only one such item (in 1937) with a circulation of no more than 4,000 copies. Evidently, neither publisher nor Party was willing to expend much energy on agitating against religion at a time when the Soviet Union was veering toward a gradual reconciliation with the Russian-Orthodox Church in the face of the rising Nazi threat. In theory, to be sure, the Communist Party did not abandon its antireligious crusade. In its conference of 1936, the All-Union Party adopted a resolution reading:

> Among the tasks of the cultural revolution, embracing the widest masses, special place is occupied by the struggle against the opiate of the people—religion—a struggle which must be carried on systematically and relentlessly. . . . At the same time the proletarian power, allowing freedom of confession and destroying the privileged position of the former state religion, conducts by all possible means antireligious propaganda, and reconstructs all upbringing and educational work on the basis of a scientific, materialistic world-view.[12]

In the second place, the largest category consisting of belles lettres whose 328 titles with a circulation of 1,147,750 amounted to nearly 40 percent of all publications, and to 20 percent of the entire distribution. The political literature (in this listing divided between so-called Marx-Lenin literature, that devoted to Party politics, and another to Soviet political documents) ran a close second in the number of titles (229 or *ca.* 25 percent), but exceeded the belles lettres in its circulation of 1,941,425 copies, or over 30 percent. Among the other categories the most important was that of textbooks, running to 69 titles and 633,750 circulation.

Much of that literature consisted of reprints of older classics or translations from foreign languages. The Soviet cultural leaders made a special point of acquainting the national minorities with one another's culture by promoting translations from one minority language into another, as well as from all of them into Russian. For one example, according to the computations of the Soviet bibliographer, A. Finkelshtain, in the first twenty years of the Revolution (1917-37) the works of Sholem Aleikhem appeared in a total of 2,107,000 copies of which 1,216,000 were in Yiddish, 405,000 in Russian, and 486,000 in six other languages. With even greater abandon L. Zinger claims that, in the years 1917-39, Sholem Aleikhem's works had appeared in ten languages and in 3,200,000 copies. A Soviet Yiddish writer, Leib Kvitko, was said to have been even more popular; in 1928-39 his works were published in 22 languages and 6,500,000 copies. Such figures are beyond any comparison with the publication of Jewish books in the West. However, in the Soviet Union they were easily overshadowed by works of popular Russian authors; indeed, of some written in relatively less prominent minority languages. According to the catalogue of the *Mezhdynarodnaia Kniga* (International Book), the 10 Russian translations from the Yiddish, published in 1938 in 2,156 pages contrasted with 24 books and 6,410 pages of such translations from the Gruzhian (Georgian) literature. The number of translations into Yiddish was also large; it actually increased in periods of rapid ideological changes, when it appeared safer to translate an old classic than to write an original work.[13]

We have furnished here, perhaps excessively, statistical data pertaining to the publication of Yiddish books. Not that quantitative measurements are decisive in matters of spirit. But the data compiled by Soviet bibliographers stress these measurements which have at least the virtue of some objectivity. No less a figure than David Bergelson (1884-1952), one of the really distinguished Yiddish novelists, who, after many years in Berlin, lived and died in the Soviet Union, applied this standard when he claimed that Soviet Yiddish literature had achieved primacy in the world of Yiddish letters. He doubtless had in mind the bibliographical account for 1925, which had appeared in his periodical and which had shown that, of the total of 451 Yiddish publications throughout the world, 208 had appeared in the Soviet Union, 163 in Poland, and only 63 in the United States. The author of that list exclaimed with great pride, "This means that, during the last year, the Soviet Union published almost as many [Yiddish] books as all other countries combined."[14]

On closer examination, however, it turns out that much of the material published then and later in a Yiddish garb was of little specifically Jewish interest. A subsequent bibliography covering the Yiddish publications during 1935 included the respectable number of 437 titles with an average circulation of 4,320 copies. But the really large editions were devoted to translations from the Russian propaganda literature, such as Stalin's speeches and the Statute of the Collective Farms (in twenty-five thousand copies each), or Molotov's address on the Constitution (eighteen thousand copies). Some pamphlets by Stalin, Molotov and other Soviet leaders were allotted fifteen thousand copies each. At the same time even propaganda works by Jewish communists, such as an information booklet and a speech on Biro-Bidzhan, or descriptions of the new Jewish agricultural colonies of Stalindorf and Novo-Zlatopol, were published in only one thousand to five thousand copies. It is also interesting that the twelve books devoted to economics, one to geography, one to natural science, and two of the three books in history, were all translations. The one original historic work, to be sure, was quite important. It was the collection of documents, entitled "Socialist Literature in Yiddish, 1875-1897," edited by S. Agurskii, Volume II, and published by the White Russian Academy in but one thousand copies. The category of medicine has an original Yiddish book, but it consists only of a popular first-aid guide. Similarly, technology is represented by one original Yiddish book, that is a handbook of Yiddish stenography, published in six hundred copies. There were many other textbooks and children's books, both original and in translation, but they could not claim any major intellectual significance. This entire output could not even remotely compare with the qualitatively rich and highly diversified intellectual harvest of Jewry in neighboring Poland on the eve of its destruction.[15]

The most important branches of Yiddish literature were poetry, novels, and essays in literary history and criticism. The 1935 list shows 141 original Yiddish works of this kind and sixty translations. Apart from the highly popular classics, especially Sholem Aleikhem, there were twenty-seven books of new poetry, and a considerable number of novels published for the most part only in one thousand to three thousand copies, only Bergelson's novel and a collection of short stories appearing in six thousand copies each. Practically all publications were now limited to Soviet authors. Such eminent Yiddish writers as Sholem Asch, H. Leivick, and Abraham Reisen living abroad, had become taboo after their visits to Russia on which they had reported in a critical vein. Typical of the extreme criticisms hurled at these foreign writers is B. Orshanskii's attack on Abraham Reisen. In connection with his discussion of the pre-War period of Yiddish literature, whose estheticism had alienated the writers from the masses, Orshanskii referred to an essay written by Samuel Niger (Charney) in 1908 which actually blamed Reisen for overstressing the ordinary sufferings and the "gray misery." At that time Reisen had indeed been a "poet of millions" though not Niger's poet. In contrast thereto, Orshanskii contended in 1931, that "now A. Reisen has betrayed the Revolution, the millions of toiling masses, and has sold himself to the yellow *Forward*; he is now in the service of the Nigers and not of the millions." While most of the Soviet authors, too, had been born and trained in the pre-Revolutionary period, some poems and stories by younger writers also made their appearance in the 1920s and 1930s.[16]

From the standpoint of content the Yiddish letters of the period followed the lead of the contemporary Russian writers. Even lyrics rarely described the personal emotions of individuals perplexed by the difficulties of life and human relations. The novels were, for the most part, written in simple black and white, the heroes representing the new type of Soviet worker, upstanding, generous, devoted to the building up of his country, contrasted with the villains harking back to the old order. Distinguished artists like Peretz (Peter) Markish (1895-1952) could not completely suppress their inner sympathy, or at least, some romantic yearnings toward the world passed by. But Markish, too, after his return in 1926 from a five-year sojourn abroad, concentrated on the victory of the socialist ideals over the outworn strivings of the past. The writers helped inspire confidence in the future among their Yiddish readers who, even more than most other Soviet citizens, faced the harsh difficulties of that era of forced cultural integration, economic scarcities, and constant appeals to sacrifices. Even their heroines are rarely described as persons motivated by the usual human emotions of love or parenthood, but as dedicated workers exceeding all their comrades in organizational zeal and effectiveness.

A highlight of Note Lurye's (1907-   ) significant novel, *Der step ruft* (The Steppe Calls), written in 1931 and describing a Jewish farm village in the Ukraine (he himself was a native of a Jewish agricultural colony), is reached with the exhortation, by the nineteen-year-old woman organizer, Elke Rudner, addressed to the Jewish farmers to join a collective. She argues most cogently by comparing their low output with that of a neighboring collectivized farm. And yet Lurye is too genuine an artist to write with unmitigated venom even about the local Jewish *kulak*. He puts into the mouth of this rich Jewish farmer a pathetic description of how he had "lived his whole life quietly and peacefully like a good farmer. Now they want to take away his house. . . . That Jews should slaughter Jews! Where had such a thing ever been heard of before?" On the other hand, Noyakh (Noah) Lurye (1885-   ) does not refrain from extolling the Secret Service's bloody suppression of counter-revolutionaries in some of his short stories included in his *Brikn brenen* (Bridges are Burning) and published in 1929.[17]

In the mid-1930s, when the large purges began and the "cult of personality" was celebrating great triumphs, Jewish authors, like their non-Jewish confreres, were in a precarious position. After much hesitation during the 1920s when, among others, Trotsky had advocated a "soft line" toward arts and the creative expression of uncontrollable subconscious feelings, the Party assumed a definite stand for submerging individual creativity to the common purpose of upbuilding socialism. Beginning in 1932, an essay by Lenin, written under totally different circumstances in 1905, began to be cited as a piece of sacrosanct revelation. Here Lenin had stated:

> For the socialist proletariat literature cannot be an instrument of gain for persons or groups; it cannot altogether be an individual matter, independent of the whole proletarian cause. Down with non-Party writers! Down with literary supermen! Literature must become *part* of the general cause of the proletariat, the "wheel and the screw" of a single great Social Democratic mechanism, set in motion by the entire politically conscious vanguard of the whole working class. Literature must become a component part of the organized, planned, united Social Democratic Party work.

So entrenched had Party control become that, in 1933, A. V. Lunacharskii completely reversed his previous "liberal" position and declared: "We know very well that we have the right to intervene in the course of culture, starting with mechanization in our country, with electrification as part of it, and ending with the direction of the most delicate forms of art."[18]

Like their non-Jewish colleagues, the Yiddish writers were particularly affected by the constant vagaries in communist ideology. Some preferred to write historical novels going back to pre-Revolutionary times, even to antiquity or the Middle Ages, because many novels dealing with contemporary subjects, however closely hewing to the momentary Party line, were later condemned for having taken the wrong ideological position. This sense of insecurity affected even literary and scholarly critics. For many a critic, who in his review had praised a certain book, was later censured together with the author. It was safer, therefore, not to write any criticisms at all and leading Yiddish literary journals now appeared without their customary review sections.

More permanently debilitating was the constant shrinkage of the Yiddish reading public. Not only were the hundreds of thousands of Jews moving to the interior of Russia increasingly estranged from their mother tongue, but even most Ukrainian and White Russian Jews gradually acquired a good knowledge of Russian, and/or the local languages. It made less and less sense now to translate for them speeches by Stalin or resolutions of the Communist Party, which they preferred to read in their Russian originals. In time an unnamed Ukrainian Jewish leader actually suggested to the Yiddish poet Isaac Fefer that perhaps Yiddish poets and novelists would do better if they submitted their Yiddish manuscripts to Russian or Ukrainian translators and had their books published only in such renditions. Since Sholem Aleikhem's works were quite popular among non-Jewish readers as well, it could be argued that such Russian translations of works dealing with Jewish subjects would fill a literary void. To some extent such practice was, indeed, adopted in the late 1930s.[19]

This was a complete reversal of the position taken earlier by the Jewish communist leadership. Most blatantly the trend toward concentration on Yiddish came to the fore in the field of Jewish scholarship. Before the First World War even the leading journals devoted to Jewish history had appeared in Russian (*Evreiskaia Starina, Perezhitoe,* and *Voskhod*). Now whatever historical scholarship was still cultivated, for the most part by scholars trained before the Revolution, appeared in such Yiddish journals as the Minsk *Zeitshrift, Ofn Shprakhfront,* and others. Here, too, there was constant attrition after 1932-33 and fewer and fewer works of that Marxist-oriented scholarship now saw the light of day. The internecine struggle between the Jewish scholars themselves, filled with denunciations of communist heterodoxy, further increased these authors' feelings of insecurity. Especially some younger research men, more politicians and Party hacks than genuine students, attacked such an old-time expert as Israel Sosis for his attempts at objectivity in the Western sense and his excessive "nationalism." Even a publicist like Hillel Aleksandrov, who had not only frequently indulged in vehement attacks on "Fascist" Jewish scholarship as repre-

sented by the Yiddish Scientific Institute in Vilna but had
also published a number of propagandist pamphlets for
communism and communist research, became the target of
sharp polemics by some younger writers who detected in
his works supposed "deviations" from the "newest" Party
line.[20]

Another revolutionary transformation took place in the
Yiddish spelling. Long before 1914 one heard suggestions
that the Yiddish orthography should be simplified by the
transcription of the Hebrew loanwords in a phonetic, rather
than etymological form. Some had even recommended the
adoption of the Latin alphabet. All such plans never ma-
terialized because of the staunch resistance of the Yiddish
readers. Now, however, these proposals were taken up
seriously. Even Jewish communists did not dare to flaunt
the public's wishes to the extent of adopting the Latin, or
later, the Cyrillic script, as was done with some two-score
other minority languages in the Union. But unhesitatingly
they introduced the phonetic transliteration of Hebrew terms.
They also eliminated the five final Hebrew letters which
always constituted a minor hardship for beginners, as well
as two other letters used only in words of Hebrew origin.
January 1, 1932, was set as the deadline for the use of the
new spelling. Apart from simplification, this move tended
to "dehebraize" Jewish culture, as well as to alienate the
Soviet readers from the Yiddish literature produced in Poland
and America. Its initiators succeeded only too well, but at
the price of digging their own graves.[21]

The same phenomenal rise and decline could also be noted
in the Yiddish theater. At the outset the democratic Revolution opened a vent for the pent-up creative energies of
talented Jewish playwrights and theatrical performers. During the First World War Moscow had become a center of
the Jewish stage, as well as of the Jewish book. One of the
highlights of all Jewish theatrical history was reached when,
under the leadership of Nahum Zemach (1887-1939), a
Hebrew theatrical group, the *Habimah*, was organized and
received the active guidance of Vakhtangov, one of Stan-
islavskii's brightest pupils. Their performance of S. An-sky's
Dybbuk in Bialik's unmatched Hebrew translation became

one of the high points of the interwar theater in any language. After Hebrew culture was pronounced taboo in the new society, the *Habimah* left, in 1926, for other countries, where it was enthusiastically received, and finally settled in Palestine. Its place was taken by the Yiddish theater which flourished in Moscow, Kiev, Minsk, and other centers. Subsidized by the government, as was the theater in other languages, the Jewish theatrical groups found themselves, for the first time on Russian soil, freed from nagging financial worries and basking in public recognition by Jews and non-Jews alike. Under the direction of the renowned actor and producer, Salomon Mikhoels, the Moscow Yiddish Theater achieved international fame. There also were Yiddish theatrical schools for the training of Yiddish actors in Moscow, Kiev, and Minsk.[22]

However, here, too, a process of attrition set in for the same reasons which stymied the development of Yiddish literature. Of the eleven Yiddish theaters which existed in the Ukraine in 1933 no more than four were still in operation five years later. By that time only twelve Yiddish theaters were still open, including one in Biro-Bidzhan and another in a Crimean *kolkhoz*. L. Zinger, in the boastful context of his praise of the cultural achievements under the Soviet regime, speaks of only ten Yiddish theaters in the Union in 1939.[23] Although the Moscow theater still performed plays with a high degree of artistic excellence, its days, too, were numbered.

RUSSIAN LETTERS

On the other hand, there was a growing influx of talented young Jews into the general Russian literature and theater. One need but mention names like Isaac E. Babel (1894-1940), Ilya G. Ehrenburg (1891-   ), and Boris Pasternak (1890-1962), in the field of literature; Sergei M. Eisenstein (1898-1948), the outstanding film producer, whose 1938 movie, *Alexander Nevskii*, focussed much of Russia's patriotic fervor shortly before the outbreak of the Second World War, and many others who have added luster to the interwar Russian arts. But most of these men, like the numerous Jews active in science and social studies, evinced little interest in Jews or Jewish affairs.

Some of these writers, to be sure, at least incidentally referred to Jewish characters or reminiscences of their youth. An outstanding example is that of Isaac Babel, whose *Red Cavalry* included many episodes from the Ukrainian Civil War, although he, too, dreamed of the amalgamation of Jews and their neighbors to the extent of depicting one of his heroes as a Jew enlisted in a Cossack regiment and in this capacity fighting for the Revolution. Yet Babel was too much of an individualist to fit into the rigidly controlled Russian literature, especially of the RAPP (Russian Association of Proletarian Writers) era. During the years 1929-32, when that organization was under the leadership of the young Jewish extremist, Leopold L. Averbakh (born in 1903), the system of repression, often later called Averbakhism, reached such an extent that Babel, together with other writers of his individualistic bent, remained altogether silent. In fact, after Averbakh was removed in 1932, to vanish from the scene completely thereafter, the more liberal First Writers' Congress of 1934 featured Babel as one of its speakers. By indirection the novelist spoke exaltingly of the right to write badly. The relaxation of literary controls did not last long, however. During the purges of 1937 Babel, too, was arrested. He died in a concentration camp sometime between 1939 and 1940.[24]

Another distinguished Jewish native of Odessa also remembered his Jewish youth. Eduard G. Bagritskii (Dzhubin, 1897-1934), generally considered one of the outstanding Russian poets of his generation, had also begun his literary career before the War. In his later masterpiece, *Duma ob Opanase* (The Song of Opanas), he described how, through a tragic concatenation of circumstances, the farmer Opanas shot down the Jewish communist Kogan who had tried to requisition his produce for the government. Even more remarkably, Joseph P. Utkin (1903-41), born in far-off Manchuria, depicted Jewish life in that distant province in his outstanding poem, *The Story of the Red-Haired Motele, the Inspector, the Rabbi Isaiah, and the Commissar Blokh,* which attracted wide attention. Less outspokenly Jewish but in their individualism also quite remote from the prevailing revolutionary enthusiasm were not only such older poets as Ossip E. Mandelshtam (1891-1942?), but also the youthful Mikhail Golodnii (pseud. for Michael S. Epshtain, 1903-49), and particularly Boris Pasternak who, though reared in a cultured Zionist home of a famous painter, friend of Leo Tolstoy, Rainer Maria Rilke, and Chaim Weizmann, gradually drifted spiritually into the world of both Russian populism and Russian-Orthodox mysticism.

At the other extreme stood out some convinced communist poets who placed the Party and its philosophy ahead of their artistic predilections. Alexander I. Bezymenskii, a native of Zhitomir (1898-   ), professed in one of his poems: "Others may care for a maiden's lips,/ But I am concerned with smoking factory chimneys." In another poem, quite reminiscent of rabbinic parables, he spoke of a communist cell, whose heart might suddenly appear in the shape of a fifty-kopeck piece. He would consider two of these kopecks as representing the element of bitterness, against forty-five kopecks symbolic of genuine joy. Many other writers, Jewish and non-Jewish, wrote less from conviction than because they had to perform their frequent acrobatic twists in order to keep up with the vagaries of communist policies. A most accomplished artist of these *salti mortali* has been Ilya Ehrenburg. His return to Jewish interests during the Second World War inspired many descriptions in the first draft of his novel, *Buria* (The Storm). But sensing the changed attitude of the literary dictators during the *zhdanovshchina* (the Zhdanov era), Ehrenburg burned his original manuscript and expurgated most pro-Jewish statements when the novel finally appeared and secured the Stalin Prize in 1948. But it evidently was this extreme pliability which saved his life during the Stalin terror.[25]

❧ 15 ❧

Second World War

RUMBLINGS OF AN approaching world war became quite loud after Hitler's rise to power in 1933. After the Nazi occupation of Czechoslovakia early in 1939, *Izvestia* fulminated: "In this struggle we ought to be inspired by the images of our glorious ancestors, Alexander Nevskii, Dmitrii Donskoi, Minin and Pozharskii, Suvorov, Kutuzov and the victorious banner of Lenin. . . . The readiness of the present generation to give everything to protect the Russian country against invaders, the struggle for its independence has deep historic roots. . . . Soviet patriotism is national and historical. National and historical has also been the Russian Revolution which has continued the tradition of the Russian nation." During the Second World War this patriotic fervor reached the high pitch of the new national anthem proclaiming to the world the

> Unbreakable union of free-born republics
> Great Russia has welded for ever to stand;
> Created in struggle, by will of the people
> United and mighty, our Soviet land.[1]

Characteristically, in its constant diatribes against Nazism and its racist doctrines, the Russian press failed to play up the Jewish issue, mainly because of the Nazis' very effective stratagem to weaken the inner unity of their prospective victims by appealing to the anti-Semites of all countries and by placing the blame of the war hysteria on Jewish "warmongering." Many persons, not only in the Soviet Union but also in France, the Netherlands, and elsewhere, fright-

ened by the steadily worsening international situation, swallowed this Nazi line. The Soviet propagandists avoided,
therefore, the anti-Jewish aspects and merely spoke of the
German barbarities against socialists, liberals, and other dis-
senters. Even Jewish organs no longer had a chance to
protest, for the national Yiddish press, especially the Moscow
Emes, had been suppressed in 1938. What remained were
such obscure publications as the Biro-Bidzhan *Shtern* (Star),
which had a very small circulation even in its native habitat,
and normally reached European Russia only two or three
weeks after publication.

NAZI-SOVIET COLLABORATION

In the midst of the sharp Nazi-Soviet exchanges exploded
the bombshell: the Molotov-Ribbentrop Treaty of August 24,
1939, a week before the Nazi invasion of Poland. It required
all the propagandistic artistry of the Soviet agencies to try to
explain this sudden reversal to their own peoples. Among
them the Jews must have been most difficult to persuade that
the enemy of yesteryear, who had shriekingly proclaimed the
elimination of European Jewry as one of his major goals,
should now be considered almost an ally. Yet the Jewish
officials active in the "information services" of the Soviet
Union, domestically and internationally, strained all their
ingenuity to explain this new turn as but a part of Marxian
dialectics which, though transcending the reasoning capacities
of average men, was fully comprehended by the superior
minds of the Soviet regime and the Third International.

Unfortunately, we have no documentary evidence for the
reaction of the rank and file of Russian Jewish communists
to the new policy. Concurrently with the feeding of the Nazi
war machine by Soviet supplies of raw materials and foodstuffs (some 500,000 tons of phosphates, 900,000 tons of oil
products, 1,500,000 tons of grain, even rubber and zinc
purchased from Germany's enemy, the British Empire) in
accordance with the treaty, all Russian organs of public
opinion observed an enforced silence on the treatment of
Jews by the Nazi conquerors in Poland between September,
1939, and June, 1941. Very few Russian Jews had access to

the information trickling through from these occupied territories. The ensuing unpreparedness of the White Russian,
Ukrainian, and other Jews for the Nazi onslaught when the
German steamroller finally started moving into Russia herself
astounded even the conquering Nazi commanders. A German
military report upon entry into White Russia in July, 1941,
stated:

> The Jews are strikingly ill-informed about our attitude
> towards them and about the treatment Jews are receiving
> in Germany or in Warsaw, places after all not too remote
> from them. If they were not, they could scarcely ask
> whether we in Germany treat Jews differently from other
> citizens. Although they do not expect to be granted equal
> rights with the Russians under the German administration,
> they do believe that we will let them alone if they apply
> themselves diligently to their work.

This lack of psychological preparedness was, in part, responsible for the extent to which the Jewish masses were trapped
beyond any ability to escape at the crucial moment.[2]

At first, even during the period of Russian "neutrality," the
War seemed to bring about a certain relaxation of the antireligious propaganda which might have accrued to the benefit
of the Jewish segment still cherishing its religious tradition.
After the Nazi invasion of June, 1941, the government not
only tolerated soldiers carrying Bibles into battle and having
priests informally accompanying military detachments but,
in a publication *Truth About Religion in Russia* issued in
1942, various writers sounded off with the contention that
the preceding strict separation of state and Church had
accrued to the benefit of the Church. What it lost in numbers
of adherents, material goods, and external prestige had been
more than made up, they contended, by the deepening of its
spiritual appeal. True, after recovering from the first shocks
of the Nazi invasion some of the old-time Bolsheviks, such as
Kalinin, still spoke of religion as "a misguiding institution"
and contended that the Party must continue to fight it
through education. But even Kalinin admitted in 1943 that,
"since religion still grips considerable sections of the population and some people are deeply religious, we cannot combat
it by ridicule." The number of Russian-Orthodox churches

was now allowed to grow from 4,225, served by 5,665 priests in August, 1941, (contrasted with 50,960 priests in 1917), to a substantial majority of the 16,000 churches of all denominations counted in the Soviet Union in June, 1945. The climax of that reconciliation came when the new patriarch of the Orthodox Church, Alexis, was installed by the government itself with great pomp and with the participation of many foreign churchmen.[3]

For Jews, too, this relaxation in the state-church tensions might have involved greater freedom of worship, reconstruction of synagogues, and fuller employment of rabbis and religious teachers. In fact, the godless agitation among them, as among the non-Jews, had long before been undermined by the government's lukewarm attitude. *Der Apikoires* (The Epicurean, the ancient Hebrew term for agnostic), the Yiddish magazine devoted to atheistic propaganda, had suspended publication in 1935. By 1937, even Emelian Yaroslavskii, the Jewish head of the Russian Godless Society, publicly admitted failure. True, the revival of Russian Orthodoxy entailed some reassertion of traditional anti-Jewish doctrines preached by the pre-Revolutionary Churches. It thus helped to resuscitate the age-old anti-Semitic feelings which now manifested themselves with ever increased vigor. But the government was still suppressing any overt internal discords and most Soviet Jews felt far less threatened by this recrudescence of old hatreds. Much as the new processions of the Communist Youth resembled the age-old Church pageants, they were not allowed to degenerate into such pre-Revolutionary anti-Semitic performances as were recorded in the case of the well-known monk, Iliodor of Tsaritsin (interveningly renamed Stalingrad). At that time the marchers had displayed a large doll dressed in a Jewish kaftan which they solemnly burned at the end of the procession.[4]

From the Jewish standpoint the immediate effect of the Molotov-Ribbentrop Treaty had a revitalizing impact for it soon brought into the Union masses of religiously and nationally conscious Jews. In September, 1939, while the Nazis were subduing the Polish armies, the Soviets occupied large stretches of eastern Poland. In June, 1940, when Germany was fully preoccupied with the conquest of Belgium, the Netherlands, and France, the Soviet Union took over the three Baltic states with practically no resistance. The Jewish population of the Union now increased from over three million in 1939, to more than five million in July, 1940. The accession of two million nationally-minded Jews helped revive the national forms of Jewish culture among the older Russian citizens as well.

However, governmental antagonism made itself immediately felt and the powerful totalitarian machinery quickly suppressed all creative manifestations of the newly annexed Jewish communities. This repression came clearly to the fore in Vilna, which had fully maintained its cultural vitality under the interwar Polish regime, as well as after October 10, 1939, when the Russian army had handed it over to the Lithuanian Republic. The size of its Jewish community had been swelled by some fifteen thousand refugees from the provinces; among them about one thousand Zionist "pioneers," men and women, who had undergone training for work in Palestine. True, the material conditions had greatly deteriorated and, with some help from the American Jewish Joint Distribution Committee, the International and American Red Cross, and other foreign relief organizations, the Jewish community had to assume tremendous new financial responsibilities. For the sake of goodwill it even supported many non-Jewish refugees, including some previously notorious Polish anti-Semites. No less than three Yiddish dailies resumed publication; a Jew was appointed vice-mayor, and four streets were renamed in honor of Mendele, Peretz, Dick, and a local communal worker, Zemach Shabad. The same experience repeated itself on a lesser scale in the other communities so long as they remained outside the Soviet Union.[5]

No sooner, however, did the Russian administration take over the Baltic States in June, 1940, than the Yiddish papers had to discontinue publication (they were temporarily replaced in August by a communist daily, *Der Vilner Emes*). Synagogues and schools were starved out of existence, if not formally suppressed. More tragically, the Soviet authorities, in closing all Zionist organizations, the Bund, and other Jewish associations, also deported most of their leaders to Siberia. Outstanding Jewish industrialists and businessmen shared that fate, together with some nationalist and business leaders of the Lithuanian people. The proportionate Jewish share, however, was much larger. It has been plausibly estimated that among the approximately twenty-five thousand Lithuanian exiles there were some four thousand Jews, far in excess of their share in the population. Nevertheless the few Jewish communists who participated in the newly established Soviet regime were conspicuous enough to fan the embers of anti-Jewish hostility among the masses. In a greatly exaggerated form this alleged Jewish preponderance in the communist administration served as an excuse for some Lithuanian nationalists in the United States and elsewhere after the World War to justify the subsequent collaboration of many Lithuanians in the wholesale extermination of Jews during the Nazi occupation. As a matter of fact, during the year of Soviet domination from June, 1940, to July, 1941, Jews had suffered even more severely than their neighbors. The same speedy attrition was noticeable in the course of 1940-41 in the other Baltic communities which had been the scene of vigorous Jewish cultural and religious life before the War.[6]

UNDER NAZI TERROR

All these difficulties were far overshadowed by the stark tragedy which befell Russian Jewry after the Nazi invasion. Although Russia had been forewarned by Hitler's speeches announcing war preparations against world communism and although Soviet and Nazi "volunteers" had already fought many battles during the Spanish Civil War of 1936-37, the Red Army was unprepared to meet the Nazi onslaught. With unprecedented speed the Nazi armies not only occupied the formerly Polish and Baltic possessions which were supposed to serve as buffers for just such an eventuality, but they also occupied all of White Russia, the Ukraine, and many provinces of the Great Russian Republic. By October, 1941, less than four months after the start of the invasion Nazi foreposts were a mere six miles from the perimeter of Moscow.

With these conquests the Nazis became the masters of most Jewish mass settlements. The speed of the German advance, combined with the Jews' lack of preparedness, resulted in their overwhelming majority finding themselves now under the Nazi heel. Only the Jewish draftees from the western areas were, at least in part, withdrawn together with the rest of the Russian armies into the deep interior, to be reformed over the winter and to resume the hostilities during the second year of the War. However, the four million war-prisoners, taken by the Germans in the first six months, and their successors in the following two years, embraced many thousands of Jews who, even less than their Gentile comrades, enjoyed the benefits of the Geneva Convention of 1929. In an agreement concluded on July 17, 1941, between the notorious Reinhardt Heydrich of the Reich Security Office and General Hermann Reinecke of the Army, professional revolutionaries, Red Army political officers, "fanatical" communists, and "all Jews" were to be implacably eliminated. Very frequently German officers condemned to death also Jewish-looking Gentiles on the basis of their facial features or because they were circumcised. In the first flush they paid little heed to the possible impact of such slaughter of circumcised Muslims upon Turkey, whose goodwill was being ardently sought by the German diplomacy.[7]

Needless to say, news of these and other atrocities committed on the war prisoners gradually trickled back to the Russian home front, nullifying whatever sympathies the anti-communist segments in the population might originally have felt toward the German "liberators." Even the Jews were at first rather meek and submissive. An officer of the German Economic Commission in the Ukraine wrote in his report of December 2, 1941:

> The attitude of the Jewish population was from the beginning rather shy and willing. They tried to avoid any conflicts with the German Administration. . . . It cannot be proved that the Jews participated in an organized manner in any sabotage action against the Germans. It cannot be asserted that the Jews represented a danger to the German Army. With the work performed by the Jews, which, of course, was stimulated by fear, the German Army and Administration was completely satisfied.

The Jews were quickly disabused, but their vast majority was hopelessly trapped behind the advancing German front. That, contrary to news spread abroad, Russian officials did not evacuate entire Jewish communities was quite evident to any informed student of the strategic situation. The Russian railway system had, from the outset, been inadequate for the tremendous task of moving millions of soldiers and their armaments to the front and then back into the interior. No one could dream of a mass evacuation of any segment of the civilian population, even if the will had been there. The American, Corliss Lamont, was taken in by the war-time propaganda when he wrote in 1945: "More than 1,000,000 [Jews] were safely evacuated from these [occupied] regions and were given priority in transportation and care, the bulk of them going to Uzbekistan." The result was that only small groups of Jews and non-Jews, considered particularly valuable for the war production or other government services, were sent away in advance of, or together with, the retreating armies.[8]

Even the Jewish collective farms in the Ukraine, whose personnel might have proved very useful for the maintenance of agricultural production in the unoccupied areas, were largely left to their own devices; they suffered nearly total annihilation by the Nazis and their Ukrainian collaborators. Only from the Crimea, which was given a breathing spell before the Nazi conquest, were the inhabitants of some Jewish *kolkhozes* evacuated in large numbers. Otherwise it was left to the individual initiative as to how many succeeded in fleeing for their lives with whatever means they had, hiding in forests, being concealed by some non-Jewish friends or, before long, in joining the ever-growing partisan detachments who fought the Germans from the rear and tried to cut their supply lines. It was fortunate for the Jews of the western Polish provinces, occupied in the first onrush of the Nazi armies in September, 1939, that hundreds of thousands had succeeded in fleeing into Russia, where most of them were assigned settlements far in the interior, often beyond the Ural. Quite a few hardy souls had traversed the entire Soviet Union and reached China or Japan (much of China was at that time occupied by the Japanese). They formed new Jewish colonies in Shanghai, Tientsin, and Kobe, many proceeding from there to the Americas, Palestine, or Australia during and after the War. In all, the Jewish population in the unoccupied parts of the Soviet Union more than doubled. From some nine hundred thousand in January, 1939, it increased to well over two million by the end of 1941.

The remaining three million left behind suffered all the pangs of hunger and aggravation inflicted upon them by the Nazi autocrats before they finally were, in their majority, deported to the gas chambers. Immediately after the occupation they were forced to wear a badge (usually a white arm band with the Star of David), segregated in ghettos under the sanction of capital punishment for unauthorized departures and given food rations far below the prevailing minima. Of course, Jews were not alone to suffer. Apart from losses on the battlefields, the Soviet Union lost many millions of her citizens liquidated by the Nazis. But in most cases non-Jews were exterminated on individual grounds, some because they had been communist officials (*Bolshewismus—jüdisches Untermenschentum* or "Bolshevism: Jewish Subhumanity," was the title of an early German war pamphlet); others because they were accused of spying or sabotage; still others because they belonged to the native intelligentsia whose destruction was writ large in the Nazi program of enslavement of Eastern Europe. As early as May 21, 1930, Hitler had told Otto Strasser that "the Nordic race has a right to rule the world and we must take this racial right as the guiding star of our foreign policy. It is for this reason that for us any cooperation with Russia is out of the question, for there on a Slav-Tartar body is set a Jewish head." Nor did the German dictator refrain from such obvious exaggerations, as his reiterated public claims that 98 percent of all leading positions in the Soviet Union in 1937-38 were held by Jews. Ultimately, the aggregate of the Slav victims of the Nazi occupation forces came quite close to the thirty million persons, predicted as desirable by Heinrich Himmler soon after the inception of the hostilities.[9]

Yet Jews were in a category by itself: the mere fact of being a Jew was sufficient ground for most brutal treatment and assassination. Many Nazis considered the cold-blooded murder of Jews a meritorious deed. So deeply ingrained had this hatred become that it swept away all utilitarian considerations. Even in White Russia where Jews monopolized entire branches of handicrafts and where, for instance, a Nazi commander himself reported that, with the removal of the Jewish shoemakers, no one was left to repair the shoes of his forced laborers, the progress of the *Einsatztruppen* proceeded unhampered. The German district commissar of Slutsk complained that, although Jewish artisans were "indispensable for the maintenance of the economy," the police had carted off all Jews, claiming "that this purge must take place for political reasons and economic considerations had never yet played a role."[10]

The domination of the racialist ideology came to the fore also after the German conquest of the Crimea and parts of the Caucasus. In the Crimea the conquerors drew a line of demarcation between the Krimchaks (old Tartar-speaking Jewish settlers) whom they considered full-blooded Jews and hence subject to extermination, and the Karaims (members of the religious Karaite sect) whom their racial specialists declared to be of non-Jewish origin. Similarly tolerant was the German attitude toward the Tats (the "Mountain Jews") of the Caucasus whom their neighbors shielded with all means at their disposal and whose outward appearance and dialect sharply differentiated them from Jewish types familiar to the Western conquerors.[11]

All these were minor exceptions, however, to the general plan of extermination of all Soviet Jews on whom the Nazi Storm Troopers could lay their hands. Their leaders actually glorified in the success of their undertaking. In his well-known address to the SS generals of October 4, 1943—at a time when the fortunes of war had already turned against Germany—Heinrich Himmler thus described the "very grave" matter of the complete extermination of Jews. He declared: "Among ourselves it should be mentioned quite frankly, and yet we will never speak of it publicly . . . I mean . . . the extermination of the Jewish race. . . . This is a page of glory in our history which has never been written and is never to be written."[12]

It has indeed been extremely difficult to assemble full information concerning the Nazi atrocities in the occupied eastern areas. From the outset these territories were divided by the German administration into a Reichskommissariat Ostland, embracing the northeastern provinces of Poland and the Baltic States, and a similar Kommissariat for the Ukraine including Podolia and Volhynia. Both these Kommissariats were under the administration of Alfred Rosenberg, the chief ideologist of the Nazi Party, who now served as minister for the East. His underlings as heads of these two Kommissariats, Heinrich Lohse and Erich Koch, outdid their chief in their barbaric treatment of Jews and, to a lesser extent, of the other inhabitants of these territories. In the Ukraine, particularly, some restraints were imposed by that faction of policy makers in Berlin who, as during the First World War, wished to build up a Ukrainian irredenta leading to the formation of an independent Ukrainian Republic under German control. They found many collaborators, and were even able to form Ukrainian auxiliary detachments under the name of the "Ukrainian Liberation Legion." They also encouraged some Russian captives to form a "Russian Army of Liberation" under the command of the collaborationist general, Andrei A. Vlasov. Some such local pro-Nazis, though not Vlasov himself, helped their masters to uncover hidden Jews and to send them to their death. In fact, a leading official in the German Ministry of Propaganda complained of Vlasov's passivity in fighting Jews. As in the past, the White Russian population was far less inclined to stage pogroms, an attitude which German officials attributed to their "political stupidity."[13]

In this great emergency the old religious and national traditions reasserted themselves. An unconfirmed story has it that the Nazi commander of a Crimean town tricked the Jewish population in 1942 by proclaiming that he wished to send them all off to Palestine. The Zionist sentiment in the population was supposed to have been so strong, even twenty-five years after the Revolution, that not a single Jew failed to appear at the appointed time. Of course, these train loads had an entirely different destination.

Be this as it may, there is no question about the considerable upsurge of religious feeling. Some heroic rabbis continued to preach to their congregations almost to their last breath. There also was much religious questioning, the ancient debates between Job and his friends being now resuscitated under different guises. A Hasidic leader, Kalonymus Kalmish Shapiro, whose homiletical work appeared posthumously in Israel, referred to a talmudic legend concerning the Ten Martyrs executed in the days of Emperor Hadrian. When angels reputedly queried the Lord whether martyrdom was indeed a proper reward for the unflinching devotion of these students of Torah, the Lord supposedly promised that, if it were to happen again, the universe would return to chaos. At this point the rabbi asked: "And now innocent children, pure as angels, as well as great and holy men in Israel, are being killed and slaughtered only because they are Jews . . . and the world's space is filled with their heart-rending shouts: 'Save us, save us!' They, too, cry, 'Is this the reward for devotion to Torah?' Yet the universe is not destroyed but remains intact, as if nothing happened." Continuing such preachments all through 1942 and early 1943, the rabbi defied destiny until his body, too, was turned into ashes in September, 1943. Deep religious and national feeling also permeated the numerous melancholy "songs of the ghetto" which have survived to attest to the unbroken spirit of heroism, however passive, of a whole people facing uncontrollable disaster. Others preferred more active resistance and, whether in partisan groups or individually, fought the Germans. Perhaps one of the most tragic manifestations of the unquenchable anti-Semitism of the period was the occasional rejection of Jewish partisans by their non-Jewish confreres.[14]

SOVIET REACTIONS

Very little of that cataclysm was reported in the Russian press. While all means of communication, in the printed word or through the radio, were set in motion to denounce the Nazi atrocities, the mass murders of the civilian population were not emphasized until very late in the War and postwar periods. Undoubtedly, the propaganda agencies felt that there would have been too much questioning of why the Red Army had retreated so deeply into the interior and left so many millions at the mercy of the Nazi assassins. Even those who believed in the doctrine of "strategic retreat" and the conscious luring of the enemy into the vast open steppes as a means for his destruction, often questioned why this method had become necessary and why the Soviet military power could not have stemmed the German steamroller closer to the frontier. Nor were the Russian memories so short as to forget the Molotov-Ribbentrop pact of 1939 and the supplies the Russians had sent into Germany which had helped build up the Nazi military power before the invasion. Only occasionally did a Russian writer find such words of sympathy, as those in Boris Gorbatov's novel, *Taras' Family,* written in 1943. Here a Jewish doctor working in a small Ukrainian factory town is depicted as a greatly beloved dedicated physician. When he first appears wearing the Nazi-imposed Star of David, he is greeted with a deep bow by the old worker, Taras, a bow intended "to you and your suffering."[15]

In any case, the specific slaughter of Jews was rarely mentioned in releases intended for domestic consumption. Once again, the Soviet leaders feared that, by siding with the Jewish victims of Nazidom, they might furnish "proof" for the Nazi contention of the alliance between the Bolshevists and the Jewish world conspiracy. Even the Soviet soldiers were not immune from the Nazi propaganda. With their accustomed thoroughness the Germans were often able to use specific data in their messages to the Russian combatants. Facing a regiment recruited from a certain area, the Nazis blared over their loudspeakers and radios names of prominent Jews from that area and then asked the Soviet soldiers whether these Jews were among them, or else had shirked their military duty and stayed behind to enrich themselves through war speculations. For the most part these were names of prominent citizens who, for that very reason, were known to the recruits. The fact that they were over-age or badly needed behind the front because of their expertness in the production of war materials or for other vital government services, was hardly considered by the unsophisticated *muzhiks* now in uniform. In other effective broadcasts the Nazis warned the Soviet soldiers not to entrust their lives to "Yankel

Kreiser," that is, to Lt.-Gen. Jacob Kreiser, one of the eminent Jewish war heros.

Whether because of the efficacy of German propaganda or because of the persistence of atavistic anti-Jewish prejudices, even Jewish partisans often found lukewarm reception among their comrades in arms. In some areas one heard the saying that Jews "merely eat and spoil the air." When on September 12, 1943, twenty-two young Jews from the Vilna ghetto wished to join a neighboring partisan force, they were asked, "Why have you not come until today? So long as the Germans had not attacked you, you have faithfully worked for them. Only now when they have started exterminating you, you have come to seek refuge among us." Such incidents occurred quite frequently, although the testimony of later writers fully bears witness to the heroism of numerous Jewish freedom fighters. Some of them, like the watchmaker Abraham Hirschfeld of Slonim, became quite legendary figures. One of the leading partisans, Colonel G. M. Linkov, devoted to Hirschfeld an entire chapter in his war-time reminiscences. In the regular Russian armies, too, no less than thirty-four thousand Jews received decorations for bravery in combat. They were the fourth-largest national group in the Red Army to merit such recognition, although their population had ranked but seventh in size. Probably, more than one hundred achieved the title of "Hero of the Soviet Union." Among outstanding individuals one need but mention Captain Israel Fisanovich who, as a submarine commander, sank thirteen enemy ships, earning also an American Navy Cross. A woman flier, Lt. Lily Litvak, distinguished herself at Stalingrad and shot down six German planes at Orel before losing her own life. At the same time, Jews occasionally suffered from anti-Semitism among both the Soviet officers and enlisted men. The number of decorated Jewish soldiers is doubly remarkable as some of them were passed over "because of the pernicious influence of the late Supreme Army Commissar Shcherbakov, member of the Politbureau . . . [and] dyed-in-the-wool anti-Semite," according to a later report by a Jewish captain.[16]

No complete statistics of Jewish casualties on Russia's battlefields are available. But the incomplete data at hand indicate that the number of Jewish victims exceeded their ratio in the population. All that may have become known in some official bureaus in Moscow, but no information to this effect was circulated either in the Red Army or among the civilians. If, in the praise of the great valor of the Soviet peoples or in the deprecation of Nazi methods Jews were mentioned at all, this was done either casually or for foreign consumption, especially in broadcasts to Britain or America.

It also was only with the view to foreign propaganda that a new Jewish organization was called into being: the Jewish Anti-Fascist Committee. The idea of such an organization was first broached by two socialist refugees from Poland, Henryk Erlich and Viktor Alter who discussed it with Lavrentii P. Beria, then Commissar of the Interior and head of Secret Service, and subsequently addressed themselves to Stalin himself. Although generally sympathetic to the idea of a Jewish organization, Stalin was evidently annoyed by their letter, which reminded him of the presence in Kuibyshev of these two former leaders of the hated Second International. He immediately noted on the letter the two words: *Rasstrieliat oboikh* (Let them both be shot). They were immediately executed, although in the following year Molotov and Vishinskii continued to reassure correspondents that the two men would soon be set free. Not until January, 1943, did Molotov admit in a reply to Albert Einstein and to the labor leaders, William Green and Philip Murray, the intervening execution of Alter and Erlich, claiming that the latter had engaged in hostile activities toward the Union and incited Soviet soldiers to make speedy peace with the Germans. Until today this calumny has not been formally repudiated by the Soviet government, although Khrushchev has publicly admitted the terroristic crimes committed by Stalin and his associates.[17]

Indirectly, nevertheless, the negotiations initiated by Erlich and Alter may well have persuaded the Soviet authorities of the worthwhileness of a Jewish organization to maintain contacts with the Jewry of the Allied lands. While the details of the formation of the Jewish Anti-Fascist Committee have never been fully revealed, by the summer of 1942 it was in operation under the presidency of Salomon M. Mikhoels, the renowned actor who was also prominent in the general Russian theatrical circles.[18]

Characteristically, this Committee was not intended to be a national organization of Soviet Jewry with any program of domestic activity. It became part and parcel of the Soviet Bureau of Information under the guidance of Solomon A. Lozovskii, director of that bureau and vice-commissar for foreign affairs. Although himself a Jew, Lozovskii specialized in the Far-Eastern area and evinced interest in the Committee only in so far as it could be used for Soviet propaganda abroad. He defined its task as consisting exclusively in helping the Allies "to stop the bloodthirsty rage of Hitler and the other fascist apes who claim to belong to a master race." In this respect the Committee's releases and radio broadcasts to the Jews of the United States and the British Commonwealth served an excellent purpose in Russia's great hour of need.

A highlight of the Committee's activity was a 1943 trip, undertaken by Mikhoels and Itzik Fefer to the West, with Stalin's personal blessings. The two men, known at least to the Yiddish-reading public through their artistic and literary achievements, received a warm welcome in the United States and, according to Fefer, raised $2,000,000-$3,000,000 for the benefit of the Russian people as a whole. Fefer also gloried in having persuaded the American Jewish Joint Distribution Committee to extend charitable aid, through the Russian Red Cross, to the downtrodden of all nationalities. Another oft-repeated early slogan of the Committee exhorted the Jews abroad to supply the Soviet Union with one thousand tanks and five hundred bombers. However, with American governmental supplies reaching the Soviets through Murmansk or Iran in much larger quantities, this particular appeal lost much of its significance. In essence, the Committee's secretary, Shakhno Epshtain, correctly described its function in an article of February, 1943:

> The basic activity of the Jewish Anti-Fascist Committee was directed towards enlightening the Jewish popular masses in all countries about the great historical accomplishments with which Soviet reality is replete. The Committee did this in writing, dispatching daily by cable, and

frequently through special mailing facilities, newspaper material, reports, short stories, songs and even lengthy plays; and it did it orally by means of four weekly radio broadcasts to foreign countries, especially to England and the United States.[19]

As part of foreign propaganda the Committee undertook to collaborate with American Jewish organizations in the preparation of a Black Book documenting Nazi atrocities, of which Yiddish and English editions were to appear in New York, while a Russian rendition was to be published in Moscow. At first there was considerable excitement within the Committee about this project. Many Soviet Jews in high positions, who had previously lost all contact with their people, rediscovered their ancient ties under the blows of Nazism which did not discriminate between Orthodox or agnostic Jews, nationalists or assimilationists, sending them all alike to gas chambers. Ilya Ehrenburg not only joined the sponsorship of the Anti-Fascist Committee but also personally collected material, mainly eyewitness reports, relating to the Nazi extermination of Jews. In sending such a collection to the prospective copublishers of the Black Book in August, 1944, he wrote in his accompanying note: "I have collected here documents telling of the annihilation of defenseless Jews by the Nazi invaders. Here is no literature. These are genuine, candid stories, letters to relatives, diaries. . . . Let all know that defenseless Jews died manfully, with words of contempt and revenge. . . . Let all know that Jews, when they could, killed their executioners. . . . Let this book burn like fire. Let it call for retribution." Active Jewish resistance to the Nazi onslaught, rather than passive martyrdom, was also extolled in Peretz Markish's wartime poems, *For the People and the Fatherland,* and his great postwar epic, *The War.*[20]

As time went on the Committee's enthusiasm for the book waned. While the American partners continued with the preparations for publication and even secured a foreword from Albert Einstein, the Moscow Committee dragged its feet. It first rejected Einstein's foreword as too Zionist in approach (a later collection of the physicist's essays was to include this "Preface That was Not Used"), and finally withdrew completely. Nor did it proceed with the implementation of its other major projects. In all these matters the Committee had to avoid the appearance of acting as a nationalist Jewish agency, instead of merely following the line laid down by the Soviet Information Bureau. If, as the only functioning nation-wide Jewish organization, it unavoidably had to deal with some problems brought to it by various Jewish groups in the country, had to extend support to unemployed Yiddish writers and artists, and occasionally engaged in some form of Jewish social work, it actually transcended its permissible range of activity. Curiously, Lozovskii who, if anything, had constantly tried to stem any such expansion into the domestic field, was later accused of complicity in this illegal endeavor, an accusation which, in part, led to his execution in 1952.

One such involuntary Jewish cultural activity consisted in the publication, by the Committee, of its own Yiddish organ, *Di Ainikeit* (Unity). Its content was mainly devoted to foreign propaganda, but it also had to report the activities of the organization itself, public meetings it held, and otherwise mention certain communal or cultural happenings within Soviet Jewry. Needless to say, this was a poor substitute for the ramified press and the educational system which had existed in the Soviet Union but a decade earlier. Even after the German invasion of June, 1941, there still appeared in the newly annexed Polish and Baltic provinces twenty-two Yiddish books and pamphlets. But these had mostly been in the press before the start of the Russo-German hostilities. In 1942, this output was reduced to a single pamphlet of sketches published in Moscow. Despite a minor recovery in the following three War years in connection with the activities of the Anti-Fascist Committee, the total three-year output was still limited to only fifty-six items, for the most part of minor significance.[21]

In part, to be sure, there existed many purely technical difficulties. Certainly, the Nazi occupation of the main centers of Yiddish printing, the headlong evacuation of Moscow which forced the publishing firm *Emes* to transfer a skeletal force to Kuibishev, general wartime shortages, the drafting of many writers into active service, and other factors made continued publication of Yiddish works extremely arduous.

But these obstacles might have been overcome, were it not for the official discouragement of Jewish cultural endeavors, such as had clearly manifested itself during the brief interval of 1939-41. A fairly authentic story has it that when Zelig Akselrod, a prominent Yiddish writer of Soviet Minsk, visited the newly annexed communities of Vilna and Kovno early in 1941, he heard complaints that the Soviet authorities were closing down all Yiddish schools. Somewhat rashly, he suggested organized petitions signed by the majority of parents as the only way of saving the Yiddish school system. Evidently denounced for this "nationalist deviation," he speedily disappeared from the scene, never to be heard of since. The totalitarian government simply brooked no interference with its own initiative, especially during the subsequent War years, when it concentrated on its single-minded objective of winning the war.

❧ 16 ❧

Postwar Reaction

WHEN GERMANY SURRENDERED in May 1945, Jews and the other Soviet citizens looked forward to an era of peace and prosperity of unprecedented dimensions. Jews, in particular, cherished the hope that, once relieved of the great menace from its Western neighbor, the Soviet Union might relax its totalitarian controls and treat them without fear of the worldwide Nazi anti-Semitic propaganda. After the great holocaust in the western provinces, the Jewish survivors were deeply grateful to the Red Army for saving them from the Nazi extermination squads. Only few realized that the war had been won by a coalition of great powers and that, without Britain's staunch resistance alone for a whole year and the subsequent entry of the United States into the war, the Nazis would not have been stopped during the invasion of Russia in 1941-42. According to the mythology, effectively developed by all organs of domestic propaganda, it was the Red Army alone which, with but minor and reluctant assistance from her Western allies, defeated the German war machine. In a *Pravda* article, Ilya Ehrenburg actually contended, without any mention of El-Alamein and the British, that even Palestinian Jewry had been saved from the Nazi onslaught by the Russians. Like the rest of the Soviet inhabitants, Jews rejoiced in the victories of the Red Army and for the most part considered it as the savior of their surviving remnant.[1]

EARLY DISENCHANTMENT

From the beginning, to be sure, clouds appeared on the horizon. When many Ukrainian, White Russian, and Baltic Jews, who had spent the war years either as combatants or as civilian workers in Soviet factories, wished to return to their homes, they not only found their old communities in shambles but they also were received coolly by their erstwhile neighbors. The memories of the German anti-Semitic propaganda were still quite fresh. Many neighbors had been outright collaborationists with the Nazis and helped them to track down prospective Jewish victims. These guilt-ridden individuals looked forward with trepidation to the investigation of their roles during the war in which the victims' surviving relatives might prove to be dangerous avengers.

Many friendly Ukrainians and others in the Nazi-occupied areas also looked askance at the returning Jews whose homes, or posts in industry or government, they had interveningly taken over. According to the law, returning refugees, particularly war veterans, could reclaim both their possessions and their prewar positions. But with the growing housing shortage in the devastated occupied cities, most new tenants refused to vacate, for the benefit of such Jewish arrivals, premises which they had acquired with much effort and the bribing of numerous Nazi or Soviet officials. Some persons allegedly muttered under their breaths that they wished the Nazis had done away with all Jews. Naturally, apologists for the Soviet authorities never lacked excuses. When an American visitor, Ben Zion Goldberg, asked Itzik Fefer whether, under similar circumstances, a returning Ukrainian war veteran would not be given back his old apartment, Fefer evaded the issue and merely claimed that the Ukrainian's difficulty would be mitigated by the presence in the community of relatives and friends who would extend to him the hospitality of their homes. The Yiddish poet failed to grasp the simple logic that, for this very reason, Jews had an even stronger case for the return of their former dwellings. A returning prosecuting attorney found that he was demoted to the role of a defense attorney. It was explained to him that, since many prosecutions would be aimed at former Ukrainian collaborationists, it would be better for the Jew to be cast in the role of defending the accused, rather than in prosecuting them.[2]

The upshot was that many Jews found life in their old habitations quite unbearable; they preferred to settle in the big cities of the interior and to make a fresh start. Even the Jewish agricultural colonies in the Ukraine and the Crimea had been totally wiped out and no effort was made to reconstitute them. Their very names, though connected with Soviet leaders, like Kalinindorf or Stalindorf, were never mentioned again in the official records.

A brighter future seemed to beckon for the Jewish autonomous region in Biro-Bidzhan. Still eager to develop that area, the Soviet regime granted prospective Jewish settlers free transportation and 300 rubles per capita; each family could also secure a government loan of 10,000 rubles. Nor were the conditions on the spot as dismal as they had been when the first colonists arrived there in the late 1920s. Now Tikhonka, renamed the city of Biro-Bidzhan, had become a sizable town of thirty to forty thousand inhabitants with broad boulevards and a good deal of free housing made available by the numerous departures during the war, while immigration had been almost totally suspended. Jewish cultural life was also resuscitated, the newspaper *Der Shtern* appearing twice, and later four times, a week. A literary journal, too, was being talked about, as was the founding of a Yiddish university, the only one in the world. It is small wonder, then, that quite a few young Jewish veterans chose to settle in that new land of promise. According to local officials, twenty thousand Jews arrived in 1947 and in the first four months of 1948. This figure may be exaggerated, but there is no question that six thousand persons were brought in by the government in regular convoys of several hundred Jews, each stemming from a particular western region.[3]

In European Russia things also seemed to be improving. Many assimilated Jews doubtless felt like Ehrenburg, who said: "I grew up in Moscow. My native tongue is Russian. I do not know the Yiddish language. I am a Russian, a

Soviet citizen, a man who cherishes the culture of Europe. But now I feel bound to the Jews because of the great misery of my Jewish people." Ehrenburg expressed dissatisfaction with the Jewish Anti-Fascist Committee for being too little Jewish, although his name continued to appear among the Committee's sponsors. In the privacy of his home Ehrenburg allowed himself even such far-reaching admissions as that the Soviet population of the occupied regions, "in particular the youth, had helped the German murderers." To Nathan Rapaport, the famous sculptor of the monument for the fighters and martyrs of the Warsaw ghetto, he conceded in 1945 that he had been unable to write frankly about the persecution of the Jews within the Soviet area, because of the prevailing anti-Semitism in the higher echelons of the Party. Nevertheless immediately after the armistice with Germany he and others could delude themselves into believing that a new era was dawning also for the Russian Jewish survivors.[4]

In 1947, an event took place which must have heartened many devoted Jews. As the Palestine crisis was drawing to its climax, the Soviet Union suddenly appeared as a champion of a Jewish state. Domestically, Zionism was still outlawed and any Zionist activity was still subject to stringent criminal prosecution. Yet Andrei Gromyko voted, together with the United States and other Western countries, for the United Nations resolution of November, 1947, pledging the partition of Palestine. After Israel's Declaration of Independence of May 14, 1948, the Soviet Union was one of the first powers to recognize the new state. Keen observers realized, of course, that the main purpose of these moves was to oust Britain from the entire Middle East. Possibly the leaders of the Union expected, as did most outside observers, that the new state would be quickly overrun by the Arab armies and that a British mandatory country would be replaced by a weak Arab alliance, offering many openings for a Russian diplomatic offensive.

When Israel proved victorious and, assured of its independence, for the most part sided with the Western alliance, the tone of the Soviet press became increasingly hostile. Once again the epithet "Zionist" became a supreme insult.

The Russian government and public opinion reverted to the old Lenin-Stalinist repudiation of Zionism. One could freely hear the quotation from Stalin's essay of 1913 when, in a footnote, he described Zionism as

> a reactionary nationalist trend of the Jewish bourgeoisie, which had followers among the intellectuals and the more backward sections of the Jewish workers. The Zionists endeavored to isolate the Jewish working-class masses from the general struggle of the proletariat.

Because of the gradual withdrawal of the Western powers from their Middle East colonies and the rise of Arab nationalism, that area offered a great temptation for the Soviet Union to move into the emergent power vacuum. Certainly, no slogan could appeal more strongly to Arab nationalists than the condemnation of the State of Israel as an outpost of Western "imperialism." The combination of anti-Zionism with general anti-Judaism by many nationalist Arabs further strengthened the inner forces operating in Russia, too, toward the reassertion of the ancient anti-Semitic heritage.[5]

At first, after reading, in the *Pravda* and *Izvestia*, the speeches of the Russian delegates at the United Nations, some Russian Jews assumed that these marked a turning point in the theretofore hostile attitude of the Soviet regime toward Zionism. The Yiddish poet, David Hofshtain, who, in his youth, had spent several years as a Zionist pioneer in Palestine and had returned to Russia after the Revolution in order to participate in the upbuilding of the socialist society, now deluded himself to the extent of asking the Ministry of Education to introduce instruction in Hebrew into the public schools. He paid dearly for this act of daring, being one of the first of the distinguished array of Yiddish poets and writers to be imprisoned and ultimately executed. Deportation was also inflicted upon hundreds of other Zionist sympathizers who thus misinterpreted the direction of the Soviet policies.[6]

"THE BLACK YEARS"

All along there was growing retrogression of Jewish cultural institutions, particularly in the reoccupied western territories.

We must not lose sight of the hundreds of thousands of Jewish survivors who had become Soviet citizens only as a result of the annexations of 1939-40 and the reoccupation of these lands in 1944-45. Most of these more recent members of the Soviet Jewish community spoke Yiddish, had much Hebrew learning, and were of the old type of nationalist and/or religious Jews. Even those who had acquired familiarity with the Lithuanian, Latvian, and Polish languages could use them now to little advantage if they settled in areas of different national majorities. For their children it was quite imperative that they attend Yiddish schools and receive instruction in a language familiar to them. We have the eyewitness testimony of Szmerl Kaczerginski, a Yiddish writer who had lived in the Vilna ghetto under the Nazi occupation and had then fought with the partisans against the Nazi armies, that he, together with like-minded Jewish leaders, began rebuilding the Jewish community as soon as the Germans left Vilna in July, 1944. With the aid of Jewish army officers they finally obtained permission from the local Russian authorities to found a Yiddish primary school of four grades. During the following year they applied for permission to open a fifth grade, but they were refused under the excuse that, having received the obligatory instruction in the Russian language during the first four years, the children should be able to enroll in a Russian school. In other communities no Yiddish school was opened at all and the interested parties were dismissed with bland promises for the future.[7]

The same contrast between provinces and capital appeared also in the publishing field. No effort whatsoever was made to revive Yiddish journalism and book publishing in the old Jewish centers of the Ukraine, White Russia, or Lithuania, together with the enlarged territories taken over from Poland, Czechoslovakia, or Rumania. In the entire three-year period of 1946-48 the Ukrainian Academy in Kiev published only one scholarly work in Yiddish, namely a 64-page study by Elias Spivak, of *The Language in the Period of the Great Patriotic War*. This paucity reflected the general growth of the nationalist spirit among the Russians and the Ukrainians which also prevented the resumption of prewar Ukrainian publications in Polish, Bulgarian, and German. The government publishing house in Minsk brought out, in 1947, a literary-artistic collection, entitled "With a Firm Step." Not that there was a shortage of Yiddish readers. According to a report in the *Ainikait* of August 17, 1948, no less than 5,000 copies of Yiddish books were sold in Odessa in the first six months of that year; among them 1,500 copies of Sholem Aleikhem's writings and 400 copies of a recent memorial volume for Mikhoels. In the same period Kiev readers spent 67,000 rubles on purchasing Yiddish books. A dedicated writer, J. Buchbinder, succeeded in collecting within four days in the relatively small community of Zhitomir no less than 320 new subscriptions for the literary almanac, *Der Shtern.* All these efforts, however, ran up against the passive resistance of the local Russian authorities, with or without prodding from above.[8]

The central authorities had decided at that time to concentrate all major Jewish publishing efforts in the capital. Since open collaboration with the Jewry abroad was still being encouraged, Moscow could display to interested visitors certain governmentally sponsored Jewish cultural activities. Apart from fine theatrical performances and public lectures, regularly attended by large throngs of people, one could display the *Emes* publishing firm and its ambitious program of publications. Among its more significant projects was a Russian-Yiddish dictionary of some forty thousand words, prepared by the Yiddish section of the Ukrainian Academy; a comprehensive memorial volume for the Soviet Yiddish writers who had fallen on the battlefields of the Second World War; and a literary collection entitled "On Soviet Paths," in commemoration of the thirtieth anniversary of the beginnings of the Soviet Yiddish literature. Most remarkably, *Emes* was prepared to publish a collection of Yiddish poems by Bialik, despite the previous fulminations by older communists against this "bourgeois-nationalist" poet. If none of these projects was carried through, the *Emes* publications during the three-year period of 1946-48 totaled some one hundred ten thousand copies of Yiddish books and pamphlets. True, this number compares unfavorably with the size and quality of publications of a single year in the mid-

1930s. But one could excuse this decline by the prevailing shortage of paper and other technical difficulties. For foreign consumption one could herald these efforts as mere beginnings of a difficult reconstruction period, beginnings out of which would develop a flowering Yiddish culture. The impression made abroad upon Soviet sympathizers is well described by an academic writer's comment in 1946,

> Meanwhile, with anti-Semitism outlawed by both the Soviet Constitution and public opinion, and cultural autonomy guaranteed where there are Jewish majorities who want it, the Jews in the Soviet Union enjoy a fully rounded ethnic democracy that no other country in the world at present gives to the Jewish people.

A year later an Anglo-Jewish writer subsumed the Jewish people under the general trend: "For all the peoples of the Soviet Union the war not only increased the intensity of their communion, but strengthened the links with their own past, and contributed to a new development of every national community."[9]

At the very moment these lines were written in the West, Jews saw themselves gradually eliminated from all positions of trust and confidence. After the departure of Lev Mekhlis in 1950, the only Jew left in the Politbureau was Lazar Kaganovich. In the course of 1948-53 no less than 63 Jewish generals, 111 colonels and 159 lt.-colonels were pensioned off and no Jew was appointed to any important Army command.[10] More generally, too, a new ice age was descending upon all Russian culture and particularly upon that of the national minorities. Under the system which came to be known as the *zhdanovshchina*, Andrei Zhdanov, with the full concurrence of Stalin, laid down the general rules under which all Soviet writers and artists had to operate. They were to forget their personal inclinations and feelings and put their pens, paint brushes, and other tools completely at the service of the Party. Great writers like Fadeev, who now became a leading official of the Soviet Writers' Union, were forced to rewrite especially their war-time novels in the sense directed by Party officials. Not a shadow was to fall on the behavior of either the local communists or the Red Army officers during the great retreat of 1941-42. In all cases this was to be presented as a well-planned withdrawal which left behind a Party apparatus able, with almost superhuman wisdom and energy, to organize the partisan groups fighting behind the German front.

It is small wonder, then, that the same Fadeev who had so greatly extolled the Jewish officer Levinson as the hero of the Siberian Civil War, now had practically no word to spare for the great Jewish tragedy in his Stalin prize-winning novel, *The Young Guard*, particularly in its final form published in 1951. The same was true of Valentin Kataev's *For Soviet Power*, although the scene of its war-time happenings was placed in the center of the old Jewish community of Odessa. Ever pliable Ehrenburg readily agreed to describe the technique called for in the "production novel." The personal attitudes of the hero and heroine are played down, while their entire energies must be placed in the service of attempting to "over-fulfill their quota." The new rewriting of history did not stop with what might have been considered more or less contemporary history. The new journal *Kultura i zhizn* (Culture and Life), especially founded to serve as a watchdog over the conformity of the Soviet writers, as early as September, 1946, sharply censured the great film producer, Eisenstein, for his direction of *Ivan the Terrible*. Eisenstein was accused of "ignorance of historical facts in representing the progressive special troops (*oprichniki*) of Ivan the Terrible as a gang of degenerates resembling the American Ku Klux Klan, and Ivan the Terrible himself, a man with a strong will and character, as characterless and weak-willed, a kind of Hamlet."[11]

Under these circumstances what could exponents of Yiddish culture expect? As the Cold War grew warmer in 1948, the Soviet leaders began looking askance at any contact between their citizens and foreigners. The American monopoly of the atomic bomb created an abysmal feeling of insecurity. Ever-suspicious Stalin must have spent sleepless nights thinking of what he would have done if, for several years, the Soviet Union had the sole possession of such an irresistible weapon. In that feeling bordering on panic, every foreigner appeared as a potential spy and any chat, however casual, with a foreigner became necessarily even more suspect than it had been in the 1930s.

In regard to Jews these suspicions were heightened when the Soviet rulers noted, to their chagrin, how deeply imbedded the Zionist sentiment still was among the Jewish masses. The spontaneous demonstration at the Moscow synagogue on the Jewish New Year (October 16, 1948) on the occasion of the arrival there of Golda Meyerson (now Meir), the first Israeli envoy to the Soviet Union, a demonstration involving thousands of Moscow Jews defying all dangers, must have appeared to the secret service men as an open rebellion. Even earlier the suggestion of the Anti-Fascist Committee that the old Jewish colonies in the Crimea, destroyed by the Nazis, be resurrected was viewed by some officials as a veiled intention of Russian Jews to create there an autonomous Jewish area where, in case of war, the Americans could readily establish a bridgehead for the occupation of southern Russia. Unbelievable though it may seem, this canard was still upheld as true by Nikita Khrushchev in his lengthy exchange with a Canadian communist delegation, including the provincial deputy I. B. Salzberg, although Khrushchev admitted that the execution of Lozovskii on this score was a clear miscarriage of justice. The glorified Biro-Bidzhan experiment itself could be interpreted as an instrument of Western imperialism intended to deliver that base to Japan, although that country was many hundreds of miles away.[12]

TOTAL ECLIPSE

To informed observers such rumblings of anti-Jewish suspicion became quite audible in 1948. The sudden death of Salomon Mikhoels on January 13, 1948, on a trip to Minsk, where he was officially to present the Stalin Prize to the White Russian State Theater, must have raised questions in the minds of wary partners on the Committee. Although his death was explained as the result of an automobile accident, he was given a solemn State funeral, and a theater was named after him, some of his colleagues suspected foul play. The suspicions against Mikhoels were nurtured by his earlier war-time trip to the United States and his continued correspondence with American Yiddish writers, mostly of pro-Soviet leanings. Not surprisingly, in the prevailing spy scare, some one conceived the idea that Mikhoels had helped to hatch the Crimean and other plots against his native land. Had not that prosaic technician, Lazar Kaganovich, suspected even Mikhoels' internationally famous presentation of *King Lear*, as an oblique criticism of the Soviet order? Mikhoels must have had premonitions of his falling from the grace of the dictator. Stalin frequently liked to be entertained by the great actor through the private recitations of distinguished dramatic roles. He even endearingly called Mikhoels from time to time his "Solomon the Wise." However, according to a story reported by a Soviet refugee in Israel, Mikhoels' friend and colleague Kachalov, another well-known Soviet actor, had told him about a conversation with Stalin in which the latter referred to "Solomon the Wise," the caricature of a Jew in Chekhov's *Steppe*. In this connection Stalin had exclaimed: "This is ·exactly like my Mikhoels, a buffoon and not a king!" That some Committee members sensed the real plot against the actor's life, could be seen from the eulogy in verse written by Peretz Markish which stressed the marks of the brutal assault on the deceased man's body and placed him among the Nazi victims.[13]

This was but an individual beginning. By late November, 1948, the ax fell upon the entire Anti-Fascist Committee. Details of that operation have never been disclosed and are still subject to much guesswork. The *Ainikait* seems to have suspended publication soon after November 20, 1948, but the Committee's official dissolution was never announced in the Russian press. Inquiries from abroad, as well as those addressed to Soviet representatives in the United States and elsewhere, were evasively answered. For a long time, indeed, foreign Jewish communists simply could not believe the reports about the new terror striking the Yiddish leaders. They finally had to admit the suppression of the Anti-Fascist Committee but explained it simply as the result of the return to normalcy after the war. They were still whistling in the dark about the Soviet recognition of Jewish national culture.

But in April, 1949, the shattering news suddenly came about the jailing of the five most eminent Yiddish writers, David Bergelson, Samuel Halkin, Peretz Markish, Der Nister, and Itzik Fefer. While Bergelson was accused of pro-Israel sympathies, no particulars were given in the other cases. Certainly, one could not accuse Fefer of lack of Soviet patriotism. He who had not only served as colonel of the Red Army during the war, but had also sung "Siberia, the Urals,/ Kaluga, and Tripolye,/ And wherever I am/ A flaming Komsomol am I," and had outdone any Russian poet in his patriotic diatribes, was now lingering in prison as a traitor to the Fatherland. These arrests were followed by a number of others and, before long, practically all Yiddish literary leaders were behind bars.

All that was accomplished in extreme secrecy and even the communist organs in other countries were kept in the dark about the fate of these Soviet patriots. Finally, in 1952, most of them were tried and executed on the same day (August 12), except for those who, like Der Nister, had died in prison. Only years thereafter did some survivors of these new purges who succeeded in getting out of the Soviet Union (in part, as a result of the Russo-Polish agreement affecting Polish citizens) disclose some of the horrors of that new wave of persecutions. Even they had only fragmentary information, much of it based on hearsay. At any rate, not only were the leaders physically exterminated, but all organs of Yiddish expression were speedily suppressed. During that bleak quinquennium of the last years of Stalin, no Yiddish paper or book was allowed to appear, except perhaps for the sporadic publication of the Biro-Bidzhan *Shtern* which reported nothing of Jewish interest, indeed nothing that had not appeared in the Russian paper of that area, the Biro-Bidzhan *Zvezda* (Star).

While these blows were aimed at the very core of Jewish intellectual life in Moscow, the provinces did not go unscathed. Particularly the Baltic countries, which still included important remnants of Jewish communities, felt the brunt of the Stalin terror. It has been estimated that, in the first three years after the Second World War, no less than 371,000 Baltic nationals were deported. Most of these, to be sure, were persons accused of collaboration with the Nazis and doubtless included a great many pogromists who had aided the Nazi extermination squads. But others were merely Lithuanian or Latvian "nationalists," a term now used as a word of opprobrium and included Jews guilty of "Jewish nationalism." Perhaps the greatest source of fear was the apparent irrationality of the persecutions. A family was deported because its little daughter had inquired in school where Israel was. A little watch repairman disappeared one day because "his name just happened to be on a list. Maybe it was confused with another name. In any event, he was shot." As a Jewish friend explained it to Harrison E. Salisbury, the correspondent of *The New York Times,* "No one even knew why, and this was what made the terror so much worse."[14]

Even more threatening became the new issue of Jewish "cosmopolitanism." Quite apart from Jewish "nationalism" or "Zionism," the very foundations of the Jews' loyalty to the Soviet Union were now questioned. Through a dialectical combination of such opposites as "cosmopolitan nationalism" Jews could be accused of trying to undermine the allegiance of the Russian people to their Fatherland. To be sure, Jews as such were not usually mentioned, but in the unceasing flow of press releases condemning prominent individuals for "cosmopolitan" associations, there invariably appeared a majority of Jewish-sounding names. This proved technique from the days of Nazis and Nazi sympathizers (when Father Coughlin, for instance, fulminated against the "international bankers" he always mentioned at least two or three Jewish banking houses by name) was now used to good advantage. No informed reader in Russia was fooled about the intent of these denunciations and yet, in the foreign propaganda, one could roundly deny any anti-Semitic aims.

No better illustration of the changed attitude of the Soviet regime need be adduced than the different treatment of Jewish problems and personalities in the successive editions of the *Large Soviet Encyclopedia,* each volume of which was edited with great care and attuned to the changing demands and moods of the Party. Like most other semiofficial publications the encyclopedia served as an instrument of com-

munist propaganda. Under the heading of "Jews" (*Evrei*),
the first edition, published in 1932, devoted no less than
150 columns to an explanation of the history, culture, and
contemporary situation of the Jewish people. In contrast
thereto, Volume XXV of the second edition, published in
1953, reduced the entire treatment to a mere four columns
(in addition to some remarks on Biro-Bidzhan), filled with
diatribes against "national Jewish culture" which is only
"a word of the order of rabbis and bourgeois, a word of the
order of our enemies." The very definition of "Jew" follows
the Party line. "Jews do not represent a nation," the author
contends, "for they do not form a stable community shaped
in the course of history on the common basis of language,
territory, economic life, and culture. They partake of the economic and cultural life of the peoples among whom they
live." Naturally the article emphasizes the great disparity
allegedly existing between the fate of Jews in Western
countries where they suffer from anti-Semitism and discrimination (the Soviet propagandists generally like to identify
capitalism with fascism and nazism), and their complete
equality in the Soviet Union.

> The "American way of life," built upon the oppression of
> classes and nationalities also finds its expression in the
> persecution of Jewish workers. In the United States it is
> the rule not to admit Jews to public service [these words
> were written long after the American Jew-baiters had
> dubbed the New Deal the "Jew-Deal" because it had
> attracted many Jewish civil servants to Washington and
> other cities]. In fact, there exist regular quotas for the
> admission of Jewish pupils to scholarly institutions. The
> Jewish sub-proletariat, like those of the other national
> minorities, lives in special closed quarters in particularly
> unsanitary conditions.

Contrasted with this lowly status, the Soviet Jews "take an
active part in the building of communism. In this fashion
the Lenin-Stalinist national policy of equality and amity
among the people has led to the disappearance of the
'Jewish question' in the U. S. S. R."

With particular venom are treated here and in a few

special articles all aspects of Zionism. "The Zionists, agents
of American and English imperialism," we are told, "are
the sworn enemies of the Jewish workers." The same line
is taken in describing Chaim Weizmann who "had placed
himself at the disposal of the American imperialists and
transformed Israel into a colony. He pursued the policy of
oppressing the Jewish working masses and the Arab minorities in order to extinguish the forces of peace and democracy." Bialik is briefly dismissed as a "reactionary poet," while
Herzl, Ahad Haam, Mendele, An-Sky, Sholem Asch, and
many others, more or less fairly treated in the first edition,
are completely omitted in the second. If some Jewish artists
are given considerable space in the new edition, this is
merely owing to their sculpting or painting of historic figures
from Russia's tsarist or communist past. But in such cases
no mention is made of their Jewish origin. A similar silent
treatment was extended even to such independent publications as that of the complete works of Maxim Gorki in 30
volumes, completed in 1957. On the whole, every little article
by Gorki is included, except his manifold attacks on anti-
Semitism, his praise of Bialik, and other pro-Jewish utterances to which reference was made above. Ignoring the Jews
and their past was pushed to such extremes that in 1954 an
author (Kovalev) could publish a textbook on the history
of the ancient world without mentioning ancient Israel.
Indeed, if the Jewish question could be eliminated by such
a "conspiracy of silence," the Russian propaganda machine
would have succeeded in disposing of it once and for all.[15]

Inconsistently, however, the Soviet regime itself was guilty
of indirectly raising the Jewish issue by referring to conspirators bearing Jewish names. Most dangerous was the
so-called doctors' plot, supposedly hatched by nine eminent
Moscow physicians, of whom six "happened" to be Jewish;
among them Dr. Wofsi, president of the Academy of Medicine and a relative of Mikhoels, whose family name had
also been Wofsi. These doctors had allegedly conspired to
poison Stalin and other Soviet leaders and thus prepare the
way for an internal upset. We need but quote Nikita

Khrushchev's secret report to the Twentieth Congress of the
Communist Party of February 24-25, 1956:

> He [Stalin] personally issued advice on the conduct of the
> investigation and the method of interrogation of the
> arrested persons. He said that the academician Vinogradov
> should be put in chains, another one should be beaten.
> Present at this Congress as a delegate is the former Min-
> ister of State Security, Comrade Ignatiev. Stalin told him
> curtly, "If you do not obtain confessions from the doctors
> we will shorten you by a head."

> Stalin personally called the investigative judge, gave him
> instructions, advised him on which investigative methods
> should be used; these methods were simple—beat, beat and,
> once again, beat.

> Shortly after the doctors were arrested, we members of the
> Political Bureau received protocols containing the doctors'
> confessions of guilt. After distributing these protocols,
> Stalin told us, "You are blind like young kittens; what
> will happen without me? The country will perish because
> you do not know how to recognize enemies."[16]

The Russian public, including its Jewish segment, did not
have to be informed of what all that meant. It still vividly
remembered how the assassination of S. M. Kirov in 1934
had set up a chain reaction resulting in the terrible purges
of the old Bolsheviki in the following three years. The
doctors' plot, too, was evidently intended to serve as an
excuse for new violent purges, except that this time Jews
would undoubtedly have been singled out for particular
retribution. A foretaste was given, for instance, by the
exclusion from the Party of one of its leading publicists,
David Zaslavskii (a former Bundist), allegedly because one
of his editorial colleagues had declared that he was unable
to work "together with the son of a people of traitors and
poisoners." Widespread rumors had it that Stalin was preparing to deport all European Jewry to the Far East. Since
during and after the War various tribes, such as the Crimean
Tartars, the Kalmyks, and the Volga Germans, had thus been
physically transplanted from Europe to Asia, where before

long most of them vanished as identifiable groups, these rumors enjoyed full credence among many Jews and non-Jews alike. One can easily visualize the terror among the Jewish masses who had but a few years before emerged from the nightmare of Nazi extermination.[17] At that particular moment the old tyrant died and, in the scuffle for succession, the accused doctors were discharged and the entire terroristic campaign was called off.

Not that this relaxation involved the immediate abandonment of the anti-"cosmopolitan" agitation. True, one could now allow himself to deplore the war-time Nazi atrocities without being exposed to such a harsh denunciation of the kind suffered in 1949 by the Ukrainian Jewish poet, Savva Golovanivskii, for a poem describing the infamous massacre of some 75,000 (more exactly 33,771) Kiev Jews in the cave of Babii-Yar in 1941. A critic in the semiofficial *Literaturnaia Gazeta* had accused Golovanivskii of "a terrible defamation of the Soviet nation" because he had described the passive behavior of the Kiev population, while the Germans marched the old Jew, Abraham, to his doom.[18]

However, any form of Jewish nationalism was still considered taboo. The American communist writer, Howard Fast, was glorified in Soviet literary circles even beyond his literary merits. During that period of adulation a complete bibliography of Fast's writings was published in Moscow with the omission of but two items, namely a short history of the Jews entitled, *Romance of a People* (1939), and a novel *My Glorious Brothers* on the Maccabean revolt (1947). Evidently, the compiler feared that, by including these two "nationalistic" Jewish items, he might lower the dignity of the writer he and his readers so greatly admired. Naturally enough, when Fast turned his back on communism, his Jewishness was suddenly discovered and made the subject of vicious attacks. All this was symptomatic of the general effort to make the Soviet Jews sever their relations with both the Jewish people the world over and their own past. Howard Fast's comments thereon are indeed pertinent:

> Equality based upon the forcible blotting out of differences and the subjugation of the group memory of minorities is

not a pleasant thing to contemplate, and little enough dignity goes along with it. . . . What a bitter thing it is to be robbed of your father's as well as of your own pride!

Yet, this was demanded of all Russian Jews who wished to retain their membership in the Communist Party or their offices in one or another governmental agency.[19]

✺ 17 ✺

After Stalin

A CONSCIENTIOUS HISTORIAN will necessarily approach the task of analyzing the latest decade of Jewish life in the Soviet Union with even greater reluctance than in dealing with the earlier periods. All sources of solid, scholarly information have practically dried up. We are limited, for the most part, to fleeting impressions accumulated by foreign visitors, narratives of refugees from some Soviet area, interviews with one or another leading Soviet statesman, and occasional reports from foreign correspondents. Apart from the general bias in evaluating almost anything pertaining to Soviet life, one need but bear in mind how erroneous often are the impressions gathered by foreign visitors to the United States, despite the availability here of a free press and broadcasting media. In the Jewish case, the American community has at its disposal a large network of periodical publications and other sources of information which enable a visitor to check and double-check any ambiguous observations. Not to speak of the freedom with which he may circulate among the masses, speak with, and listen freely to, any casual acquaintance, probe as deeply as he wishes in interviewing responsible leaders, and sift contradictory evidence hurled at him even without asking by all sorts of interested parties. And yet, how often have such visitors gone askew in interpreting the basic trends in general and Jewish life in America!

Most fundamentally, there is a fateful dearth of basic Soviet scientific data. Long before the Jewish lyre was muted with the imprisonment of the Jewish writers and poets in 1948, long before the suspension in that year of the last

organs of Jewish public opinion, Jewish scholarly investigations had come to a halt. The last fairly scholarly publication,
Lev Zinger's *Dos banaite Folk* (The Rejuvenated People),
appeared in 1941 on the eve of the German invasion of the
Soviet Union. Much as the underlying data failed to measure
up to Western standards of research and greatly hampered as
the author was by Party line shackles, this volume furnished,
at least, some statistical data on the population trends and
occupational distribution of Soviet Jewry as reflected, in part,
by the census of 1939. Even then Zinger's attempt was a
singular exception, the other Jewish sociologists and historians
having been silenced during the purges of the mid-1930s.
Since 1941 (except for Zinger's own half-hearted attempt to
bring his study slightly up to date seven years later) no
effort at all was made by Jews or non-Jews to ascertain the
basic facts of Jewish life in the Union.[1]

Everyone working in the contemporary Jewish field knows
how difficult it is to evaluate the dynamic changes in any
community without the solid cooperation of local Jewish
scholars having free access to the archives and libraries of
their country. Their interpretation of these data may sometimes be lacking in long-range perspectives but it has the
virtue of being based on intimate living experience. In a
country as vast as the Soviet Union, in a Jewish community
which had undergone such a cataclysmic decline during the
War and the Nazi occupation, and a population which had
been subjected to the severe strains of inner migration, economic reconstruction, and cultural adjustments in the midst
of a growing spiritual vacuum, only the persistent efforts of
a whole generation of well-trained and dedicated scholars
might have produced some fundamental facts upon which to
base general conclusions. As it was, for more than two
decades not one Jewish or non-Jewish author has published
a book or monograph based upon thoroughgoing research.
One need but contrast the vast outcropping of analytical
studies probing the Jewish aspects of the census of 1926 in
the three or four years after its publication, with the total
absence of such investigations of the census of 1959, to realize
how shaky the ground is over which one may try to erect
any structure of scholarly evaluation.[2]

And yet, however reluctantly, one must come to grips with the great enigma of Soviet Jewish life today. In the following pages we shall try not only to summarize what might be considered the best state of available knowledge, but perhaps also venture into the ever perilous domain of prediction concerning the shape of things to come.

RADICAL CHANGES

The 1959 census showed how totally the Jewish situation had changed since the preceding census twenty years earlier. To the surprise of many outsiders no less than 2,269,000 persons answered the enumerators' questions by registering as members of the Jewish nationality. While some persons may have been afraid of giving replies at variance with the national identifications on their passports, others undoubtedly believed the much-publicized promise that these answers would not be divulged to anyone outside the Census Bureau, reinforced by the order to the enumerators to accept the statements of their interlocutors without verification by documentary evidence. In any case, it stands to reason that an unspecified number, perhaps several hundred thousands, preferred to list themselves as belonging to the Russian, Ukrainian, or some other nationality. This doubtless was the case, in particular, of the numerous Jews who had intermarried, or lived in small isolated groups in the scattered mining and industrial areas. Certainly, the countless European Jews employed as executives and white-collar workers in the rapidly expanding industrial enterprises of the Asiatic republics were generally considered by the local population as part and parcel of the "Russian" managerial class, rather than as Jews. Be this as it may, the official figures showed a reduction of the Jewish ratio in the total population from 1.78 percent in 1939, to 1.09 percent twenty years later.

Even more drastic were the dislocations within the various parts of the Soviet Union. Now the largest group of 875,000 Jews, or 38.1 percent of all Soviet Jewry, resided in the Russian Republic. Although declining in absolute figures by some 94,000 (always bearing in mind that perhaps more than that number were among those unidentified as Jews), their ratio had increased from 32.1 percent in 1939. The Ukraine now held second place. Its 840,000 Jews had diminished from 1,533,000 in 1939 and amounted to but 37.4 percent of the whole Jewish population in the Union. This ratio contrasted with 50.8 percent in 1939, and 58.7 percent in 1926. White Russia lagged even further behind. Its 150,000 Jews, or 7.0 percent of Soviet Jewry, were in sharp contrast with the 375,000 and 12.4 percent of 1939, and the 407,000 or 15.2 percent of 1926. The old Jewish communities of Lithuania, not surprisingly, suffered the greatest devastation, being reduced to a mere 25,000 or 1.1 percent of Soviet Jewry. On the other hand, the newly incorporated Republic of Moldavia retained much more of its prewar Jewish community (95,000 or 4.4 percent of the total). At the same time Uzbekistan, with about the same number of Jews, revealed how the tremendous war-time influx of Jewish refugees from Poland and other parts had again ebbed away in the fourteen years since the cessation of hostilities. In the list of Soviet nationalities, nevertheless, the Jewish community still ranked as the eleventh largest (it had been the seventh largest in 1939).[3]

These broad figures, incomplete as they appear to be, give us but an inkling of Jewish life in contemporary Russia. We are limited to mere guesswork even in regard to the proportion of urban to rural Jews in the new society, although it is quite certain that the large majority of the 875,000 Jews in Greater Russia still are concentrated in Moscow and Leningrad. Unofficial estimates sometimes give the Jewish populations of Odessa and Kiev as 200,000 each, but the official figures of 118,000 or 17 percent for Odessa, and 154,000 or 15 percent for Kiev are closer to the truth. The other large communities include Kharkov with 80,000 (9 percent) and Minsk with 38,000 Jews (7 percent). With the destruction of the agricultural colonies in southern Russia and the slow development of Biro-Bidzhan the overwhelming majority of Russian Jewry thus live in the respective metropolitan areas. Under favorable conditions such local concentration might have favored an intensive development of Jewish cultural life. But in the hostile clime of the contemporary Soviet environment it has merely given an additional impetus to the forces of assimilation.

CONTINUED DISCRIMINATION

Despite official denials few outsiders still doubt that anti-Semitism has continued to play a great role in shaping the Jewish destinies in the post-Stalin era as well. Even the most obdurate defenders of the existing system could not deny the fact that, in his long indictment of Stalin's crimes, Khrushchev never referred to the crimes committed by the deceased dictator and his henchmen against Jews or the Jewish community. Not even in his denunciation of the handling of the alleged doctors' plot, we recall, did he make the slightest allusion to the Jewishness of the majority of the victims. More, the entire record of his behavior toward Jews seems to betray the atavistic hostility of Khrushchev's Ukrainian environment. True, in 1913, he, together with other socialists, helped quell an anti-Jewish riot in Marinpol. However, during his long-term leadership of the Party in the Ukraine during and after the Second World War, he did nothing to help Ukrainian Jewry during its greatest hour of trial.

Stalin, too, may have harbored anti-Jewish prejudices from his early days in Georgia; occasionally he may have indulged in such private remarks as were heard by Edward Stettinius during Stalin's conversation with Roosevelt at Yalta. In reply to Roosevelt's statement that he intended to review the entire Palestine question with King Ibn Saud, "Stalin observed that the Jewish problem was extremely difficult. The Soviet Union had tried to establish a national home for the Jews, but they had stayed only two or three years before returning to the cities." Yet publicly the iron-fisted dictator was, as a rule, on his guard and from time to time even strongly went on record against anti-Semitism, as in his famous reply to the Jewish Telegraphic Agency of January 12, 1931, in which he called it "a survival of the barbarous practices of the cannibalistic period." No such public denunciation of Jew-baiting came from Khrushchev's lips; at the most he publicly denied to foreign journalists the presence of anti-Semitism in his country and pointed out that he himself had a Jewish daughter-in-law, widow of his son Leonid who had died as a fighter pilot in the War. On the other hand, during his visit to Warsaw in 1956 for the funeral of President Boleslav Bierut, he did not hesitate to lecture his Polish comrades on the contrast between the Russian Party which had been able completely to eliminate Jews from its leadership, and the Polish Party which still harbored a disproportionate number of Jews in its Central Committee. Almost directly pointing at the chairman of the Committee, Roman Zambrowski (formerly Zuckerman), Khrushchev emphasized, "There are among you many leaders named 'ski,' but an Abramovich always remains an Abramovich." Even more bluntly he attacked the Jewish leadership upon his arrival in Warsaw during the great Polish upheaval of 1956 which brought to the helm Wladyslaw Gomulka. Having been kept in the air cruising over the Warsaw airport until the change in the Polish leadership became a *fait accompli*, Khrushchev, upon touching ground, delivered himself of his famous three words: *"Zhidam budiete pomagat?"* (Do you wish to help the Yids?). The very term *zhid* had long become a term of opprobrium, rarely used in official statements even by the tsarist administration. Yet at this crucial historical moment, this erstwhile peasant, now elevated to a position of undisputed power in the Soviet Union, thus gave vent to his deep-rooted prejudice against Jews.[4]

Khrushchev was too much of a politician, however, to allow these prejudices to be publicly proclaimed as the foundation stone of the Soviet international or domestic policies. Espousal of racial and ethnic equality had been not only too integral a part of the Marxist-Leninist ideology, but also the most effective foreign propaganda instrument against Nazi racialism and Western colonialism. Khrushchev and his associates preferred, therefore, to pursue the postwar Stalinist policy of quietly introducing discriminatory measures, while publicly singing the praises of equality and nondiscrimination. To begin with, completing the work begun during the great purges of the 1930s, Jews were completely ousted from the top leadership of the Party and the higher echelons of the governmental bureaucracy. With the removal, in 1957, of

Lazar M. Kaganovich, the last Jewish member departed from the Politbureau or Party Praesidium. It was but recently (November, 1962) that a Jew was appointed chairman of the Soviet State Planning Committee and Deputy Premier. But the selection of a largely nonpolitical engineer, Veniamin E. Dymshit, who had mainly distinguished himself as the builder of the Soviet-financed steel plant in India, indicated that no basic change in policy was intended. These purges of Jewish leaders went down to the lowest local levels. Soviet apologists have often countered this argument by pointing out that no less than 7,623 Jews had recently been elected to local soviets. But when one weighs that number against the total of 1,800,000 local leaders elected in 1960, one realizes that the quota of less than 0.5 percent is much below the Jewish ratio of 1.1 percent in the total population. In fourteen of the fifteen republics the Jews were thus underrepresented in the local councils. This was even more true in the supreme soviets of the respective republics: in the Russian Republic there were only 0.12 percent of Jewish members (population ratio: 0.7 percent), in the Ukraine 0.22 percent (as against 2.00 percent), in White Russia 0.45 percent (as against 1.90 percent) and so forth.[5]

Apart from Stalin's or Khrushchev's personal leanings, it is quite evident that, once again, anti-Semitism had begun to be used as an instrument of public policy to divert the disaffection of the people to the Jewish scapegoat. As in tsarist times the far-flung bureaucracy, even larger and more powerful now, had revealed the usual signs of corruption. Lord Acton's famous saying, "Power corrupts, absolute power corrupts absolutely," came true in the case of Soviet officialdom which, despite occasional purges and executions, has largely been a self-perpetuating class. Only its constant numerical expansion to provide for the new technological and social services, and the ensuing recruitment of younger trained personnel, has thus far prevented its total resemblance to the old tsarist group of *chinovniks*. Nevertheless, connivance of officials in evading the law has become quite commonplace.

Although the economy had progressed markedly from the days of the Second World War and consumer goods had become much more readily available especially in the major cities, there still were innumerable examples of persistent shortages, shoddy quality, breakdowns in distribution and other economic ills—all of which encouraged black markets, currency speculation, and other prohibited practices. Since many Jews, especially in the older communities, still engaged in some form or other of merchandising, it was easy enough to place the blame on them as the economic criminals mainly responsible for these shortcomings in the Soviet economy. Such economic "subversion" was now placed among the capital crimes because of its long-range counterrevolutionary effects. While there also were many non-Jewish economic criminals, in all public announcements Jews were singled out with great frequency. Even the numerous culprits who had Russianized their names were cited with their Jewish names in parentheses, so that no reader or broadcast listener could mistake their ethnic identity. According to a recent, evidently incomplete, computation, of the one-hundred and sixty-three "economic criminals" condemned to death in eighty-one trials in forty-eight different cities between July, 1961 and August, 1963, no less than eighty-eight (and possibly ninety-six), that is 55-60 percent were easily identified as Jews. The latest trial of the so-called Shakerman ring, ended in February, 1964, apparently involved eighteen Jews among the twenty-three defendants. Moreover, many of these trials resulted in the execution of the Jewish culprits while the non-Jewish defendants were usually let off with longer or shorter prison terms. Among the condemned Jews, not perchance, were also leaders of the religious Jewish communities of Leningrad and Moscow, whose arrest achieved wide publicity both in the country and abroad.[6]

All along there has also been a growing discrimination against Jews in public employment and in admission to schools of higher learning. Without facing the old formal *numerus clausus*, Jews, as a rule, had to be more gifted and more industrious in order to be chosen ahead of non-Jewish applicants; promotions were also becoming more difficult to secure. Not only have Jews been ousted, for instance, from the diplomatic service in which they had once played a major role, but they even found advancement in the more ordinary occupations more and more difficult to achieve.

Regrettably, these reports by foreign observers cannot easily be verified. The government has constantly denied any discriminatory policy. In a recent release it quoted statistics showing that Russian Jewry, constituting but a little more than 1.1 percent of the population, nevertheless furnished 14.7 percent of the country's doctors, 10.4 percent of lawyers and judges, 10 percent of the scientists, 8.5 percent of journalists and writers, 7 percent of workers in graphic and theatrical arts, and 3.1 percent of university students. If these statistics are accurate, they would indeed attest a considerable measure of equality. Even the obvious decline from 9 percent of the student body in the 1930s to 3 percent today might be explained by the enormous increase of the general student population throughout the country, as for the first time in Russian history, urbanites now outnumber their rural brethren. On the other hand, we are told by informed observers that Jews are discriminated against in the admission to the more desirable schools of higher learning or to particular departments. Nor does the high Jewish percentage in certain professions—Jews are also supposed to constitute fully 19 percent of all doctors of science in the Union—really prove much for the present-day practice, since these statistics reflect the effects of decades of earlier training.[7]

On the other hand, there have also been some manifestations of a growing opposition to anti-Semitism among the younger intelligentsia. Evgenii Evtushenko's poem, *Babii Yar,* once again describing the notorious Kiev massacre, has been hailed with extraordinary enthusiasm in the literary circles and in the numerous clubs where it has been recited. This wide acceptance contrasted sharply with the cool reception extended to the similar poem by Savva Golovanivskii a decade earlier. Here Evtushenko identifies himself with the Jewish people:

. . . It seems to me that I am as old
As the Jewish people itself.
It seems to me that I am a Jew.
I am tramping through ancient Egypt

I am dying, crucified on the cross
And till this time I have traces of the nails.
It seems to me that I am Dreyfus. . . .
It seems to me that I am a youngster in Bialystok
Whose blood is running over the floors
The victim of the hooliganism of the leaders from the
    saloons. . . .
It seems to me that I am Anne Frank. . . .
Over Babii-Yar there is the hum of the thick grass
The trees look powerful, like judges
Everything screams silently here, and, removing my hat,
I feel that I am growing gray slowly
And that I am myself a totally soundless shriek
Over the thousands of thousands who are buried.
I am each old man that was slaughtered here
I am each child that was slaughtered here.
Nothing in me can forget this.
Let the "Internationale" sound out joyously
When the last anti-Semite on earth will be buried. . . .

This poem understandably aroused the ire of the authorities
which had long tried to blot out the difference between the
Jewish and non-Jewish victims of the Nazis. In fact, in Kiev
proper, a monument was erected for the Nazi victims on
another hill, while the gully of Babii Yar was allowed to be
overgrown by brush and filled with refuse.

Partly in protest against these governmental restrictions,
partly as a repudiation of anti-Semitism, and partly out of
idolization of the young poet, thousands of young Muscovites
foregathered to listen to Evtushenko's recitation of this poem
in Moscow's Mayakovskii Square on Poets' Day of 1961. At
midnight dispersed by the police, carried away in vans
twenty miles out of town and dumped on distant roads, many
of these youngsters returned the following day to participate
in a similar demonstration. The police handled them with
equal roughness the second time. The great composer Dmitrii
Shostakovich joined the procession of the poet's admirers and
included *Babii Yar,* together with Evtushenko's four other
poems, in his Thirteenth Symphony. The authorities reacted
violently—the composer had already before drawn upon his
head the censure of musical party hacks—and suspended any
further performances after the second concert. At that point

both poet and composer yielded and by inserting the two lines: "I am proud of the Russia which stood in the path of the [Nazi] bandits," and "Here together with Russians and Ukrainians, lie Jews," they came close enough to the accepted Party position to be allowed to resume their concerts.[8]

ENFORCED SILENCE

Any expression of Jewish national feeling continued to be considered essentially subversive even after the days of Stalin and the ensuing "thaw" (this title of an Ehrenburg novel had become the designation of the new era). Typical of the attitude of litterateurs and literary critics, long after the general relaxation of the Zhdanov system, was a meeting held by a local Writers' Union in Chernovtsy (formerly Czernowitz or Cernauti) early in 1960. That meeting ruthlessly condemned as "an alien voice" the work of a local Yiddish poet, Meir Kharatz, whose poem, "The Wanderer," was considered as an outright anti-Soviet slander. The report in the Bukovina paper did not spell it out, but it appears that the Union's Jewish members were among the assailants of the "daring" poet. Although, in the somewhat less tense atmosphere of 1960, such denunciations did not spell a death sentence, as they might have a decade earlier, the fate of one so violently attacked could still become extremely unpleasant. Perhaps such rigidity of a provincial group may have merely reflected the usual time lag between the new reformist relaxation in the two centers of Moscow and Leningrad as compared with the unswerving submission to Stalinist directives still dominant in the provinces. Yet Jewish "bourgeois nationalism" continued to be stigmatized as even more unpatriotic than the same sentiments harbored by other nationalities.[9]

Combined with this sharp antagonism to any manifestation of Jewish national feeling also was the Soviet Union's unwavering hostility toward the State of Israel, a hostility shared by few of its Jewish citizens. On the contrary, just as the arrival of the first envoy from Israel, in 1948, had led to a series of spontaneous outbursts of enthusiasm, a decade later (1959), the Israel representatives at a Youth Festival were hailed at every stop from the Black Sea port to Moscow by sufficiently intrepid Jews to cause consternation among the local autocrats. It mattered little that the official propaganda from time to time denounced a few of Israel's lower-ranking diplomatic representatives as spies for the United States, and condemned every Soviet citizen's contact with them as part of a conspiracy against the state. Jews and most informed non-Jews, including the authorities themselves, knew very well the baselessness of these accusations. They realized that rejoicing in the rise and growth of the new state did not in the slightest impinge upon Soviet patriotism.

A great many Soviet Jews have in fact been mentally pre-pared to emigrate to Israel. To discourage such aspirations the Soviet press constantly drummed into the ears of its readers tales of woe of what happened to recent immigrants in the new state. It widely displayed letters, both authentic and spurious, received by Russian relatives from a number of maladjusted new settlers complaining about the hardships they had suffered in the new land and the callous treatment they had received from the Israel authorities and the public. It was claimed that most Soviet Jews, after reaching Israel, applied for permission to return to the Union, although no reliable figures of such returnees were ever given. On the other hand, emigration from the Soviet Union was absolutely barred by law. The same Russian press which was vocifer-ously denouncing the American State Department for refusing a passport to Paul Robeson or Howard Fast (in his com-munist days) considered it perfectly legitimate for its own government to refuse passports to the hundreds of thousands of Russian Jews who wished to go to Israel or to the United States. The extent to which even the assimilated Russian Jews, particularly government officials, were affected by the anti-Zionist line is demonstrated by the following testimony of Howard Fast. He claims to have received a letter from Boris Izakov, member of the Foreign Department of the Soviet Writers' Union stating "that he would gladly volunteer to take up arms with Egypt against Israel."[10]

When Nikita Khrushchev was asked in Vienna in July, 1960, why the Soviet Union had refused exit permits even to the few older Jews wishing to join close relatives already settled in Israel, he roundly denied that any Soviet citizen had expressed such a desire. In reply Golda Meir, Israel's foreign minister, informed the Israel Parliament that, in the preceding five years alone, no less than 9,236 Israelis had applied, through the international Red Cross, to the Soviet authorities for permission for their families to rejoin them in Israel. Almost invariably these requests had been turned down. Nor is there any expectation for a change in this adamant policy in the foreseeable future, unless it were to become the subject of some new international convention. At a recent session of a United Nations subcommission on human rights a resolution was unanimously adopted, the representative of the Soviet Union alone abstaining, that no citizen be ever forbidden to leave, or to return to, his own country. In the meantime, however, an appeal like that voiced by the Australian delegate, H. D. White, before the United Nations Assembly on November 1, 1962, "should the U. S. S. R. find difficulty in according the Soviet Jewry full freedom to practice their religion, it should, we believe, permit them to leave the country," was curtly dismissed by the Soviet delegate as based on "filthy calumnies." An interesting description of a synagogue service held in Moscow on a Saturday morning was given by Yizhar Smilansky, a recent Israel visitor to the Moscow Peace Conference. No less than five hundred Jews had assembled for the services; for the most part they were elderly persons.

> When the members of the Israel embassy walked in, a spark was lit in the worshipers' eyes. They rose to their feet to honor them. There was a dramatic contrast between the festive garb of the embassy people and their solemn entry on the one hand, and the drab, beggarly appearance of the synagogue. The guests and the members of the embassy sit on a special dais removed from the congregation. The bond between the guests and the congregants is the bond of the eyes and of glances. This goes on all the time as a silent, shattering experience, which envelops you and does not leave you throughout the whole service.[11]

Curiously, under the vagaries of Soviet policy, the attitude toward Jews turned full circle. At the beginning of the Revolution the "godless" agitators tried to persuade Jews to repudiate their religion and to adopt in its place a purely secular national culture. Now this national culture has been repressed while, the reality of the Jewish people remaining undeniable, the main mark of identification shifted back to the Jewish religion. With all their cultural institutions, including schools, the press, and the theater remaining closed, Jews are still allowed to worship in synagogues, of which there exist, according to varying official computations, between 150 and 450 in the vast expanses of the Soviet Union. These places of worship are usually located in dilapidated buildings in some fairly inaccessible districts. Manned by frequently unlearned rabbis or cantors, they hold little attraction for the Russian youth. Nevertheless, at least on High Holidays, they usually are overcrowded. More recently, even that modicum of Jewish religious loyalty has annoyed certain official circles. While the godless propaganda has generally been toned down, attacks on Judaism as a religion have been stepped up, especially in the Ukraine, that old focus of anti-Judaism. A professor of philosophy, M. K. Kichko, in particular, was given free rein to assail the ethics of the Bible and post-biblical Judaism in several essays and a book *Yudaizm* (Judaism Without Embellishment), published in Kiev in 1963 under the official sponsorship of the Ukrainian Academy of Science.

Most remarkably, while Hebrew had so long been outlawed, in contrast to the Yiddish culture which had been lovingly fostered by the government in the 1920s and early 1930s, now the Yiddish authors remained silent (some observers spoke of a fairly substantial body of letters circulating in manuscripts as in the Middle Ages, or even in oral form as in remote antiquity), while a few Hebrew books were allowed to appear. In 1956, Rabbi Solomon Schliefer of the Moscow synagogue was given permission to publish, in a rather inferior photo-offset reproduction, a prayerbook consisting of selections from the traditional Jewish liturgical pieces. Some omissions were quite as significant as were such additions as "a prayer for peace," since peace had become a slogan widely bandied about by the Soviet authorities. The prayer begins: "Our Father in Heaven! Bless the Government of the USSR, the shield of peace throughout the world, Amen." The three thousand to five thousand copies thus reproduced quickly disappeared from the market, satisfying only a small part of a long pent-up demand, especially in the provincial communities. For several years the authorities also permitted the publication of an annual Jewish calendar which not only contained data on holidays, but also reproduced certain prayers such as the Mourners' *Kaddish* or the *Yizkor* services for deceased relatives in both the original Hebrew-Aramaic texts and Russian transliterations. In 1963 also appeared a Hebrew-Russian dictionary, based on the recognition of Hebrew as a living language. Evidently, these crumbs had to be thrown to the irresistible filiopietistic desires of the Jewish masses.

However, Jews were still forbidden to publish Hebrew Bibles in either the original or a Russian translation (none have indeed appeared since 1917), whereas, for instance, the Baptist denomination, not much larger in size than the Jewish population, was permitted in 1957 to issue a Protestant Bible in an edition of ten thousand copies. Similarly, the Baptist and other denominations were allowed to establish seminaries for the training of religious personnel, the Baptists allegedly maintaining fully five hundred pastors. The Russian Orthodox Church with which the Soviet regime had made peace during the Second World War, once again maintained a far-flung, ramified ecclesiastical establishment. In contrast thereto, the Jews succeeded only with great effort in erecting a tiny school for rabbis in the Moscow synagogue, although it was opened in 1957 with much propagandistic fanfare for foreign consumption. Rabbi Schliefer was allowed to assemble only at best thirteen pupils, eleven of them over forty years old. This number dwindled in April, 1962, to four, when the authorities refused permission to some Asiatic students to return to Moscow, allegedly because they had no residential permits in the capital. Nor were the Jewish theologians allowed to study abroad or to attend any international gatherings of Jewish religious leaders, concessions readily granted to the clergy of the Christian and Muslim faiths. In fact, the Russian Orthodox and other Eastern, as well as the Protestant, Churches were allowed formally to join the membership of the World Council of Churches.[12]

Not that the practice of the Jewish religion and the domestic religious institutions totally escaped the brunt of the new antagonistic policy. In March, 1962, the baking of unleavened bread for Passover was suddenly outlawed, showing how deeply irked the Soviet authorities were by that festival of ancient Jewish national liberation and its immemorial links to Israel. This prohibition was repeated in 1963. Nor was there any official interference with the radio program of a lesser Ukrainian station in which the old Jewish religious doctrine of the Chosen People was held up for public contumely. Taking biblical and liturgical phrases out of their religious context, the broadcaster denounced the Jews for aspiring to world domination—that good old anti-Semitic shibboleth, made doubly popular by the Nazi propaganda. Recurrent attacks by vandals on the Moscow Central Synagogue and other houses of worship led to few official reprisals. More recently, even the two leading Jewish religious communities of Moscow and Leningrad suffered from another twist of the official policy. This time the major attack was aimed at alleged "espionage" of their lay leaders who were condemned to long prison terms after a secret trial. Nor was there any diminution in either the frequency or the intensity of the perennial attacks on Jewish ritual circumcision as a barbaric custom and a danger to health.[13]

Tiny concessions in a few details, combined with large-scale repression, were finally made also to the Yiddish cultural effort. For many years after Stalin's death no Yiddish book or magazine at all was allowed to be printed. But in 1959-60, there appeared one reprint each of Sholem Aleikhem's, Mendele's, and Peretz's works and a single new volume to commemorate the twenty-fifth anniversary of Biro-Bidzhan. At the end of 1961 a new Yiddish literary journal, *Dos Sovietishe Haimland,* made its appearance. Its editor, Aron Vergelis, has become the chief apologist for the Soviet treatment of Jews, insisting also in speeches and interviews in the United States in November, 1963, that there was no anti-Jewish discrimination in the Soviet Union. He and his associates, moreover, interpret the term "literary" so precisely that they refrain from including any news item pertaining to Jewish religious, communal or political life. At the same time another editor, Avron Gontar, reputedly answering a letter from an American, Joseph Hoffman, has gloried in the publication of that journal in twenty-five thousand copies, a circulation never reached by any Yiddish literary magazine in either the United States or Israel. In the same statement Gontar contended that *Dos Sovietishe Haimland* "unites over one hundred authors, members of the Soviet Writers' Union. They write in Yiddish. In the last seven years publishing houses in various parts of the country produced about two hundred of their works in a total of twelve million copies." None of these assertions have been borne out by any other evidence, not even if one were to include the Russian translations from Yiddish authors, which in the late 1950s had begun reappearing in the market and which, in 1961, suddenly gushed forth from the Moscow and other presses. These translations included some works by Sholem Aleikhem, Mendele, and Peretz, as well as by rehabilitated authors like Peretz Markish and new writers whose works had never appeared in Yiddish. As was pointed out, the discrimination against the Yiddish-speaking public, of which 472,000, or 20.8 percent of all those registered as Jews, had formally designated Yiddish as their language, can easily be noted if one compares its treatment to that of the 504,000 primitive Asian Maris and 236,000 equally primitive Yakuts. In 1961 alone, the Soviet authorities helped to publish 17 Mari and 28 Yakut newspapers, as well as 62 Mari and 144 Yakut books.[14]

Biro-Bidzhan was no exception. Not only were the Jews too few in number—the highest estimate, undoubtedly exaggerated, set the Jewish population at about one-half of the 163,000 inhabitants of the region counted in the census of 1959—to develop an independent culture of their own, but they were not even given the opportunity to maintain a single school or to publish a book in the Yiddish language. Apart from the anemic *Shtern*, circulating in but a thousand copies, the only reminders of the Hebrew alphabet have been a few signs in Yiddish on street corners and stations, left over from the previous more friendly era. In his much-quoted interview with Serge Groussard of 1958, Khrushchev admitted failure of the entire enterprise of erecting a Jewish autonomous region and blamed it on Jewish "individualism." Although subsequent Soviet propaganda tried to tone down that admission, the facts have fully been confirmed by the few foreign visitors allowed into the region in recent years. Perhaps that small Jewish community is a bit more overtly Jewish than any comparable Jewish settlement in European Russia, but the high hopes attached to this "noble experiment" in the Far East thirty years ago by the Soviet Jewish leaders and their sympathizers abroad have clearly not been fulfilled.[15]

Nor does the frequent official answer that Jews no longer care for their Yiddish or Hebrew letters carry much conviction. Certainly, the twenty-five thousand Jews still found in 1959 in Lithuania must include a substantial number of survivors from the Hebrew and Yiddish school systems which had flourished in that country before 1940. After all, more than 80 percent of Jewish parents of that period had sent their children to Hebrew or Yiddish schools. That they should have suddenly lost all interest in their great heritage is extremely unlikely. On the other hand, some eager youngsters, prevented from acquiring any kind of Hebrew or Yiddish training, could at least partially satisfy their hunger for Jewish values by reading translations. In essence, the Russian Jewish public embraces a number of highly intelligent and well-educated groups which had weathered all storms of persecution and discrimination and succeeded in joining the highest ranks of Russian science, technology, and arts. Perhaps it is indeed symbolic that the only two Russians found worthy of Nobel prizes in recent years were the poet, Boris Pasternak, and the physicist Lev Landau, both Jews.[16] Equally Jewish have been the two chess champions of the world in recent decades, Mikhail Botvinnik and Mikhail Tal, the pride and glory of Russia's greatest national pastime. Yet it is quite evident to any impartial observer that, like Polish Jewry in the 1930s, that of the Soviet Union twenty years later might have supplied much manpower to the general intellectual endeavors of society at large, while at the same time continuing to cultivate on a high level the ramified domains of its Hebrew and Yiddish learning and letters, both traditional and modern.

✺18✺

No End of Road

EVER SINCE THE BEGINNING of the communist regime voices were heard that it spelled the end of the Jewish people in Russia. Some spoke of it joyously in the messianic terms of an approaching end of days when all peoples would lose their identity and be submerged within one common ocean of humanity. Others regretfully commented on the forthcoming disappearance of that ancient people with its ancient civilization as the unavoidable price of the great liberation of the toiling masses. Still others spoke of the mere revival of Russian anti-Semitism under a new guise. But the clamor that history was writing the final chapter in the long annals of the Jewish people was sounded by many observers, both friends and foes of the new regime.

VANISHING PEOPLE

Its friends, particularly West-European communists like Otto Heller, theorized that such a "decline of Judaism" was but the realization of an old Marxian prediction and the necessary consequence of the final victory of Marxian ideology. By referring to Marx's own bitter comments on the Jewish question of 1843, and by selecting a few appropriate interpretations of Marxism by both Lenin and Stalin, while disregarding all contradictory utterances by the three men—the accepted technique of dialecticians of all ages—Otto Heller and, less bluntly, some leaders of the *Yevsektsiia* asserted with extreme confidence that Jewish history was drawing to an end. Heller taught that, in Marxian terms, throughout recorded history diaspora Judaism had been but a "superstructure" of Jewry's social contributions as a merchandising agent and, with the disappearance of merchandise as a vital social function, there was no longer any future for the Jewish group as such. Only such a small remnant might survive as might settle in the Jewish autonomous territory (or ultimately Jewish state) in Biro-Bidzhan. After assimilating even there to the mores and modes of living of the other nations, this remnant might retain sufficient linguistic and cultural identity to continue in some residual fashion the traditions of the ancient people.

Opponents of the communist experiment, on the other hand, viewed the assimilatory pressures exerted by the Soviet regime upon its Jewish subjects as a telling denial of human freedoms. Unblinded by the Soviets' early repudiation of anti-Semitism and their recognition of the Jewish nationality, which was to enjoy the full protection of minority rights, these opponents freely predicted that this new "nationality" could not long survive being deprived of its traditional moorings in religion, Hebrew culture, and its old or new messianic-Zionist goals. They insisted that, no matter how many Jewish children might attend schools with the Yiddish language of instruction, no matter how many local soviets or courts of justice might use Yiddish as their official medium of communication, in the end that new secular nationality would still have to discard some three millennia of its Hebraic history and religious Weltanschauung; it would still have to limit itself to a small cultural segment of its heritage, created in the form of belles lettres by a few outstanding poets and writers of two or three prerevolutionary East European generations. At the same time this Jewish minority would be exposed to the powerful impact of the great cultural attainments of the Russian people of both the tsarist and the communist era. Combined with the indoctrination in the new communist Weltanschauung this overwhelming pressure of the great outside culture could not possibly long be resisted with the meager survivalist tools at the disposal of the downtrodden community.

These dire predictions seemed to come true as early as the 1930s when the autonomous cultural Jewish structure, built up with so much devotion in the 1920s, had begun to crumble in the severe clime of the Nazi-Communist controversy. Beginning in 1934, fewer and fewer Yiddish books were allowed to be published, Yiddish school attendance declined sharply within a few years, and more and more of the Yiddish cultural institutions were dismantled. The terror, moreover, spreading through all classes of society in that era of early purges muted the protests of communal organs and thus deprived them of even the negative solidarity engendered by such complaints in unison. This process of attrition was briefly interrupted by the Soviet occupation of eastern Poland and the Baltic countries whose Jewish communities, together with some hundreds of thousands of refugees from Nazi-occupied Poland, injected a powerful rejuvenating factor into Soviet Jewish life. But the situation was completely reversed when the Nazi armies overran all these and many additional Soviet territories, physically exterminating millions of Jews they now controlled. Even among the remaining segments of the Soviet Jewish communities all manifestations of cultural vitality were quickly expunged by the enforced silence imposed upon them during the "black years" of the Stalinist terror. There seemed, indeed, to be little hope for any Jewish survival; certainly for any meaningful survival based upon the cultivation of one's religio-cultural heritage.

RIVAL RELIGION

Far beyond these external pressures the intrinsic forces of Jewish survival were seriously sapped by the new communist ideology. It has long been recognized that, while appearing as a scientific, materialistic movement, communism had in itself all the features of a new religion, promising its believers a glittering messianic future and threatening all infidels or sectarian deviationists with fire and brimstone. No less a student of the Russian mentality than Nicholas Berdyaev, a former Marxist become one of the leading Russian philosophers of religion, once observed:

> Communism, both as a theory and as a practice, is not only a social phenomenon, but also a spiritual and religious phenomenon. And it is formidable precisely as a *religion*.

It is as a religion that it opposes Christianity and aims at ousting it. . . . It has its dogmas and its dogmatic morals, has even the beginnings of its own cult; it takes possession of the whole soul and calls forth enthusiasm and self-sacrifice.

It is this religious exclusivity which has accounted for both the great expansive power of the communist credo and its severe denominational limitations. At the outset, its basically universalist message greatly appealed to members of all nationalities and easily displaced in the minds of many all particularist, or historically and nationally confined, religions. To many younger Jews, especially, who had grown impatient with the "narrow" particularist traditions of their own Orthodox mode of living, this universalist message sounded like the long-expected clarion call to a boundless humanitarian embrace and the ultimate liberation movement for all men.[1]

If, in the past, Judaism had effectively resisted the encroachments of other faiths, although it had at one time or another surrendered segments of its population to the on-rushing universalist waves of early Christianity or early Islam in their truly heroic stages, it now faced a rival religion which seemed the more persuasive as it denied being a religion. By emphasizing secularism, fully in consonance with the secularist trends of the modern era, and by refraining from demanding any particular religious initiation which necessarily placed upon each convert the formal sign of betrayal of his former faith, communism could indeed appear as the all-human new civilization to which Jews, and others, might readily surrender their identity.

As time went on, however, Russian communism was forced, by historic circumstances, to shed more and more of its universalist features and to emphasize its particularist Russian characteristics. In the titanic Second World War its very survival depended on the appeal to the traditional Russian patriotism, and in a far lesser degree to that of the minorities. The Great Patriotic War thus clinched an evolution which had become increasingly evident after the death of Lenin and the defeat of Trotsky: the Soviets' return to the traditional moorings of the Russian soil and the Russian national spirit.

By the last years of Stalin the wheel of history had made a complete turn. Despite the tremendous revolutionary changes which seemed to have transformed society and its outlook from the bottom up, the early 1950s were not so far apart from the early 1850s as they appeared to superficial observers. Uvarov's famous guidelines for Nicholas I's regime, "Orthodoxy, Autocracy and [Russian] Nationality," applied now to Stalin's Russia under new guises. Of course, Orthodoxy now meant not conformity with the teachings of the Russian-Orthodox Church, but one with the even more inviolable dogmas of the Communist Party and their exclusively valid interpretations by the Holy Synod of its Politbureau. Autocracy was even stronger than it had been, because it was buttressed by the state's full control over the means of production, its far greater ability to uproot and deport entire populations, and its much more pervasive police surveillance than that of the tsarist gendarmerie. Only with respect to Russian nationalism was the Stalinist regime less explicitly demanding in theory. In practice, however, Russification was progressing with gigantic steps and, notwithstanding all the mouthings of the principle of minority rights, it celebrated far more rapid victories than it had in any such short span of time during the Romanov era.

Above all, there has been under both regimes an overriding, all-benumbing terror. What the keen French observer, Marquis Astolphe L. de Custine, wrote about the Russia of 1839 applied no less to the "black years" of the Stalinist terror:

> The affectation of resignation is the lowest depth of abjectness into which an enslaved nation can fall: revolt or despair would be doubtless more terrible, but less ignominious. Weakness so degraded that it dare not indulge itself even in complaint, . . . fear calmed by its own excess—these are moral phenomena which cannot be witnessed without calling forth tears of horror.[2]

Jews, too, found themselves facing an implacable regime quite reminiscent of that of a century earlier. As under Nicholas I the aim remained to denationalize and completely to absorb the Jewish minority, if need be with the aid of the mailed fist. Under Nicholas it was the combination of the seizure of Jewish children for long-term military service, the removal of Jews from frontier districts, and the closing of the *kahal*, with the liberal admission of Jews to Western-type schools, and other measures, both overtly forcible or deceptively friendly, which was to lead to the Christianization of the Jewish masses and their ultimate disappearance as an identifiable group apart. On its part, the Stalinist regime in its last phases tried to achieve substantially the same purpose through the deportation of recalcitrant individuals for long-term forced labor, the uprooting of large groups of temporarily declassed persons, the suppression of all Jewish communal organs, the physical destruction of their intellectual leadership, and the total silencing of any cultural form of expression, combined with the promises of full self-determination in distant Biro-Bidzhan. Instead of having to turn Christian in order to become good Russians, Jews now had to become devout communists, equally forgetful of their own heritage. Even less than in the days of Nicholas, were Jews free to choose the alternative of leaving the country. Once again the frontiers were closely watched and, except for the flight of a few individuals, most Jews, and for that matter, also non-Jews, felt permanently immured behind invisible but no less impregnable walls under the watchful eyes of a capricious dictator.

New Marranos

It did not escape the keen eyes of outsiders that this denial of one's heritage forced a great many Russian Jews to live a double life, reminiscent of that of the Spanish and Portuguese Marranos. In the Iberian Peninsula, too, Jews had long cherished the hope of being able to develop their autonomous culture under conditions of relative freedom. But an intolerant regime, even more nationalistically than Church oriented, finally told them that they had to conform and be assimilated by the majority through adopting the latter's beliefs and modes of life. If, in 1492, Spain still left the Jews the alternative of a harried, unhappy and dangerous departure, Portugal five years later gave them no such choice but forced them all to adopt Christianity. The result was that, particularly in the smaller kingdom, the Jews maintained their secret life for generations thereafter.

Nor was this a singular exception. Throughout medieval and early modern history it happened time and again that, while individual Jews, converted to Christianity or Islam, were rather quickly absorbed by the body politic of the majority, any mass conversion of Jews resulted in the perpetuation within that body of an alien group retaining memories of its Jewish past. Four centuries after the so-called expulsion from Portugal thousands of Marranos living in and around Oporto still sufficiently retained the traces of their former Jewishness for many to find their way back to the Jewish community during the 1920s. Nor, one could argue, would any Russian secret service be more enduringly effective in ferreting out all secret forms of nonconformity than had been the Iberian Inquisition.

Fortunately, it appears that no generations of secret living will be required before the Soviet regime will realize that its methods are totally self-defeating. Khrushchev and his associates have already conceded many grave errors committed during the Stalinist terror; they have already purged the Lenin mausoleum of Stalin's body and, either physically or at least in the memory of men, they have rehabilitated at least some of the dictator's victims. In the Jewish case this reversal has thus far been painfully slow and incomplete. For reasons not yet fully explained, the new administration still persists along the Stalinist denial of any legitimate outlets for Jewish education, literary and artistic creativity, and even simple religious observance or daily modes of life.

It stands to reason, however, that such illogical behavior will not long endure. It certainly is not too sanguine to expect that, before very long, the Soviet Union will be prepared to sign and ratify the international convention guaranteeing the right of every individual to leave his native land and to return thereto. It may not be likely that, so long as it prohibits other citizens from emigrating, it will make an exception for the Jews, yet we must not forget that, while the tsarist regime, too, during most of the nineteenth century had outlawed mass emigration in any form, it saw itself forced to open the floodgates first to a Jewish and, then, to a lesser extent, to a non-Jewish exodus during the last decades before the First World War.

More significantly, in the titanic struggle for control over humanity, both physical and mental, the Soviet Union can no more afford to waste the great human energies, potentially dormant in a suppressed people like the Jews, than can any Western power consistently pursue discriminatory racial policies. To all keen observers of our modern scene it has become manifest that not the possession of ever increasing chunks of property, or its denial—these overriding issues of the nineteenth century—but rather that of knowledge, imaginative, creative knowledge of the universe and its potentialities, has become the real source of power. To dispense in the long run with the fullest contribution that the Jewish people of Russia can make to the widening of the frontiers of human knowledge, because of some atavistic desires for discrimination, would clearly be even more self-defeating than the persistent racial segregation of the Southern Negroes in the United States. Even now there is less anti-Jewish discrimination in the basic fields of Soviet science and technology, especially nuclear physics and space exploration.

True, our prognosis may turn out to be overoptimistic. We need but remember the tremendous eruption of irrational forces into all human affairs in our generation. Yet we must not overlook the very basic assumption of both American democracy and Russia's materialistic conception of history, namely, that in any long historic process reason must ultimately prevail.

NOTES

CHAPTER 1 (pages 1-14)

1. St. Jerome, *Commentary* on Zechariah 10:11, in Migne's *Patrologia latina*, XXV, 1568 f.

2. Muqaddasi, *Descriptio imperii islamici*, ed. by De Goeje, Leiden, 1877, p. 355; Ibn an-Nadim, *K. al-Fihrist* (Book of the List: a Bibliography), ed. by G. Flügel, 2 vols., Leipzig, 1872, I, 20. On the complex problems of the Khazars and the Khazar origins of East-European Jewry, *see* the vast literature, cited in the author's *A Social and Religious History of the Jews*, 2d ed. rev., Vols. I-VIII and Index thereto, New York, 1952-60, esp. Vol. III, pp. 196 ff., 323 ff.

3. Adam of Bremen, *Gesta Hammaburgensis ecclesiae pontificum*, ii. 19, ed. by Johann M. Lappenberg, Hanover, 1846, in *Monumenta Germaniae historica*, Scriptores, VII, 312 f.

4. *The Russian Primary Chronicle*, Laurentian Text, English trans. by Samuel H. Cross and Olgerd P. Sherbovitz-Wetzor, Cambridge, Mass., 1953 (Publications of the Mediaeval Academy of America, LX), pp. 96 ff.

5. Johannes Schiltberger, *The Bondage and Travels . . . in Europe, Asia and Africa, 1396-1427*, English trans. by J. Buchan Telfer, with notes by P. Brunn, London, 1879. Works issued by the Hakluyt Society, LVIII, pp. 49, 176 n. 7.

6. Julius Brutzkus, "Zechariah, the Prince of Taman" (Russian), *Evreiskaia Starina*, X (1918), 132-43.

7. The origins and evolution of the important sect of *Judaizanti* have long intrigued scholars. *See* the extensive older literature cited by D. Oljancyn in his "Aus dem Kutur-und-Geistesleben der Ukraine, I: Was ist die Häresie der 'Judaisierenden'?" *Kyrios*, I (1936), 176-89, although that author's own hypothesis that it was a native movement without any Jewish influence appears untenable. However, many problems still await clarification, especially in connection with the underground survivals of the sect beyond the early sixteenth century and their impact on the continued hostility of the Russian leaders to the possible missionary effects of the admission of Jews to Russia.

8. Vittore Colorni, "Note per la biografia di alcuni dotti ebrei vissuti a Mantova nel secolo XV," *Annuario di studi ebraici*, I (1934), 172 ff.

9. Julius Hessen, *Istoriia evreiskago naroda v Rossii* (A History of the Jewish People in Russia), 2 vols., Leningrad, 1925-27, I, 39; *idem*, "Jews in Courland (XVI-XVIII Centuries)" (Russian), *Evreiskaia Starina*, VII (1914), 145 ff. On this and other phases of Russian-Jewish history, *see also* the older sources and studies listed in the *Sistematicheskii ukazatel literatury o Evreiakh* (A Systematic Guide to the Literature on Jews), St. Petersburg, 1883.

10. "From the Archives of the Yiddish Scientific Institute (YIVO)" (Yiddish), *YIVO Studies in History*, II (1937), 667 f.

11. More details about these two noteworthy social climbers are furnished by Saul M. Ginsburg in his *Historishe Verk* (Historical Works), new series, Vol. II: "Converts in Tsarist Russia: Studies in History of Russian Jewry," New York, 1946, pp. 11-33. *See also*, more generally, Robert Stupperich, *Staatsgedanke und Religionspolitik Peters des Grossen*, Breslau, 1936. Osteuropäische Forschungen, n.s. XXII.

12. Jacob Gurland, "An Episode from the History of the Expulsion of the Jews from Russia in 1727" (Russian), *Evreiskaia Starina*, II (1909), 246-50.

13. Hessen, *Istoriia*, I, 51 f.

CHAPTER 2 (pages 15-30)

1. Mikhail M. Speransky, *Proekty i zapiski* (Projects and Memoirs), ed. by A. I. Kopanev *et al.*, Moscow, 1961 (U. S. S. R. Academy of Science, Historical Section), pp. 86 ff. *See also* Marc Raeff, *Michael Speransky, Statesman of Imperial Russia, 1772-1839*, The Hague, 1957, esp. pp. 204 ff., 222 ff.

2. *See* the author's *The Jewish Community: Its History and Structure to the American Revolution*, 3 vols., Philadelphia, 1942, II, 274 f.; III, 190 ff. n. 31; and such monographs as Jacob Galant, "The Debts of Jewish Kahals in Podolia and Volhynia" (Russian), *Zbirnyk prats* (Collection of Papers) of the Jewish Historical and Archaeological Commission, II (1929), 119-27. *See also* below, Chap. VII. n. 2.

3. Gabriel R. Derzhavin, *Sochineniia* (Works), 2d ed., with notes by Yakob Grot, 7 vols., St. Petersburg, 1868-78, VI, 688 ff.; VII, 261-355. *See also ibid.*, VI, 122 ff., 688 ff., 761 ff., etc.

4. The text of this law is reproduced in the *Polnoe sobranie zakonov rossiiskoi imperii* (Complete Collection of Laws of the Russian Empire), 1st ser. XXVIII No. 21,547; and, from there, in Vitalii O. Levanda's *Polnyi khronologicheskii sbornik zakonov* (Complete Chronological Collection of Laws and Ordinances Relating to Jews, 1649-1873), St. Petersburg, 1874, pp. 53 ff. No. 59.

5. N. M. Gelber, "La Police autrichienne et le Sanhédrin de Napoléon," *Revue des études juives*, LXXXIII (1927), 137, App. 2.

6. Alexeiev's report, cited by Simon M. Dubnow in his *History of the Jews in Russia and Poland from the Earliest Times until the Present Day*, English trans. from the Russian by Israel Friedlander, 3 vols., Philadelphia, 1916, I, 347 f. Sonnenberg and Dillon, theretofore unofficial representatives, were later to play a considerable role among the elected "Deputies of the Jewish People." *See* Julius Hessen and D. G. Maggid's pertinent essays cited below n. 10., and Chap. VII, n. 4.

7. Chaim Borodiansky, "Poems of Eulogy in Honor of Catherine II and Their Authors" (Yiddish), *Yivo Historishe Shriftn* (Yivo Studies in History), II (1937), 531-37; "From the Archives of the Yiddish Scientific Institute (Yivo)," *ibid.*, pp. 680 f. (reproducing in facsimile the title page and first Hebrew page of a poem published by the Vilna community in 1802 in honor of Alexander I).

8. Saul M. Ginsburg, *Otechestvennaia voina 1812 goda i russkiie evreii* (The Patriotic War of 1812 and the Russian Jews), St. Petersburg, 1912, p. 30; Asriel Nathan Frenk, *Yehude Polin bi-yeme milhamot Napoleon* (Polish Jews during the Napoleonic Wars), Warsaw, 1912.

9. August Fournier, *Die Geheimpolizei auf dem Wiener Kongress. Eine Auswahl aus ihren Papieren*, Vienna, 1913, p. 164 n. 2; Max J. Kohler, "Jewish Rights at the Congresses of Vienna (1814-1815) and Aix-la-Chapelle (1818)," *Publications of the American Jewish Historical Society*, XXVI (1918), 82 ff., 116 ff. *See also*, more generally, the author's *Die Judenfrage auf dem Wiener Kongress auf Grund von zum Teil ungedruckten Quellen dargestellt*, Vienna, 1920.

10. The Slutsky affair is described on the basis of the Synod's own archival data by Saul M. Ginsburg in "A Forced Conversion of a Rabbi's Daughter" (Yiddish) in his *Historishe Verk*, III, 162-77. On the deputies, *see* Julius I. Hessen, "The 'Deputies of the Jewish People' in the Days of Alex-

ander I" (Russian), *Evreiskaia Starina*, II (1909), 17-29, 196-206; and below, Chap. VII, n. 4.

11. *See* Julius Hessen, "On the Origin of the Ritual Murder Literature in the Russian Language" (Russian), *Evreiskaia Letopis*, I (1923), 3-17. *See* Chap. III.

CHAPTER 3 (pages 31-50)

1. Jacques Ancelot, *Six mois en Russie: lettres écrites à M. X.-B. Saintines en 1826*, Paris, 1827, p. 184; Nicholas I's Diary reproduced by N. Schilder in "The Grand Duke Nicholas Pavlovich" (Russian), *Russkaia Starina*, VI (1901), 465 f. It may be noted that the term *zhid* (Jew) had long acquired a pejorative connotation and, ever since Catherine II, had been replaced by *evrei* (Hebrew) in official parlance. *See also* S. Beilin, "From Historical Journals, IV: a Statement of the Grand Duke Nicholas Pavlovich about the Jews" (Russian), *Evreiskaia Starina*, IV (1911), 589-90.

2. *See* Saul M. Ginsburg, *Historishe Verk*, n.s. II, 34 ff.; and, more generally, Mikhail Osipovich Zetlin, *The Decembrists*, English trans. by George Parin, with a Preface by Michael Karpovich, New York, 1958.

3. The text of this remarkable oath, followed by signatures of Jewish witnesses and judges, is reproduced by Saul M. Ginsburg in his *Historishe Verk*, II, p. 10. The text of the law of August 26, 1827 is reproduced from the *Polnoe sobranie* in Levanda's *Polnyi . . . sbornik*, pp. 102 ff. No. 154, while Nicholas I's lengthy instructions to the priests in charge of cantonist institutions concerning the conversion of Jews are published in the Appendix to Ginsburg, III, 357-69.

4. Alexander Herzen, *Byloye i dumy* (Reminiscences and Meditations) in Constance Garnett's English trans. entitled *My Past and Thoughts*, 6 vols., New York, 1924-26, I, 270 ff.

5. This Yiddish folksong, included in Saul M. Ginsburg and P. Marek's collection of *Evreiskie narodnye pesni* (Jewish Folksongs), St. Petersburg, 1901, No. 50, is cited in an English trans. by Isaac Levitats in *The Jewish Community in Russia, 1772-1844*, New York, 1943, p. 65.

6. Hugh Y. Reyburn, *The Story of the Russian Church*, London, 1924, pp. 8 f.

7. *See* the author's Hebrew article, "A Vilna Excommunication and the Great Powers," *Horeb*, XII (1956), 62-69. The text of that ban could not be located in any Russian archive.

Even its German translation used in the internal exchanges in Prussia, still available to the author at the Geheimes Preussisches Staatsarchiv between the two wars, seems to have disappeared during the Second World War.

8. Jacob Jacobson, "Eine Aktion für die russischen Grenzjuden in den Jahren 1843/44," *Festschrift . . . Simon Dubnow*, Berlin, 1930, pp. 237-50; N. M. Gelber, "The Intercession of Baron Salomon Rothschild of Vienna in Behalf of the Russian Jews in 1846" (Yiddish), *YIVO Historische Shriftn*, I (1929), 803-10.

9. The provisions here cited form but a small selection of the 121 articles included in the statute of 1835 and printed in the *Polnoe sobranie*, 2d ser. X, No. 8,054. The text is reproduced by Levanda in his *Polnyi . . . sbornik*, pp. 359 ff. No. 304.

10. Pinhas Kon, "The Attitude of the Tsarist Authorities to Maimonides" (Yiddish), *Yivo Bleter*, XIII (1938), 577-82.

11. David Philipson, "Max Lilienthal in Russia," *Hebrew Union College Annual*, XII-XIII (1937-38), 829, 833, 838; *idem, Max Lilienthal, American Rabbi, Life and Writings*, New York, 1915, esp. pp. 12 ff.; Julius Hessen, "Die russische Regierung und die westeuropäischen Juden (Zur Schulreform in Russland 1840-44). Nach archivalischen Materialien," *Monatsschrift für Geschichte und Wissenschaft des Judentums*, LVII (1913), 257-71, 482-500 (also reprint).

12. Philipson, *Max Lilienthal*, p. 264. The Vilna community went so far as to address, on July 10, 1842, a letter to Lilienthal's father, Judah, in Munich, trying to induce him to restrain his overzealous son. This letter was intended to counteract another, sent to that father by some progressive leaders of Berdichev which had been full of praise for young Lilienthal's endeavors. Published in a German trans. in the *Allgemeine Zeitung des Judentums* (VI, 1942, 715 f.), the Berdichev epistle had helped to reinforce the erroneous impression among the Western Jews. Philipson, pp. 33 ff.; Saul M. Ginsburg, "Max Lilienthal's Activities in Russia: New Documents," *Publications of the American Jewish Historical Society*, XXXV (1939), 45 ff. *See also* below, Chap. VIII.

13. Nicholas Hans, *History of Russian Educational Policy (1701-1917)*, London, 1931 (Diss. University of London), pp. 73 f., 85 ff., in part based on Beletskii's "Jewish Education under Nicholas I" (Russian), *Russkaia shkola*, IV (1893).

14. *Diaries of Sir Moses Montefiore and Lady Montefiore,* ed. by L. Loewe, 2 vols., Chicago, 1890, I, 317 f., 328 ff.; Saul M. Ginsburg, *Historishe Verk,* II, 163-202, 292-305 (on Montefiore), 203-19, 304-5 (on Altaras); Theodor Schiemann, *Geschichte Russlands unter Kaiser Nikolaus I,* 4 vols, Berlin, 1908-19, IV, 79 f., also quoting another English official's exaggerated statement, "As to the poor Jews themselves, they look upon him [Montefiore] and actually call him their Messiah" (p. 80 n. 1).

15. Albert M. Hyamson, ed., *The British Consulate in Jerusalem in Relation to the Jews of Palestine, 1838-1914,* 2 vols., London, 1939-41, I, pp. xlviii ff., 109 ff. Nos. 68 and 71, 130 f. No. 80, 146 ff. No. 96.

16. Osip Rabinovich's editorial in *Razsvet,* 1860, vi. 85; his other publicist writings and programmatic stories, collected in his *Sochineniia* (Works), 3 vols., St. Petersburg, 1880-88; Louis Greenberg, *The Jews in Russia,* 2 vols., New Haven, 1944-59, I, 83, 85. See also below, Chap. IX, n. 19.

17. See N. M. Gelber, *Die Juden und der polnische Aufstand 1863,* Vienna, 1923, esp. p. 165; Jacob Shatzky, "Jews in the Polish Uprising of 1863" (Yiddish), *Yivo Historishe Shriftn,* I (1929), 423-68; D. Fajnhauz, "The Jewish Population in Lithuania and White Russia in the Uprising of January 1863" (Polish), *Biuletyn* of the Zydowski Instytut Historyczny in Warsaw, XXXVIII (1961), 39-68; and the telling anecdotes reported by Ezekiel Kotik in *Maine Zikhroines* (My Reminiscences), 2 vols., Berlin, 1922, I, 271.

18. Jacob Brafman, *Kniga Kahala* (The Book of the Kahal), 2d ed., 2 vols., St. Petersburg, 1875-82. With its motto taken from Friedrich Schiller's statement, "The Jews form a state within the state," this book furnished much ammunition for Jew-baiters in the following decades. It was published for the same purpose in a German trans. by Siegfried Passarge, under the title *Das Buch vom Kahal,* 2 vols., Leipzig, 1928. On the modicum of its trustworthiness, *see* Isaac Levitats, "The Authenticity of Brafman's Book of the Kahal" (Hebrew), *Zion,* III (1938), 170-78.

19. *See* the first-hand observations by Henry (Genrikh) B. Sliozberg in his "Baron G. [H.] O. Günzburg and the Legal Status of Jews" (Russian), *Perezhitoe,* II (1910), 94-115; the full-length biography cited below, Chap. VI, n. 23; and Julius Hessen's "On the Lot of Jewish Physicians in Russia" (Russian), *Evreiskaia Starina,* III (1910), 612-23.

CHAPTER 4 (pages 51-75)

1. Much documentation on the Russian pogroms has been assembled by A. Linden (pseud. for Leo Motzkin), *et al.*, in *Die Judenpogrome in Russland*, ed. by the Zionistischer Hilfsfond in London, 2 vols., Cologne, 1910; G. Krasnii-Admoni (with the cooperation of Simon M. Dubnow), ed., *Materialy dlia istorii anti-evreiskikh pogromov v Rossii* (Materials for the History of Anti-Jewish Pogroms in Russia), 2 vols., Petrograd, 1919-23; and the three Yiddish essays by Elias Tscherikower, "New Materials about the Pogroms in Russia at the Beginning of the 1880s"; N. M. Gelber, "The Pogroms in Russia in the Light of Austrian Diplomatic Correspondence"; and I. L. Lipshitz, "The Intervention of the United States about the Pogroms in Russia in 1881-1882" in *YIVO Historishe Shriftn*, II (1937), 444-65, 466-96, 497-516. *See also* Mina Goldberg's dissertation, *Die Jahre 1881-1882 in der Geschichte der russischen Juden*, Berlin, 1934.

2. Alexander III's marginal notations on these government reports have been published from archival sources after the Revolution by R. M. Kantor in his "Alexander III on the Anti-Jewish Pogroms of 1881-83" (Russian), *Evreiskaia Letopis*, I (1923), 149-58.

3. Constantin Pobedonostsev, *L'Autocratie russe. Mémories politiques, correspondance officielle et documents inédits (1881-1894)*, Paris, 1927, pp. 61 f.; Nadezhda Jaffe, "Molodetskii's Assault on the Russian Dictator Count M. Loris-Melikov in 1880: From New Sources" (Yiddish), *Di Zukunft*, XLIII (1938), 89-93; Nikolai P. Ignatev's memorandum of August 22, 1881, more fully cited, in a somewhat different English trans., in Dubnow's *History*, II, 271 f. On Goldenberg, see his "Confession," published in Russian by R. Kantor in *Krasnii Arkhiv*, XXX (1928), 117-83; and other sources cited by Elias Tcherikower in his "Jews—Revolutionaries in Russia in the 1860s and 1870s" (Yiddish), *Yivo Historishe Shriftn*, III (1939), 145 ff., 815 f. *See also ibid.*, pp. 142 ff.

4. Wickham Hofman's report to the Department of State of April 29, 1882, in *Papers Relating to the Foreign Relations of the United States*, 1882, p. 452. The figure of 5,000,000 Jews at that time was exaggerated. *See infra*, Chap. V. Characteristically, a well-substantiated rumor had it that Ignatev himself delayed the issuance of the May Laws until he made certain that the Jewish managers of his estates

in the Kiev province had signed new twelve-year contracts and thus became exempt from the operation of these laws. *See* Harold Frederic, *The New Exodus: a Study of Israel in Russia,* London, 1892, p. 130. Ignatev's devious policies, his attempt to use the Jewish leaders for his purposes and his expectation to receive a *douceur* of 2,000,000 rubles, are analyzed in Benzion Dinur's recent Hebrew essay, "Ignatiev's 'Projects for the Solution of the Jewish Question' and the Meetings of Representatives of the Jewish Communities in St. Petersburg in 1881-82," *He-Abar,* X(1963), 5-82.

5. Countess Mariia E. Kleinmichel, *Memories of a Shipwrecked World,* English trans. by Vivian le Grand, London, 1923, pp. 129 f. A survey of Russian Jewry's disabilities in the 1890s was offered by the Belgian professor, Leo Errera, in *The Russian Jews: Extermination or Emancipation?* With a Prefatory Note by Theodor Mommsen. Trans. from the French by Bella Löwy, London, 1894. Of course, Errera advocated complete emancipation in preference to its sole alternative: extermination. A more detailed legal analysis of the conditions in the following decade is found in Genrikh (Henry) B. Sliozberg's *Pravovoe i ekonomicheskoe polozhenie Evreev v Rossii* (The Legal and Economic Status of the Jews in Russia: From Materials on the Jewish Question), St. Petersburg, 1907.

6. The protracted Jewish struggle to salvage the Moscow synagogue in 1891-1906 is described by A. S. Katsnelson in his "From the Martyrdom of the Moscow Community" (Russian), *Evreiskaia Starina,* I (1909), 175-88.

7. Benjamin Harrison's Third Annual Message to Congress of December 9, 1891, in James A. Richardson's *A Compilation of the Messages and Papers of the Presidents, 1789-1908,* 11 vols., Washington, D. C., 1909, IX, 188; Dubnow, *History,* II, 408 ff.; III, 10.

8. Pobedonostsev's letter to Alexander III of February 11, 1888, in *L'Autocratie russe,* p. 523; Arnold White, "Jewish Colonization and the Russian Persecution," *New Review,* V (1891), 97-105. Hirsch himself explained, in part, his personal motivations in "My Views of Philanthropy," reprinted from the *North-American Review* of July, 1891, in Samuel Joseph's *History of the Baron de Hirsch Fund,* Philadelphia, 1935, pp. 275-77.

9. D. Zaslavskii, "Jews in Russian Literature" (Russian), *Evreiskaia Letopis,* I (1923), 59-86; Joshua Kunitz, *Russian Literature and the Jew: a Sociological Inquiry into the Nature*

and Origin of Literary Patterns, New York, 1929 (Diss. Columbia University); Feivel Goetz's analysis of *Der Philosoph W. Solowioff und das Judentum,* Riga, 1927; F. Häusler, "V. G. Korolenkos Kampf gegen den Antisemitismus," *Wissenschaftliche Zeitschrift der Martin-Luther-Universität,* X (1961), 237-48. See also below, Chap. IX, n. 8.

10. Alexander Kornilov, *Modern Russian History,* 2 vols., New York, 1917, II, 278.

11. Dubnow's *History,* III, 26 f.; above, n. 5.

12. N. Chmerkine (Shmerkin), *Les Conséquences de l'antisémitisme en Russie,* with a Foreword by M. G. de Molinari, Paris, 1897; Martin Philippson, *Neueste Geschichte des jüdischen Volkes,* 3 vols., Frankfort, 1907-11, III, 172 ff.

13. Herman Bernstein, *The Truth about "The Protocols of Zion": a Complete Exposure,* New York, 1935, pp. 36 f. See also V. L. Burtsev, *Protokoly sionskikh mudretsov* (The Protocols of the Elders of Zion), Paris, 1938; John Shelton Curtis, *An Appraisal of the Protocols of Zion,* New York, 1942; and, more generally, Mark Vishniak, "Antisemitism in Tsarist Russia: a Study in Government-Fostered Antisemitism" in Koppel S. Pinson, ed., *Essays on Antisemitism,* 2d ed., New York, 1946, pp. 121-44.

14. Michael Davitt, *Within the Pale: the True Story of Anti Semitic Persecution in Russia,* New York, 1903, p. 126; *Memoirs of a Russian Governor, Prince Serge Dmitriyevich Urussov,* ed. and trans. into English by Herman Rosenthal, New York, 1908, esp. pp. 42 ff., 142 ff. See also above, n. 1. On the reaction in other countries, see esp. Cyrus Adler, *The Voice of America on Kishineff,* Philadelphia, 1903.

15. Alexander B. Tager, *The Decay of Czarism: the Beiliss Trial,* Philadelphia, 1935, pp. 10 f.; Urussov, *Memoirs,* p. 55.

16. Maxim Gorki, "Kishineff Mob Were Led by Men of Cultivated Society" in the English trans. by William Curtis Stiles in his *Out of Kishineff: The Duty of the American People to the Russian Jew,* New York, [1903], pp. 276 ff. See also Leo Tolstoy's comment, *ibid.,* pp. 274 f.; and below, n. 19.

17. Simeon Samuel Frug, "The Resurrection," in the English trans. by Maurice Samuel in Edmond Fleg, *The Jewish Anthology,* New York, 1925, pp. 387 f. It may be noted that, in order to live in St. Petersburg, Frug had to register with the police as a valet to one of the local attorneys.

18. *Pravo,* 1905, No. 19, here cited, with some variations, from the English trans. by L. Greenberg in *The Jews in*

Russia, II, 114. *See also* L. Rubinov, "The Jewish Self-Defense in Southern Russia during the First Revolution" (Yiddish), *Fun nuenten Ovar* (From the Recent Past), I (1938), 322-32; and, on the Jewish part in the Revolution, S. Dimanshtain, *Di revolutsionere bavegung ba yidishe masn in di revolutsie fun 1905 yor* (The Revolutionary Movement among the Jewish Masses in 1905), Moscow, 1929.

19. These developments are well summarized from the Stenographic Protocols of the Duma and the contemporary Russo-Jewish press by Sidney S. Harcave in "The Jewish Question in the First Russian Duma," *Jewish Social Studies*, VI (1944), 155-76. The report concerning the Bialystok pogrom, the Duma debates, and resolution are reproduced here from an English trans. in the *American Jewish Year Book*, 5667 (1906-1907), pp. 70-89. *See also* Jakob Jaffé's dissertation, *Ursachen und Verlauf der Juden-Pogrome in Russland im Oktober 1905*, Bern, 1916, which includes a number of references to expressions of non-Jewish leaders (pp. 69 ff.).

20. Nicholas' statement reported by the then Finance Minister Vladimir N. Kokovtsov in his *Memoirs*, trans. into English by Laura Matveev and ed. by H. H. Fischer under the title *Out of My Past: Memoirs of Count Kokovtsov*, Stanford, California, 1935 (Hoover War Library Publications, VI), p. 167; Tager, *The Decay of Czarism*, p. 14.

21. Tager, *The Decay*, pp. 20, 58; A. Chernovskii, *Soiuz russkago naroda* (Union of the Russian People: According to the Materials of the Extraordinary Investigating Commission of the Provisional Government of 1917), Moscow, 1929, *passim*.

22. Ivan Sergeevich Aksakov, "Judaism as a World-Wide Phenomenon" (Russian), reprinted in his *Polnoe sobranie sochinenii* (Complete Collection of Works), 7 vols., Moscow, 1886-87, III, 725-35 (also his attacks on the Alliance Israélite, *ibid.*, pp. 819 ff., 827 ff., 843 ff.); Lamsdorf's memorandum trans. (from the Russian text published in the Secret Documents issued by the Soviet Commission of Foreign Affairs, Vol. VI) by Lucien Wolf in his *Notes on the Diplomatic History of the Jewish Question*, London, 1919, pp. 57-62. On the earlier activities of the Alliance in Russia and Poland and its attitude toward the Russian government, *see* Zoza Szajkowski. "The Alliance Israélite Universelle and East-European Jewry in the '60s," *Jewish Social Studies*, IV (1942), 139 ff., 148 ff.

23. *See* the amply documented story of the Beiliss affair in A. B. Tager, *The Decay of Czarism*. Interesting sidelights are also thrown by the reminiscences of the chief defense counsel Oscar O. Gruzenberg in his *Vchera* (Yesterday), Paris, 1938. Of more general interest are the essays, in part based upon personal reminiscences, on various aspects of Russian Jewish life between 1860 and 1917 published by the Union of Russian Jews in New York under the title, *Kniga o russkom evreistve* (Book on Russian Jewry), New York, 1960, with the comments thereon by Elias Hurwicz in his "Zur Psychologie und Problematik des russischen Judentums," *Zeitschrift für Politik*, VIII (1961), 256-70. *See also* E. Lifshitz, "Repercussions of the Beilis Trial in the United States" (Hebrew), *Zion*, XXVIII (1963), 206-222.

CHAPTER 5 (pages 76-89)

1. The results of the 1897 census are comprehensively analyzed in the *Sbornik materialov ob ekonomicheskom polozhenii Evreev v Rossii* (Collection of Materials relating to the Economic Conditions of the Jews in Russia), published by the Jewish Colonization Association, 2 vols., St. Petersburg, 1904; and briefly summarized by J. G. Lipman and Herman Rosenthal in "Russia: Census Statistics," *Jewish Encyclopedia*, X, 529-34. The figures differ slightly in Jacob Lestchinsky, *Dos yidishe folk in tsifern* (The Jewish People in Numbers), Berlin, 1922, whose pioneering effort in this field, though subject to some corrections in detail, still offers the most acceptable data, some of which are utilized in this chapter.

2. The data for European Russia's population, quite unreliable as they appear to be, are cited here from Ludwig Elster's computations in his section of the article "Bevölkerungswesen, III" in the *Handwörterbuch der Staatswissenschaften*, 4th ed., Vol. II, Jena, 1924, pp. 688 f. Somewhat different estimates are given by Paul N. Miliukov and Alexander Kornilov. *See* the latter's *Modern Russian History*, II, 123 ff.

3. Arnold White in *New Review*, V, 98; Robert Lyall, *Travels in Russia, the Krimea, the Caucasus and Georgia*, 2 vols., London, 1825, I, 162; and, more generally, E. Lifshitz, "English Travelers at the Beginning of the Nineteenth Century on East-European Jews" (Yiddish), *Yivo Bleter*, XVI (1940), 59-66.

4. These problems were discussed also outside Russia as early as 1887. In a statistically documented essay, "Les Juifs dans le service militaire," included in his collection *Les Juifs de Russie: Recueil d'articles et d'études sur leur situation légale, sociale et économique*, Paris, 1891, pp. 321 ff., an anonymous author proved that Jews were drafted beyond their ratio in the population. *See also ibid.*, pp. 346 ff.; and other passages listed in the Index, *s.v.* Service militaire. It may be noted that, after the Russo-Japanese War and the Revolution of 1905, a reactionary Vilna deputy to the Third Duma suggested the complete elimination of Jews from the armed services. *See* the counterarguments offered by the Jewish deputy, Leonid N. Nisselovich (Nisselowitsch), trans. into German under the title, *Die Judenfrage in Russland*, Berlin, 1909, pp. 15 ff.

5. Robert Pinkerton, *Russia, or, Miscellaneous Observations on the Past and Present State of that Country and Its Inhabitants. Compiled from Notes Made on the Spot. . . ,* London, 1833, pp. 88, 101 f.; J. de le Roi, "Judentaufen im 19. Jahrhundert. Ein statistischer Versuch," *Nathanael*, XV (1899), 65-118.

6. The figures here cited follow J. Lestchinsky's computations. *See* above, n. 1. It may be noted that Odessa Jewry's rapid expansion attracted the attention of its distant American coreligionists as early as 1857. *See* the *Jewish Messenger*, I (New York, 1857), 38.

7. *See* above, Chap. III, n. 14.

8. Mary Antin, *From Plotzk to Boston*. With a Foreword by Israel Zangwill, Boston, 1899, pp. 12 f.; Leo Shpall, "A List of Selected Items of American Interest in the Russian-Jewish Press, 1860-1932," *Publications of the American Jewish Historical Society*, XXXVIII (1948-49), 239-48, 305-16; XXXIX (1949-50), 87-113.

9. *See* the pertinent documentation in Cyrus Adler and Aaron M. Margalith, *With Firmness in the Right: American Diplomatic Action Affecting Jews, 1840-1945*, New York, 1946, pp. 281 ff.; and the analyses by Louis Marshall (the main architect of the abrogation) and Max J. Kohler in the "American Supplementary Chapters" appended to Luigi Luzzati's *God in Freedom: Studies in the Relations between Church and State*, New York, 1930, pp. 705 ff., 714 ff. *See also* Naomi W. Cohen, "The Abrogation of the Russo-American Treaty of 1832," *Jewish Social Studies*, XXV (1963), 3-41.

10. Cited by Zosa Szajkowski in his "How the Mass Migration to America Began," *Jewish Social Studies*, IV (1942), 309 n. 93.

11. These figures follow the computations by Samuel Joseph in his *Jewish Immigration to the United States from 1881 to 1910*, New York, 1914 (Columbia University, Studies in History, LIX), p. 164 Tables xii-xiii. *See also* Mark Wischnitzer, *To Dwell in Safety: the Story of Jewish Migrations since 1800*, Philadelphia, 1948, esp. pp. 288 ff. and the additional bibliography listed there.

12. Lloyd P. Gartner, *The Jewish Immigrant in England, 1870-1914*, London, 1960.

CHAPTER 6 (pages 90-118)

1. Ivan S. Blioch, *Sravnenie materialnago i nravstennago blagosostoianiia* (A Comparison of the Material and Moral Well-Being of the Western, Greater Russian and By-Vistula [Polish] Provinces), 5 vols., St. Petersburg, 1901 (analyzed by A. Subbotin in *Evreiskaia Biblioteka*, X [1903], 63-123); and other sources listed by Louis Greenberg in *The Jews in Russia*, I, 170 f. *See also* the memorandum submitted in 1894 by Sergei Y. Witte and published by the editor (Simon M. Dubnow) in "The Jewish Question or the Introduction of the Alcohol Monopoly" (Russian), *Evreiskaia Starina*, VIII (1915), 405-10.

2. *See* above, Chap. II. Among the later eloquent exponents of a Jewish return to the soil was the influential Hebrew writer Isaac Baer Levinsohn, especially in his *Te'udah be-Yisrael* (Admonition unto Israel), Vilna, 1828 (written in 1823), which, partly for this reason, received a government prize of one thousand rubles.

3. The fullest information on Jewish agricultural colonization in tsarist Russia and, to a lesser extent, on Jewish individual farming is supplied by V. N. Nikitin in his *Evrei zemledeltsy* (Jewish Farmers, 1807-1887), St. Petersburg, 1887; and by Saul Y. Borovoi, *Evreiskaia zemledelcheskaia kolonizatsiia v staroi Rossii* (Jewish Agricultural Colonization in Old Russia: Politics, Ideology, Economics, Daily Life. From Archival Sources), Moscow, 1928.

4. It should be noted that Benckendorff was not personally a Jew-baiter. On more than one occasion he is said to have calmed down the tsar's outbursts against Jews and Poles.

See Sidney Monas, *The Third Section: Police and Society under Nicholas I,* Cambridge, Mass., 1961, p. 92.

5. *See* J. M. Isler, *Rückkehr der Juden zur Landwirtschaft. Beitrag zur Geschichte der landwirtschaftlichen Kolonisation der Juden in verschiedenen Ländern,* Frankfort, 1929, pp. 14 ff.

6. J. B. Weber and W. Kempter, *Report of the Commissioners of Immigration upon the Causes which Incite Immigration to the United States,* Washington, D. C., 1892, pp. 34 ff. This section relating to Russian Jewry was also published in a French trans. entitled *La situation des Juifs en Russie,* n. p., n. d.

7. *See* the "Official Correspondence on the Discontinuation of the Jewish Colonization in Neo-Russian Territories (1862)," published with his comments by I. Galant (Russian), *Evreiskaia Starina,* V (1912), 330-34. On the Jewish colonization movement in the Kingdom of Poland, to which we could but briefly allude here, *see* Jacob Shatzky, "Contributions to the History of Jewish Colonization in the Kingdom of Poland" (Yiddish), *Yivo Bleter,* VI (1934), 209-32.

8. Tisserand's report, reproduced in the Jewish Colonization Association's *Rapport* for 1908.

9. Jacob Lestchinsky lends in general excessive credence to these computations, but he himself shows that a similar listing in the province of Minsk alone in 1808 gives Jewish artisans a ratio of 19.9 percent. *See* his study in Yivo *Shriftn far ekonomik,* I (1928), 56 f. During the decade of 1808-18 there was a general increase in the Jewish artisan class.

10. Philipp Friedmann, "Wirtschaftliche Umschichtungsprozesse und Industrialisierung in der polnischen Judenschaft 1800-1870," *Jewish Studies in Memory of George A. Kohut,* New York, 1935, p. 185.

11. Usher Margulis, *Geshikhte fun Yidn in Rusland* (A History of the Jews in Russia: Studies and Documents), Vol. I: 1772-1881, Moscow, 1930, pp. 42 ff., 246 ff. Nos. 32-37. On the Jewish guilds as part of the communal structure, *see* Isaac Levitats, "The Jewish Association in Russia in the First Half of the Nineteenth Century" (Yiddish), *The Jewish Review,* I (1943), 83-112. *See also* Boris Brutzkus, "Die wirtschaftliche und soziale Lage der Juden in Russland vor und nach der Revolution," *Archiv für Sozialwissenschaft und Sozialpolitik,* LXI (1929), 266-321, esp. pp. 275 ff.

12. E. B. Lanin, "Jewish Colonization and the Russian

Persecution," *New Review*, V (1891), 113 f. *See* Vasilii
Rosenthal's succinct analysis (largely based on the *Sbornik*
cited above, Chap. V, n. 1) in "Russia: Artisans," *Jewish
Encyclopedia*, X (1905), 534-38, esp. the illuminating break-
down of the various branches by provinces (p. 537); and
S. B. Weinryb, *Neueste Wirtschaftsgeschichte der Juden
in Russland und Polen*, Vol. I: 1772-1881, Breslau, 1934
(Historische Untersuchungen, XII), pp. 93 ff., 115 ff.

13. Gheron Netta, *Die Handelsbeziehungen zwischen
Leipzig und Ost- und Südosteuropa bis zum Verfall der
Warenmessen*, Diss. Zurich, 1920, pp. 40, 139 ff. On some
conflicting data *see* Weinryb, *Neueste Wirtschaftsgeschichte*,
p. 32 n. 2.

14. Count Fryderyk Florian Skarbek, *Dzieje Polski* (History of Poland), Vol. III: Congress Poland after the November Revolution, Poznan, 1877, p. 96; Friedmann in
Jewish Studies . . . Kohut, pp. 214 ff.

15. S. B. Weinryb, *Neueste Wirtschaftsgeschichte*, p. 41.

16. Margulis, *Geshikhte fun Yidn*, I, 276 No. 63.

17. A. Yuditskii, *Yidishe burzhoazie un yidisher proletariat*
(Jewish Bourgeoisie and Jewish Proletariat in the First Half
of the Nineteenth Century), Kiev, 1930, pp. 103 ff. App. 8;
Weinryb, *Neueste Wirtschaftsgeschichte*, I, 52 n. 1; Isaac
Meier Dick, *Feigele der Maggid* (Feigele the Preacher),
Vilna, 1860.

18. *See* the data assembled, from archival sources, by
Yuditskii in his *Yidishe burzhoazie*, esp. pp. 17 f., 35 ff.,
56 f., 96 ff. App. 5.

19. H. Landau, "The Jewish Share in the Russo-Ukrainian
Sugar Industry" (Yiddish), *Yivo Shriftn far ekonomik*, I
(1928), 98-104. As early as 1868, the government recognized that Jews often were the only entrepreneurs competent
to develop that industry in the western provinces and, for
this purpose, relaxed the existing prohibition for landlords to
lease their facilities to Jews. *See* the decree of January 29,
1868, reproduced by V. O. Levanda in his *Polnyi khronologicheskii sbornik*, pp. 1092 f. No. 1004. *See also* P. Tchefra-
noff's (Chefranov's), "Industrie sucrière," included in the
semiofficial publication prepared for the Paris Exposition,
La Russie à la fin du 19e siècle, ed. by M. W. de Kovalevsky,
Paris, 1900, pp. 365-74, from which the statistics cited in
the next paragraph are also taken.

20. P. Friedmann in *Jewish Studies . . . Kohut*, pp. 230
ff.; H. Landau, "Jews and the Development of the Credit

and Transport System in Russia" (Yiddish), *Yivo Ekonomishe Shriftn*, II (1932), 93-105.

21. Pobedonostsev, *L'Autocratie russe*, pp. 364 ff., 427 f., 473 ff., 477 ff.

22. H. Landau, "The Jews in the Oil Industry and Trade in Tsarist Russia" (Yiddish), *Yivo Bleter*, XIV (1939), 269-85; A. A. Fursenko, "The Paris Rothschilds and Russian Oil" (Russian), *Voprosy istorii*, 1962, No. 8, pp. 29-42; and, more generally, the twin essays by D. Mendéléeff (Mendeleev), "Industrie du naphte et des produits chimiques" and by S. Goulichambaroff (Gulichambarov), "Industrie du naphte," in M. W. de Kovalevsky's *La Russie*, pp. 333-42, 510-21.

23. A. Goloubeff (Golubev), "Establissements de banque," in Kovalevsky, *ibid.*, pp. 804-22; Pierre Renouvin, "Finances et politique. L'emprunt russe d'avril 1906 en France," *Etudes suisses d'historie générale*, XVIII-XIX (1960-61), 507-15 (in part based on an unpublished archival study by Jean Servonnat); the correspondence cited by Cyrus Adler in his biography of *Jacob H. Schiff: His Life and Letters*, 2 vols., New York, 1929, I, 212 ff. (quoting a long memorandum by Korekiyo Takahashi, vice-governor of the Bank of Japan). Schiff's anti-Russian activities, starkly exaggerated, form a major chapter in A. Netchvolodov's anti-Semitic study, *L'Empereur Nicolas II et les Juifs. Essais sur la revolution russe dans ses rapports avec l'activité universelle du Judaïsme contemporain*, trans. from the Russian by I. M. Narischkina, Paris, 1924. Understandably, the subsequent Triple Entente between Russia, France, and England caused much grief to the Western Jewish patriots. *See*, for instance, Max Beloff, *Lucien Wolf and the Anglo-Russian Entente, 1907-1914*, London, 1951. On one of the leading Jewish bankers, as well as communal leaders of the period, *see* Henry (Genrikh) B. Sliozberg, *Baron Horace O. de Gunzbourg, sa vie et son oeuvre*, trans. from the Russian by Prince Vladimir Bariatinsky, Paris, 1933.

24. B. Miliutin, *Ustroistvo i sostoianie evreiskiikh obshchestv v Rossii* (Structure and Status of the Jewish Communities in Russia), St. Petersburg, 1849-50, pp. 225 ff.; and other sources cited by L. Greenberg in *The Jews in Russia*, I, 160 ff.

25. *See* above, Chap. V, n. 1; and this chapter, n. 12.

26. The inadequacy of Russo-Jewish labor statistics is well illustrated by the older, yet still valuable, study by Leonty Soloweitschik, *Un Prolétariat méconnu: Etude sur la*

situation sociale et économique des ouvriers juifs, Brussels, 1898, where many more data for the Western than the Russian Jewish proletariat are given. But of some interest still are particularly the tentative statistical tables for Jewish artisans (p. 93) and for the Bialystok workers (p. 100).

CHAPTER 7 (pages 119-134)

1. The millennial history of Jewish self-governmental institutions, which helps explain their great tenacity and vast range, is described in the author's *The Jewish Community: its History and Structure to the American Revolution,* 3 vols., Philadelphia, 1942.

2. I. Galant, "The Debts of Jewish Kahals in Podolia and Volhynia" (Russian), *Zbirnyk prats* of the Jewish Historical Archaeological Commission, II (1929), 119-37; the author's *The Jewish Community,* II, 273 f.; III, 190 ff. nn. 31-32; Robert Anchel, *Napoléon et les Juifs,* Paris, 1928, pp. 579 ff.

3. *Polnoe sobranie zakonov,* X, No. 8,054; XIX, No. 18,545; Levanda, *Polnyi khronologicheskii sbornik zakonov,* pp. 355 ff. No. 301, 577 ff. No. 509; Max Lilienthal, *Allgemeine Zeitung des Judentums,* XI (1847), 226; and other data analyzed by Isaac Levitats in *The Jewish Community in Russia, 1772-1844,* New York, 1943, esp. pp. 35 ff.

4. David G. Maggid, "From My Archive" (Russian), *Perezhitoe,* IV (1913), 188 ff.; above, Chap. II, nn. 7 and 10.

5. *Polnoe sobranie zakonov,* XIX, No. 13,850 (omitted by Levanda in his *Polnyi . . . sbornik,* p. 23); Levitats, *The Jewish Community in Russia,* pp. 24 ff., 198 ff.

6. Abraham Jacob Paperna, "From the Era of Nicholas I: Reminiscences" (Russian), *Perezhitoe,* II (1910), 1-53. *See also* his *Zikhronot* (Memoirs) in *Sefer ha-Shanah* (Yearbook), ed. by Nahum Sokolow, I (1900), 60-75 (on his student years in Zhitomir).

7. Saul M. Ginsburg, "The Ushitsa Case" (Yiddish) in his *Historishe Verk,* III, 178-87.

8. Robert Pinkerton, *Russia,* p. 90; Mendele Mokher Seforim, *Fishke der Krumer* in *Kol kitbei* (Collected Works), 7 vols., Berlin, 1922, I, 69 f. On the ancient origins of that institution and its gradual degeneration even before the nineteenth century, *see* the author's *The Jewish Community,* II, 328 f.; III, 211 n. 44.

9. Yekhezkel (Ezekiel) Kotik, *Maine Zikhroines* (Mem-

oirs), 2 vols., Warsaw, 1913, I, 189 f. *See also* A. J. Paperna's reminiscences in *Perezhitoe*, II, 38 ff.

10. Cited, from documents published by the Ukrainian Academy, by Saul M. Ginsburg in his *Historishe Verk*, III, 20.

CHAPTER 8 (pages 135-157)

1. The text of the Warsaw ordinance of 1838 is reproduced in the Hebrew original in Saul M. Ginsburg's *Historishe Verk*, I, 301 ff. App. iii. On the general background, *see* Jacob Shatzky, *Geshikhte fun Yidn in Varshe* (A History of the Jews in Warsaw), Vols. I-III, New York, 1947-53. Similar regulations were enacted from time to time also by other communities within the Pale.

2. *See* Abraham Menes's brief survey of "Learning in Lithuania in the Nineteenth Century" (Yiddish), *Lite* (Lithuania), ed. by Mendel Sudarsky, *et al.*, Brooklyn, New York, 1951, pp. 483-526.

3. *Polnoe sobranie zakonov*, X, No. 8,054; Levanda, *Polnyi . . . sbornik*, pp. 359 ff. No. 304; *Allgemeine Zeitung des Judentums*, VI (1942), 185; Levitats, *The Jewish Community in Russia*, pp. 148 ff., 178 ff.

4. A. J. Paperna's aforementioned reminiscences in *Perezhitoe*, II, 31 f.; the correspondence from Vitebsk in *Voskhod* of 1894, cited by J. G. Lipman in the *Jewish Encyclopedia*, X, 547.

5. Benzion Dinur, "The Historical Image of Russian Jewry and Problems Connected with Its Study" (Hebrew), *Zion*, XXII (1957), 107 n. 46.

6. Pauline Wengeroff, *Memoiren einer Grossmutter: Bilder aus der Kulturgeschichte der Juden Russlands im 19. Jahrhundert*, 2d ed., 2 vols., Berlin, 1913-19, I, 5, 9, 143 ff.; minutes of the Grodno Mishnah Association, cited from a Jerusalem MS by Levitats in *The Jewish Community in Russia*, p. 192.

7. S. Posner, *Evrei v obshchei shkole* (Jews in the General Schools), St. Petersburg, 1914; Jacob Shatzky, *Kultur-Geshikhte fun der haskoleh in Lite* (Cultural History of Jewish Enlightenment in Lithuania), Buenos Aires, 1950, p. 58; Elias Tcherikower, *Istoriia Obshchestva dlia rasprostraneniia prosveshcheniia mezhdu evreiamii v Rossii* (A History of the Society for the Promotion of Enlightenment among the Jews

of Russia), 2 vols., St. Petersburg, 1913, I, 129. *See also* the figures for the later years, cited above, this chapter, n. 5; and Chap. III, nn. 10-11.

8. Mordecai Teitelbaum, *Ha-Rab mi-Ladi u-mifleget Habad* (The Rabbi of Ladi and the Sect Habad), 2 vols., Warsaw, 1910-13; Simon M. Dubnow, *Toledot ha-hasidut* (A History of Hasidism), 3 parts, Tel Aviv, 1930-32 (also in a German trans. by A. Steinberg, entitled *Geschichte des Chassidismus*, 2 vols., Berlin, 1931-32).

9. Nahman ben Simhah of Bratslav, *Shibhe ha-Ran* (On His Life and Teachings), new ed., Lwów, 1901, Chap. on his journey to Palestine, vi; Israel Friedmann of Ruzhin, *Irin kaddishin* (Holy Angels: Selections of Homilies by Him and His Son, Abraham Jacob of Sadagóra), Warsaw, 1885, pp. 105, 92, also cited by Levitats in *The Jewish Community in Russia,* p. 166. On Nahman's enthusiastic praise of the Holy Land, *see also* the excerpts included in Louis I. Newman (in collaboration with Samuel Spitz), *The Hasidic Anthology: Tales and Teachings of Hasidism,* New York, 1934, p. 299.

10. Louis Ginzberg, *Students, Scholars and Saints,* Philadelphia, 1928, esp. pp. 145 ff., 278 (on Israel Salanter); Kopul Rosen, *Rabbi Israel Salanter and the Musar Movement,* London, 1943; Dov Katz, *Tenu'at ha-musar* (The Musar Movement: Its History, Leaders and Ideas), 4 vols., Tel Aviv, 1952-57; B. Dinur in *Zion,* XXII, 109 f.

11. Israel Zinberg, *Di Geshikhte fun der literatur bay Yidn* (The History of Jewish Literature), 8 vols., Vilna, 1929-37, VIII, Part 2, pp. 13 ff., 251 f. App. i.

12. The extraordinary difficulties under which Levinsohn labored throughout his literary career, as did many of his progressive confreres, come to the fore in various letters. *See,* for instance, that written on Shebat 18, 5603 (January 19, 1843) to Jacob Reifmann, in which he expressed his satisfaction over the sympathy evinced for his struggles by so distant a colleague as Abraham Geiger in Breslau. This letter is included in the collection, *Be'er Yizhak* (Isaac's Well: Letters by and to Levinsohn), ed. by David Baer ben Yehudah Nathanson, Warsaw, 1899, pp. 93 ff. *See also* Louis S. Greenberg's brief study, *A Critical Investigation of the Works of Rabbi Isaac Baer Levinsohn,* New York, 1930. Diss. Columbia University.

13. Zinberg, *Geshikhte,* VIII, Part 2, pp. 104 ff., 254 ff.

App. iii. On the resistance of the Jewish population to any changes in attire also in Congress Poland, *see* J. Shatzky, *Geshikhte fun Yidn in Varshe,* II, 81 ff.

14. *See* Reuben Brainin's extensive biography of *Abraham Mapu hayyav u-sefarav* (A. M. His Life and Works), 2 vols., Pietrków, 1900; and, more generally, Joseph Klausner's comprehensive *Historiah shel ha-sifrut ha-ibrit ha-hadashah* (A History of Modern Hebrew Literature), 6 vols., Jerusalem, 1930-50, to be consulted also in connection with the other Hebrew writers discussed in this and the next chapter. *See also* the pertinent chapters in Meyer Waxman, *A History of Jewish Literature,* new ed. rev. and enlarged, 5 vols., New York, 1960.

15. Much light on Gordon's personality and his time is shed by his letters, collected under the title, *Iggerot YeLaG,* 2 vols., Warsaw, 1894-95; and a brief diary (*Yoman*), ed. by Saul M. Ginsburg in *He-Abar,* I (1917), 1-32; II (1918), 3-33, esp. II, 8, 32. The episode of "Y. L. Gordon's Arrest and Deportation" is described by S. M. Ginsburg in his *Historishe Verk,* I, 121-39. *See also* the brief biographical sketches of Gordon by Abraham Benedict Rhine in his *Leon Gordon: an Appreciation,* Philadelphia, 1910; and by Shalom Spiegel in his *Hebrew Reborn,* New York, 1930 (paperback, Cleveland, 1962), pp. 174-87; and, more generally, Jacob S. Raisin, *The Haskalah Movement in Russia,* Philadelphia, 1913.

16. *See* Meir Wiener *et al.,* bio-bibliographical sketches in the Intro. to Aksenfeld's *Verk* (Works), ed. by Wiener, 2 vols., Kharkov and Moscow, 1931-38 (the editor tries in vain, however, to explain away the religious overtones in Aksenfeld's letter to Levinsohn of 1840, congratulating the latter on the publication of his *Bet Yehudah,* pp. 345 ff.); S. M. Ginsburg, *Historishe Verk,* I, 75 ff.; Zalman Reisen's (Rejzen's) comprehensive *Leksikon fun der yidisher literatur, prese un filologie* (Lexicon of the Yiddish Literature, Press and Philology), 3d rev. ed., 4 vols., Vilna, 1928-29, I, 159-62; and, more generally, the essays assembled in *Tsu der geshikhte fun der yidisher literatur in 19tn yorhundert* (On the History of Yiddish Literature in the Nineteenth Century: Studies and Materials), Kiev, 1940. On "The Social Import of Aksenfeld's Creativity" *see* Max Erik's pertinent Yiddish article in the Minsk *Zeitshrift,* V (1931), 125-69, with additional documents reproduced by J. Riminik, *ibid.,* pp. 171-80.

17. Reisen, *Leksikon,* I, 8-37; Samuel Niger, *Mendele*

Mokher Seforim, New York, 1937. The numerous Soviet publications on Mendele are listed in Khana Shmeruk, ed., *Pirsumim yehudiim bi-brit ha-moesot* (Jewish Publications in the Soviet Union, 1917-1960), Jerusalem, 1961, under the numbers listed in the Index, p. 474. On the large earlier literature *see* esp. the informative review article by A. Gurstein, "Bird's-Eye View of Mendele Studies" (Yiddish), *Zeitshrift,* II-III (1928), 485-524.

18. *See* the well-documented outline by Peter S. Marek, *Ocherki po istorii prosveshcheniia Evreev v Rossi* (A Survey of the History of Jewish Enlightenment in Russia), Moscow, 1909 (on the period of 1844-73), with Simon M. Dubnow's remarks thereon in his review of that volume entitled "Echoes of the Last Century" (Russian) in *Evreiskaia Starina,* I (1909), 302-308. It may be noted that, despite governmental assistance, all efforts at injecting Christian doctrines into some sectarian movements within the Jewish community achieved but minor results. *See* the twin essays by N. A. Buchbinder, "From the History of Sectarian Trends among Russian Jews" (Russian), *ibid.,* XI (1924), 238-65; XIII (1930), 116-30.

19. Moshe Perlmann, "*Razsvet* 1860-1861: the Origins of the Russian Jewish Press," *Jewish Social Studies,* XXIV (1962), 162-82 (with extensive bibliographical references); and, more generally, S. L. Zinberg, *Istoriia evreiskoi pechati v Rossii* (A History of the Jewish Press in Russia), Petrograd, 1915. *See also* the same author's Yiddish essays on "The History of the Russo-Jewish Press (1860-1880)" and "The *Kol mebasser* [Voice of the Herold, ed. by Alexander Zederbaum] and Its Time" in his *Kultur-historishe Shtudien* (Studies in Culture and History), New York, 1949, pp. 87-158, 159-81; and A. Kirzhnitz's bibliography, chronologically arranged, of *Di yidishe presse in der gevezener ruslendisher imperie* (The Yiddish Press in the Former Russian Empire, 1823-1916), Moscow, 1930. The first periodical here mentioned is *Der Beobakhter an der Vaiksel* (The Observer on the Vistula), a weekly published in Warsaw from Dec. 3, 1823 to Sept. 29, 1824; it suspended publication after the appearance of the thirty-ninth issue. A little-known effort to found in 1871 a new Russo-Jewish periodical for the combating of anti-Semitism, is described by its initiator, Jacob Teitel in "Aus meinen Memoiren," *Festschrift Moritz Schäfer,* Berlin, 1927, pp. 237-40.

CHAPTER 9 (pages 158-186)

1. The history of that society was described by one of its founders, Leon Rosenthal (1817-87) in his *Toledot Hebrat Marbe ha-haskalah be-Yisrael* (History of the Society for the Promotion of Enlightenment among the Jews), 2 parts, St. Petersburg, 1885 (reproducing the early protocols of the Society); and, more fully, by Elias Tcherikower in his *Istoriia Obshchestva*, cited above Chap. VIII, n. 7.

2. Moses Leib Lilienblum, *Hatot ne'urim* (Sins of Youth; an autobiographical sketch) in his *Kol kitbe* (Collected Works), ed. with an Intro. by Joseph Klausner, 4 vols., Cracow-Odessa, 1910-13, II, 201-410; Klausner, *Yotserim u-bonim* (Creators and Builders; biographical sketches), 3 vols., Jerusalem, 1925-29, I, 80-123; below, n. 18.

3. Abraham Uri Kovner, Letters to Paperna and Y. L. Gordon in *Hed ha-zeman*, 1909, p. 132; Leonid Grossmann, *Die Beichte eines Juden in Briefen an Dostojewski*, ed. by René Fülöp-Miller and Friedrich Eckstein, Munich, 1927; S. M. Ginsburg, *Historishe Verk*, n.s. II, 157-93; J. Bronstein, "Avrom Uri Kovner (1842-1909)" (Yiddish), *Zeitshrift*, V (1931), 211-43.

4. Of the extensive literature on Klaczko we need but refer to Count Stanislaw Tarnowski's comprehensive Polish biography, *Julian Klaczko*, 2 vols., Cracow, 1919.

5. Herman Rosenthal, "Blioch (Bloch), Ivan Stanislavovich," *Jewish Encyclopedia*, III, 250-52; S. M. Ginsburg, *Historishe Verk*, n.s. II, 119-56, 209-21; Daniel Chwolson, *Corpus inscriptionum hebraicarum*, St. Petersburg, 1882; *idem, Das letzte Passamahl Christi und der Tag seines Todes*, new impression revised, Leipzig, 1908 (based on a Russian ed. of 1875); *idem, Die Blutanklage und sonstige mittelalterliche Beschuldigungen der Juden, Eine historische Undersuchung nach den Quellen*, German trans. from the 2d Russian ed., Frankfort, 1901; A. E. Harkavy's works listed in the *Festschrift* in his honor published in St. Petersburg, 1908.

6. Dimitrii S. Mirsky, *A History of Russian Literature*, ed. and abridged by Francis J. Whitefield, new impression, New York, 1958, pp. 223 ff.; and other literature listed by L. Greenberg in *The Jews in Russia*, I, 172 ff., 182 f.

7. Pobedonostsev, *L'Autocratie russe*, pp. 359 f.; Catherine Drinker Bowen, *"Free Artist": the Story of Anton and*

Nicholas Rubinstein, Boston, 1939, pp. 308 f. *See also* pp. 73, 151, 183, 222 f.

8. Henry B. Sliozberg, *Dela minuvshikh dnei* (Affairs of Days Past: Notes of a Russian Jew), 3 vols., Paris, 1933-34, I, 132 ff., 207, 267 f.; *80 Years of ORT: Historical Materials, Documents and Reports,* Geneva, 1960, emphasizing that much of the original archives was lost during the Russian Revolution and the Nazi occupation.

9. Fiodor Mikhailovich Dostoevsky's letter to Kovner of February, 1877, reproduced in a German trans. by L. Grossmann in *Die Beichte eines Juden,* p. 119; other literature listed by Avrahm Yarmolinsky in his *Dostoevsky: a Life,* New York, 1934, pp. 156, 342, 436; Leo Nikolaevich Tolstoy's letter, cited from an earlier English trans. by Joseph L. Baron in his *Stars and Sand: Jewish Notes by Non-Jewish Notables,* Philadelphia, 1943, pp. 45 f. Otherwise Tolstoy generally avoided the Jewish issue in his writings. *See* Joshua Kunitz, *Russian Literature and the Jew,* pp. 139 ff.; and above, Chap. IV, n. 9.

10. Sergei Y. Witte, *Memoirs,* trans. from the original Russian manuscript and ed. by Abraham (Avrahm) Yarmolinsky, Garden City, 1927, pp. 381 f.; the biographical and other essays included in the memorial volume, *M. M. Vinaver i ruskaia obshchestvennost* (M. M. V. and Russian Society at the Beginning of the Twentieth Century), ed. by P. M. Miliukov, *et al.,* Paris, 1937; Vinaver's own *Nedavnee* (Not Long Ago: Reminiscences and Characteristics), 2d ed., Paris, 1926; H. (G.) B. Sliozberg, *Dela minuvshikh dnei;* O. O. Gruzenberg, *Vchera; idem, Ocherki i rechi* (Sketches and Addresses), ed. by Alexander Goldenweiser, New York, 1944; Julius Brutzkus "Bramson—Organizer of Russian Jewry" (Russian), *Evreiskii Mir,* II (New York, 1944), 14-24; and other essays in that volume.

11. Pavel B. Akselrod (Paul Axelrod), *Perezhitoe i peredumanoe* (Experiences and Meditations), Berlin, 1923; *idem, Die russische Revolution und die sozialistische Internationale. Aus dem literarischen Nachlass,* Jena, 1932; Samuel Loeb Zitron (Citron), *Drai literarishe doires* (Three Literary Generations: Reminiscences concerning Jewish Writers), 4 vols., Vilna, 1920-23, II, 104 ff. Even the distinguished early socialist, Peter Lavrov who, though denying the existence of a Jewish nationality, was sympathetic to the Jewish workers' demands, nevertheless advised against too sharp protests against the Russian pogroms of 1881-82 on tactical grounds.

He persuaded Akselrod to desist from publishing an intended pamphlet on this subject, lest it interfere with the party's objective "to establish closer contacts with the [Russian] people and to arouse them against the government." *See* his letter of April 11, 1882, cited by E. Tcherikower in his "Peter Lavrov and the Jewish Socialist Emigrés," *YIVO Annual of Jewish Social Science,* VII (1952), 133. *See also* S. Agurskii's ideologically interesting reconstruction of "The Character of the Socialist Movement among the Jewish Workers until the Rise of the Russian Social Democratic Labor Party" (Yiddish), *Zeitshrift,* IV (1930), 237-54 (also citing Lev Daitch's postscript to Peter Lavrov's letter to Akselrod, p. 248); with the interesting editorial comment thereon, *ibid.,* pp. 254-55; and, more generally, Avrahm Yarmolinsky, *Road to Revolution: a Century of Russian Radicalism,* London, 1957.

12. Eliakum Zunser, *A Jewish Bard,* Yiddish text of his autobiography with an English trans. by Simon Hirsdansky, New York, 1905, pp. 43 (Yiddish), 32 (English). On this eminent folk poet see also Sol Liptsin's biography, *Eliakum Zunser: Poet of His People,* New York, 1950.

13. The absence of any consciously Jewish motivation among the Jewish *narodniki* is well illustrated by a small Yiddish hectograph paper, entitled *Arbeter-Tsaitung,* published in a few copies in January, 1881. It is essentially a trans. of a similar sheet in Russian and does not even mention Jews. *See* L. Greenberg, *The Jews,* pp. 148 f.; Elias Tcherikower, "The 'Arbeter-Tsaitung' of the Narodnaya Volia (1881)" (Yiddish), *Yivo Historishe Shriftn,* III, 604-609. *See also* the other valuable essays by Abraham Menes, Elias Tcherikower, *et al.,* in that comprehensive volume devoted to the history of "The Socialist Movement among the Jews up to 1897"; and below n. 17. From another angle, *see* the somewhat exaggerated account by Usher Margulis of "The Participation of the Jewish Masses in the Famine 'Disturbances' of 1891" (Yiddish), *Forpost,* VII (1938), 127-45.

14. The facsimile of Liberman's prospectus, reproduced by S. Ts. in *Evreiskaia Starina,* XIII (1930), 164-70; G. E. Gurevich, "The Trial of Jewish Socialists in Berlin (1878-79)," *ibid.,* X (1918), 151-74; N. M. Gelber, *Aus zwei Jahrhunderten,* Vienna, 1924, pp. 185-92. See also, more generally, Elias Tcherikower, "The Beginnings of the Jewish Socialist Movement" (Yiddish), *YIVO Historishe Shriftn,*

I (1929), 469-532, together with "The Minute Book of the Society of Hebrew Socialists in London (1876)," *ibid.*, cols. 533-94; Boris Sapir, "Liberman et le socialisme russe," *International Review for Social History*, III (1938), 25-88 (includes several letters to and by Valerian Smyrnov, secretary of the small but influential *Vperiod* [Forward] movement); Dov (Bernard) Weinryb, "The Ideological Evolution of A. S. Liberman" (Hebrew), *Zion*, IV (1939), 317-48.

15. Chaim Zhitlowsky, *Gezamelte Shriftn* (Collected Works), 10 vols., New York, 1912-19 (VI, 11-55: "A Jew to Jews"); Simon M. Dubnow, *Nationalism and History: Essays on Old and New Judaism*, ed. with an Introductory Essay by Koppel S. Pinson, Philadelphia, 1958 (paperback, Cleveland, 1961). On the early hesitant moves of these two founders of Jewish diaspora nationalism, see also their autobiographical descriptions in Zhitlowsky's *Zikhroines fun main leben* (Reminiscences from My Life), Vols. I-III, New York, 1935-40; Dubnow's *Kniga zhizni* (Book of Life: Reminiscences and Reflections. Materials for the History of My Time), 2 vols., Riga, 1934-35 (to 1922; also in a Hebrew trans.); and letters by and essays on him, ed. by Simon Rawidowicz in *Sefer Shimeon Dubnow*, London, 1954. *See also*, Aaron Steinberg, ed., *Simon Dubnow, The Man and His Work*, Paris, 1963.

16. Koppel S. Pinson, "Arkady Kremer, Vladimir Medem and the Ideology of the Jewish Bund," *Jewish Social Studies*, VII (1945), 233-64; and, more generally, Jacob Sholem Hertz, ed., *Doires Bundistn* (Generations of Bundists), New York, 1956 (including more than 300 biographical sketches with a listing of the main biographies); *idem, Di Geshikhte fun Bund* (The History of the Bund), Vol. I, New York, 1960; *idem, The Jewish Labor Bund: a Pictorial History, 1897-1957* (English and Yiddish), New York, 1958. *See also* Henry J. Tobias's brief report on "The Archives of the Jewish Bund. New Materials on the Revolutionary Movement," *American Slavic and East-European Review*, XVII (1958), 81-85.

17. *Encyclopédie socialiste, syndicale et coopérative de l'Internationale ouvrière*, 8 vols., Paris, 1912-13, V, 377, 385 f., 397 f.; articles on "Bund" and "VKP(B)" (All-Russian Communist Party), both in Russian, in *Bolshaia sovetskaia entsiklopedia*, 1st ed., VIII, 113; XI, 531; Vladimir Medem, *Fun main leben* (An Autobiography), 2 vols., New York, 1923, II, 86 ff.; and, more fully, Oscar I. Janowsky, *The*

Jews and Minority Rights (1893-1919), with a Foreword by Julian W. Mack, New York, 1933 (Diss. Columbia University), pp. 72 ff., 88 n. 1, 122 ff. *See also*, more generally, Lev Deich (Daitch), *Rol Evreev v russkom revolutsionnom dvizhenii* (The Jews' Role in the Russian Revolutionary Movement), Vol. I (only), 2d ed., Moscow, 1925 (partly recording personal experiences); A. L. Patkin, *The Origins of the Russian-Jewish Labour Movement*, Melbourne, 1947; the articles on "The Jewish Socialist Movement in Russia and Poland (1870s-1897) and "(1897-1919)" by Abraham Menes and Raphael R. Abramovich in *The Jewish People, Past and Present*, II (1948), 355-68 and 369-98; and Leonard Shapiro's perceptive lecture, "The Role of the Jews in the Russian Revolutionary Movement," *Slavonic and East-European Review*, XL (1961), 148-67. Additional data may be gleaned from Aryeh Tartakower's comprehensive review of *Toledot tenuat ha-obdim ha-yehudit* (History of the Jewish Labor Movement), 2 vols., Warsaw, 1929-30; and the two recent English dissertations, thus far inaccessible to the author: J. Frankel, *Socialism and Jewish Nationalism in Russia 1897-1907*, Diss. Cambridge, 1960; and H. Shukman, *The Relations between the Jewish Bund and the RSDRP [Russian Social-Democratic Labor Party], 1897-1908*, Diss. Oxford, 1960 (both in typescript).

18. Moses Leib Lilienblum, "The Future of Our People" in his *Kol Kitbe* (Collected Works), 4 vols., Cracow-Odessa, 1910-13, cited here with variations, from Arthur Hertzberg, *The Zionist Idea: an Historical Analysis and Reader*, with a Foreword by Emanuel Neumann, New York, 1959, p. 173 (also paperback). *See also* Zalman Epstein, *Mosheh Leib Lilienblum, shittato ve-halakh mahshevotav* (M. L. L.: His Doctrine and the Evolution of His Thoughts on Religion and the Rebirth of the People of Israel in the Land of Its Fathers), Tel Aviv, 1935.

19. Leo Pinsker, *Auto-Emancipation*, trans. from the German by David S. Blondhein, New York, 1906, p. 2 (here cited with variations in the English rendition). *See also* the rich collection of *Ketabim le-toledot hibbat Siyyon* (Documents for the History of "Love of Zion" and Palestine Colonization), ed. by A. Druyanov, 3 vols., Odessa-Tel Aviv, 1910-32.

20. Theodor Herzl, *Tagebücher*, 3 vols., Berlin, 1923, III, 460 ff.; in the English trans. by Harry Zorn, entitled *Complete Diaries of Theodor Herzl*, ed. by Raphael Patai, 5 vols.,

New York, 1960, IV, 1517 ff. *See also* Alex Bein, *Theodor Herzl: a Biography,* trans. from the German by Maurice Samuel, Philadelphia, 1941 (also paperback, Cleveland, 1962), pp. 447 ff.; and Saul Ginsburg, "Theodor Herzl's Trip to St. Petersburg" (Russian), *Evreiskii Mir,* II (1944), 197-209. Of interest in this connection is also the subsequent interview by the non-Zionist Lucien Wolf with Plehve, reported by the former in his "Mr. Plehve and the Jewish Question," *The Times* (London) of Feb. 6, 1904.

21. *See* esp. Joseph Klausner, *Menahem Ussishkin: His Life and Work,* New York, 1942, pp. 65 ff. Interesting data on the intellectual evolution of a young Russian Jew who ultimately became an outstanding Zionist leader are offered by Shmarya Levin in his autobiographical *Childhood in Exile* and *Youth in Revolt,* both in the English trans. by Maurice Samuel, New York, 1929-30.

22. Ahad Ha-Am (pseud. for Asher Ginzberg), "The Negation of the Diaspora" in his Hebrew essays collected under the title *Al parashat derakhim* (At the Crossroads), 4 vols., 3d ed., Berlin, 1921, IV, 106 ff., 108; here cited from the English trans. by Leon Simon in his *Ahad Ha-Am: Essays, Letters, Memoirs,* Oxford, 1946 (East and West Library), p. 215. *See also* Ahad Ha-Am's *Iggerot* (Letters), 6 vols., Tel Aviv, 1923-25; his *Pirqe zikhronot ve-iggerot* (Memoirs and Letters), Tel Aviv, 1931; and in an English trans., *Basic Writings of Ahad Haam,* ed. with an Intro. by Hans Kohn, New York, 1962.

23. Janowsky, *The Jews and Minority Rights,* pp. 106 ff. *See also* M. N. Syrkin's report on the earlier "Zionist Conference in Minsk" of 1902 in his Hebrew essay in *Sefer ha-Shanah,* ed. by Nahum Sokolow, IV (1902-1903), 11-24.

24. Nachman Syrkin, *Geklibene tsionistish-sotsialistishe Shriftn* (Selected Zionist-Socialist Writings), 2 vols., New York, 1925-26 (with a biographical sketch by Isaac Zar); *idem, Kitbe* (Writings), ed. by Berl Katzenelson and Judah Kaufmann, Vol. I, Tel Aviv, 1939; Marie Syrkin, *Nachman Syrkin Socialist Zionist: Biographical Memoir. Selected Essays,* New York, 1961 (*see* esp. p. 304); Ber Borochov, *Geklibene Shriftn* (Selected Writings), 2 vols., New York, 1920-28; *idem, Ketabim* (Works), in the Hebrew trans. by D. Ben Nahum, *et al.* in L. Levita's and his ed., 2 vols., Tel Aviv, 1957-58 (II, 399 ff. includes an interesting documentary appendix relating to the early history of the Labor-Zionist movement); *idem, Nationalism and the Class Strug-*

gle: a Marxian Approach to the Jewish Problem, ed. by Moshe Cohen, New York, 1937 (includes Abraham G. Duker's essay on "Ber Borochov's Theories and Their Place in the History of the Jewish Labor Movement"); Aaron David Gordon, *Kitbe* (Writings), 5 vols., Tel Aviv, 1925-28 (includes biographical sketch by Joseph Aronowich); idem, *Selected Essays,* trans. from the Hebrew by Frances Burnce and ed. by N. Teradyon and A. Shohat. With a biographical sketch by Eisig Silberschlag, New York, 1938.

25. On the beginnings of the Mizrahi (or Mizrachi) movement, *see* esp. Judah Leb Fishman, "The History and Evolution of the Mizrahi Organization" (Hebrew), *Sinai,* I (1937), 260-67, 361-68; II (1938), 63-72; III (1938), 301-15, 478-81. *See also* Isaac Jacob Reines's *Or hadash al Siyyon* (New Light on Zion), Vilna, 1902, expounding the principles of the new movement; and the essays ed. in memory of Reines by J. L. Fishman under the title *Sefer ha-Mizrahi* (The Book of Mizrahi), Jerusalem, 1946. On Mohilever, see the collection of Hebrew essays by I. Nissenbaum, *et al., R. Shemuel Mohilever,* Warsaw, 1938. Other early Russian Zionists belonging to the various groups are included in Samuel L. Citron's *Leksikon siyyoni* (Zionist Handbook: Biographies of Leaders who Distinguished Themselves in the Zionist Movement), Warsaw, 1924.

26. Jacob Rosenheim, *Ausgewählte Aufsätze und Ansprachen,* 2 vols., Frankfort, 1930, esp. II, 159-318.

27. Chaim Nachman Bialik, *Kitbe u-mibhar targumav* (Writings and Selected Translations), 4 vols., Berlin, 1923, esp. I, 287 ff., 320 ff., 341 ff.; *idem, Iggerot* (Letters), assembled and ed. with notes by Fischel Lachover, 5 vols., Tel Aviv, 1938-39. Some of his poems are available in the English trans. by Leonard Victor Snowman, entitled *Poems from the Hebrew,* with an Intro. by Vladimir Jabotinsky, London, 1924, esp. pp. 66 ff., 77 ff.; and by Maurice Samuel in Bailik's *Selected Poems,* New York, 1926, esp. pp. 45 ff., 67 ff. The full-length Hebrew biography by Fischel Lachover, *Chaim Nachman Bialik* (C. N. B.: His Life and Works), Tel Aviv, 1936; the perceptive Hebrew essays on *Ch. N. Bialik u-bene doro* (C. N. B. and His Contemporaries) by the distinguished poet Zalman Shneur, Tel Aviv, 1953; may be supplemented by the general histories of modern Hebrew literature by Joseph Klausner, Lachover, and Shalom Spiegel (*Hebrew Reborn,* pp. 295 ff.); and by a host of monographs. *See* esp. the penetrating essay by Moses Kleinman in his

Demuyot ve-komot (Portraits and Personalities: Essays on Modern Hebrew Literature), 2d ed., London, n.d., pp. 279 ff.

28. Micah Joseph Bin Gorion (Berdichevski), *Kitbe* (Writings), 2 vols., Tel Aviv, 1960; *idem, Yiddishe kesovim* (Yiddish Writings), 6 vols., Berlin, 1924; Rachel and Emanuel Bin Gorion, *Gedächtnisschrift zum zehnten Todestage von Micha Josef Bin Gorion*, Berlin, n.d.; Yeshurun Keshet (Koplowitz), *Mikhah Yosef Berdichevski* (biography, in Hebrew), Jerusalem, 1959; Saul Tchernichovski, *Shirim* (Poems), collected by the author, 12th ed., Tel Aviv, 1959, esp. pp. 317 ff.; Leonard V. Snowman, *Tchernichowsky and His Poetry*, London, 1929 (includes English translations of poems, including that cited, with variations, in the text); Joseph Klausner, *Shaul Tchernikhovski: ha-adam ve-ha-meshorer* (S. T.: the Man and the Poet), Jerusalem, 1947. Of interest are also Jacob ben Yeshurun's (Kitaiksher's) succinct observations on *Ha-Shirah ha-russit ve-hashpaatah al ha-shirah ha-ibrit* (Russian Poetry and Its Influence on Hebrew Poetry), with an Intro. by Joseph Klausner, Tel Aviv, 1955.

29. Isaac Leb Peretz, *Ale Verk* (Complete Works, in Yiddish), 11 vols., New York, n.d.; *idem, Kol kitbe* (Collected Works, in Hebrew), 8 vols., Tel Aviv, 1948-52; *Briv un Redes* (Letters and Addresses), ed. and trans. by Nachman Meisel, New York, 1944; *idem, Yizchok Leibush Peretz un zein dor shreiber* (Y. L. P. and Contemporary Writers), New York, 1951; Reisen, *Leksikon*, II, 974-1043; A. A. Roback, *I. L. Peretz, Psychologist of Literature*, Cambridge, Mass., 1935; Maurice Samuel, *Prince of the Ghetto*, Philadelphia, 1948. However, many of the lacunae stressed by A. Gurstein in his Yiddish essay, "The Present State of a Peretz Biography (On the Published Biographical Materials)," *Zeitshrift*, I (Minsk, 1926), still await answers.

30. Sholom Aleikhem's works appeared in many editions and translations. See esp. his *Ale Verk* (Collected Works), 28 vols., New York, 1923; Melech Graftein's illustrated *Sholom Aleichem Panorama*, London, n.d. (includes translations of selected stories and essays by various authors on S. A.); and Maurice Samuel, *The World of Sholom Aleichem*, New York, 1943. See also Reisen, *Leksikon*, IV, 673-736; below, Chaps. XIV and XVII; and, more generally, A. A. Roback, *The Story of Yiddish Literature*, New York, 1940.

31. Jacob Shatzky, ed., *Goldfaden Bukh*, published by the Yiddish Theater Museum in New York, 1926; Nachman

Meisel, *Abraham Goldfaden, 1840-1908* (biography, in Yiddish), New York, 1938; and, more generally, B. Gorin (J. Guido), *Di Geshikhte fun yiddishen teater* (History of the Jewish Theater: Two Thousand Years of Theater among Jews), 2 vols., New York, 1918; and the various essays included in the *Arkhiv far der geshikhte fun yiddishen teater un drame* (Archive for the History of the Jewish Theater and Drama), ed. by J. Shatzky, Vol. I, Vilna, 1930.

32. Karl Lamprecht, *Americana. Reiseeindrücke, Betrachtungen, geschichtliche Gesamtansicht,* Freiburg i. B., 1906, pp. 61 f.

CHAPTER 10 (pages 187-200)

1. *Russkii Invalid,* 1858, No. 39, cited by Joseph L. Baron in *Stars and Sand,* pp. 227 f.

2. These Russian edicts are reproduced in a German trans. in *Die Juden im Kriege. Denkschrift des Jüdischen Sozialistischen Arbeiterverbandes Poale-Zion and das Internationale Sozialistische Bureau,* submitted in The Hague, November, 1915, pp. 49 ff. A dramatic story of these ruthless acts of the conquerors was told, partly on the basis of direct observation, by the famous playwright, S. An-Sky (pseud. for Salomon Rapoport) in his *Hurban ha-Yehudim be-Polin, Galitsia u-Bukovina* (Ruin of the Jews of Poland, Galicia and the Bukovina), trans. into Hebrew by S. L. Citron, 4 parts, Tel Aviv, [n.d.].

3. Maxim Gorki, "Anti-Semitism" (1929) in his collection of essays entitled *Culture and the People,* English trans. from the Russian, New York, 1939, p. 67.

4. Ludendorff's and other manifestos were reprinted by J. Barkai in his "Proclamations Issued by the German and Austrian Armies to the Jews of Poland" (Hebrew), *Reshumot,* VI (1930), 459-65. *See also* the Hebrew and Yiddish texts of the leaflets dropped from airplanes over Warsaw and other cities and reproduced in An-Sky's *Hurban,* I, 39 ff., and, more generally, Paul P. Roth and Wilhelm Stein, *Die politische Entwicklung in Kongress-Polen während der deutschen Okkupation,* Leipzig, 1919, esp. pp. 170 ff. (by Stein); and Janusz Pajewski, "The Policy of the Central Powers toward Poland during the First World War" (Polish), *Roczniki historyczne,* XXVIII (1962), 9-56.

5. A partial story of that semivoluntary labor enlistment is told by Julius Berger, who had made valiant efforts to

mitigate its hardships, in his *Ostjüdische Arbeiter im Kriege. Ein Beitrag zur Arbeitervermittlung unter Juden,* Berlin, 1919 (reprinted from *Volk und Land,* a Jewish weekly).

6. Zalman Reisen, ed., *Pinkos far Geshikhte fun Vilne* (Record Book of the History of [the Jews of] Vilna in the Years of War and Occupation), Vilna, 1922, pp. 133 ff. (article by Z. Shabad); Israel Cohen, *Vilna,* 1943 (Jewish Communities Series), pp. 361 ff.; S. Weissenberg, "Zur Biotik der südrussischen Juden," *Archiv für Rassen- und Gesellschafts-Biologie,* IX (1912), 200-206; *idem,* "The Russian Jews during the War and Revolution" (Yiddish), *Bleter far yidishe demografie,* I (1924), 17-20, esp. Table I. *See also* the interesting data on "Births, Deaths, and Marriages among the Jews of Odessa, 1892-1919" (Yiddish), assembled by Jacob Lestchinsky, *ibid.,* pp. 70-74.

7. N. Hans, *History of Russian Educational Policy,* pp. 204 f.

8. *See* the data assembled by S. M. Dubnow in his "From the 'Black Book' of Russian Jewry. Sources for the History of the War, 1914-1915" (Russian), *Evreiskaia Starina,* X (1918), 195-296; Louis Stein, "The Exile of the Lithuanian Jews in the Conflagration of the First World War (1914-1918)" (Yiddish), *Lite* (Lithuania), ed. by M. Sudarsky, *et al.,* pp. 89-118; and, more generally, Abraham G. Duker's succinct survey of *Jews in World War I: a Brief Historic Sketch,* New York, [1939] (reprinted from *Contemporary Jewish Record,* II, No. 5).

9. *See The National Question in the Russian Duma: Speeches by Professor Milyukoff, Dzubinsky, Tschkeidze, Freedman, Djafaroff, Kerensky, etc., etc.,* trans. and arranged by E. L. Minsky, London, 1915; *The Jews and the War in Russia,* New York, 1916, pp. 81, 84; *The Jews in the Eastern War Zone,* published by the American Jewish Committee in New York, 1916, pp. 49, 70 ff. *See also* the documentary appendix to the aforementioned memorandum of the Poale-Zion (above n. 2); and, more generally, C. Jay Smith, Jr., *The Russian Struggle for Power: a Study of Russian Foreign Policy during the First World War,* New York, 1957.

10. *Shchit* (The Shield), ed. by Maxim Gorki, *et al.,* trans, into English by Avrahm Yarmolinsky, with a Foreword by William English Walling, New York, 1917, pp. 5 f., 8, 24, 57 f., 68, 70 f., 86, 90 f.; *The Jews in the Eastern War Zone,* p. 119. *See also* Gorki's earlier brief description of a "Pogrom" (1901-1903), in his *Sobranie sochinenii* (Col-

lected Works), 30 vols., Moscow, 1949-55, V, 328-33, 486.

11. D. Movshovitch, "A Page of Modern Jewish History (1915-1917)" (Yiddish), *Yivo Historishe Shriftn*, II (1937), 549-62 (with a note by E. Tcherikower).

12. René Fülöp-Miller, *Rasputin, the Holy Devil*, trans. from the German by F. S. Flint and D. F. Tait, Garden City, N. Y., 1928. A Star Book, pp. 61, 227 ff., 282.

CHAPTER 11 (pages 201-222)

1. The text of this appeal is reproduced in a German trans. in *Die Judenfrage der Gegenwart: Dokumentensammlung*, ed. by Leon Chasanowitsch and Leo Motzkin, Stockholm, 1919, pp. 35 ff.

2. This preeminence of Jews in the early communist regime understandably attracted world-wide attention from friend and foe alike. The various anti-Semitic movements in the West kept on denouncing the new world-wide revolutionary propaganda as a tool of an alleged Jewish conspiracy to take over the world domination. Among the numerous pamphlets on this theme one need but mention J. F. (Fedor Izmailevich) Roditschew and Alfred Nossig, *Bolschewismus und Juden*, ed. by Davis Eintracht, Berlin, 1922; Daniel S. Pasmanek, *Russkaia revolutsiia i evreistvo* (The Russian Revolution and Jewry), Paris, 1923; Dimitrii Bulaschow (pseud. for Benjamin Segel), *Bolschewismus und Judentum*, 3d. ed. rev. of *Die Nutzniesser des Bolschewismus*, Berlin, 1923; and the later violent Nazi diatribes by Herman Fehst, *Bolschewismus und Judentum. Das jüdische Element in der Führerschaft des Bolschewismus*, Berlin, 1934; and by Rudolf Kommoss, *Juden hinter Stalin: die jüdische Vormachtstellung in der Sowjetunion, auf Grund amtlicher Sowjetquellen dargestellt*, 3d ed., Berlin, 1942. More serious, though also permeated with Nazi bias, are Reinhart Maurach's *Russische Judenpolitik*, Berlin, 1939; and Peter Heinz Seraphim's comprehensive study of *Das Judentum im osteuropäischen Raum*, Essen, 1938.

3. In his purported diary Litvinov referred to a conversation he had allegedly had with Lazar Kaganovich about the appointment of a Jewish communist to serve as Secretary-General of the Party in Kazakhstan. Kaganovich objected because the man had been a member of a left-wing Jewish organization, whereupon Litvinov jokingly suggested that, perhaps, they ought to introduce a *numerus clausus* into

the Party. *See* Maxim Litvinov, *Notes for a Journal*. Intro.
by E. H. Carr, and a Prefatory Note by Walter Bedell Smith,
New York, 1955, pp. 39 f. True, the authenticity of this document has rightly been impugned. *See*, for instance, Philip
E. Mosely's review of this volume in *The New York Times* of
November 6, 1955; and Bertram D. Wolfe, "The Litvinov
'Diaries' Literary Detective Story," *Commentary*, XXII (1956),
164-71. Doubts were voiced by Carr himself in the Introduction. Yet some of these alleged dialogues approximate the
truth. *Se non a vero*. . . . On Litvinov (Meir Genokh Moisee-
vich Wallach, 1876-1952), his Jewish family in Bialystok and
his almost exclusive use of Yiddish in his early years, *see*
Arthur Upham Pope, *Maxim Litvinov*, New York, 1943, pp.
35 ff. In contrast thereto, *see* Leon Trotsky, *My Life: an
Attempt at an Autobiography*, New York, 1930, p. 292.

4. Leonard Schapiro in the *Slavonic and East-European
Review*, XL esp. p. 165.

5. N. Gergel, "Jews in the Russian Communist Party and
the Communist Youth Organization" (Yiddish), *Yivo Bleter*,
I (1931), 62-70. Slightly different data are cited by Abraham Heller in *Die Lage der Juden in Russland von der
Märzrevolution 1917 bis zur Gegenwart*, Breslau, 1935.
Schriften der Gesellschaft zur Förderung der Wissenschaft
des Judentums, XXXIX, pp. 107 ff. Fuller answers to these
and other problems will be supplied only after the enormous
amount of the documentary materials, published and unpublished, extant in the Russian archives is carefully sifted
and analyzed. According to G. A. Below's "Dokumentarische
Quellen zur Epoche der Oktoberrevolution in den staatlichen
Archiven der UdSSR" in *Die Oktoberrevolution und Deutschland: Referate und Diskussion*, ed. by Albert Schreiner,
Berlin, 1958, pp. 369-79, the Central Government Archives
of the October Revolution alone had accumulated more
than 6,000,000 documents. In addition there are many more
millions scattered in the numerous other archives throughout
the Union. Nor is the habit of many scholars to publish
individual documents in the daily and weekly press throughout the country really helpful so long as there are no
satisfactory bibliographical guides to these scattered publications.

6. Vladimir Ilich Lenin, (Ulianov), "The Position of the
Bund in the Party" (Russian), reprinted from the *Iskra*
of Oct. 22, 1903 in his *Sochineniia* (Works), 4th ed., 40
vols., Moscow, 1941-62, VII, 76-86; in the authorized Eng-

lish trans. of his *Collected Works* published by the Marx-
Leninist Institute of the Central Committee of the Communist
Party, Moscow, 1960-62, VII, 92-103, esp. 99, 101. *See also*
his earlier article (in *Iskra* of Feb. 15, 1903), "Does the
Jewish Proletariat Need an 'Independent Political Party'?"
reproduced in *Sochineniia*, VI, 295-300; and *Collected Works*,
VI, 330-35; and other communist statements against the
Bund, cited by Khatskel Dunets in his *Kegn sotsial-
fashistishn Bund* (Against the Social-Fascist Bund: Against
the Idealization of Bundism), Minsk, 1932.

7. This Declaration of the Rights of Nationalities, signed
by V. Ulianov (Lenin) and Joseph Djugashvili (Stalin), is
reproduced in the pamphlet, *Lenin on the Jewish Question*,
issued by the International Publishers in New York, 1936.
See also Alfred D. Low, *Lenin on the Question of Nationality*, New York, 1958; and Richard Pipes's comprehensive
analysis of *The Formation of the Soviet Union: Communism
and Nationalism, 1917-1923*, Cambridge, Mass., 1954. Great
inconsistencies of the Marxist nationalist doctrines had been
manifest already in Marx himself; *see* Solomon F. Bloom,
*The World of Nations: a Study of the National Implications
in the Work of Karl Marx*, New York, 1941; and the author's
brief review of that work in *Jewish Social Studies*, III (1941),
438-39. On the Lithuanian developments *see* Alfred Erich
Senn, "Die bolschewistische Politik in Litauen, 1917-1919,"
Forschungen zur osteuropäischen Geschichte, V (1957), 93-
118.

8. N. S. Timasheff, "Russian Nationalism under the Soviets," *Thought*, XX (1945), 443 f.: Joseph Stalin, *Political
Report to the Sixteenth Party Congress of the Russian Communist Party*, English trans. from the Russian, New York,
1930, p. 191.

9. The proceedings and resolutions of that Second Con-
ference are extensively reproduced by S. Agurskii in *Di
yidishe komisariatn un di yidishe komunistishe sektsies* (The
Jewish Commisariats and Communist Sections: Protocols,
Resolutions and [Other] Documents, 1918-1921), Minsk,
1928 (published by the *Histpart* at the Central Committee
of the White Russian Communist Party), esp. p. 228; L.
Zenziper's *Eser shnot redifot* (Ten Years of Persecutions: a
Story of the Persecutions of the Zionist Movement in the
Soviet Union), Tel Aviv, 1930, pp. 97 ff., 269 ff. App. iv;
Lenin's article of Feb., 1903, cited above, n. 6. Typical
of the numerous publicist attacks on Zionism are the pam-

phlets by "Hadad," *Der Tsionizm vi er iz* (Zionism as It Is), 2d ed., Moscow, 1925; Alexander Chemeriski, *Tsionistishe Traiberaien* (Zionist Cabals: a Collection of Essays), Moscow, 1926; and P. Minski, *Vi lebt un kempt der arbeter in Palestine* (How the Worker Lives and Struggles in Palestine), Minsk, 1932, with such characteristic chapter headings as "50 Years of Imperialist-Zionist Colonization" or "Zionist Cities and Colonies—Strategic Outposts of British Imperialism." *See also* Dan Pines, *He-Halus be-kur ha-mahapekhah* (The Haluts Movement in the Crucible of the Revolution), Vol. I: 1917-1924, Tel Aviv, 1924; and Guido G. Goldman, *Zionism under Soviet Rule (1917-1928),* New York, 1960.

10. S. Dimanshtain, "The Beginnings of Communist Work among the Jewish Laborers" (1919), a report in Yiddish, prepared for an intended volume *A yor arbet* (A Year's Work), the proofs of which were destroyed in 1920. This report was later published in Agurskii's *Di yidishe komisariatn,* pp. 1-16. Curiously, Agurskii found it necessary, in the light of intervening developments, to correct Dimanshtain semilaudatory reference to the more passive opposition of Labor Zionists (p. 4 n.). *See also ibid.,* pp. 423 ff.

11. Agurskii, *ibid.,* pp. 19 ff., 59f.; and, more generally, his succinct summary on "Evsektsii" in *Bolshaia sovetskaia entsiklopedia,* 1st ed., XXIV (1932), 337-38. Curiously, he was able to cite in the bibliography exclusively Yiddish books.

12. Lenin, "Socialism and Religion," in the English trans. in his *Selected Works,* 12 vols., New York, [n.d.], XI, 658, 661; P. V. Gidulianov, *Otdelenie tserkvi od gosudarstva v S. S. S. R.* (Separation of State and Church in the Soviet Union), 3d ed., Moscow, 1926; William Chauncey Emhardt, *Religion in Soviet Russia: Anarchy,* Milwaukee, 1929; and other literature listed in the author's *Modern Nationalism and Religion,* pp. 197 ff., 331 ff.

13. Cited in an English trans. from the 16th ed. by Julius F. Hecker in his *Religion and Communism: a Study of Religion and Atheism in Russia,* London, 1933, p. 275 App. I.

14. Elisha Rudin, *Bi-fe'at nekhar* (In Foreign Parts: Poems and Reflections), Tel Aviv, 1938, pp. 23, 38 (the author's trans.). At the same time the poet made it clear that he had no use whatsoever for the counterrevolution which "hangs," rather than "shoots," its opponents. *Ibid.,* pp. 63 ff.

15. *Alfarbandishe beratung fun di yidishe sektsies* (All-Union Conference of the Jewish Sections of the Communist Party of December, 1926), Moscow, 1927, pp. 130 f. This

greatly abbreviated report of the Conference proceedings is analyzed by Solomon M. Schwarz in *The Jews in the Soviet Union*. With a Foreword by Alvin Johnson, Syracuse, 1951, pp. 122 ff.

16. Lenin, *Sochineniia* (Works), 2d ed., XXIV (1932), 203 (repeated in the new ed. XXIX, 227-28); the translation of the 1918 decree in *Lenin on the Jewish Question*, p. 23; Schwarz, *The Jews in the Soviet Union*, pp. 274 ff., 289 n. 14. *See also* Anatolii V. Lunacharskii, *Ob antisemitizme* (On Antisemitism), Moscow, 1929; and I. Larin (pseud. for M. A. Lurye), *Evrei i antisemitizm v SSSR* (Jews and Antisemitism in the USSR), Moscow, 1929.

17. I. Zilberman, "The Court in Its Struggle against Antisemitism" (Russian), *Ezhenedelnik sovetskoi iustitsii* (Weekly of the Soviet Judiciary), 1929, No. 4, p. 148, cited in an English trans. by S. M. Schwarz in *The Jews*, pp. 276 ff.; Larin, *Evrei*, pp. 277 f.; Maxim Gorki, cited by Reuben Ainsztein in his "Jewish Tragedy and Heroism in Soviet War Literature," *Jewish Social Studies*, XXIII (1961), 68. *See also* L. Rodishchev, *Yad* (Poison: on Contemporary Antisemitism), Leningrad, 1930.

18. The Ukrainian legislation and its practical applications were cited in full and analyzed by some of the most active Jewish politicians who participated in these early Ukrainian liberation movements. *See* esp. M. Zilberfarb, *Dos yidishe ministerium un di yidishe avtonomie in Ukraine* (The Jewish Ministry and Jewish Autonomy in the Ukraine: a Page of History), Kiev, [1918] (with an extensive documentary appendix); Salomon Goldelmann, *Juden und Ukrainer (Briefe und Dokumente)*, Vienna, 1921; A. Rewutski, *In di shvere teg oif Ukraine* (In the Difficult Days in the Ukraine: Memoirs of a Jewish Minister), Berlin, 1924. *See also* his more recent essay, "Patterns of Life of an Ethnic Minority," *Annals* of the Ukrainian Academy of Arts and Sciences in the U. S., VII (1959 Arnold Margolin Memorial Vol.), 1567-85. On its part, the Ukrainian nationalist leaders distributed, through their press service in Western lands, a brochure, *Die Lage der Juden in der Ukraine. Eine Dokumentensammlung*, ed. by Wladimir Lewitzkyj and Gustav Specht, Berlin, 1920. Here various decrees, appeals by Ukrainian and Jewish groups, etc. were reproduced in a German trans., including Margolin's and Mark Wischnitzer's interviews published in the *Jewish Chronicle* (London) of May 16, and September 19, 1919. *See also* the extensive documentation supplied by

Di idishe avtonomie un der natsionaler sekretariat in Ukraine
(Jewish Autonomy and the National Secretariat in the
Ukraine: Materials and Documents), Kiev, 1920. This volume
was ed. for the Secretariat by M. Grossmann, *et al.*, at a time
when most regulations had become obsolete.

19. The proclamation of 1917 is cited, from the *Razsvet*
of Sept. 6, 1917, by Elias Tcherikower in his *Antisemitizm
un pogromen in Ukraine* (Antisemitism and Pogroms in the
Ukraine 1917-1918: A Contribution to the History of
Ukrainian-Jewish Relations. With a Foreword by Simon
Dubnow), Berlin, 1923, p. 52. It may be noted that, in reply
to a Jewish delegation which contrasted the relative absence
of anti-Jewish excesses in Kolchak's army with the disturbances under Denikin, the latter's collaborator, Gen. Shkura,
explained Kolchak's restraint by his consideration for "the
all-controlling American Jews." Cited from a memorandum
by the Jewish Central Committee to the Zionist Actions
Committee by Lewitskyj and Specht in *Die Juden*, pp. 75 f.

20. Nikolai Ostrowskii, *The Making of a Hero*, English
trans. by Alec Brown, New York, 1937, p. 77; S. Goldelmann,
Juden und Ukrainer, pp. 49 f.; A. Rewutski, *In di shvere teg*,
pp. 290 f. The regime's equivocation came fully to the fore
during the Paris trial of Samuel Schwartzbard, the 1926
assassin of Petliura. *See Documents sur les pogromes en
Ukraine et l'assassinat de Simon Petlura à Paris*, Paris, 1927,
the materials for which were largely supplied by Elias
Tcherikower. *See* the next notes.

21. Tcherikower, *Antisemitizm*, pp. 275 ff.; Isaac Babel,
Gedali, in Alexander Kaun's English trans. in his "Babel:
Voice of New Russia," *Menorah Journal*, XV (1928), 412.
See N. Gergel, "The Pogroms in the Ukraine in the Years
1918-1921" (Yiddish), *Yivo Shriftn far ekonomik*, I (1928),
106-13, esp. p. 111. *See also*, more generally, Arthur E.
Adams, "The Bolsheviks and the Ukrainian Front in 1918-
1919," *Slavonic and East-European Review*, XXXVI (1958),
396-417; and John S. Reshetar, *The Ukrainian Revolution,
1917-1920: A Study in Nationalism*, Princeton, 1952 (Diss.
Harvard University).

22. In addition to the studies listed in the previous notes,
see Elias Heifetz, *The Slaughter of the Jews in the Ukraine
in 1919*, New York, 1921 (by the former chairman of the
All-Ukrainian Relief Committee for the Victims of Pogroms);
A. D. Rosenthal, *Megillat ha-tebah* (Scroll of Slaughter:
Materials for the History of the Pogroms and Slaughter of

the Jews in the Ukraine, Greater Russia, and White Russia), 3 vols., Jerusalem, 1929-31 (arranged in the alphabetical order of the destroyed communities); and, more comprehensively, Elias Tcherikower, *Yehudim be-ittot ha-mahapekhah* (Jews in Revolutionary Periods). With a Foreword by Ben Zion Dinur, Tel Aviv, 1957. *See also* the additional data and literature supplied by Abraham Heller in *Die Lage der Juden in Russland, passim.* On the economic effects, *see* the succinct summary in Jacob Lestschinsky, *La Situation économique des Juifs depuis la guerre mondiale (Europe orientale et centrale)*, Paris, 1934 (Cahiers of the Comité des delegations juives, XI-XIV), pp. 48 f.

23. Richard Pipes, *The Formation of the Soviet Union: Communism and Nationalism, 1917-1923,* p. 152. *See* the data presented by the anonymous study, *Evreiskie pogromy* (Anti-Jewish Pogroms, 1918-1919: Materials), Moscow, 1926, pp. 22 ff. Dramatic testimony of excesses committed by Polish troops in the occupied territories was presented to Sir Stuart Samuel. *See* his *Report on My Mission to Poland,* London, 1920. Foreign Office, Miscellanies, X.

24. *See* the illustrations cited by B. Orshanskii in his "Yiddish Poetry in White Russia After the Revolution" (Yiddish), *Zeitshrift,* V (Minsk, 1931), 1-83, esp. pp. 39 ff.; Nikolai Ostrovskii, *Kak zakalialas stal* (How the Steel Was Tempered), in the English trans. from the Russian by R. Prokofieva, 2 vols., Moscow, 1952. Library of Selected Soviet Literature; Alexander A. Fadeev, *Razgrom* (The Debacle), in the English trans. by R. D. Charques entitled *The Nineteen,* New York, 1929; Ainsztein in *Jewish Social Studies,* XXIII, 68 ff. On Babel's *Red Cavalry, see* below Chap. XIV, n. 24. Not that these writers were unaware of the widespread anti-Semitic sentiment even among the Red soldiers. In Fadeev's novel the first page records the reaction of Levinson's orderly, Morozka, who, upon receiving an unpleasant assignment, thinks silently, "All Jews are scoundrels!" But such responses were dismissed as temporary relapses to a bygone era.

CHAPTER 12 (pages 223-243)

1. Yakov Kantor, *Natsionalnoe stroitelstvo sredi Evreev v SSSR* (National Reconstruction among the Jews of the Soviet Union), ed. by E. Ostrovskii, Moscow, 1934, pp. 21 ff.,

27 f., etc.; S. M. Schwarz, *The Jews in the Soviet Union,* pp. 149 ff.

2. Kantor, *op. cit.,* pp. 29 ff.; Schwarz, *op. cit.,* pp. 156 ff.

3. Yakov Kantor, *Ratenboiung in der yidisher svive* (Soviet Reconstruction in the Jewish Environment) Kiev, 1928 (written in July 1927), pp. 18, 51; *idem, Natsionalnoe stroitelstvo, passim; Yidn in FSSR* (Jews in the Soviet Union: Atlas and Graphs), Moscow, 1930, p. 127; Otto Heller, *Der Untergang des Judentums: Die Judenfrage—ihre Kritik— Lösung durch den Sozialismus,* Vienna, 1931, pp. 192 ff.

4. Joseph Stalin (Djugashvili), *Marxism and the National and Colonial Question: a Collection of Articles and Speeches,* New York, n. d., Marxist Library, XXXVIII; *idem, Political Report to the Sixteenth Party Congress,* English trans. cited above, Chap. XI, n. 8. *See also* S. Dimanshtain's rather tortured review of "Stalin as a Bolshevist Theoretician of the National Question" (Yiddish), *Zeitshrift,* IV (1930), pp. vii-xxi. See also his ed. of *Revolutsiia i natsionalnyi vopros* (The Revolution and the National Question: Documents and Materials for the History of the National Question in Russia and the Soviet Union in the Twentieth Century), collected by I. Levin and E. Drabkin, Moscow, 1930; and above, Chap. XI, nn. 6-7.

5. *Bolshaia sovetskaia entsiklopedia,* 1st ed., Moscow, 1932, XXIV, 338.

6. Kalinin's speech of November, 1926, first appeared in the stenographic transcript of the proceedings at the *Pervii vsesoiuznii siezd OZET v Moskve* (First All-Soviet Congress of the *OZET* in Moscow, November 15-20, 1926). Republished, together with his reply to a Crimean community, in both Russian and Yiddish in the *Izvestia* and the *Emes* of July 11, 1926, it was widely heralded in Jewish circles in the Soviet Union and abroad. It was distributed in a Yiddish trans. by the GEZERD (OZET) under Kalinin's name in a brochure entitled *Yidn Erd-Arbeter* (Jewish Workers in the USSR), Moscow, 1927.

7. *See* Dimanshtain's and other statements excerpted by D. Zalbefert, *et al.,* in their *Birobidzhanish* (Biro-Bidzhan Matters: a Small Anthology on the Jewish Autonomous Region), Vilna, 1935, pp. 22 ff. The editors admit not only the general incompleteness of their materials, but also their total disregard of voices opposing that scheme.

8. *Ibid.,* p. 26.

9. *Ibid.*, p. 23; Dimanshtain, *Yidishe Avtonome gegend* (Jewish Autonomous Region: a Child of the October Revolution), Moscow, 1934; Dudley L. A. Lord Marley, *Birobidjan as I Saw It*, New York, 1934, ICOR Library, II. Marley's statement was, understandably, cited in the propaganda brochure, *Birobidjan, the Jewish Autonomous Territory*, published by the American Committee for the Settlement of Jews in Birobidjan (Ambijan), New York, 1936, p. 8.

10. I. Sudarskii, *Biro-Bidzhan* (Yiddish), Kharkov, 1933, esp. pp. 19, 22 ff., 66 ff. *See also* ICOR's equally overoptimistic English pamphlet, *Biro Bidjan Today and Tomorrow*, New York, n. d.; and Sol Almazov's review of *Ten Years of Biro-Bidjan*, trans. from the Yiddish by Nathan Farber, New York, 1938.

11. Viktor Fink, "Biro-Bidzhan" (Russian) in *Sovetskoe Stroitelstvo* of May, 1930, p. 117; Sudarskii, *Biro-Bidzhan*, pp. 70, 75 f.,; the GEZERD's semiofficial publication *Birobidzhan in itstikn moment* (B. at the Present Time) by A. Kantorovich, Moscow, 1933; and other data carefully sifted by S. M. Schwarz in *The Jews in the Soviet Union*, pp. 174 ff.

12. A. Kantorovich, *Tsvaiter 5-yor plan* (The Second Five-Year Plan for Biro-Bidzhan), 2d ed., New York, 1932.

13. *See* esp. the statements made by Gine Medem and O. Pressman and excerpted in *Birobidzhanish*, pp. 28, 30 f.; the Ambijan's *Birobidjan*, p. 6.

14. A. Powell, "The Nationalist Trend in Soviet Historiography," *Soviet Studies*, II (1950-51), 372-77; Robert H. McNeal, "Soviet Historiography on the October Revolution: a Review of Forty Years," *American Slavic and East-European Review*, XVII (1958), 269-81.

15. *Pravda* of November 7, 1938, cited by Nicholas S. Timasheff in his "Russian Nationalism under the Soviets," *Thought*, XX (1945), 447; and, more fully, in his *The Great Retreat: the Growth and Decline of Communism in Russia*, New York, 1946, pp. 151 ff., 168; Frank Lorimer, *The Population of the Soviet Union: History and Prospects*, Geneva, 1946, pp. 137 ff.; and other sources mentioned in the author's *Modern Nationalism and Religion*, pp. 203 ff., 332 f. nn. 71-73. *See also* Vincas Rastenis's succinct observation on "The Russification of Non-Russian Peoples in the Russian Empire under the Czars and under the Soviets," *Lituanus*, VI (1959), 103-107.

16. Kalinin's speech cited above, n. 6; Joseph Roth, *Juden auf Wanderschaft,* Berlin, 1927, Berichte aus der Wirklichkeit, IV, p. 104; Otto Heller, *Der Untergang des Judentums,* pp. 198, 238; Kloinimus in *Komunistishe Velt,* 1919, Nos. 3-4, cited by Orshanskii in *Zeitshrift,* V, 15 f. See also Larin's *Evrei i antisemitizm v SSSR, passim.*

17. S. Y. Chutskaev, "Ten Years of Biro-Bidzhan" (Russian), *Vlast Sovetov,* April, 1938, p. 18; *Emes* of June 3, 1937; S. M. Schwarz, *The Jews,* pp. 180 ff.; and the literature cited above, nn. 10-11.

18. Report of the Royal (Peel) Commission, London, 1937. Cmd. 5479.

19. Otto Heller, *Der Untergang,* pp. 231 ff.

20. *See* the interesting statistical table (IX), largely compiled from official Soviet sources, by S. M. Schwarz in *The Jews,* p. 302.

21. Zbigniew Brzezinski, *The Permanent Purge: Politics in Soviet Totalitarianism,* Cambridge, 1956. Harvard University Research Center, Studies, XX, esp. pp. 65 ff., 106, 217 n. 126.

CHAPTER 13 (pages 244-267)

1. *See* the illuminating statistical table (V) in S. M. Schwarz, *The Jews in the Soviet Union,* p. 15, based on sources listed by him, p. 22 n. 23.

2. Arthur Ruppin, *Soziologie der Juden,* 2 vols., Berlin, 1930, I, 175 Table XX, 240 Table XXXIII; L. Zinger, *Dos banaite Folk* (The People Reborn), Moscow, 1941, pp. 33 ff., 40; Jacob Lestchinsky, "The Evolution of the Jewish People during the Last One-Hundred Years" (Yiddish), *YIVO Shriftn far ekonomik,* I (1928), 24; Friedrich Hermann Zanders, *Die Verbreitung der Juden in der Welt: Statistische Beiträge zu den Fragen der Zeit,* Berlin, 1937, pp. 63 ff. (somewhat colored and unreliable). See also J. A. Nillesen's comprehensive review of *De sociale Toestand der Joden in Rusland* (The Social Status of the Jews in Russia under the Tsars and the Soviets: a Contribution to the Study of the Jewish Question), Nijmegen, 1939.

3. I. Koralnik, "Jewry in Poland and Russia according to the Latest Censuses" (Yiddish), *YIVO Shriftn far ekonomik,* I, 211-28; L. Zinger, *Evreiskoe naseleniie v Sovetskom Soyuze* (Jewish Population in the Soviet Union), Moscow, 1932, pp. 104 ff.; Schwarz, *The Jews,* pp. 168, 172 f. n. 44.

4. Yurii M. Larin, *Evrei i antisemitizm,* p. 133.

5. Zinger, *Dos banaite Folk*, pp. 41 ff.

6. M. Kipper, *Dos yidishe shtetl in Ukraine* (The Jewish Hamlet in the Ukraine), Kharkov, 1929, pp. 97 ff.; Larin, *Evrei*, pp. 68 ff., 156; Yakov Kantor, *Di yidishe bafelkerung in Ukraine* (The Jewish Population in the Ukraine: According to the Census of 1926), Kharkov, 1929; *Evrei v S.S.S.R.* (Jews in the Soviet Union: Texts and Studies), published by the ORT, Moscow, 1929, pp. 10 ff.; Genrikh I. Neiman, ed., *Vnutrennaia torgovliia SSSR* (The Soviet Union's Internal trade), ed. by E. I. Kviring, Moscow, 1935, pp. 145 f.; above, Chap. VI, n. 10.

7. *See,* for instance, Mikhail Chumandrin, *Fabrika Rable* (Rable's Factory), Leningrad, 1929; and L. Radishchev's critique thereof, both cited by Bernard J. Choseed in "The Soviet Jew in Literature," *Jewish Social Studies*, XI (1949), 262 f.; Jacob Lestchinsky, "Jewish Commercial Employees in the Soviet Ukraine" (Yiddish), *Yivo Bleter*, X (1936), 197-231 (mainly based on the official *Perepis* published in Kiev, 1936); John A. Armstrong, *Ukrainian Nationalism, 1939-1945*, New York, 1958. Studies of the Russian Institute of Columbia University, p. 227 n. 2; Boris Brutzkus, "Die wirtschaftliche und soziale Lage der Juden in Russland vor und nach der Revolution," *Archiv für Sozialwissenschaft und Sozialpolitik*, LXI (1929), 266-321, esp. pp. 301 ff.

8. Numerous such excerpts from the *Emes* and other Soviet newspapers and journals are reproduced by Jacob Lestchinsky in *Der Emes vegn di Yidn in Rusland* (The Truth about the Jews in Russia), Berlin, 1925, esp. pp. 34 ff.

9. Kantor, *Di yidishe bafelkerung*, pp. 44 f. Table 25. Evidently using somewhat different definitions, a pamphlet, *Evrei v kustarno remeslennoi promyshlennosti SSSR* (Jews in the Home Industry of the Soviet Union), published by the ORT in Moscow, 1928, counted those employed in crafts, homework, and petty industry as constituting 25.2 percent of all gainfully employed Jews in the Ukrainian Republic. Of those 52 percent worked by themselves, 23.6 percent together with their families (including those family members themselves) and only 6.2 percent employed outside labor. The others consisted of factory workers and office personnel. *See* the summary in Ruppin's *Soziologie*, I, 438 f. *See also* Abraham Heller, *Die Lage der Juden in Russland*, pp. 78 ff.

10. Brutzkus in *Archiv für Sozialwissenschaft*, LXI, 302 f.;

The Jews under Soviet Rule, published by the Institute of Jewish Affairs, New York, 1941.

11. A. Heller, *Die Lage,* pp. 82 ff. *See also* Brutzkus in *Archiv für Sozialwissenschaft,* LXI, 266-321.

12. *See* the telling data summarized by Ruppin in his *Soziologie,* I, 441 Table LII; and by A. Heller in *Die Lage,* pp. 78 f. Table XX, both following the ORT's *Evrei v S.S.S.R.,* pp. 10 ff. Somewhat different statistical computations, based on different classifications, are offered for the Ukraine alone by Kantor in *Di yidishe bafelkerung,* pp. 50 ff. Tables 28 and 30.

13. S. N. Prokopowicz, *Russlands Volkswirtschaft unter den Sowjets,* German trans. from the Russian manuscript by W. Jollos, Zurich, 1944, pp. 198 ff.; L. Zinger, *Dos banaite Folk,* pp. 49 ff.; *idem, Dos ufgerikhte Folk* (The Reconstructed People: the Socioeconomic Restratification of the Jewish Population in the Soviet Union), Moscow, 1948, p. 39. To be sure, some of these data are highly conjectural and Solomon Schwarz's strictures thereon (in *The Jews,* pp. 169 ff.) are quite justified. But they clearly indicate the tremendous transformations in the Russo-Jewish economic structure within half a generation.

14. Perctz Markish, *Der finfter horizont* (The Fifth Level); and H. Orland, *Aglomerat,* cited by Choseed in *Jewish Social Studies,* XI, 266; Zinger, *Dos banaite Folk,* pp. 63, 68 f.

15. Armstrong, *Ukrainian Nationalism,* p. 242. *See also* P. Kretzer's dissertation, *Die beruflichen und sozialen Verhältnisse der Juden in der UdSSR,* Berlin, 1931.

16. Zinger, *Dos banaite Folk,* pp. 103 ff., 106; Institute for Jewish Affairs, *The Jews under Soviet Rule.* Zinger concedes the tentative nature of these computations and expresses the hope that furthcr detailed investigations of the results of the 1939 census would amplify and modify his findings. Yet he remained, during the portentous years of 1939-41, the sole fairly competent, if biased, student of the Jewish aspects of that census with relatively easy access to the primary materials. There is almost no possibility now for an independent recheck of his statistics. *See also* below, n. 19.

17. B. Brutzkus, *Di yidishe landvirtshaft in Mizrakh-Eirope* (Jewish Agriculture in Eastern Europe), Berlin, 1926, pp. 57 ff.

18. *Ibid.;* Isler, *Rückkehr der Juden zur Landwirtschaft,* pp. 40 ff.; S. N. Prokopowicz, *Russlands Volkwirtschaft,* pp.

63 ff., in the main following the data presented by the Soviet economist, B. N. Knipovich. The ill-will of many peasants toward their new Jewish neighbors is well reflected in such stories as Samuel Persov's *Tog un nakht* (Day and Night), Moscow, 1933, esp. p. 150.

19. Larin, *Evrei i antisemitizm*, p. 308; *Pratsi* (Proceedings) of the First All-Russian Conference of Marxist Agrarian Political Scientists, December, 1929, Vol. I, Moscow, 1930, pp. 74 ff.

20. N. L. Semashko, "A New Man is Born" (Yiddish), in S. Dimanshtain, ed., *Yidn in FSSR* (Jews in the Soviet Union: a Symposium), Moscow, 1935, p. 49; above, Chap. XI, n. 8; *Emes* of December 19, 1924 and other sources, cited by J. Lestchinsky in *Der Emes vegn di Yidn*, pp. 49 ff.; *idem*, "Die soziale und wirtschaftliche Lage der Ostjuden nach dem Kriege," *Weltwirtschaftliches Archiv*, XXIV (1926), 39-62.

21. *See* the ORT's publication *Evrei v S.S.S.R.*, pp. 67 f.; Artur Ruppin, "Die jüdische landwirtschaftliche Kolonisation in Russland," *Palästina*, XI (1928), 2-28. *See also* A. Rovner's report, *The ICOR and the Jewish Colonization in the U. S. S. R.*, New York, 1934. ICOR Library, III. The original preponderance of grain cultivation in the Ukrainian Jewish colonies is well illustrated by the Statistical Table (36) in Y. Kantor's *Di yidishe bafelkerung in Ukraine*, p. 56. But even then it was less pronounced in the Crimea. On the varying fortunes of the Jewish participants in the American communist movement, see Melech Epstein, *The Jew and Communism: the Story of Early Communist Victories and Ultimate Defeats in the Jewish Community, U. S. A., 1919-1941*, New York, [1959].

22. L. Zinger and B. Engel, *Yidishe bafelkerung fun FSSR* (Jewish Population in the Soviet Union: Tables and Diagrams), Moscow, n. d., Tables I,2; II,2; III,8, etc. On the frequent inconsistencies in the data supplied by Zinger in his various studies, *see* S. M. Schwarz in *The Jews*, pp. 164 ff., 171 f.

23. Zinger, *Dos banaite Folk*, pp. 85 ff. In his enthusiasm for the achievements of Jewish agriculturists in the 1930s Zinger mentions that the wheat production of the Crimean colonies had increased elevenfold between 1926 and 1938. He not only fails to indicate that in 1926 Jewish colonization there still was in its infancy, but also that the number of colonists had simultaneously increased by 436 percent. Under-

standably, with the progressive acquisition of both skills and equipment, the productivity of these Jewish farms increased greatly; in 1935-38 alone from 8 to 14 tons of wheat per hectar. In the latter year the Crimean Jews were able to deliver 2,500,000 poods (some 41,000 metric tons) of grain and 1,000,000 tons of fruits to the state.

CHAPTER 14 (pages 268-289)

1. See Elias Tcherikower's interesting Yiddish essay, "Communist Fighters for Hebrew in Turkestan" in the collection, *In der tekufe fun revolutsie* (In the Revolutionary Period: Memoirs, Materials and Documents), Vol. I, Berlin, 1924, pp. 356-66.

2. Judah Dardak, "Our Educational Achievements in Fifteen Years of the October Revolution" (Yiddish) in *Tsum 15 yortog fun der Octiabrrevolutsie* (To the Fifteenth Anniversary of the October Revolution: Socioeconomic Essays), Minsk, 1932, pp. 172 f., also cited with variations by S. M. Schwarz in *The Jews in the Soviet Union*, p. 131.

3. Nahum Gergel, *Di lage fun di Yidn in Rusland* (The Situation of the Jews in Russia), Warsaw, 1929; A. Heller, *Die Lage*, pp. 119 f. *See also* the data marshaled by Bernard Weinryb in "Das jüdische Schulwesen in Sowjetrussland," *Monatsschrift für Geschichte und Wissenschaft des Judentums*, LXXV (1931), 455-62.

4. These and other data have been assembled, with some inner contradictions and obscurities, by Yakov Kantor in his *Natsionalnoe stroitelstvo*, esp. pp. 170 ff. *See also* the statistical tables in S. M. Schwarz, *The Jews*, pp. 14 ff.

5. Weinryb in *Monatsschrift*, LXXV, 458; Jacob Lestchinsky, *Dos sovietishe yidentum* (Soviet Jewry, Its Past and Present), New York, 1941, pp. 323 ff., largely based on newspaper clippings from the *Emes* and other Soviet papers, since no serious Soviet study of Jewish education after 1933 had appeared. *See*, however, A. Kirzhnitz's obviously overoptimistic evaluation of the progress of Yiddish education during the First Five-Year Plan of 1928-32 in his succinct survey of "The Culture Upbuilding among the Jewish Masses" in *Yidn in FSSR*, ed. by Dimanshtain, pp. 257-67.

6. A. Heller, *Die Lage*, pp. 121 f.; Zinger, *Dos banaite Folk*, p. 108.

7. *See* Yehudah Slutski's comprehensive bibliographical study of "The Hebrew Publications in the Soviet Union in

the Years 1917-1960" in Khana Shmeruk, ed., *Pirsumim yehudiim bi-Berit ha-Moesot* (Jewish Publications in the Soviet Union, 1917-1960), compiled by Y. Y. Cohen and M. Piekarz, Jerusalem, 1961, pp. xix-liv.

8. H. N. Bialik, *Iggerot* (Letters), collected and ed. with notes by Fishel Lachover, 5 vols., Tel Aviv, 1938-39, II, 183 No. 327, 189 No. 333; Slutski, *op. cit.*, pp. xxiii ff.

9. *See* Bialik's *Iggerot*, II, 207 ff. Nos. 348-49. A member of that group of Hebrew emigré writers, Ben Zion Dinaburg (Dinur), the historian and later minister of education in Israel, dramatically describes these vicissitudes in his autobiographical *Bi-yeme milhamah u-mahapekhah* (In the Days of War and Revolution: Reminiscences and Impressions, 1914-1921), Jerusalem, 1960, esp. pp. 285 ff., 320 ff., 476 ff., 519 ff. *See also* above, Chap. IX, n. 28.

10. *See* the early bibliographical survey of "Hebrew Printing in the Soviet Union" (Hebrew) by [Saul] B[orovoi] in *Kirjath Sepher*, V (1928-29), 250-54 (of the 53 numbers, representing 35 books, 24 were simple prayerbooks and only four secular books, including 3 volumes of communist poetry); Slutski, *op. cit.*, pp. xxxv ff.; and the excerpts from the communist press of 1928 attesting the continued "vitality of religion" at that time, cited by William Chancey Emhardt in his *Religion in Soviet Russia: Anarchy*, Milwaukee, 1928, pp. 281 ff., 293.

11. Nahum Rubinshtain, comp., *Dos yidishe bukh in Sovietfarband* (The Jewish Book in the Soviet Union) for 1932, 1933, 1934, 1935, Minsk, 1933-36, esp. yearbook 1934, pp. xxiii f.; Khana Shmeruk, "Yiddish Publications in the Soviet Union, 1917-1960" (Hebrew) in her ed. of *Pirsumim yehudiim*, pp. lv ff., lxi ff., lxxxviii ff., 13 Nos. 97-100; S. M. Schwarz, *The Jews*, p. 139 Table XIV.

12. Paul B. Anderson, *People, Church and State in Modern Russia*, New York, 1944, p. 62. See also Adolf Ziegler, *Die russische Gottlosenbewegung*, Munich, 1932.

13. *See* esp. A. Finkelshtain, "The Book Production of the *Emes* Publishing House during the Second Five Year Plan (1933-1937)" (Yiddish), *Sovietish-literarisher Almanakh*, VII-VIII (1938), 416-27; Zinger, *Dos banaite Folk*, pp. 109 f.

14. D[avid] B[ergelson], "Three Centers" (Yiddish), *In Shpan*, I (Vilna, 1926), 84-96; "Chronicle" (Yiddish), *ibid.*, p. 165, both cited by K. Shmeruk in *Pirsumim*, pp. lxxxviii f. n. 35.

15. *See* the list in N. Rubinshtain's bibliography for 1935 (above n. 11), summarized by K. Shmeruk in *Pirsumim,* pp. cxiii ff. On the Polish-Jewish publications, *see,* for instance, the author's *Bibliography of Jewish Social Studies, 1938-39,* New York, 1941. Jewish Social Studies, Publications, I; and his *From a Historian's Notebook: European Jewry Before and After Hitler* (a memorandum prepared for the author's testimony at the Eichmann trial in April, 1961; reprinted from the *American Jewish Year Book,* LXIII, 1962, 3-53).

16. B. Orshanskii in *Zeitshrift,* V, 21.

17. Zalman Reisen, *Leksikon,* II, 105 ff., 348 ff.; Bernard J. Choseed, "The Soviet Jew in Literature," *Jewish Social Studies,* XI, 277 f. *See also* such monographic studies as Yehezkal Dobrushin's "Benjamin Susskin and the Types in Soviet Drama" (Yiddish), *Forpost,* VI (1938), 205-23; and Noah Isaac Gotlib's more comprehensive review of *Sovetishe shraiber* (Soviet Writers), Montreal, 1945 (a collection of articles published in 1934-44; includes material on non-Jewish Soviet writers discussing aspects of Jewish life).

18. Lenin's essay of 1905 and Lunacharskii's statement of 1933, cited in the English trans. by Robert M. Hankin in his informative analysis of the "Main Premises of the Communist Party in the Theory of Soviet Literary Controls" in *Continuity and Change in Russian and Soviet Thought,* ed. with an Intro. by Ernest J. Simmons, Cambridge, Mass., 1955, pp. 433-50, esp. pp. 445, 449. Developments in the Yiddish literature naturally paralleled those in general Russian letters. On these ever tightening controls, restored after a brief intermission of the War years in 1946, see Avrahm Yarmolinsky's *Literature under Communism: the Literary Policy of the Communist Party of the Soviet Union from the End of World War II to the Death of Stalin,* [Bloomington, Ind., 1957]. Russian and East European Series of Indiana Univ., XX. *See also* below, n. 21.

19. This conversation of 1939 is reported in the reminiscences relating to a leading Soviet writer, Der Nister (The Occult, pseud. for Pinhas Kahanovich; 1884-*ca.*1948) by H. Bloshtain, which were published under the telling title, "He Would Now Be Seventy-Five Years Old (Some Reminiscences about Der Nister)" (Yiddish) in *Yidishe Kultur,* XXI, No. 8 (1959), 20-23. *See* K. Shmeruk in *Pirsumim,* p. xc n. 54.

20. *See,* for instance, the sharp attack on Sosis's objec-

tivity and nationalism by Leib Holmstock and Yakov Rubin in their "On the Front of Jewish Historiography" (Yiddish) in *Tsum 15tn yortog fun der Oktiabr revolutsie* (On the Fifteenth Anniversary of the October Revolution: an Historical Collection), published by the White Russian Academy of Science, Minsk, 1932, pp. 147, 152; Hillel Aleksandrov, "The Economic and Statistical Research of the Yiddish Scientific Institute" (Yiddish), *Zeitshrift*, IV (1930), 296-331 (attacking in particular Jacob Lestchinsky's demographic studies); his, Sosis's and others' articles in *Fashizirter yidishizm* (Fascist Yiddishism and Its Science), published by the White Russian Academy of Science, Minsk, 1930; Judah Rosenthal, "Jewish Historiography in Soviet Russia and Simon Dubnow" (Hebrew) in Simon Rawidowicz, ed., *Sefer Shimeon Dubnow*, London, 1954, pp. 201-220; and, more generally, Alfred Abraham Greenbaum, *Jewish Scholarship in Soviet Russia, 1918-1941*, Boston, 1959; *idem*, "Jewish Historiography in Soviet Russia," *Proceedings* of the American Academy for Jewish Research, XXVIII (1959), 57-76; *idem*, "Nationalism as a Problem in Soviet Jewish Scholarship," *ibid.*, XXX (1962), 61-77.

21. See *Yidishe ortografie* (Yiddish Orthography: Projects and Materials Prepared for the Second All-Union Yiddish Culture Conference), Kiev, 1928; A. Zaretski, *Far a proletarisher sprakh* (For a Proletarian Language), Kharkov, 1931, esp. pp. 21 ff.; and other writings listed by Uriel and Beatrice Weinreich in their *Yiddish Language and Folklore: a Selective Bibliography for Research*, The Hague, 1959. *Janua linguarum*, X; Shmeruk in *Pirsumim*, pp. cxxv ff. See also Yudel Mark, ed., *Yuda A. Yofe-bukh* (Studies Presented to Judah A. Joffe), New York, 1958, esp. pp. 207-20 (Roman Jakobson, "The Yiddish Sound Structure in Its Slavic Environment") and 236-56 (Yehuda Elzet, "Discourses on Hebrew-Yiddish and Yiddish-Hebrew").

22. See the report by Salomon Mikhoels himself, together with Yeheskel Dobrushin, "Jewish Theater Culture in the Soviet Union" (Yiddish) included in Simeon Dimanshtain, ed., *Yidn in FSSR* (Jews in the Soviet Union: a Collection of Essays), Moscow, 1935, pp. 149-62.

23. Zinger, *Dos banaite Folk*, p. 109.

24. See esp. Alexander Kaun, "Babel: Voice of New Russia," *Menorah Journal*, XV (1928), 400-413 (includes trans. of Babel's *Gedali*); Lionel Trilling, "The Fate of Isaac Babel," *The London Magazine*, III (1956), 40-58. See also the recent

Italian rendition of Babel's *Opere*, including Vol. III, *Racconti proibiti e lettere intime*, ed. by Maria Olsonfiera, Milan, 1961. I Narratori di Feltrinelli, X.

25. See Gleb Struve, *Soviet-Russian Literature 1917-50*, Norman, Okla., 1951, in the revised and more up-to-date German trans. of this work by Horst Neerfeld and Günter Schäfer entitled, *Geschichte der Sowjetliteratur*, Munich, 1958 (up to 1957), pp. 172 ff., 212 ff., 217 ff., 223 ff., 225 ff.; Mark Slonim, "Jewish Writers in Soviet Literature" (Russian), *Evreiskii Mir*, II (New York, 1944), 146-64; and Ainsztein in *Jewish Social Studies*, XXIII, 72 f. The extent of "Averbakhism" in 1931 is well illustrated by Mikhail Sholokhov's complaint to Gorki that, if he were to accept the RAPP's criticisms of the manuscript of the third part of his *Tikhii Don* (The Silent Don)—later celebrated as a classic of the rank of Tolstoy's *War and Peace*—he would have to discard three-fourths of the volume. See Ernest J. Simmons, *Russian Fiction and Soviet Ideology: Introduction to Fedin, Leonov, and Sholokhov*, New York, 1958, pp. 171 f.

CHAPTER 15 (pages 290-308)

1. *Izvestia* of April 17, 1939, cited by N. S. Timasheff in *Thought*, XX, 455. See also Max M. Laserson's remarks on the Soviet "rehabilitation of national history" in his *Russia and the Western World: the Place of the Soviet Union in the Comity of Nations*, New York, 1945, pp. 138 ff.; and above. Chap. XI, n. 7.

2. The German report cited from an archival source by S. M. Schwarz in *The Jews in the Soviet Union*, p. 310; Ihor Kamenetsky, *Hitler's Occupation of the Ukraine (1941-1944): a Study of Totalitarian Imperialism*, Milwaukee, 1956. Marquette Slavic Studies, II, esp. pp. 19 ff., 35 ff. See also the extensive documentation in E. M. Carroll and F. T. Epstein, eds., *Deutschland und die Sowjetunion, 1939-1941*, Washington, D. C., 1948; Angelo Rossi (Tasca), *The Russo-German Alliance, August 1939-June 1941*, trans. from the French by John and Michelin Gullen, Boston, 1954; and, from the legal aspects, George Ginsburg, "The Soviet Union as a Neutral, 1939-1941," *Soviet Studies*, X (1958), 12-35.

3. See the author's *Modern Nationalism and Religion*, pp. 205 f., 333 f. nn. 77-78; P. B. Anderson, *People, Church and State*, pp. 213 f.

4. René Fülöp-Miller, *Rasputin, the Holy Devil*, English

trans. cited *supra*, Chap. X, n. 12; Ziegler, *Die russische Gottlosenbewegung*, p. 157 n.

5. Israel Cohen, *Vilna*, pp. 469 ff.

6. *See* Samuel Gringauz (Grinhaus), "The Last Year of Jewish Life in Lithuania" (Yiddish) in *Lite*, ed. by M. Sudarsky, *et al.*, I, 153-62, also citing from the *Lithuanian Bulletin*, III, No. 5 (1945), 20 ff. the interesting official Soviet listing of the alleged "counterrevolutionary" organizations in Lithuania (compiled in April, 1941). Here, too, the Jewish groups are assigned a disproportionate role. On Latvia, *see* Max Kaufmann, *Die Vernichtung der Juden Lettlands (Churban Lettland)*, Munich, 1947.

7. Raul Hilberg, *The Destruction of the European Jews*, Chicago, 1961, pp. 219 ff. On the overt mistreatment of Jewish and other Russian war-prisoners, which the Germans legalistically justified by the Soviet Union's refusal to ratify the Geneva Convention, *see also* the extensive documentary material assembled by the Soviets in *Dokumenty obviniaiut* (Documents Accuse), 2 vols., Moscow, 1943-45. *See also* the *Soviet Government Statements on Nazi Atrocities*, London, 1946; the German analysis by Karl I. Albrecht, *Sie aber werden die Welt zerstören*, Munich, 1954, pp. 201 ff.; and the graphic description of the shooting of 231 Jewish war-prisoners in a camp near Proskurov by Vladimir Bondarets in his "Notes from Captivity" (Russian), *Novy Mir*, Nos. 9-10 (Sept.-Oct. 1959), extensively cited in an English trans. by R. Ainsztein in *Jewish Social Studies*, XXIII, 82 ff.

8. *Trial of the Major War Criminals before the Nuremberg International Tribunal*, 42 vols., Washington, D. C., 1949, XXXII, 72 ff.; Corliss Lamont, *The Peoples of the Soviet Union*, New York, [1946], p. 85. *See also* the critique of similar assertions by B. Z. Goldberg in 1946-47 in S. M. Schwarz, *The Jews*, pp. 228 ff.

9. Philip Friedman, "The Jewish Badge and the Yellow Star in the Nazi Era," *Historia judaica*, XVII (1955), 41-70; *Bolschewismus—jüdisches Untermenschentum*, published by the Reich Security Office; Adolf Hitler's letter to Otto Strasser of May 21, 1930, cited by the latter in his *Ministersessel oder Revolution?* pp. 12 ff. and the address in Nuremberg of 1937-38, summarized in English in Norman H. Baynes, ed., *The Speeches of Adolf Hitler, April 1922-August 1939*. An English trans. of Representative Passages Arranged under Subjects, 2 vols., London, 1942, I, 700,

713; II, 988 f.; Himmler's address early in 1941, cited in the *Trial of Major War Criminals*, IV, 482. *See also* J. A. Newth, "Some Trends in the Soviet Population 1939 to 1956 (with Particular Reference to the RSFSR)," *Soviet Studies*, X (1958-59), 252-78; and Karol Marian Popieszalski, "The Extermination of the Jewish People and the Hitlerite Intentions to Destroy the Slavs" (Polish), *Przegląd zachodni*, X (1954), 527-41, largely based upon Artur Eisenbach's comprehensive monograph, *Hitlerowska polityka eksterminacji Zydów* (The Hitlerite Policy of Exterminating Jews in the Years 1939-1945 as One of the Manifestations of German Imperialism), Warsaw, 1953.

10. The Slutsk report and other data analyzed by Alexander Dallin in his *German Rule in Russia 1941-1945: a Study of Occupation Policies*, London, 1957, pp. 205 ff.

11. *See* Rudolf Loewenthal, "The Judeo-Tats in the Caucasus," *Historia judaica*, XIV (1952), 61-82; *idem*, "The Extinction of the Krimchaks in World War II," *American Slavic and East-European Review*, X (1951), 130-36.

12. Heinrich Himmler's address of October 4, 1943, cited by William L. Shirer in *The Rise and Fall of the Third Reich: a History of Nazi Germany*, New York, 1960, p. 966. *See also* Hilberg, *The Destruction*, p. 652.

13. Dallin, *German Rule*, pp. 215, 649 f. According to an official German report of December 2, 1941, "the population of the Crimea is anti-Jewish and in some cases spontaneously brings Jews to *Kommandos* to be liquidated. The *starosts* [village elders] ask for permission to liquidate the Jews themselves." Cited by Hilberg in *The Destruction*, p. 202 n. 76. *See also* J. A. Armstrong, *Ukrainian Nationalism, 1939-1945*; and, more generally, Alexander Dallin's "interim report" on *Popular Attitudes and Behavior under the German Occupation, 1941-1944*, Cambridge, Mass., 1944. Harvard University Russian Research Center.

14. Kalonymus Kalmish Shapiro, *Sefer Or Kodesh* (The Holy Fire: Homilies Delivered in Warsaw during the Years of the Catastrophe, 1942-44), Jerusalem, 1960; Shmerke Kaczerginski, comp., *Lider fun gettos un lagern* (Songs of Ghettos and Camps), ed. by H. Leivik, New York, 1948. The great tragedy of Soviet and, more generally, of European Jewry could be mentioned here only with utmost brevity. It has been the subject of many primary and secondary publications, the bibliographical listing of which

alone has been a prodigious task. *See* esp. the comprehensive works by Gerald Reitlinger, *The Final Solution: an Attempt to Exterminate the Jews of Europe 1939-1945*, New York, 1953 (also in a revised German trans. by J. W. Brügel, entitled *Die Endlösung*, Berlin, 1956); Léon Poliakov, *Harvest of Hate. The Nazi Program for the Destruction of the Jews of Europe*, New York, 1954; and Raul Hilberg, *The Destruction*. A host of other publications are listed by Jacob Robinson and Philip Friedman in their *Guide to Jewish History under Nazi Impact*, with Forewords by Benzion Dinur and Salo W. Baron, New York, 1960; and in Friedman's ed. of *Bibliografiah shel ha-sefarim ha-ibrim al ha-sho'ah* (Bibliography of Books in Hebrew on the Jewish Catastrophe and Heroism in Europe), Jerusalem, 1960, together forming the Bibliographical Series, I-II, of the Joint Projects of Yad Washem and the Yivo. *See also* the author's memorandum on "European Jewry Before and After Hitler," cited above, Chap. XIV, n. 15.

15. Boris Gorbatov, *Semia Tarasa* (Taras' Family), English trans. from the Russian by Elizabeth Donnelly, London, 1944, p. 21; Choseed in *Jewish Social Studies*, XI, 281 f.

16. Moshe Kahanovich, *Milhemet ha-partizanim ha-yehudim* (The Struggle of the Jewish Partisans in Eastern Europe), Tel Aviv, 1954, pp. 173 ff., 179; G. M. Linkov, *Voina v tylu vraga* (War in the Enemy's Rear), Moscow, 1947; and other data, cited by Reuben Ainsztein in his "Jewish Tragedy and Heroism in Soviet War Literature," *Jewish Social Studies*, XXIII, 70 n. 2, 73 ff.; Carol Jacobson, "The Jews in the USSR," *American Review of the Soviet Union*, VI, No. 4 (1944-45), 50-68, esp. p. 64; the anonymous report of an Army captain summarized by A. R. L. Gurland in *Glimpses of Soviet Jewry: 1,000 Letters from the USSR and DP Camps*. Report on Material Collected by the Union of Russian Jews, Inc., New York, 1948, p. 55. *See also* D. Karov, *Partizanskoe dvizhenie v SSSR v 1941 gg* (Partisans' History during the Years of 1941-45), Munich, 1954. *Posledovaniia* (Texts and Studies of the Institute for Research into the History and Culture of the Soviet Union), 1st ser., XI; and, from retrospect evaluations, below, Chap. XV, n. 1. Although superseded in many details, the following Russian studies published in 1944 in the New York *Evreiskii Mir*, II are still worthy of note: Joseph Schechtman, "Soviet

Jewry in the Soviet-German War" (pp. 221-40); and E. Stalinskii, "Jews in the Red Army" (pp. 240-54).

17. Léon Leneman, *La tragédie des Juifs en U. R. S. S.*, Paris, 1959. Questions actuelles, pp. 103 ff.; the report in *Unzer Tsait* of July, 1943, pp. 26 ff.

18. The Committee itself traced its origin back to a meeting of Jewish representatives in Moscow on August 24, 1941, at which, among others, Ilya Ehrenburg had made a dramatic declaration of being a Jew: "We are hated by Hitler above all others and this is a source of pride for us." His speech was reported in *Pravda* of August 25, 1941. *See* the pamphlets, *Brider Yidn fun der gantser velt* (Brother Jews All Over the World), Moscow, 1941 (also in Russian); and *The Second Jewish Anti-Fascist Meeting, Moscow, May 24, 1942*, Moscow, 1942. *See also* the Committee's semi-official report, *Evreiskii narod v borbe protiv fashizma* (The Jewish People in the Struggle against Fascism: Materials for the Third Antifascist Meeting), Moscow, 1945; and the literary anthology, *Tsum zig* (Toward Victory), Moscow, 1944, with significant contributions by Bergelson, Markish, Der Nister, and many others. On Mikhoels, *see* above, Chap. XIV, n. 22.

19. Shakhno Epshtain in the Committee's organ, *Ainikait*, of February 7, 1943, cited, together with other sources, by S. M. Schwarz in *The Jews*, pp. 202 ff. Like most of the older communists, Epshtain had traveled a great distance from the time he had written on *Y. L. Peretz als sotsialer dikhter* (Peretz as a Social Poet), New York, 1916, emphasizing, in particular, Peretz's "spirit of freedom" (p. 5).

20. Peretz Markish, *Far Folk un haimland* (For the [Jewish] People and the [Russian] Fatherland), Moscow, 1943; *idem, Milkhome* (The War), Moscow, 1948 (a poem of 660 pages). Ehrenburg's note is cited by B. Z. Goldberg, one of the chief American partners in the preparation of the Black Book, in *The Jewish Problem in the Soviet Union: Analysis and Solution*, with a Foreword by Daniel Mayer, New York, 1961, pp. 65 f. Ehrenburg attempted to controvert the accusation, frequently heard then and later, that Jews had too meekly submitted to the Nazi assassins. This accusation has once again been answered in K. Shabbetai's recent essay, *As Sheep to the Slaughter*, with a Foreword by Gideon Hausner, Bet Dagan, Israel, 1962.

21. K. Shmeruk in *Ha-Pirsumim*, pp. xcv ff.

CHAPTER 16 (pages 309-326)

1. Ilya Ehrenburg, "On the Occasion of a Letter" (Russian), *Pravda* of September 21, 1948, cited by S. M. Schwarz in *The Jews in the Soviet Union*, p. 209; and, more generally, Matthew P. Gallagher, *The Soviet History of World War II: Myths, Memoirs and Realities*, New York, 1963.

2. B. Z. Goldberg, *The Jewish Problem in the Soviet Union*, pp. 61 ff.

3. These figures were given by A. Bakhmutskii, Secretary of the Biro-Bidzhan Communist Party, esp. in his enthusiastic report, "In the United Soviet Family of Nations" (Yiddish), *Ainikait* of April 10, 1948; S. M. Schwarz, *The Jews*, pp. 185 ff.

4. Carol Jacobson in the *American Review of the Soviet Union*, VI, No. 4, pp. 62 f.; Shmerl Kaczerginski, *Tsvishn hamer un serp* (Between the Hammer and the Sickle: a Contribution to the History of the Liquidation of Jewish Culture in Soviet Russia), Paris, 1949; and other data cited by R. Ainsztein in *Jewish Social Studies*, XXIII, 72 f.

5. Stalin, "Marxism and the National Question (1913)," reprinted in his *Works*, Moscow, 1953, II, 300 f., 418 n. 131. The same position had been taken in 1945 by the semi-official description of "Zionism" by A. Shainberg in the *Bolshaia sovetskaia entsiklopedia*, LI (1945), 191-92 where it was defined as a "reactionary nationalist-political organization" of the Jewish bourgeoisie, whose aim was, as already observed by Lenin, to divert the masses of Jewish workers from the class struggle, the revolution, and socialism.

6. Marc Jarblum, *Le problème juif dans la théorie et la pratique du communisme*, Paris, 1953; Léon Leneman, *La tragédie des Juifs en URSS*, pp. 275 ff., citing anonymous letters in the Tel Aviv *Davar* and other sources. Although overtly written in terms of special pleading and often inaccurate in details, Leneman's volume offers a most comprehensive summary of the anti-Jewish persecutions in the Soviet Union after World War II. Its author who had spent some seven years in the Union, several of them in prison and labor camps, was released as a result of the Russo-Polish agreement for the return of Polish refugees to their home country. Some telling illustrations are offered here as eye-witness accounts. *See also* above, Chaps. XI, n. 9; XII, nn. 7-8; and on the prewar flirtations with the Arab world, the pro-Nazi

essay by Mohammed Sabry, *Islam—Judentum—Bolschewismus*, Berlin, 1938. Schriften der Hochschule für Politik.

7. Kaczerginski, *Tsvishn hamer un serp*, *passim*.

8. Elias Spivak, *Di shprakh in di teg fun der foterlendisher milkhome* (The Language in the Period of the Great Patriotic War), Kiev, 1946; *Mit festn trit* (With a Firm Step: Literary-Artistic Collection by Soviet Yiddish Writers of White Russia), Minsk, 1947; K. Shmeruk in *Pirsumim yehudiim*, pp. xcvii ff. *See also* Robert S. Sullivant, *Soviet Politics in the Ukraine, 1917-1957*, New York, 1962 (Diss. Chicago University).

9. Corliss Lamont, *The Peoples of the Soviet Union*, pp. 91 f.; Walter Zander, *Soviet Jewry, Palestine and the West*, London, 1947, p. 61.

10. Joseph B. Schechtman, *Star in Eclipse: Russian Jewry Revisited*, New York, 1961, citing a conversation with a "bemedaled former officer" in Odessa in 1959. There is no way to verify these figures.

11. Alexander Fadeev (Fadeyev), *Molodaia Gvardiia* (The Young Guard: a Novel), Moscow, 1959; in the English trans. by Violet Dutt, ed. by David Skvirsky, Moscow, n.d.; Valentin Kataev, *Za vlast sovetov* (For Soviet Power), Moscow, 1951; Ilya Ehrenburg, "On the Writer's Work" (Russian), *Znamia*, 1953, No. 10, pp. 160-83; *Kultura i zhizn* of September 10, 1946; and other data cited by A. Yarmolinsky in his *Literature under Communism*, esp. pp. 19, 52 ff., 64 ff.; Ainsztein in *Jewish Social Studies*, XXIII, 77 ff. *See also*, more generally, M. P. Gallagher, *The Soviet History of World War II*, esp. pp. 57 ff. on the criticisms leveled at the early edition of Fadeev's *The Young Guard*, despite its author's high standing in Party circles; the stimulating papers published in the *Proceedings* of the [Second] Conference of the Institute for the Study of the History and Culture of the USSR, New York, 1953; Harold Swayze, *Political Control of Literature in the USSR, 1946-1959*, Cambridge, 1962. Studies of Harvard University's Russian Research Center, XLIV; and above, Chap. XIV, n. 18.

12. *See* the widely publicized picture of the Jewish throngs extending their hearty and courageous, though imprudent, welcome to the first Israel envoy to the Soviet Union in L. Leneman, *La tragédie*, illustration No. 288 A, facing p. 280. *See also ibid.*, pp. 130 ff.

13. These and other stories illustrative of widespread

Soviet anti-Semitism are included in Mendel Man's *Bai di toirn fun Moskve* (At the Gates of Moscow), New York, 1958; and *Bai der Waiksel* (At the Vistula), Tel Aviv, 1958; Leneman, pp. 130 ff.

14. *See* the early report (trans. by Aaron Antonovsky from the Yiddish article in *Di Goldene Kait*, Tel Aviv, 1956) by Bernard Turner, "With the Yiddish Writers in Siberia," *Dissent*, IV (1957), 88-91; and other moving testimonies of various survivors cited by Leneman in *La tragédie, passim*; Casimir M. Smogrorzewski, "The Russification of the Baltic States," *World Affairs*, IV (1950), 168-81; "The Sovietization of the Baltic States," *Annals* of the American Academy of Political Science, CCCXVII (1958), 123-29; Roman Smal Stocki, *The Nationality Problem of the Soviet Union and Russian Communist Imperialism*. With a Preface by Lew E. Dobriansky, Milwaukee, 1952, esp. pp. 199 ff; Harrison E. Salisbury, *To Moscow—and Beyond: a Reporter's Narrative*, New York, 1959, pp. 65 f., 69, 78 f. *See also* Z. Brzezinski, *The Permanent Purge*, pp. 132 ff. On Stalin's changing attitudes even toward such older nationalist movements as that in White Russia, *see* S. Krushinsky's *Byelorussian Communism and Nationalism: Personal Recollections*, New York, 1954. Columbia University's Research Program on the USSR, Mimeographed Series, No. 34. In all such personal reminiscences the individual bias must be discounted. Yet this volume offers insights unavailable from other sources.

15. The article "Evrei" in the *Bolshaia sovetskaia entsiklopedia*, new ed., XV (1952), 377-79 is reproduced in a French trans. by François Fejtö in *Les Juifs et l'antisémitisme dans le pays communistes (entre l'intégration et la sécession), suivi de documents et de témoignages*, Paris, 1960. Les documents de "Tribune libre," pp. 101 ff. Here are also reproduced the critical comments on that article, courageously published by the Polish Jewish communist, Michael Mirsky, in the Warsaw Yiddish paper, *Folks-Shtime* of January 24-26, 1957 (pp. 107 ff.). It may be noted that the article in the *Encyclopedia* on "Evréiskaia avtonómnaia oblást" (Jewish Autonomous Region = Biro-Bidzhan) occupies an equal amount of space in addition to several photographs (cols. 379-81). A more comprehensive analysis of the Jewish aspects of the two editions of the *Bolshaia sovetskaia entsiklopedia* is offered in M. Jarblum's aforementioned *Le problème juif*, pp. 29 ff., 43 ff. *See also* Schechtman, *Star*

in Eclipse, pp. 114, 183f.; and Alexander Weissberg, *Conspiracy of Silence*, English trans. by Edward Fitzgerald, with a Preface by Arthur Koestler, London, 1952. While mainly a dramatic narrative of the author's own experiences during the purges of the 1930s, it helps explain the public complacency and the inactivity of the Jewish masses during the Stalinist terror of 1948-52 as well.

16. *See* the text of Khrushchev's Secret Report, reproduced and analyzed by Bertram D. Wolfe in his *Khrushchev and Stalin's Ghost: Text, Background and Meaning of Khrushchev's Secret Report to the Twentieth Congress on the Night of February 24-25, 1956*, New York, 1957. While the underlying text is taken from an evidently modified version, sent from Moscow to the communist leadership of one of the satellite countries, and subsequently used by the United States Department of State for its translation, it does represent in essence Khrushchev's seven-hour peroration. *See* esp. pp. 202 ff. Never controverted by the Soviet authorities, it was further amplified by new Khrushchev "revelations" at the Twenty-Second Party Congress of October, 1961, which ended in the removal of Stalin's body from the Lenin mausoleum. How easily Stalin could have persuaded the Russian public of the doctors' guilt may be seen from the following, probably typical, remark of a Moscow taxi driver to Harrison E. Salisbury. When in April, 1953, the driver learned about the innocence of the alleged plotters, he exclaimed: "Those *svoloch* [rascals]! They got away this time. But their day will come. We will get those yids!" *See* Salisbury's *To Moscow—and Beyond*, p. 77. On the first impression generally made by the public revelation of the "Doctors' Plot" in *Pravda, see* Salisbury, *American in Russia*, New York, 1955, pp. 140 ff.

17. The Zaslavskii dismissal cited by Solomon Goldelmann in his "Zur Frage der Assimilierung und Denationalisierung der Juden in der Sowjetunion," *Sowjet Studien*, X (1961), 29-58, esp. p. 39; and, more generally, *idem, Das Schicksal der Juden in der Sowjetunion*, Jerusalem, 1958. On the threat of the mass deportation *see* Schechtman, *Star in Eclipse*, pp. 41 f.; and the various essays in *Genocide in the USSR: Studies in Group Destruction*, ed. by Nikolai K. Deker and Andrei Lebed, English trans., ed. by Oliver J. Frederiksen for the Munich Institute for the Study of the USSR, New York, 1958, esp. pp. 20 ff., 30 ff., 49 ff. Next to the groups subjected to complete destruction a number of others suffered

partial annihilation. Among these are counted here the Jews
too, on whom *see* Solomon Goldelmann's pertinent essay,
ibid., pp. 94-110.

18. L. Dmiterko, "The Situation and Tasks of Theatrical
and Literary Criticism in the Ukraine," *Literaturnaia Gazeta*
of March 9, 1949, cited by S. M. Schwarz in *The Jews*, p.
359. The policy of enforced silence with respect to Babii Yar
has continued to the present day. Joseph Schechtman
graphically describes the obstacles placed by the Russian
authorities in the paths of foreign visitors wishing to visit
that neglected ravine, of which he also offers a telling photo-
graph. *See* his *Star in Eclipse*, pp. 99 ff. and the illustrations
following pp. 120 ff.; and below, Chap. XVII, n. 8.

19. Howard Fast, "A Matter of Validity," *Midstream*, IV
(1958), 7-18, esp. p. 10; also under the title, "The Soviet
Hatred of Jewish Jews," in the *Jewish Digest*, III, No. 11
(1958), 1-15. *See also* Fast's *The Naked God: the Writer
and the Communist Party*, London, 1958; and below, Chap.
XVII, n. 16.

CHAPTER 17 (pages 327-344)

1. L. Zinger, *Dos banaite Folk*, Moscow, 1941; *idem, Dos
ufgerikhte Folk* (The Reconstructed People: the Social-
Economic Restratification of the Jewish Population in the
Soviet Union), Moscow, 1948 (includes a 23-page superficial
survey of "The Soviet Jews in the Years of the Great Patriotic
War and the Postwar Period").

2. Our information is therefore mainly derived from the
few studies and a host of personal observations, necessarily
fragmentary, by such foreign scholars as S. M. Schwarz, L.
Leneman, B. Z. Goldberg, J. B. Schechtman, K. Shmeruk, and
others mentioned in our earlier notes. *See also* Gregorii Y.
Aronson, *Soviet Russia and the Jews*, New York, 1949; Elliot
E. Cohen, ed., *The New Red Anti-Semitism: a Symposium*,
Boston, 1953; "Jews in the Soviet Union." Special issue of
the *New Leader*, XXXVI (Sept. 14, 1959); several essays in
the Israel Hebrew periodical *Gesher*; and François Fejtö, *Les
Juifs et l'antisémitisme dans les pays communistes*. Some
additional sidelights may also be obtained from the studies
relating to the Jews of neighboring lands, such as Peter
Meyer, *et al.*, *The Jews in the Soviet Satellites*, Syracuse,
1953.

3. *See* Mark Neuweld, "The Latest Soviet Census and the Jews," *Commentary*, XXIX (1960), 426-29, largely based upon the preliminary reports published in *Pravda*; Mark Geffen, "Jews in the Soviet Union: Results of the Population Census," *Bitfutzot hagolah*, II (1960), 109-17; Zvi Rudy, "The Jews of the Soviet Union as Reflected in Soviet Ethnography" (Hebrew), *Gesher*, VI No. 4 (1960-61), 47-53; Moshe Abramovich, "Jews in the Soviet Census, 1959" (Hebrew), *Molad*, XVIII Nos. 144-45 (1960), 320-29; Schechtman, *Star in Eclipse*, pp. 27 ff.; *The New York Times* of October 23, 1962; Alec Nove, "Jews in the Soviet Union," *Jewish Journal of Sociology*, III (1961), 108-20. *See also* the earlier, somewhat overspeculative, observations by Francis Bower on "The Population of Soviet Russia," *Contemporary Review*, CLXXX (1951), 337-43.

4. Edward R. Stettinius, *Roosevelt and the Russians: the Yalta Conference*, ed. by Walter Johnson, Garden City, New York, 1949, p. 278; Stalin's reply to the Jewish Telegraphic Agency of January 12, 1931 (not publicized in the Soviet Union until 1936, when it was quoted from a Molotov speech in *Pravda*), cited by S. M. Schwarz in *The Jews*, pp. 292, 305 nn. 4-5; and the data assembled by Leneman in *La tragédie*, pp. 166 ff.; and by Schechtman in his *Star in Eclipse*, pp. 78 ff. Some of the numerous official denials of the existence of anti-Semitism in the Soviet Union, emanating from Khrushchev, Mikoyan (who once bluntly asserted before United Nations correspondents that there existed no Jewish question in the USSR), and others are summarized by F. Fejtö in *Les Juifs*, pp. 121 ff.

5. Peter N. Juviler, "Representatives of Nationalities and Occupations in the Soviets," *Annals* of the Ukrainian Academy of Arts and Sciences in the United States, IX (1961), 201-24, esp. p. 219; Moshe Decter, "The Status of the Jews in the Soviet Union," *Foreign Affairs*, XLI (1962-63), 420-30; Alec Nove, "A Note on the Proportion of Jews in Republican and Local Soviets, U. S. S. R.," *Jewish Journal of Sociology*, III (1961), 276; and, more generally, Anatole Goldstein, *The Soviet Attitude towards Territorial Minorities and the Jews*, New York, 1957. It may be noted that the percentage of Jewish elective officials, as well as of industrial managers, is somewhat higher (relative to population) in the Asiatic republics. Evidently Jews are viewed there

primarily as "Russians." However, with the growth of local talent, the gradual process of displacement of these "alien" leaders by native officials and managers is likely to hit the Jews in both capacities as Jews and as Russians.

6. "Soviet Union: 'Show-Trial' or Showdown," *Jews in Eastern Europe*, II, No. 4 (1964), 12-22, esp. p. 17; Decter in *Foreign Affairs*, XLI, 429 f.; *The New York Times*, February 27, 1964, pp. 3, 6. Interesting materials on the various aspects of the present situation of Soviet Jewry were also assembled by Moshe Decter in the "Conference Papers" submitted to the *Conference on the Status of Soviet Jews* held in New York on October 12, 1963.

7. The statistics here given are quoted from news dispatches in the *Congress Bi-Weekly*, XXIX, No. 10 (1962), p. 4. Substantially the same figures were supplied by Georgii M. Korniyenko, Counsellor of the Soviet Embassy in Washington, to Moses I. Socachewsky, president of the Jewish Nazi Victims Organization. The variants of 15.7 percent of doctors, and 3.2 of students are not significant. *See* the report in *The New York Times* of October 11, 1962, p. 6. *See also* some other figures cited in Schechtman's *Star in Eclipse*, pp. 53 ff.; and in *Jews in Eastern Europe*, II, No. 4, pp. 40 f. Surprisingly, there have also existed some Jewish apologists for these restrictive policies. Harking back to the old ideology of "productivization" of the Jewish people, a retired Jewish medical professor in Leningrad told B. Z. Goldberg in 1959: "Look here, on my faculty I had fifty-seven professors and forty-six of them were Jews. Do you think this was natural? Was this good for the Jews? Would you want the Soviet Jews to become a nation of professors? We want fewer Jewish professors and more Jewish plain workers." *See* Goldberg's *The Jewish Problem*, p. 157. On the improvement in Soviet statistical accounts in recent years and the earlier difficulties in their interpretation, *see* Harry Schwartz, "The Renaissance of Soviet Statistics," *Review of Economics and Statistics*, XL (1958), 122-26.

8. Evgenii Evtushenko (Yevtushenko), *Babii Yar* in his *Selected Poems*, trans. with an Intro. by Robin Miller-Gulland and Peter Levi, New York, 1962, pp. 82 ff.; here cited from the somewhat different English excerpts, reproduced in Harry Schwartz's column, "Moscow Papers Assail Writer" in *The New York Times* of September 28, 1961, p. 22; Harrison E. Salisbury, "Fear Grows among Soviet Jews at Resurgence

of Anti-Semitism," *ibid.*, February 8, 1962, p. 4; Arthur P. Reed, Jr., "Soviet Culture: Its Ups and Downs," *New York Standard,* February 17, 1963, p. 133. *See also* above, Chap. XVI, n. 18; and the interesting report on Evtushenko's encounter with Khrushchev, published from somewhat dubious transcripts, in "Russian Art and Anti-Semitism: Two Documents," *Commentary* of December, 1963 (with a critical analysis by Moshe Decter).

9. Schechtman, *Star in Eclipse,* pp. 38 f. n. 2; Alfred D. Low, "Patriotism, 'Bourgeois Nationalism' and the Nationality Policy of the USSR after Stalin," *Annals* of the Ukrainian Academy of Arts and Sciences in the United States, IX (1961), 126-46. *See also* the illustrations offered by Leopold H. Haimson in "The Solitary Hero and the Philistine: a Note on the Heritage of the Stalin Era" and by Max Hayward in "The Thaw and the Writers" in Richard Pipes's ed. of *The Russian Intelligentsia,* New York, 1961, pp. 101-10, 111-21.

10. Howard Fast, "The Ordeal of Boris Pasternak," *Midstream,* V (1959), 38-44, esp. p. 42. *See* such reports as that published under the telling title, "Israel: 'Hell' or 'Paradise'" (Russian) in *Sovetskaia Kultura* of March 25, 1958; and the other harangues, selected from Russian publications in 1957-59 by F. Fejtö in *Les Juifs,* pp. 155 f. Typical of the official view was a sharply anti-Israel study, published by the State Publishing House in Moscow, 1958 under the title, *Gosudarstvo Izrail* (The State of Israel, Its Location and Policies) by Ivanov and Z. Sheinis. *See* the facsimile of its title page in Schechtman's *Star,* p. 194. *See also* the *New Leader,* XXXVI (Sept. 14, 1959), 27 ff.

11. *The New York Times* of November 2, 1962, p. 13; Yizhar Smilansky, "Behind the Red Curtain: Impressions of a Sabra Writer," *Jewish Frontier* of January 1963, Section II, p. 32. This report, originally published in Hebrew in Israel journals, is more fully reproduced in the *Hadoar,* XLIII, No. 2, of November 9, 1962, pp. 19 ff.

12. M. Decter in *Foreign Affairs,* XLI, 424 ff. The picture of Rabbi Schliefer opening the rabbinical school is reproduced by Leneman in *La tragédie,* p. 16 A. *See also,* more generally, Alexander A. Bogolepov, *Tserkov pod vlastiu kommunizma* (The Church under Communist Domination), Munich, 1958. Institute for the Study of the USSR, Studies, 1st ser., XLII (reviews also the conditions in the satellite countries).

13. *The New York Times* of December 20, 1959 (Kirova-grad broadcast); *ibid.*, of October 23, 1962, p. 11 (an interview with the new Moscow chief rabbi, Yehudah Leb Levin). *See also* the attack on "The Reactionary Nature of the Jewish Religion" (Russian) published in the Lwów *Pravda* and trans. into French, together with several other similar press notices, by F. Fejtö in *Les Juifs*, pp. 157 ff.

14. *See* David Miller's extensive report on "Russia's Defense on Jewish Bias Charges" in the *New York Herald Tribune* of November 24, 1962, pp. 1-2; Decter in *Foreign Affairs*, XLI, 421 ff. On the spurt of Russian translations from the Yiddish in 1961, *see* the list in *Kirjath Sepher*, XXXVIII (1962-63), pp. 79 ff. Nos. 761-79. *See also* S. Goldelmann's studies cited above, Chap. XVI, n. 16. This process contrasted sharply with the far slower process of Russification even in recent years, for instance of the Ukrainians on which *see* Robert S. Sullivant, *Soviet Politics and the Ukraine, 1917-1957*, pp. 294 ff. *See*, however, above, n. 13.

15. *See* Khrushchev's interview with Serge Groussard, published in the Paris *Figaro* of April 9, 1958 and reproduced by F. Fejtö in *Les Juifs*, pp. 124 ff. Although denounced in the Soviet press as a "provocative forgery," this interview clearly reflects Khrushchev's essential reasoning. Of considerable interest also were the rather penetrating observations on the spot by the Polish communist, Dominik Horodynski, published in the Warsaw magazine, *Swiat* of December 7, 1958 and trans. into French by Fejtö, *ibid.*, pp. 131 ff. Subsequent reports by several visitors, including direct observations of his own on two visits to Biro-Bidzhan in 1934 and 1959, are summarized by B. Z. Goldberg in *The Jewish Problem in the Soviet Union*, pp. 170 ff.

16. It is well known that Pasternak's Nobel prizewinning novel, *Doctor Zhivago*, could not appear in Russia, because the editors of the *Novii Mir* (New World) rejected it as too critical of the Revolution. In 1958, the officials of the Writers' Union, after the award of the Nobel Prize, expelled Pasternak from the Union. At that time the original rejection of the novel was publicized in the *Literaturnaia Gazeta* of October 25, 1958 and therefrom reproduced in an English trans. in the *Current Digest of the Soviet Press* of December 3, 1958. This lengthy document is now readily available in *The Russian Intelligentsia*, ed. by R. Pipes, pp. 208-26. *See also* Howard Fast's perceptive essay on "The Ordeal of Boris Pasternak," *Midstream*, V. (1959), 38-44.

CHAPTER 18 (pages 345-352)

1. Nicholas Berdyaev (Berdiaev), *The Russian Revolution, Two Essays on Its Implications in Religion and Psychology,* English trans. from the Russian with an Intro. by D. B., London, 1932. Essays in Order, VI, pp. 59 f. *See also* Robert C. Tucker, "Marxism: Is It Religion?" *Ethics,* LXVIII (1957-58), 125-30. Still germinal in Marx's own teachings, despite Ludwig Feuerbach's exclamation in 1842, "Politics must become our religion," the religious brand of Soviet communist fanaticism had become more and more marked.

2. Marquis Astolphe L. L. de Custine, *Russia* [1839], abridged trans. from the French, 3 vols., London, 1844, I, 160 f. *See also* various essays on *Continuity and Change in Russian and Soviet Thought,* ed. by Ernest J. Simmons, including Adam Ulam's "Stalin and the Theory of Totalitarianism," also referring to the use of undercover anti-Semitism in the struggle against Trotsky, Zinoviev, and Kamenev (pp. 165 ff.).

INDEX

Index

D

Decembrists, 32, 33

"Declaration of Jewish Citizens," 71

Denikin, General Anton I., 219

Devier, Count Anton, 11, 12

Diderot, Denis, 16

Dimanshtain, Simeon, 206, 209, 231, 233, 240; leadership in Jewish community, 206, 263

Dimitrii (pretender), 9, 10

Dostoevsky, Fiodor M., 62, 63, 70, 164

Dreyfus Affair, 62

Duma, First, 71, 72, 141; Fourth, 73; Second, 73; Third, 73, 74, 197

Dybbuk, 286

E

Education, establishment of secondary schools, 41, 155; *gymnasia*, 43; Jewish schools, 41-44; progress in, 48, 141; 143

Ehrenburg, Ilya G., 287, 306, 309, 311, 317, 337; award of Stalin Prize to, 289; extreme pliability of, 289

Eisenstein, Sergei M., 287, 317

Elizabeth Petrovna, 13

Emes, 241, 251, 252, 270, 279, 291, 302, 315

Emigration, increase in, 87; mass, 58, 60, 115; peak of,
89; to United States, 80, 82, 85, 88, 100, 193

Enlightenment, 33, 135, 156

Erlich, Henryk, 304

Evtushenko, Evgenii, 335, 336

F

Fast, Howard, 323, 338

Fefer, Itzik, 285, 305, 310

G

Gamarnik, General Jan, 243

General Jewish Workers' League, the, *see* Bund

Gennadius, 8

Gerasimov, Dimitri, 9

German Occupation, 193 ff.

Giovio, Paolo, 9

Gogol, Nikolai Vasilievich, 61

Golovanivskii, Savva, 325

Gorbatov, Boris, 302

Gorki, Maxim, 61, 70, 182, 191, 327

Grand Dukes, Leopold (Emperor Leopold II) 18; Nicholas Nikolaevich, 189, 190, 197; Sviata-Polk II, 6; Vladimir Monomakh, 6

Great Patriotic War, the, *see* Second World War

Greek-Orthodox Church *see* Russian Orthodoxy

107, 120; industrialization of, 95; in industry, 235; influence of on Khazar Empire, 3, 4; in oil fields, 110, 111; in Russian letters: Babel, Ehrenburg, Eisenstein, Pasternak, 287; in sugar industry, 100 ff.; intermarriage among, 214; in transport (rail and water), 108 ff.; loyalty to Crown, 124; mass evacuation of, 190; "May laws" against *see* "May Laws"; migration *see* Emigration; participation in First Duma, 71, 72; participation in municipalities of, 18; pogroms *see* Pogroms; prohibition of settlement of, 5, 10, 11, 12; religious influence of, 5, 6; repatriation of, 45-46; resentment of, 65; resettlement of, 45-46; restrictions on, 40; schools of, 41-44; secular schools for, 41; secularization of, 21; separation of, 144, 150; smuggling by, 10, 12; vitality of, 254; welfare organizations of, 128 ff.

Joseph II, 16

Judaizanti, condemnation of, 8; heresy of, 8

K

Kaganovich, Lazar M., 243, 316, 333

kahal, 20, 37, 39, 119, 120, 121, 123, 125, 128, 140

Kalinin Mikhail, 204, 229, 239, 292, 293

Kantor, Yakov, 224, 225

Karaites, 2, 299

Kataev, Valentin, 317

Kerensky, Alexander F., 196, 218

Khazar Empire, 3, 4; adoption of Judaism, 4; destruction of, 4; orthodoxy of, 4; use of Hebrew in, 3

Kiev, 6, 29, 30, 41, 47, 52, 53, 64, 65, 68, 75, 92, 133, 166, 218, 325, 336

Kolchak, General Alexander V., 215

Korolenko, V. G., *Yom Kippur*, 61

Krushchev, Nikita, 324, 331, 332, 333, 338, 343, 351

L

Large Russian Encyclopedia, 171, 229, 230, 321; treatment of Jews in, 322-323

League for the Attainment of Jewish Rights, 71

Lenin, V. I., 170, 202, 203, 284, 348; on Jews, 205, 206, 210, 351

Lermontov, Mikhail Yurievich, 61

Lilienthal, Dr. Max, 41, 42, 44, 123, 155

Lithuania, 8, 9, 12, 82, 314, 321, 330, 344

Lozovsky, Solomon A., 305, 307

V

Y

Date Due